AWS CERTIFIED SOLUTIONS ARCHITECT ASSOCIATE 2020

390 TOP-NOTCH QUESTIONS
THE LATEST SAA-CO2 CERTIFICATION BLUEPRINT

THOMAS HOWELL

Welcome Fellow AWS Professionals!

Congratulations, you have just gained access to the highest quality Practice Tests for the AWS Certified Solutions Architect Associate Certification Exam.

Be an AWS Solutions Architect! AWS Certified Solutions Architect Associate Practice Tests with new SAA-C02 topics!

FULLY UPDATED to the new SAA-C02 - AWS Certified Solutions Architect Associate exam version!

These practice tests contain the new SAA-C02 topics such as AWS Global Accelerator, Amazon FSx for Lustre, Elastic Fabric Adapter (EFA), Direct Connect Gateway and many others.

July 2020 Update: Completed the integration of the new SAA-C02 topics in all of our 6 practice tests.

These AWS Certified Solutions Architect Associate practice tests are patterned after the latest exam format and were crafted based on the feedback of our 70,000+ students on what appeared in the actual exam. Our AWS Certified Solutions Architect practice tests are TOP-NOTCH and the CLOSEST to the actual exam, as demonstrated by over 13,000++ reviews on our course.

✔ Each question has detailed explanations at the end of each set that will help you gain a deeper understanding of the AWS services.

✔ The explanation provides an overview of the topic, reference links to AWS docs and a rationale on why the option is correct or incorrect

✔ MOBILE-COMPATIBLE - so you can conveniently review everywhere, anytime with your smartphone!

What's the difference between SAA-C01 vs SAA-C02 exam?

I took both exam versions and in my professional opinion, the SAA-C02 exam is about 70% similar to the previous exam. Amazon Aurora Serverless, AWS Global Accelerator, Amazon FSx for Lustre, Elastic Fabric Adapter (EFA), Direct Connect Gateway, HPC and many new topics were added in the latest SAA-C02 exam. It is more verbose than the previous version with longer scenarios and options. But again, the majority of the topics covered (S3, EBS, EC2, etc) are similar to the previous one.

Can I take the SAA-C02 exam online at my home?

Yes, you can. AWS announced last March 2020 that you can the new SAA-C02 exam, as well as the other AWS certification exams at the comforts of your home. Take note that this is only supported by Pearson Vue, and not PSI.

How can I schedule my SAA-C02 exam?

You can go to the official AWS Solutions Architect Associate Certification page and then click the "Schedule Exam" button to book your SAA-C02 test. Alternatively, you can directly login to your AWS Certification account to schedule the exam.

The AWS Certified Solutions Architect Associate is consistently among the top-paying IT certifications, considering that Amazon Web Services (AWS) is the leading cloud services platform in the world with almost 50% market share! Earn over $150,000 per year with an AWS Solutions Architect certification!

But before you become an AWS Certified Solutions Architect Professional, it is recommended for you to pass the AWS Solutions Architect Associate certification exam first, and this is where AWS practice tests come in. It is possible that you have read all of the available AWS documentation online yet still fail the exam! These AWS practice tests simulate the actual certification exam and ensure that you indeed understand the subject matter.

This AWS Certified Solutions Architect Associate (SAA-C02) Practice Exam course offers the following features:

✔ FULLY UPDATED TO THE NEW SAA-C02 version - Most practice tests out there are already obsolete and advertised as "updated", but in reality, they are not! We have already integrated the new SAA-C02 topics such as AWS Global Accelerator, Amazon FSx for Lustre, Elastic Fabric Adapter (EFA), Direct Connect Gateway, HPC and many more in our sets.

✔ 390 TOP-NOTCH Questions - has 6 sets of AWS Practice Tests with 65 UNIQUE questions and a 130-minute time limit for each set.

✔ SIMULATES ACTUAL EXAM ENVIRONMENT - mimics the actual, and the latest AWS Solutions Architect Associate certification exam to help you AWS exam!

✔ DETAILED EXPLANATIONS, AND REFERENCE LINKS, our answer keys at the end of each set have full and detailed explanations along with complete reference links so you can check and verify yourself that the answers are correct.

✔ MOBILE-COMPATIBLE - so you can conveniently review everywhere, anytime with your smartphone!

✔ CLEAR AND ERROR-FREE QUESTIONS - Each item has a reference link that can validate the answer but you can also post in the QA section so we can discuss any issues.

✔ Prepared by an AWS Certified Solutions Architect Professional who has actually passed the actual SAA-C02 exam!

These AWS Solutions Architect practice exams are designed to focus on the important exam topics (such as EC2, EBS, S3, and many others) hence, the aforementioned topics have more questions than the other AWS knowledge areas. The number of questions on each topic is carefully selected based on the 4 domains of the actual AWS certification exam.

Some people are using brain dumps for the AWS Certified Solutions Architect certification exam which is totally absurd and highly unprofessional because these dumps will not only hinder you to attain an in-depth AWS knowledge, these can also result with you failing the actual AWS certification exam since Amazon regularly updates the exam coverage.

Please also note that these AWS Certified Solutions Architect practice tests are not exam dumps and since Amazon shuffles the actual exam content from a question bank with hundreds to thousands of questions, it is nearly impossible to match what you can see here with the actual tests. Again, the key to passing the exam is a good understanding of AWS services and this is what our AWS Certified Solutions Architect Associate practice tests are meant to do.

There are a lot of existing AWS Practice Tests in the market however, most of them contain both technical and grammatical errors that may cause you to fail the actual exam. There are also official certification practice exams provided by AWS but these only have 20 or 40 questions and cost 20 or 30 USD -- a price that is comparable with having these 390 Unique and Timed Amazon Web Services practice questions!

When I was reviewing for my AWS Certified Solutions Architect Associate exam, I had a hard time finding comprehensive practice tests to help me pass my exam. I bought some of them in the market but I was disappointed because there are a lot of technical and grammatical errors in the questions. This is why I created these AWS practice tests to help my fellow IT professionals in the industry.

We gave a considerable amount of effort to create and publish these AWS practice tests, including the laborious task of checking each item for any errors. We are confident that this will significantly help you pass your CSA-Associate exam. Wishing you all the best with your AWS Certification exam.

All the best!

IMPORTANT NOTE

These AWS Certified Solutions Architect Associate practice exams have a passing score of 72% but I highly encourage you to repeat taking these exams again and again until you consistently reach a score of 90% or higher on each exam.

Remember that using this product alone does not guarantee you will pass the AWS exam as you still need to do your own readings and hands-on exercises in AWS. Nonetheless, these Amazon Web Services practice exams provide a comprehensive assessment on which knowledge area you need improvement on and even help you achieve a higher score!

What you'll learn

✔ Increase your chances of passing the new (SAA-C02) version of the AWS Certified Solutions Architect Associate Exam

✔ Learn the new AWS technologies in the SAA-C02 exam such as AWS Global Accelerator, AWS Directory Service, Elastic Fabric Adapter, High-Performance Computing and many more!

✔ Take the practice exams again and again on your mobile or laptop, unlike the AWS-provided practice exam which you can only do once

✔ Answer and solve tricky scenario-based AWS Solutions Architect Associate questions under time pressure

✔ Validate your answers and do further readings with the provided reference links from the Official AWS documentation

✔ Learn the AWS concepts in-depth with the comprehensive explanations included in each answer plus bonus cheat sheets!

✔ Become an AWS Certified Solutions Architect Associate!

Are there any course requirements or prerequisites?

✔ If you have a computer or a smartphone then you are ready to go!

✔ An AWS Account (You can also get the Free-Tier!)

Who this course is for:

✔ For those who are about to take the AWS Certified Solutions Architect Associate (SAA-C02) exam

✔ For all IT Professionals who want to gauge their AWS Knowledge for their upcoming job interview

✔ For anyone who want to take their career, and salary, to a whole new level with an AWS certification!

TABLE OF CONTENTS

PRACTICE TEST 1

AWS CERTIFIED SOLUTIONS ARCHITECT ASSOCIATE

AWS CERTIFIED SOLUTIONS ARCHITECT ASSOCIATE PRACTICE TEST 1

Question 1:

You are using a combination of API Gateway and Lambda for the web services of your online web portal that is being accessed by hundreds of thousands of clients each day. Your company will be announcing a new revolutionary product and it is expected that your web portal will receive a massive number of visitors all around the globe. How can you protect your backend systems and applications from traffic spikes?

1. API Gateway will automatically scale and handle massive traffic spikes so you do not have to do anything.
2. Use throttling limits in API Gateway
3. Deploy Multi-AZ in API Gateway with Read Replica
4. Manually upgrade the EC2 instances being used by API Gateway

Answer(s): 1, 2

Explanation

Amazon API Gateway provides throttling at multiple levels including global and by a service call. Throttling limits can be set for standard rates and bursts. For example, API owners can set a rate limit of 1,000 requests per second for a specific method in their REST APIs, and also configure Amazon API Gateway to handle a burst of 2,000 requests per second for a few seconds.

Amazon API Gateway tracks the number of requests per second. Any requests over the limit will receive a 429 HTTP response. The client SDKs generated by Amazon API Gateway retry calls automatically when met with this response.

The option that says: API Gateway will automatically scale and handle massive traffic spikes so you do not have to do anything is incorrect because although it can scale using AWS Edge locations, you still need to configure the throttling to further manage the bursts of your APIs.

Manually upgrading the EC2 instances being used by API Gateway is incorrect because API Gateway is a fully managed service and hence, you do not have access to its underlying resources.

Deploying Multi-AZ in API Gateway with Read Replica is incorrect because RDS has Multi-AZ and Read Replica capabilities, and not API Gateway.

Reference:

https://aws.amazon.com/api-gateway/faqs/#Throttling_and_Caching

Question 2:

A government entity is conducting a population and housing census in the city. Each household information uploaded on their online portal is stored in encrypted files in Amazon S3. The government assigned its Solutions Architect to set compliance policies that verify sensitive data in a manner that meets their compliance standards. They should also be alerted if there are compromised files detected containing personally identifiable information (PII), protected health information (PHI) or intellectual properties (IP).

Which of the following should the Architect implement to satisfy this requirement?

1. Set up and configure Amazon GuardDuty to monitor malicious activity on their Amazon S3 data.
2. Set up and configure Amazon Rekognition to monitor and recognize patterns on their Amazon S3 data.
3. Set up and configure Amazon Macie to monitor and detect usage patterns on their Amazon S3 data.
4. Set up and configure Amazon Inspector to send out alert notifications whenever a security violation is detected on their Amazon S3 data.

Answer(s): 3

Explanation

Amazon Macie is an ML-powered security service that helps you prevent data loss by automatically discovering, classifying, and protecting sensitive data stored in Amazon S3. Amazon Macie uses machine learning to recognize sensitive data such as personally identifiable information (PII) or intellectual property, assigns a business value, and provides visibility into where this data is stored and how it is being used in your organization.

Amazon Macie continuously monitors data access activity for anomalies, and delivers alerts when it detects risk of unauthorized access or inadvertent data leaks. Amazon Macie has ability to detect global access permissions inadvertently being set on sensitive data, detect uploading of API keys inside source code, and verify sensitive customer data is being stored and accessed in a manner that meets their compliance standards.

Hence, the correct answer is: Set up and configure Amazon Macie to monitor and detect usage patterns on their Amazon S3 data.

The option that says: Set up and configure Amazon Rekognition to monitor and recognize patterns on their Amazon S3 data is incorrect because Rekognition is simply a service that can identify the objects, people, text, scenes, and activities, as well as detect any inappropriate content on your images or videos.

The option that says: Set up and configure Amazon GuardDuty to monitor malicious activity on their Amazon S3 data is incorrect because GuardDuty is just a threat detection service that continuously monitors for malicious activity and unauthorized behavior to protect your AWS accounts and workloads.

The option that says: Set up and configure Amazon Inspector to send out alert notifications whenever a security violation is detected on their Amazon S3 data is incorrect because Inspector is basically an automated security assessment service that helps improve the security and compliance of applications deployed on AWS.

References:

https://docs.aws.amazon.com/macie/latest/userguide/what-is-macie.html

https://aws.amazon.com/macie/faq/

https://docs.aws.amazon.com/macie/index.html

Question 3:

A company has an On-Demand EC2 instance that is transferring large amounts of data to an Amazon S3 bucket in the same region. Your manager is worried about infrastructure cost considering the vast amounts of data being transferred to the bucket.

What will you say to justify this architecture?

1. Transferring data from an EC2 instance to an S3 bucket in the same region has no cost at all.
2. You are only using an On-Demand EC2 instance which is exactly the same price as Spot EC2 instance, launched by a persistent Spot request.
3. Transferring data from an EC2 instance to an S3 bucket in the same region has a 50% discount based on the AWS Pricing.
4. You are only using an On-Demand EC2 instance so the cost will be lower than a Spot instance.

Answer(s): 1

Explanation

Transferring data from an EC2 instance to Amazon S3, Amazon Glacier, Amazon DynamoDB, Amazon SES, Amazon SQS, or Amazon SimpleDB in the same AWS Region has no cost at all. Refer to the Amazon EC2 Pricing on the link below for reference.

4

The options that say: You are only using an On-Demand EC2 instance which is exactly the same price as Spot EC2 instance, launched by a persistent Spot request and You are only using an On-Demand EC2 instance so the cost will be lower than a Spot instance are incorrect since an On-Demand instance costs more than a Spot instance.

The option that says: Transferring data from an EC2 instance to an S3 bucket in the same region has a 50% discount based on the AWS Pricing is incorrect as there is no such thing as 50% discount when transferring data from an EC2 instance to an S3 bucket in the same region.

Reference:

https://aws.amazon.com/ec2/pricing/on-demand/#Data_Transfer

Question 4:

A content management system (CMS) is hosted on a fleet of auto-scaled, On-Demand EC2 instances which use Amazon Aurora as its database. Currently, the system stores the file documents that the users uploaded in one of the attached EBS Volumes. Your manager noticed that the system performance is quite slow and he has instructed you to improve the architecture of the system.

In this scenario, what will you do to implement a scalable, high throughput POSIX-compliant file system?

1. Use EFS
2. Create an S3 bucket and use this as the storage for the CMS
3. Use ElastiCache
4. Upgrade your existing EBS volumes to Provisioned IOPS SSD Volumes

Answer(s): 1

Explanation

Amazon Elastic File System (Amazon EFS) provides simple, scalable, elastic file storage for use with AWS Cloud services and on-premises resources. When mounted on Amazon EC2 instances, an Amazon EFS file system provides a standard file system interface and file system access semantics, allowing you to seamlessly integrate Amazon EFS with your existing applications and tools. Multiple Amazon EC2 instances can access an Amazon EFS file system at the same time, allowing Amazon EFS to provide a common data source for workloads and applications running on more than one Amazon EC2 instance.

This particular scenario tests your understanding of EBS, EFS, and S3. In this scenario, there is a fleet of On-Demand EC2 instances that stores file documents from the users to one of the attached EBS Volumes. The system performance is quite slow because the architecture doesn't provide the EC2 instances a parallel shared access to the file documents.

Remember that an EBS Volume can be attached to one EC2 instance at a time, hence, no other EC2 instance can connect to that EBS Provisioned IOPS Volume. Take note as well that the type of storage needed here is a "file storage" which means that S3 is not the best service to use because it is mainly used for "object storage", and S3 does not provide the notion of "folders" too. This is why using EFS is the correct answer.

Upgrading your existing EBS volumes to Provisioned IOPS SSD Volumes is incorrect because the scenario requires you to set up a scalable, high throughput storage system that will allow concurrent access from multiple EC2 instances. This is clearly not possible in EBS, even with Provisioned IOPS SSD Volumes. You have to use EFS instead.

Using ElastiCache is incorrect because this is an in-memory data store that improves the performance of your applications, which is not what you need since it is not a file storage.

Reference:

https://aws.amazon.com/efs/

Here's a short video tutorial on Amazon EFS:

https://youtu.be/AvgAozsfCrY

Question 5:

You are designing a multi-tier web application architecture that consists of a fleet of EC2 instances and an Oracle relational database server. It is required that the database is highly available and that you have full control over its underlying operating system.

Which AWS service will you use for your database tier?

1. Amazon EC2 instances with data replication in one Availability Zone
2. Amazon RDS
3. Amazon EC2 instances with data replication between two different Availability Zones
4. Amazon RDS with Multi-AZ deployments

Answer(s): 3

Explanation

To achieve this requirement, you can deploy your Oracle database to Amazon EC2 instances with data replication between two different Availability Zones. Hence, this option is the correct answer. The deployment of this architecture can easily be achieved by using CloudFormation and Quick Start. Please refer to the reference link for information.

The Quick Start deploys the Oracle primary database (using the preconfigured, general-purpose starter database from Oracle) on an Amazon EC2 instance in the first Availability Zone. It then sets up a second EC2 instance in a second Availability Zone, copies the primary database to the second instance by using the DUPLICATE command, and configures Oracle Data Guard.

Amazon RDS and Amazon RDS with Multi-AZ deployments are both incorrect because the scenario requires you to have access to the underlying operating system of the database server. Remember that Amazon RDS is a managed database service, which means that Amazon is the one that manages the underlying operating system of the database instance and not you.

The option that says: Amazon EC2 instances with data replication in one Availability Zone is incorrect since deploying to just one Availability Zone (AZ) will not make the database tier highly available. If that AZ went down, your database will be unavailable.

References:

https://aws.amazon.com/quickstart/

https://docs.aws.amazon.com/quickstart/latest/oracle-database/architecture.html

http://docs.aws.amazon.com/dms/latest/userguide/CHAP_Introduction.Replicatio nInstance.html

Question 6:

An application hosted in EC2 consumes messages from an SQS queue and is integrated with SNS to send out an email to you once the process is complete. The Operations team received 5 orders but after a few hours, they saw 20 email notifications in their inbox.

Which of the following could be the possible culprit for this issue?

1. The web application is set to short polling so some messages are not being picked up
2. The web application is not deleting the messages in the SQS queue after it has processed them.
3. The web application is set for long polling so the messages are being sent twice.
4. The web application does not have permission to consume messages in the SQS queue.

Answer(s): 2

Explanation

Always remember that the messages in the SQS queue will continue to exist even after the EC2 instance has processed it, until you delete that message. You have to ensure that you delete the message after processing to prevent the message from being received and processed again once the visibility timeout expires.

There are three main parts in a distributed messaging system:

1. The components of your distributed system (EC2 instances)

2. Your queue (distributed on Amazon SQS servers)

3. Messages in the queue.

You can set up a system which has several components that send messages to the queue and receive messages from the queue. The queue redundantly stores the messages across multiple Amazon SQS servers.

Refer to the third step of the SQS Message Lifecycle:

Component 1 sends Message A to a queue, and the message is distributed across the Amazon SQS servers redundantly.

When Component 2 is ready to process a message, it consumes messages from the queue, and Message A is returned. While Message A is being processed, it remains in the queue and isn't returned to subsequent receive requests for the duration of the visibility timeout.

Component 2 deletes Message A from the queue to prevent the message from being received and processed again once the visibility timeout expires.

The option that says: The web application is set for long polling so the messages are being sent twice is incorrect because long polling helps reduce the cost of using SQS by eliminating the number of empty responses (when there are no messages available for a ReceiveMessage request) and false empty responses (when messages are available but aren't included in a response). Messages being sent twice in an SQS queue configured with long polling is quite unlikely.

The option that says: The web application is set to short polling so some messages are not being picked up is incorrect since you are receiving emails from SNS where messages are certainly being processed. Following the scenario, messages not being picked up won't result into 20 messages being sent to your inbox.

The option that says: The web application does not have permission to consume messages in the SQS queue is incorrect because not having the correct permissions would have resulted in a different response. The scenario says that messages were properly processed but there were over 20 messages that were sent, hence, there is no problem with the accessing the queue.

References:

https://docs.aws.amazon.com/AWSSimpleQueueService/latest/SQSDeveloperGuid e/sqs-message-lifecycle.html

https://docs.aws.amazon.com/AWSSimpleQueueService/latest/SQSDeveloperGuid e/sqs-basic-architecture.html

Question 7:

A web application is using CloudFront to distribute their images, videos, and other static contents stored in their S3 bucket to its users around the world. The company has recently introduced a new member-only access to some of its high quality media files. There is a requirement to provide access to multiple private media files only to their paying subscribers without having to change their current URLs.

Which of the following is the most suitable solution that you should implement to satisfy this requirement?

1. Create a Signed URL with a custom policy which only allows the members to see the private files.
2. Configure your CloudFront distribution to use Match Viewer as its Origin Protocol Policy which will automatically match the user request. This will allow access to the private content if the request is a paying member and deny it if it is not a member.
3. Configure your CloudFront distribution to use Field-Level Encryption to protect your private data and only allow access to members.
4. Use Signed Cookies to control who can access the private files in your CloudFront distribution by modifying your application to determine whether a user should have access to your content. For members, send the required Set-Cookie headers to the viewer which will unlock the content only to them.

Answer(s): 4

Explanation

CloudFront signed URLs and signed cookies provide the same basic functionality: they allow you to control who can access your content. If you want to serve private content through CloudFront and you're trying to decide whether to use signed URLs or signed cookies, consider the following:

Use signed URLs for the following cases:

- You want to use an RTMP distribution. Signed cookies aren't supported for RTMP distributions.

- You want to restrict access to individual files, for example, an installation download for your application.

- Your users are using a client (for example, a custom HTTP client) that doesn't support cookies.

Use signed cookies for the following cases:

- You want to provide access to multiple restricted files, for example, all of the files for a video in HLS format or all of the files in the subscribers' area of a website.

- You don't want to change your current URLs.

Hence, the correct answer for this scenario is the option that says: Use Signed Cookies to control who can access the private files in your CloudFront distribution by modifying your application to determine whether a user should have access to your content. For members, send the required Set-Cookie headers to the viewer which will unlock the content only to them.

The option that says: Configure your CloudFront distribution to use Match Viewer as its Origin Protocol Policy which will automatically match the user request. This will allow access to the private content if the request is a paying member and deny it if it is not a member is incorrect because a Match Viewer is an Origin Protocol Policy which configures CloudFront to communicate with your origin using HTTP or HTTPS, depending on the protocol of the viewer request. CloudFront caches the object only once even if viewers make requests using both HTTP and HTTPS protocols.

The option that says: Create a Signed URL with a custom policy which only allows the members to see the private files is because Signed URLs are primarily used for providing access to individual files, as shown on the above Explanation. In addition, the scenario explicitly says that they don't want to change their current URLs which is why implementing Signed Cookies is more suitable than Signed URL.

The option that says: Configure your CloudFront distribution to use Field-Level Encryption to protect your private data and only allow access to members is incorrect because Field-Level Encryption only allows you to securely upload user-submitted sensitive information to your web servers. It does not provide access to download multiple private files.

Reference:

https://docs.aws.amazon.com/AmazonCloudFront/latest/DeveloperGuide/private-content-choosing-signed-urls-cookies.html

https://docs.aws.amazon.com/AmazonCloudFront/latest/DeveloperGuide/private-content-signed-cookies.html

Question 8:

An application that records weather data every minute is deployed in a fleet of Spot EC2 instances and uses a MySQL RDS database instance. Currently, there is only one RDS instance running in one Availability Zone. You plan to improve the database to ensure high availability by synchronous data replication to another RDS instance.

Which of the following performs synchronous data replication in RDS?

1. RDS Read Replica
2. CloudFront running as a Multi-AZ deployment
3. DynamoDB Read Replica
4. RDS DB instance running as a Multi-AZ deployment

Answer(s): 4

Explanation

When you create or modify your DB instance to run as a Multi-AZ deployment, Amazon RDS automatically provisions and maintains a synchronous standby replica in a different Availability Zone. Updates to your DB Instance are synchronously replicated across Availability Zones to the standby in order to keep both in sync and protect your latest database updates against DB instance failure.

RDS Read Replica is incorrect as a Read Replica provides an asynchronous replication instead of synchronous.

DynamoDB Read Replica and CloudFront running as a Multi-AZ deployment are incorrect as both DynamoDB and CloudFront do not have a Read Replica feature.

Reference:

https://aws.amazon.com/rds/details/multi-az/

Here is a quick introduction to Amazon RDS:

https://youtu.be/eMzCI7S1P9M

Question 9:

A tech company that you are working for has undertaken a Total Cost Of Ownership (TCO) analysis evaluating the use of Amazon S3 versus acquiring more storage hardware. The result was that all 1200 employees would be granted access to use Amazon S3 for storage of their personal documents.

Which of the following will you need to consider so you can set up a solution that incorporates single sign-on feature from your corporate AD or LDAP directory and also restricts access for each individual user to a designated user folder in an S3 bucket? (Select TWO.)

1. Set up a matching IAM user for each of the 1200 users in your corporate directory that needs access to a folder in the S3 bucket.
2. Map each individual user to a designated user folder in S3 using Amazon WorkDocs to access their personal documents.
3. Use 3rd party Single Sign-On solutions such as Atlassian Crowd, OKTA, OneLogin and many others.
4. Configure an IAM role and an IAM Policy to access the bucket.
5. Set up a Federation proxy or an Identity provider, and use AWS Security Token Service to generate temporary tokens.

Answer(s): 4,5

Explanation

The question refers to one of the common scenarios for temporary credentials in AWS. Temporary credentials are useful in scenarios that involve identity federation, delegation, cross-account access, and IAM roles. In this example, it is called enterprise identity federation considering that you also need to set up a single sign-on (SSO) capability.

The correct answers are:

- Setup a Federation proxy or an Identity provider

- Setup an AWS Security Token Service to generate temporary tokens

- Configure an IAM role and an IAM Policy to access the bucket.

In an enterprise identity federation, you can authenticate users in your organization's network, and then provide those users access to AWS without creating new AWS identities for them and requiring them to sign in with a separate user name and password. This is known as the single sign-on (SSO) approach to temporary access. AWS STS supports open standards like Security Assertion Markup Language (SAML) 2.0, with which you can use Microsoft AD FS to leverage your Microsoft Active Directory. You can also use SAML 2.0 to manage your own solution for federating user identities.

Using 3rd party Single Sign-On solutions such as Atlassian Crowd, OKTA, OneLogin and many others is incorrect since you don't have to use 3rd party solutions to provide the access. AWS already provides the necessary tools that you can use in this situation.

Mapping each individual user to a designated user folder in S3 using Amazon WorkDocs to access their personal documents is incorrect as there is no direct way of integrating Amazon S3 with Amazon WorkDocs for this particular scenario. Amazon WorkDocs is simply a fully managed, secure content creation, storage, and collaboration service. With Amazon WorkDocs, you can easily create, edit, and share content. And because it's stored centrally on AWS, you can access it from anywhere on any device.

Setting up a matching IAM user for each of the 1200 users in your corporate directory that needs access to a folder in the S3 bucket is incorrect since creating that many IAM users would be unnecessary. Also, you want the account to integrate with your AD or LDAP directory, hence, IAM Users does not fit these criteria.

References:

https://docs.aws.amazon.com/IAM/latest/UserGuide/id_roles_providers_saml.html

https://docs.aws.amazon.com/IAM/latest/UserGuide/id_roles_providers_oidc.html

https://aws.amazon.com/blogs/security/writing-iam-policies-grant-access-to-user-specific-folders-in-an-amazon-s3-bucket/

Question 10:

You have triggered the creation of a snapshot of your EBS volume attached to an Instance Store-backed EC2 Instance and is currently on-going. At this point, what are the things that the EBS volume can or cannot do?

1. The volume can be used as normal while the snapshot is in progress.
2. The volume can be used in write-only mode while the snapshot is in progress.
3. The volume can be used in read-only mode while the snapshot is in progress.
4. The volume cannot be used until the snapshot completes.

Answer(s): 1

Explanation

EBS snapshots occur asynchronously which makes the option that says: The volume can be used as normal while the snapshot is in progress the correct answer. This means that the point-in-time snapshot is created immediately, but the status of the snapshot is pending until the snapshot is complete (when all of the modified blocks have been transferred to Amazon S3), which can take several hours for large initial snapshots or subsequent snapshots where many blocks have changed. While it is completing, an in-progress snapshot is not affected by ongoing reads and writes to the volume hence, you can still use the volume.

The rest of the options are incorrect because you will still be able to perform normal read and write operations on your EBS volume even while a snapshot is ongoing. Although you can take a snapshot of a volume while a previous snapshot of that volume is in the pending status, having multiple pending snapshots of a volume may result in reduced volume performance until the snapshots complete.

Reference:

https://docs.aws.amazon.com/AWSEC2/latest/UserGuide/ebs-creating-snapshot.html

Question 11:

In a government agency that you are working for, you have been assigned to put confidential tax documents on AWS cloud. However, there is a concern from a security perspective on what can be put on AWS.

What are the features in AWS that can ensure data security for your confidential documents? (Select TWO.)

1. Public Data Set Volume Encryption
2. S3 Server-Side Encryption
3. S3 Client-Side Encryption
4. EBS On-Premises Data Encryption
5. S3 On-Premises Data Encryption

Answer(s): 2, 3

Explanation

You can secure the privacy of your data in AWS, both at rest and in-transit, through encryption. If your data is stored in EBS Volumes, you can enable EBS Encryption and if it is stored on Amazon S3, you can enable client-side and server-side encryption.

Public Data Set Volume Encryption is incorrect as public data sets are designed to be publicly accessible.

EBS On-Premises Data Encryption and S3 On-Premises Data Encryption are both incorrect as there is no such thing as On-Premises Data Encryption for S3 and EBS as these services are in the AWS cloud and not on your on-premises network.

References:

https://docs.aws.amazon.com/AmazonS3/latest/dev/UsingEncryption.html

https://docs.aws.amazon.com/AWSEC2/latest/UserGuide/EBSEncryption.html

https://docs.aws.amazon.com/AWSEC2/latest/UserGuide/using-public-data-sets.html

Question 12:

An online cryptocurrency exchange platform is hosted in AWS which uses ECS Cluster and RDS in Multi-AZ Deployments configuration. The application is heavily using the RDS instance to process complex read and write database operations. To maintain the reliability, availability, and performance of your systems, you have to closely monitor how the different processes or threads on a DB instance use the CPU, including the percentage of the CPU bandwidth and total memory consumed by each process.

Which of the following is the most suitable solution to properly monitor your database?

1. Use Amazon CloudWatch to monitor the CPU Utilization of your database.
2. Check the CPU% and MEM% metrics which are readily available in the Amazon RDS console that shows the percentage of the CPU bandwidth and total memory consumed by each database process of your RDS instance.
3. Enable Enhanced Monitoring in RDS.
4. Create a script that collects and publishes custom metrics to CloudWatch, which tracks the real-time CPU Utilization of the RDS instance, and then set up a custom CloudWatch dashboard to view the metrics.

Answer(s): 3

Explanation

Amazon RDS provides metrics in real time for the operating system (OS) that your DB instance runs on. You can view the metrics for your DB instance using the console, or consume the Enhanced Monitoring JSON output from CloudWatch Logs in a monitoring system of your choice. By default, Enhanced Monitoring metrics are stored in the CloudWatch Logs for 30 days. To modify the amount of time the metrics are stored in the CloudWatch Logs, change the retention for the RDSOSMetrics log group in the CloudWatch console.

Take note that there are certain differences between CloudWatch and Enhanced Monitoring Metrics. CloudWatch gathers metrics about CPU utilization from the hypervisor for a DB instance, and Enhanced Monitoring gathers its metrics from an agent on the instance. As a result, you might find differences between the measurements, because the hypervisor layer performs a small amount of work. Hence, enabling Enhanced Monitoring in RDS is the correct answer in this specific scenario.

The differences can be greater if your DB instances use smaller instance classes, because then there are likely more virtual machines (VMs) that are managed by the hypervisor layer on a single physical instance. Enhanced Monitoring metrics are useful when you want to see how different processes or threads on a DB instance use the CPU.

Using Amazon CloudWatch to monitor the CPU Utilization of your database is incorrect because although you can use this to monitor the CPU Utilization of your database instance, it does not provide the percentage of the CPU bandwidth and total memory consumed by each database process in your RDS instance. Take note that CloudWatch gathers metrics about CPU utilization from the hypervisor for a DB instance while RDS Enhanced Monitoring gathers its metrics from an agent on the instance.

The option that says: Create a script that collects and publishes custom metrics to CloudWatch, which tracks the real-time CPU Utilization of the RDS instance and then set up a custom CloudWatch dashboard to view the metrics is incorrect because although you can use Amazon CloudWatch Logs and CloudWatch dashboard to monitor the CPU Utilization of the database instance, using CloudWatch alone is still not enough to get the specific percentage of the CPU bandwidth and total memory consumed by each database processes. The data provided by CloudWatch is not as detailed as compared with the Enhanced Monitoring feature in RDS. Take note as well that you do not have direct access to the instances/servers of your RDS database instance, unlike with your EC2 instances where you can install a CloudWatch agent or a custom script to get CPU and memory utilization of your instance.

The option that says: Check the CPU% and MEM% metrics which are readily available in the Amazon RDS console that shows the percentage of the CPU bandwidth and total memory consumed by each database process of your RDS instance is incorrect because the CPU% and MEM% metrics are not readily available in the Amazon RDS console, which is contrary to what is being stated in this option.

References:

https://docs.aws.amazon.com/AmazonRDS/latest/UserGuide/USER_Monitoring.OS.html#USER_Monitoring.OS.CloudWatchLogs

https://docs.aws.amazon.com/AmazonRDS/latest/UserGuide/MonitoringOverview.html#monitoring-cloudwatch

Question 13:

An online medical system hosted in AWS stores sensitive Personally Identifiable Information (PII) of the users in an Amazon S3 bucket. Both the master keys and the unencrypted data should never be sent to AWS to comply with the strict compliance and regulatory requirements of the company.

Which S3 encryption technique should the Architect use?

1. Use S3 client-side encryption with a client-side master key.
2. Use S3 client-side encryption with a KMS-managed customer master key.
3. Use S3 server-side encryption with customer provided key.
4. Use S3 server-side encryption with a KMS managed key.

Answer(s): 1

Explanation

Client-side encryption is the act of encrypting data before sending it to Amazon S3. To enable client-side encryption, you have the following options:

- Use an AWS KMS-managed customer master key.

- Use a client-side master key.

When using an AWS KMS-managed customer master key to enable client-side data encryption, you provide an AWS KMS customer master key ID (CMK ID) to AWS. On the other hand, when you use client-side master key for client-side data encryption, your client-side master keys and your unencrypted data are never sent to AWS. It's important that you safely manage your encryption keys because if you lose them, you can't decrypt your data.

This is how client-side encryption using client-side master key works:

When uploading an object - You provide a client-side master key to the Amazon S3 encryption client. The client uses the master key only to encrypt the data encryption key that it generates randomly. The process works like this:

1. The Amazon S3 encryption client generates a one-time-use symmetric key (also known as a data encryption key or data key) locally. It uses the data key to encrypt the data of a single Amazon S3 object. The client generates a separate data key for each object.

2. The client encrypts the data encryption key using the master key that you provide. The client uploads the encrypted data key and its material description as part of the object metadata. The client uses the material description to determine which client-side master key to use for decryption.

3. The client uploads the encrypted data to Amazon S3 and saves the encrypted data key as object metadata (x-amz-meta-x-amz-key) in Amazon S3.

When downloading an object - The client downloads the encrypted object from Amazon S3. Using the material description from the object's metadata, the client determines which master key to use to decrypt the data key. The client uses that master key to decrypt the data key and then uses the data key to decrypt the object.

Hence, the correct answer is to use S3 client-side encryption with a client-side master key.

Using S3 client-side encryption with a KMS-managed customer master key is incorrect because in client-side encryption with a KMS-managed customer master key, you provide an AWS KMS customer master key ID (CMK ID) to AWS. The scenario clearly indicates that both the master keys and the unencrypted data should never be sent to AWS.

Using S3 server-side encryption with a KMS managed key is incorrect because the scenario mentioned that the unencrypted data should never be sent to AWS, which means that you have to use client-side encryption in order to encrypt the data first before sending to AWS. In this way, you can ensure that there is no unencrypted data being uploaded to AWS. In addition, the master key used by Server-Side Encryption with AWS KMS–Managed Keys (SSE-KMS) is uploaded and managed by AWS, which directly violates the requirement of not uploading the master key.

Using S3 server-side encryption with customer provided key is incorrect because just as mentioned above, you have to use client-side encryption in this scenario instead of server-side encryption. For the S3 server-side encryption with customer-provided key (SSE-C), you actually provide the encryption key as part of your request to upload the object to S3. Using this key, Amazon S3 manages both the encryption (as it writes to disks) and decryption (when you access your objects).

References:

https://docs.aws.amazon.com/AmazonS3/latest/dev/UsingEncryption.html

https://docs.aws.amazon.com/AmazonS3/latest/dev/UsingClientSideEncryption.html

Question 14:

You are working as a Solutions Architect for a major telecommunications company where you are assigned to improve the security of your database tier by tightly managing the data flow of your Amazon Redshift cluster. One of the requirements is to use VPC flow logs to monitor all the COPY and UNLOAD traffic of your Redshift cluster that moves in and out of your VPC.

Which of the following is the most suitable solution to implement in this scenario?

1. Use the Amazon Redshift Spectrum feature.
2. Enable Enhanced VPC routing on your Amazon Redshift cluster.
3. Enable Audit Logging in your Amazon Redshift cluster.
4. Create a new flow log that tracks the traffic of your Amazon Redshift cluster.

Answer(s): 2

Explanation

When you use Amazon Redshift Enhanced VPC Routing, Amazon Redshift forces all COPY and UNLOAD traffic between your cluster and your data repositories through your Amazon VPC. By using Enhanced VPC Routing, you can use standard VPC features, such as VPC security groups, network access control lists (ACLs), VPC endpoints, VPC endpoint policies, internet gateways, and Domain Name

System (DNS) servers. Hence, enabling Enhanced VPC routing on your Amazon Redshift cluster is the correct answer.

You use these features to tightly manage the flow of data between your Amazon Redshift cluster and other resources. When you use Enhanced VPC Routing to route traffic through your VPC, you can also use VPC flow logs to monitor COPY and UNLOAD traffic. If Enhanced VPC Routing is not enabled, Amazon Redshift routes traffic through the Internet, including traffic to other services within the AWS network.

Enabling Audit Logging in your Amazon Redshift cluster is incorrect because the Audit Logging feature is primarily used to get the information about the connection, queries, and user activities in your Redshift cluster.

Using the Amazon Redshift Spectrum feature is incorrect because this is primarily used to run queries against exabytes of unstructured data in Amazon S3, with no loading or ETL required.

Creating a new flow log that tracks the traffic of your Amazon Redshift cluster is incorrect because, by default, you cannot create a flow log for your Amazon Redshift cluster. You have to enable Enhanced VPC Routing and set up the required VPC configuration.

Reference:

https://docs.aws.amazon.com/redshift/latest/mgmt/enhanced-vpc-routing.html

Question 15:

You are a Solutions Architect for a leading Enterprise Resource Planning (ERP) solutions provider and you are instructed to design and set up the architecture of your ERP application in AWS. Your manager instructed you to avoid using fully-managed AWS services and instead, only use specific services which allows you to access the underlying operating system for the resource. This is to allow the company to have a much better control of the underlying resources that their systems are using in the AWS cloud.

Which of the following services should you choose to satisfy this requirement? (Select TWO.)

1. DynamoDB
2. Amazon EC2
3. Amazon Neptune
4. Amazon Athena '
5. Amazon EMR

Answer(s): 2, 5

Explanation

Amazon EC2 provides you access to the operating system of the instance that you created.

Amazon EMR provides you a managed Hadoop framework that makes it easy, fast, and cost-effective to process vast amounts of data across dynamically scalable Amazon EC2 instances. You can access the operating system of these EC2 instances that were created by Amazon EMR.

Amazon Athena, DynamoDB, and Amazon Neptune are incorrect as these are managed services, which means that AWS manages the underlying operating system and other server configurations that these databases use.

References:

https://aws.amazon.com/ec2/

https://aws.amazon.com/emr/

Question 16:

You are a Solutions Architect in your company working with 3 DevOps Engineers under you. One of the engineers accidentally deleted a file hosted in Amazon S3 which has caused disruption of service.

What can you do to prevent this from happening again?

1. Enable S3 Versioning and Multi-Factor Authentication Delete on the bucket.
2. Use S3 Infrequently Accessed storage to store the data.
3. Set up a signed URL for all users.
4. Create an IAM bucket policy that disables delete operation.

Answer(s): 1

Explanation

To avoid accidental deletion in Amazon S3 bucket, you can:

- Enable Versioning

- Enable MFA (Multi-Factor Authentication) Delete

Versioning is a means of keeping multiple variants of an object in the same bucket. You can use versioning to preserve, retrieve, and restore every version of every object stored in your Amazon S3 bucket. With versioning, you can easily recover from both unintended user actions and application failures.

If the MFA (Multi-Factor Authentication) Delete is enabled, it requires additional authentication for either of the following operations:

- Change the versioning state of your bucket

- Permanently delete an object version

Using S3 Infrequently Accessed storage to store the data is incorrect. Switching your storage class to S3 Infrequent Access won't help mitigate accidental deletions.

Setting up a signed URL for all users is incorrect. Signed URLs give you more control over access to your content, so this feature deals more on accessing rather than deletion.

Creating an IAM bucket policy that disables delete operation is incorrect. If you create a bucket policy preventing deletion, other users won't be able to delete objects that should be deleted. You only want to prevent accidental deletion, not disable the action itself.

Reference:

http://docs.aws.amazon.com/AmazonS3/latest/dev/Versioning.html

Question 17:

An application is hosted in an AWS Fargate cluster that runs a batch job whenever an object is loaded on an Amazon S3 bucket. The minimum number of ECS Tasks is initially set to 1 to save on costs, and it will only increase the task count based on the new objects uploaded on the S3 bucket. Once processing is done, the bucket becomes empty and the ECS Task count should be back to 1.

Which is the most suitable option to implement with the LEAST amount of effort?

1. Set up an alarm in CloudWatch to monitor CloudTrail since this S3 object-level operations are recorded on CloudTrail. Set two alarm actions to update ECS task count to scale-out/scale-in depending on the S3 event.
2. Set up a CloudWatch Event rule to detect S3 object PUT operations and set the target to a Lambda function that will run Amazon ECS API command to increase the number of tasks on ECS. Create another rule to detect S3 DELETE operations and run the Lambda function to reduce the number of ECS tasks.
3. Set up a CloudWatch Event rule to detect S3 object PUT operations and set the target to the ECS cluster with the increased number of tasks. Create another rule to detect S3 DELETE operations and set the target to the ECS Cluster with 1 as the Task count.
4. Set up an alarm in CloudWatch to monitor CloudTrail since the S3 object-level operations are recorded on CloudTrail. Create two Lambda functions

for increasing/decreasing the ECS task count. Set these as respective targets for the CloudWatch Alarm depending on the S3 event.

Answer(s): 3

Explanation

You can use CloudWatch Events to run Amazon ECS tasks when certain AWS events occur. You can set up a CloudWatch Events rule that runs an Amazon ECS task whenever a file is uploaded to a certain Amazon S3 bucket using the Amazon S3 PUT operation. You can also declare a reduced number of ECS tasks whenever a file is deleted on the S3 bucket using the DELETE operation.

First, you must create a CloudWatch Events rule for the S3 service that will watch for object-level operations – PUT and DELETE objects. For object-level operations, it is required to create a CloudTrail trail first. On the Targets section, select the "ECS task" and input the needed values such as the cluster name, task definition and the task count. You need two rules – one for the scale-up and another for the scale-down of the ECS task count.

Hence, the correct answer is: Set up a CloudWatch Event rule to detect S3 object PUT operations and set the target to the ECS cluster with the increased number of tasks. Create another rule to detect S3 DELETE operations and set the target to the ECS Cluster with 1 as the Task count.

The option that says: Set up a CloudWatch Event rule to detect S3 object PUT operations and set the target to a Lambda function that will run Amazon ECS API command to increase the number of tasks on ECS. Create another rule to detect S3 DELETE operations and run the Lambda function to reduce the number of ECS tasks is incorrect because although this solution meets the requirement, creating your own Lambda function for this scenario is not really necessary. It is much simpler to control ECS task directly as target for the CloudWatch Event rule. Take note that the scenario asks for a solution that is the easiest to implement.

The option that says: Set up an alarm in CloudWatch to monitor CloudTrail since the S3 object-level operations are recorded on CloudTrail. Create two Lambda functions for increasing/decreasing the ECS task count. Set these as respective targets for the CloudWatch Alarm depending on the S3 event is incorrect because using CloudTrail, CloudWatch Alarm, and two Lambda functions creates an unnecessary complexity to what you want to achieve. CloudWatch Events can directly target an ECS task on the Targets section when you create a new rule.

The option that says: Set up an alarm in CloudWatch to monitor CloudTrail since this S3 object-level operations are recorded on CloudTrail. Set two alarm actions to update ECS task count to scale-out/scale-in depending on the S3 event is incorrect because you can't directly set CloudWatch Alarms to update the ECS task count. You have to use CloudWatch Events instead.

References:

https://docs.aws.amazon.com/AmazonCloudWatch/latest/events/CloudWatch-Events-tutorial-ECS.html

https://docs.aws.amazon.com/AmazonCloudWatch/latest/events/Create-CloudWatch-Events-Rule.html

Question 18:

You are leading a software development team which uses serverless computing with AWS Lambda to build and run applications without having to set up or manage servers. You have a Lambda function that connects to a MongoDB Atlas, which is a popular Database as a Service (DBaaS) platform and also uses a third party API to fetch certain data for your application. You instructed one of your junior developers to create the environment variables for the MongoDB database hostname, username, and password as well as the API credentials that will be used by the Lambda function for DEV, SIT, UAT and PROD environments.

Considering that the Lambda function is storing sensitive database and API credentials, how can you secure this information to prevent other developers in your team, or anyone, from seeing these credentials in plain text? Select the best option that provides the maximum security.

1. There is no need to do anything because, by default, AWS Lambda already encrypts the environment variables using the AWS Key Management Service.
2. Create a new KMS key and use it to enable encryption helpers that leverage on AWS Key Management Service to store and encrypt the sensitive information.
3. AWS Lambda does not provide encryption for the environment variables. Deploy your code to an EC2 instance instead.
4. Enable SSL encryption that leverages on AWS CloudHSM to store and encrypt the sensitive information.

Answer(s): 2

Explanation

When you create or update Lambda functions that use environment variables, AWS Lambda encrypts them using the AWS Key Management Service. When your Lambda function is invoked, those values are decrypted and made available to the Lambda code.

The first time you create or update Lambda functions that use environment variables in a region, a default service key is created for you automatically within AWS KMS. This key is used to encrypt environment variables. However, if you wish to use encryption helpers and use KMS to encrypt environment variables after your

Lambda function is created, you must create your own AWS KMS key and choose it instead of the default key. The default key will give errors when chosen. Creating your own key gives you more flexibility, including the ability to create, rotate, disable, and define access controls, and to audit the encryption keys used to protect your data.

The option that says: There is no need to do anything because, by default, AWS Lambda already encrypts the environment variables using the AWS Key Management Service is incorrect because although Lambda encrypts the environment variables in your function by default, the sensitive information would still be visible to other users who have access to the Lambda console. This is because Lambda uses a default KMS key to encrypt the variables, which is usually accessible by other users. The best option in this scenario is to use encryption helpers to secure your environment variables.

The option that says: Enable SSL encryption that leverages on AWS CloudHSM to store and encrypt the sensitive information is also incorrect since enabling SSL would encrypt data only when in-transit. Your other teams would still be able to view the plaintext at-rest. Use AWS KMS instead.

The option that says: AWS Lambda does not provide encryption for the environment variables. Deploy your code to an EC2 instance instead is incorrect since, as mentioned, Lambda does provide encryption functionality of environment variables.

References:

https://docs.aws.amazon.com/lambda/latest/dg/env_variables.html#env_encrypt

https://docs.aws.amazon.com/lambda/latest/dg/tutorial-env_console.html

Question 19:

A newly hired Solutions Architect is assigned to manage a set of CloudFormation templates that is used in the company's cloud architecture in AWS. The Architect accessed the templates and tried to analyze the configured IAM policy for an S3 bucket.

```
{
"Version": "2012-10-17",
"Statement": [
{
"Effect": "Allow",
"Action": [
"s3:Get*",
```

"s3:List*"

],

"Resource": "*"

},

{

"Effect": "Allow",

"Action": "s3:PutObject",

"Resource": "arn:aws:s3:::tutorialsfree/*"

}

]

}

What does the above IAM policy allow? (Select THREE.)

1. An IAM user with this IAM policy is allowed to write objects into the tutorialsfree S3 bucket.
2. An IAM user with this IAM policy is allowed to read and delete objects from the tutorialsfree S3 bucket.
3. An IAM user with this IAM policy is allowed to read objects in the tutorialsfree S3 bucket but not allowed to list the objects in the bucket.
4. An IAM user with this IAM policy is allowed to change access rights for the tutorialsfree S3 bucket.
5. An IAM user with this IAM policy is allowed to read objects from all S3 buckets owned by the account.
6. An IAM user with this IAM policy is allowed to read objects from the tutorialsfree S3 bucket.

Answer(s): 1, 5, 6

Explanation

You manage access in AWS by creating policies and attaching them to IAM identities (users, groups of users, or roles) or AWS resources. A policy is an object in AWS that, when associated with an identity or resource, defines their permissions. AWS evaluates these policies when an IAM principal (user or role) makes a request. Permissions in the policies determine whether the request is allowed or denied. Most policies are stored in AWS as JSON documents. AWS supports six types of policies: identity-based policies, resource-based policies, permissions boundaries, AWS Organizations SCPs, ACLs, and session policies.

IAM policies define permissions for an action regardless of the method that you use to perform the operation. For example, if a policy allows the GetUser action, then a user with that policy can get user information from the AWS Management Console, the AWS CLI, or the AWS API. When you create an IAM user, you can choose to allow console or programmatic access. If console access is allowed, the IAM user can sign in to the console using a user name and password. Or if programmatic access is allowed, the user can use access keys to work with the CLI or API.

Based on the provided IAM policy, the user is only allowed to get, write and list all of the objects for the 'tutorialsfree' s3 bucket. The s3:PutObject basically means that you can submit a PUT object request to the S3 bucket to store data.

Hence, the correct answers are:

- An IAM user with this IAM policy is allowed to read objects from all S3 buckets owned by the account.

- An IAM user with this IAM policy is allowed to write objects into the 'tutorialsfree' S3 bucket.

- An IAM user with this IAM policy is allowed to read objects from the 'tutorialsfree' S3 bucket.

The option that says: An IAM user with this IAM policy is allowed to change access rights for the 'tutorialsfree' S3 bucket is incorrect because the template does not have any statements which allow the user to change access rights in the bucket.

The option that says: An IAM user with this IAM policy is allowed to read objects in the 'tutorialsfree' S3 bucket but not allowed to list the objects in the bucket is incorrect because it can clearly be seen in the template the there is a s3:Get* which permits the user to list objects.

The option that says: An IAM user with this IAM policy is allowed to read and delete objects from the 'tutorialsfree' S3 bucket is incorrect because although you can read objects from the bucket, you cannot delete any objects.

References:

https://docs.aws.amazon.com/AmazonS3/latest/API/RESTObjectOps.html

https://docs.aws.amazon.com/IAM/latest/UserGuide/access_policies.html

Question 20:

A retail website has intermittent, sporadic, and unpredictable transactional workloads throughout the day that are hard to predict. The website is currently hosted on-premises and is slated to be migrated to AWS. A new relational database is needed that autoscales capacity to meet the needs of the application's peak load and scales back down when the surge of activity is over.

Which of the following option is the MOST cost-effective and suitable database setup in this scenario?

1. Launch an Amazon Redshift data warehouse cluster with Concurrency Scaling.
2. Launch an Amazon Aurora Serverless DB cluster then set the minimum and maximum capacity for the cluster.
3. Launch a DynamoDB Global table with Auto Scaling enabled.
4. Launch an Amazon Aurora Provisioned DB cluster with burstable performance DB instance class types.

Answer(s): 2

Explanation

Amazon Aurora Serverless is an on-demand, auto-scaling configuration for Amazon Aurora. An Aurora Serverless DB cluster is a DB cluster that automatically starts up, shuts down, and scales up or down its compute capacity based on your application's needs. Aurora Serverless provides a relatively simple, cost-effective option for infrequent, intermittent, sporadic or unpredictable workloads. It can provide this because it automatically starts up, scales compute capacity to match your application's usage and shuts down when it's not in use.

Take note that a non-Serverless DB cluster for Aurora is called a provisioned DB cluster. Aurora Serverless clusters and provisioned clusters both have the same kind of high-capacity, distributed, and highly available storage volume.

When you work with Amazon Aurora without Aurora Serverless (provisioned DB clusters), you can choose your DB instance class size and create Aurora Replicas to increase read throughput. If your workload changes, you can modify the DB instance class size and change the number of Aurora Replicas. This model works well when the database workload is predictable, because you can adjust capacity manually based on the expected workload.

However, in some environments, workloads can be intermittent and unpredictable. There can be periods of heavy workloads that might last only a few minutes or hours, and also long periods of light activity, or even no activity. Some examples are retail websites with intermittent sales events, reporting databases that produce reports when needed, development and testing environments, and new applications with uncertain requirements. In these cases and many others, it can be difficult to configure the correct capacity at the right times. It can also result in higher costs when you pay for capacity that isn't used.

With Aurora Serverless , you can create a database endpoint without specifying the DB instance class size. You set the minimum and maximum capacity. With Aurora Serverless, the database endpoint connects to a proxy fleet that routes the workload to a fleet of resources that are automatically scaled. Because of the proxy fleet, connections are continuous as Aurora Serverless scales the resources automatically based on the minimum and maximum capacity specifications. Database client applications don't need to change to use the proxy fleet. Aurora Serverless manages the connections automatically. Scaling is rapid because it uses a pool of "warm" resources that are always ready to service requests. Storage and processing are separate, so you can scale down to zero processing and pay only for storage.

Aurora Serverless introduces a new serverless DB engine mode for Aurora DB clusters. Non-Serverless DB clusters use the provisioned DB engine mode.

Hence, the correct answer is: Launch an Amazon Aurora Serverless DB cluster then set the minimum and maximum capacity for the cluster.

The option that says: Launch an Amazon Aurora Provisioned DB cluster then set the minimum and maximum capacity for the cluster is incorrect because an Aurora Provisioned DB cluster is not suitable for intermittent, sporadic, and unpredictable transactional workloads. This model works well when the database workload is predictable because you can adjust capacity manually based on the expected workload. A better database setup here is to use an Amazon Aurora Serverless cluster.

The option that says: Launch a DynamoDB Global table with Auto Scaling enabled is incorrect because although it is using Auto Scaling, the scenario explicitly indicated that you need a relational database to handle your transactional workloads. DynamoDB is a NoSQL database and is not suitable for this use case. Moreover, the use of a DynamoDB Global table is not warranted since this is primarily used if you need a fully managed, multi-region, and multi-master database that provides fast, local, read and write performance for massively scaled, global applications.

The option that says: Launch an Amazon Redshift data warehouse cluster with Concurrency Scaling is incorrect because this type of database is primarily used for online analytical processing (OLAP) and not for online transactional processing (OLTP). Concurrency Scaling is simply an Amazon Redshift feature that automatically and elastically scales query processing power of your Redshift cluster to provide consistently fast performance for hundreds of concurrent queries.

References:

https://docs.aws.amazon.com/AmazonRDS/latest/AuroraUserGuide/aurora-serverless.how-it-works.html

https://docs.aws.amazon.com/AmazonRDS/latest/AuroraUserGuide/aurora-serverless.html

Question 21:

A suite of web applications is hosted in an Auto Scaling group of EC2 instances across three Availability Zones and is configured with default settings. There is an Application Load Balancer that forwards the request to the respective target group on the URL path. The scale-in policy has been triggered due to the low number of incoming traffic to the application.

Which EC2 instance will be the first one to be terminated by your Auto Scaling group?

1. The EC2 instance launched from the oldest launch configuration
2. The EC2 instance which has been running for the longest time
3. The EC2 instance which has the least number of user sessions
4. The instance will be randomly selected by the Auto Scaling group

Answer(s): 1

Explanation

The default termination policy is designed to help ensure that your network architecture spans Availability Zones evenly. With the default termination policy, the behavior of the Auto Scaling group is as follows:

1. If there are instances in multiple Availability Zones, choose the Availability Zone with the most instances and at least one instance that is not protected from scale in. If there is more than one Availability Zone with this number of instances, choose the Availability Zone with the instances that use the oldest launch configuration.

2. Determine which unprotected instances in the selected Availability Zone use the oldest launch configuration. If there is one such instance, terminate it.

3. If there are multiple instances to terminate based on the above criteria, determine which unprotected instances are closest to the next billing hour. (This helps you maximize the use of your EC2 instances and manage your Amazon EC2 usage costs.) If there is one such instance, terminate it.

4. If there is more than one unprotected instance closest to the next billing hour, choose one of these instances at random.

The following flow diagram illustrates how the default termination policy works:

References:

https://docs.aws.amazon.com/autoscaling/ec2/userguide/as-instance-termination.html#default-termination-policy

https://docs.aws.amazon.com/autoscaling/ec2/userguide/as-instance-termination.html

Question 22:

A leading utilities provider is in the process of migrating their applications to AWS. Their Solutions Architect created an EBS-Backed EC2 instance with ephemeral0 and ephemeral1 instance store volumes attached to host a web application that fetches and stores data from a web API service.

If this instance is stopped, what will happen to the data on the ephemeral store volumes?

1. Data is automatically saved as an EBS snapshot.
2. Data will be deleted.
3. Data is automatically saved in an EBS volume.
4. Data is unavailable until the instance is restarted.

Answer(s): 2

Explanation

The word ephemeral means "short-lived" or "temporary" in the English dictionary. Hence, when you see this word in AWS, always consider this as just a temporary memory or a short-lived storage.

The virtual devices for instance store volumes are named as ephemeral[0-23]. Instance types that support one instance store volume have ephemeral0. Instance types that support two instance store volumes have ephemeral0 and ephemeral1, and so on until ephemeral23.

The data in an instance store persists only during the lifetime of its associated instance. If an instance reboots (intentionally or unintentionally), data in the instance store persists. However, data in the instance store is lost under the following circumstances:

- The underlying disk drive fails

- The instance stops

- The instance terminates

Hence, the option that says: Data will be deleted is the correct answer.

The option that says: Data is automatically saved in an EBS volume is incorrect since instance store volumes and EBS volumes are two different storage types. An Amazon EBS volume is a durable, block-level storage device that you can attach to a single EC2 instance. An instance store provides temporary block-level storage and is located on disks that are physically attached to the host computer. No automatic backup will be performed.

The option that says: Data is unavailable until the instance is restarted is incorrect because once you stop an instance, the data in the ephemeral instance store volumes will be gone.

The option that says: Data is automatically saved as an EBS snapshot is incorrect because just like in the option above, instance store volumes and EBS volumes are two different storage devices. There is no automated snapshot that will be created.

Reference:

http://docs.aws.amazon.com/AWSEC2/latest/UserGuide/InstanceStorage.html?shortFooter=true#instance-store-lifetime

Question 23:

There was an incident in your production environment where the user data stored in the S3 bucket has been accidentally deleted by one of the Junior DevOps Engineers. The issue was escalated to your manager and after a few days, you were instructed to improve the security and protection of your AWS resources.

What combination of the following options will protect the S3 objects in your bucket from both accidental deletion and overwriting? (Select TWO.)

1. Enable Versioning
2. Provide access to S3 data strictly through pre-signed URL only
3. Disallow S3 Delete using an IAM bucket policy
4. Enable Amazon S3 Intelligent-Tiering
5. Enable Multi-Factor Authentication Delete

Answer(s): 1, 5

Explanation

By using Versioning and enabling MFA (Multi-Factor Authentication) Delete, you can secure and recover your S3 objects from accidental deletion or overwrite.

Versioning is a means of keeping multiple variants of an object in the same bucket. Versioning-enabled buckets enable you to recover objects from accidental deletion or overwrite. You can use versioning to preserve, retrieve, and restore every version of every object stored in your Amazon S3 bucket. With versioning, you can easily recover from both unintended user actions and application failures.

You can also optionally add another layer of security by configuring a bucket to enable MFA (Multi-Factor Authentication) Delete, which requires additional authentication for either of the following operations:

- Change the versioning state of your bucket

- Permanently delete an object version

MFA Delete requires two forms of authentication together:

- Your security credentials

- The concatenation of a valid serial number, a space, and the six-digit code displayed on an approved authentication device

Providing access to S3 data strictly through pre-signed URL only is incorrect since a pre-signed URL gives access to the object identified in the URL. Pre-signed URLs are useful when customers perform an object upload to your S3 bucket, but does not help in preventing accidental deletes.

Disallowing S3 Delete using an IAM bucket policy is incorrect since you still want users to be able to delete objects in the bucket, and you just want to prevent accidental deletions. Disallowing S3 Delete using an IAM bucket policy will restrict all delete operations to your bucket.

Enabling Amazon S3 Intelligent-Tiering is incorrect since S3 intelligent tiering does not help in this situation.

Reference:

https://docs.aws.amazon.com/AmazonS3/latest/dev/Versioning.html

Question 24:

A travel photo sharing website is using Amazon S3 to serve high-quality photos to visitors of your website. After a few days, you found out that there are other travel websites linking and using your photos. This resulted in financial losses for your business.

What is the MOST effective method to mitigate this issue?

1. Use CloudFront distributions for your photos.
2. Store and privately serve the high-quality photos on Amazon WorkDocs instead.
3. Configure your S3 bucket to remove public read access and use pre-signed URLs with expiry dates.
4. Block the IP addresses of the offending websites using NACL.

Answer(s): 3

Explanation

In Amazon S3, all objects are private by default. Only the object owner has permission to access these objects. However, the object owner can optionally share objects with others by creating a pre-signed URL, using their own security credentials, to grant time-limited permission to download the objects.

When you create a pre-signed URL for your object, you must provide your security credentials, specify a bucket name, an object key, specify the HTTP method (GET to download the object) and expiration date and time. The pre-signed URLs are valid only for the specified duration.

Anyone who receives the pre-signed URL can then access the object. For example, if you have a video in your bucket and both the bucket and the object are private, you can share the video with others by generating a pre-signed URL.

Using CloudFront distributions for your photos is incorrect. CloudFront is a content delivery network service that speeds up delivery of content to your customers.

Blocking the IP addresses of the offending websites using NACL is also incorrect. Blocking IP address using NACLs is not a very efficient method because a quick change in IP address would easily bypass this configuration.

Storing and privately serving the high-quality photos on Amazon WorkDocs instead is incorrect as WorkDocs is simply a fully managed, secure content creation, storage, and collaboration service. It is not a suitable service for storing static content. Amazon WorkDocs is more often used to easily create, edit, and share documents for collaboration and not for serving object data like Amazon S3.

References:

https://docs.aws.amazon.com/AmazonS3/latest/dev/ShareObjectPreSignedURL.html

https://docs.aws.amazon.com/AmazonS3/latest/dev/ObjectOperations.html

Question 25:

There are many clients complaining that the online trading application of an investment bank is always down. Your manager instructed you to re-design the architecture of the application to prevent the unnecessary service interruptions. To ensure high availability, you set up the application to use an ELB to distribute the incoming requests across an auto-scaled group of EC2 instances in two single Availability Zones. The Auto Scaling group is configured with default settings.

In this scenario, what happens when an EC2 instance behind an ELB fails a health check?

1. The ELB stops sending traffic to the EC2 instance
2. The EC2 instance is replaced automatically by the ELB.
3. The EC2 instance will automatically be deregistered from the default Placement Group.
4. The EC2 instance gets terminated automatically by the ELB.

Answer(s): 1

Explanation

In this scenario, the load balancer will route the incoming requests only to the healthy instances. When the load balancer determines that an instance is unhealthy, it stops routing requests to that instance. The load balancer resumes routing requests to the instance when it has been restored to a healthy state.

There are two ways of checking the status of your EC2 instances:

1. Via the Auto Scaling group

2. Via the ELB health checks

The default health checks for an Auto Scaling group are EC2 status checks only. If an instance fails these status checks, the Auto Scaling group considers the instance unhealthy and replaces. If you attached one or more load balancers or target groups to your Auto Scaling group, the group does not, by default, consider an instance unhealthy and replace it if it fails the load balancer health checks.

However, you can optionally configure the Auto Scaling group to use Elastic Load Balancing health checks. This ensures that the group can determine an instance's health based on additional tests provided by the load balancer. The load balancer periodically sends pings, attempts connections, or sends requests to test the EC2 instances. These tests are called health checks.

If you configure the Auto Scaling group to use Elastic Load Balancing health checks, it considers the instance unhealthy if it fails either the EC2 status checks or the load balancer health checks. If you attach multiple load balancers to an Auto Scaling group, all of them must report that the instance is healthy in order for it to consider the instance healthy. If one load balancer reports an instance as unhealthy, the Auto Scaling group replaces the instance, even if other load balancers report it as healthy.

The scenario said that the Auto Scaling group is configured with default settings. This means that it is using the EC2 health check type. Hence, the correct answer is: The ELB stops sending traffic to the EC2 instance.

The option that says: The EC2 instance gets terminated automatically by the ELB is incorrect because this action will not be done by ELB.

The option that says: The EC2 instance will automatically be deregistered from the default Placement Group is incorrect because in the first place, an EC2 instance is not associated with a Placement Group by default. A Placement group is simply a logical placement of a group of interdependent EC2 instances to meet the low-latency network performance needs of your workload.

The option that says: The EC2 instance is replaced automatically by the ELB is incorrect because the scenario clearly states that the Auto Scaling group is configured with default settings. The default health check type is the EC2 checks, which means that the ELB will stop sending traffic to the EC2 instance.

References:

https://docs.aws.amazon.com/elasticloadbalancing/latest/classic/elb-healthchecks.html

https://docs.aws.amazon.com/autoscaling/ec2/userguide/as-add-elb-healthcheck.html

Here is an additional training material on why an Amazon EC2 Auto Scaling group terminates a healthy instance:

Question 26:

A startup based in Australia is deploying a new two-tier web application in AWS. The Australian company wants to store their most frequently used data in an in-memory data store to improve the retrieval and response time of their web application.

Which of the following is the most suitable service to be used for this requirement?

1. DynamoDB
2. Amazon Redshift
3. Amazon RDS
4. Amazon ElastiCache

Answer(s): 4

Explanation

Amazon ElastiCache is a web service that makes it easy to deploy, operate, and scale an in-memory data store or cache in the cloud. The service improves the performance of web applications by allowing you to retrieve information from fast, managed, in-memory data stores, instead of relying entirely on slower disk-based databases.

DynamoDB is incorrect because this is primarily used as a NoSQL database which supports both document and key-value store models. ElastiCache is a more suitable service to use than DynamoDB, if you need an in-memory data store.

Amazon RDS is incorrect because this is mainly used as a relational database and not as a data storage for frequently used data.

Amazon Redshift is incorrect because this is a data warehouse service and is not suitable to be used as an in-memory data store.

References:

https://aws.amazon.com/elasticache/

https://aws.amazon.com/products/databases/

Question 27:

A cryptocurrency trading platform is using an API built in AWS Lambda and API Gateway. Due to the recent news and rumors about the upcoming price surge of Bitcoin, Ethereum and other cryptocurrencies, it is expected that the trading platform would have a significant increase in site visitors and new users in the coming days ahead.

In this scenario, how can you protect the backend systems of the platform from traffic spikes?

1. Move the Lambda function in a VPC.
2. Use CloudFront in front of the API Gateway to act as a cache.
3. Switch from using AWS Lambda and API Gateway to a more scalable and highly available architecture using EC2 instances, ELB, and Auto Scaling.
4. Enable throttling limits and result caching in API Gateway.

Answer(s): 4

Explanation

Amazon API Gateway provides throttling at multiple levels including global and by service call. Throttling limits can be set for standard rates and bursts. For example, API owners can set a rate limit of 1,000 requests per second for a specific method in their REST APIs, and also configure Amazon API Gateway to handle a burst of 2,000 requests per second for a few seconds. Amazon API Gateway tracks the number of requests per second. Any request over the limit will receive a 429 HTTP response. The client SDKs generated by Amazon API Gateway retry calls automatically when met with this response. Hence, enabling throttling limits and result caching in API Gateway is the correct answer.

You can add caching to API calls by provisioning an Amazon API Gateway cache and specifying its size in gigabytes. The cache is provisioned for a specific stage of your APIs. This improves performance and reduces the traffic sent to your back end. Cache settings allow you to control the way the cache key is built and the time-to-live (TTL) of the data stored for each method. Amazon API Gateway also exposes management APIs that help you invalidate the cache for each stage.

The option that says: Switch from using AWS Lambda and API Gateway to a more scalable and highly available architecture using EC2 instances, ELB, and Auto Scaling is incorrect since there is no need to transfer your applications to other services.

Using CloudFront in front of the API Gateway to act as a cache is incorrect because CloudFront only speeds up content delivery which provides a better latency experience for your users. It does not help much for the backend.

Moving the Lambda function in a VPC is incorrect because this answer is irrelevant to what is being asked. A VPC is your own virtual private cloud where you can launch AWS services.

Reference:

https://aws.amazon.com/api-gateway/faqs/

Here is an in-depth tutorial on Amazon API Gateway:

https://youtu.be/XwfpPEFHKtQ

Question 28:

You have identified a series of DDoS attacks while monitoring your VPC. As the Solutions Architect, you are responsible in fortifying your current cloud infrastructure to protect the data of your clients.

Which of the following is the most suitable solution to mitigate these kinds of attacks?

1. Using the AWS Firewall Manager, set up a security layer that will prevent SYN floods, UDP reflection attacks and other DDoS attacks.
2. A combination of Security Groups and Network Access Control Lists to only allow authorized traffic to access your VPC.
3. Use AWS Shield to detect and mitigate DDoS attacks.
4. Set up a web application firewall using AWS WAF to filter, monitor, and block HTTP traffic.

Answer(s): 3

Explanation

For higher levels of protection against attacks targeting your applications running on Amazon Elastic Compute Cloud (EC2), Elastic Load Balancing(ELB), Amazon CloudFront, and Amazon Route 53 resources, you can subscribe to AWS Shield Advanced. In addition to the network and transport layer protections that come with Standard, AWS Shield Advanced provides additional detection and mitigation against large and sophisticated DDoS attacks, near real-time visibility into attacks, and integration with AWS WAF, a web application firewall.

AWS Shield Advanced also gives you 24x7 access to the AWS DDoS Response Team (DRT) and protection against DDoS related spikes in your Amazon Elastic Compute Cloud (EC2), Elastic Load Balancing(ELB), Amazon CloudFront, and Amazon Route 53 charges.

The option that says: Using the AWS Firewall Manager, set up a security layer that will prevent SYN floods, UDP reflection attacks and other DDoS attacks is incorrect because the AWS Firewall Manager is mainly used to simplify your AWS WAF administration and maintenance tasks across multiple accounts and resources. It does not protect your VPC against DDoS attacks.

The option that says: Set up a web application firewall using AWS WAF to filter, monitor, and block HTTP traffic is incorrect because even though AWS WAF can help you block common attack patterns to your VPC such as SQL injection or cross-site scripting, this is still not enough to withstand DDoS attacks. It is better to use AWS Shield in this scenario.

The option that says: A combination of Security Groups and Network Access Control Lists to only allow authorized traffic to access your VPC is incorrect because although using a combination of Security Groups and NACLs are valid to provide security to your VPC, this is not enough to mitigate a DDoS attack. You should use AWS Shield for better security protection.

References:

https://d1.awsstatic.com/whitepapers/Security/DDoS_White_Paper.pdf

https://aws.amazon.com/shield/

Question 29:

You are managing a suite of applications in your on-premises network which are using trusted IP addresses that your partners and customers have whitelisted in their firewalls. There is a requirement to migrate these applications to AWS without requiring your partners and customers to change their IP address whitelists.

Which of the following is the most suitable solution to properly migrate your applications?

1. Set up a list of Elastic IP addresses to map the whitelisted IP address range in your on-premises network.
2. Set up an IP match condition using a CloudFront web distribution and AWS WAF to whitelist a specific IP address range in your VPC.
3. Submit an AWS Request Form to migrate the IP address range that you own to your AWS Account.
4. Create a Route Origin Authorization (ROA) then once done, provision and advertise your whitelisted IP address range to your AWS account.

Answer(s): 4

Explanation

You can bring part or all of your public IPv4 address range from your on-premises network to your AWS account. You continue to own the address range, but AWS advertises it on the Internet. After you bring the address range to AWS, it appears in your account as an address pool. You can create an Elastic IP address from your address pool and use it with your AWS resources, such as EC2 instances, NAT gateways, and Network Load Balancers. This is also called "Bring Your Own IP Addresses (BYOIP)".

To ensure that only you can bring your address range to your AWS account, you must authorize Amazon to advertise the address range and provide proof that you own the address range.

A Route Origin Authorization (ROA) is a document that you can create through your Regional internet registry (RIR), such as the American Registry for Internet Numbers (ARIN) or Réseaux IP Européens Network Coordination Centre (RIPE).

It contains the address range, the ASNs that are allowed to advertise the address range, and an expiration date. Hence, Option 3 is the correct answer.

The ROA authorizes Amazon to advertise an address range under a specific AS number. However, it does not authorize your AWS account to bring the address range to AWS. To authorize your AWS account to bring an address range to AWS, you must publish a self-signed X509 certificate in the RDAP remarks for the address range. The certificate contains a public key, which AWS uses to verify the authorization-context signature that you provide. You should keep your private key secure and use it to sign the authorization-context message.

Setting up a list of Elastic IP addresses to map the whitelisted IP address range in your on-premises network is incorrect because you cannot map the IP address of your on-premises network, which you are migrating to AWS, to an EIP address of your VPC. To satisfy the requirement, you must authorize Amazon to advertise the address range that you own.

Setting up an IP match condition using a CloudFront web distribution and AWS WAF to whitelist a specific IP address range in your VPC is incorrect because the IP match condition in CloudFront is primarily used in allowing or blocking the incoming web requests based on the IP addresses that the requests originate from. This is the opposite of what is being asked in the scenario, where you have to migrate your suite of applications from your on-premises network and advertise the address range that you own in your VPC.

Submitting an AWS Request Form to migrate the IP address range that you own to your AWS Account is incorrect because you don't need to submit an AWS request in order to do this. You can simply create a Route Origin Authorization (ROA) then once done, provision and advertise your whitelisted IP address range to your AWS account.

Reference:

https://docs.aws.amazon.com/AWSEC2/latest/UserGuide/ec2-byoip.html

Question 30:

You have a web application deployed in AWS which is currently running in the eu-central-1 region. You have an Auto Scaling group of On-Demand EC2 instances which are using pre-built AMIs. Your manager instructed you to implement disaster recovery for your system so in the event that the application goes down in the eu-central-1 region, a new instance can be started in the us-west-2 region.

As part of your disaster recovery plan, which of the following should you take into consideration?

1. In the AMI dashboard, add the us-west-2 region to the Network Access Control List which contains the regions that are allowed to use the AMI.

2. None. AMIs can be used in any region hence, there is no problem using it in the us-west-2 region.
3. Copy the AMI from the eu-central-1 region to the us-west-2 region. Afterwards, create a new Auto Scaling group in the us-west-2 region to use this new AMI ID.
4. Share the AMI to the us-west-2 region.

Answer(s): 3

Explanation

In this scenario, the EC2 instances you are currently using depends on a pre-built AMI. This AMI is not accessible to another region hence, you have to copy it to the us-west-2 region to properly establish your disaster recovery instance.

You can copy an Amazon Machine Image (AMI) within or across an AWS region using the AWS Management Console, the AWS command line tools or SDKs, or the Amazon EC2 API, all of which support the CopyImage action. You can copy both Amazon EBS-backed AMIs and instance store-backed AMIs. You can copy encrypted AMIs and AMIs with encrypted snapshots.

The options that say: In the AMI dashboard, add the us-west-2 region to the Network Access Control List which contains the regions that are allowed to use the AMI and Share the AMI to the us-west-2 region are incorrect because the AMI does not have a Network Access Control nor a Share functionality.

The option that says: None. AMIs can be used in any region hence, there is no problem using it in the us-west-2 region is incorrect as you can use a unique or pre-built AMI to a specific region only.

Reference:

http://docs.aws.amazon.com/AWSEC2/latest/UserGuide/CopyingAMIs.html

Here is a quick tutorial on how to create an AMI from EBS-backed EC2 instance:

https://youtu.be/vSKWBBrEbNQ

Question 31:

A tech company has a CRM application hosted on an Auto Scaling group of On-Demand EC2 instances. The application is extensively used during office hours from 9 in the morning till 5 in the afternoon. Their users are complaining that the performance of the application is slow during the start of the day but then works normally after a couple of hours.

Which of the following can be done to ensure that the application works properly at the beginning of the day?

1. Configure a Dynamic scaling policy for the Auto Scaling group to launch new instances based on the CPU utilization.
2. Set up an Application Load Balancer (ALB) to your architecture to ensure that the traffic is properly distributed on the instances.
3. Configure a Dynamic scaling policy for the Auto Scaling group to launch new instances based on the Memory utilization.
4. Configure a Scheduled scaling policy for the Auto Scaling group to launch new instances before the start of the day.

Answer(s): 4

Explanation

Scaling based on a schedule allows you to scale your application in response to predictable load changes. For example, every week the traffic to your web application starts to increase on Wednesday, remains high on Thursday, and starts to decrease on Friday. You can plan your scaling activities based on the predictable traffic patterns of your web application.

To configure your Auto Scaling group to scale based on a schedule, you create a scheduled action. The scheduled action tells Amazon EC2 Auto Scaling to perform a scaling action at specified times. To create a scheduled scaling action, you specify the start time when the scaling action should take effect, and the new minimum, maximum, and desired sizes for the scaling action. At the specified time, Amazon EC2 Auto Scaling updates the group with the values for minimum, maximum, and desired size specified by the scaling action. You can create scheduled actions for scaling one time only or for scaling on a recurring schedule.

Hence, configuring a Scheduled scaling policy for the Auto Scaling group to launch new instances before the start of the day is the correct answer. You need to configure a Scheduled scaling policy. This will ensure that the instances are already scaled up and ready before the start of the day since this is when the application is used the most.

Configuring a Dynamic scaling policy for the Auto Scaling group to launch new instances based on the CPU utilization and configuring a Dynamic scaling policy for the Auto Scaling group to launch new instances based on the Memory utilization are both incorrect because although these are valid solutions, it is still better to configure a Scheduled scaling policy as you already know the exact peak hours of your application. By the time either the CPU or Memory hits a peak, the application already has performance issues, so you need to ensure the scaling is done beforehand using a Scheduled scaling policy.

Setting up an Application Load Balancer (ALB) to your architecture to ensure that the traffic is properly distributed on the instances is incorrect. Although the Application load balancer can also balance the traffic, it cannot increase the instances based on demand.

Reference:

https://docs.aws.amazon.com/autoscaling/ec2/userguide/schedule_time.html

Question 32:

You are working as a Solutions Architect for a government project in which they are building an online portal to allow people to pay their taxes and claim their tax refunds online. Due to the confidentiality of data, the security policy requires that the application hosted in EC2 encrypts the data first before writing it to the disk for storage.

In this scenario, which service would you use to meet this requirement?

1. Elastic File System (EFS)
2. EBS encryption
3. AWS KMS API
4. Security Token Service

Answer(s): 3

Explanation

AWS Key Management Service (AWS KMS) is a managed service that makes it easy for you to create and control the encryption keys used to encrypt your data. The master keys that you create in AWS KMS are protected by FIPS 140-2 validated cryptographic modules. AWS KMS is integrated with most other AWS services that encrypt your data with encryption keys that you manage. AWS KMS is also integrated with AWS CloudTrail to provide encryption key usage logs to help meet your auditing, regulatory and compliance needs

The scenario mentions that you have to encrypt the data before writing it to disk for storage. What this means is that you will have to temporarily store the data in memory and not persist it on the disk, then encrypt it on the fly before finally storing it. The end result would be an encrypted data in your disk EBS Volume, and the EBS Encryption would be the secondary layer of protection/encryption for your sensitive data.

You can configure your application to use the KMS API to encrypt all data before saving it to disk. Hence, AWS KMS API is the correct answer.

Security Token Service is incorrect because AWS Security Token Service (STS) is a web service that enables you to request temporary, limited-privilege credentials for AWS Identity and Access Management (IAM) users or for users that you authenticate (federated users). It is not used for encrypting data unlike KMS.

EBS encryption is incorrect because although EBS encryption provides additional security for the EBS volumes, the application could not use this service to encrypt or decrypt each individual data that it writes on the disk. It is better to use KMS API instead to automatically encrypt the data before saving it to disk for maximum security, rather than after.

Elastic File System (EFS) is incorrect because EFS is a storage service and does not provide encryption services unlike KMS API.

References:

https://docs.aws.amazon.com/kms/latest/developerguide/programming-top.html

https://docs.aws.amazon.com/kms/latest/developerguide/concepts.html#data-keys

Question 33:

A company has a hybrid cloud architecture that connects their on-premises data center and cloud infrastructure in AWS. They require a durable storage backup for their corporate documents stored on-premises and a local cache that provides low latency access to their recently accessed data to reduce data egress charges. The documents must be stored to and retrieved from AWS via the Server Message Block (SMB) protocol. These files must immediately be accessible within minutes for six months and archived for another decade to meet the data compliance.

Which of the following is the best and most cost-effective approach to implement in this scenario?

1. Launch a new file gateway that connects to your on-premises data center using AWS Storage Gateway. Upload the documents to the file gateway and set up a lifecycle policy to move the data into Glacier for data archival.
2. Launch a new tape gateway that connects to your on-premises data center using AWS Storage Gateway. Upload the documents to the tape gateway and set up a lifecycle policy to move the data into Glacier for archival.
3. Use AWS Snowmobile to migrate all of the files from the on-premises network. Upload the documents to an S3 bucket and set up a lifecycle policy to move the data into Glacier for archival.
4. Establish a Direct Connect connection to integrate your on-premises network to your VPC. Upload the documents on Amazon EBS Volumes and use a lifecycle policy to automatically move the EBS snapshots to an S3 bucket, and then later to Glacier for archival.

Answer(s): 1

Explanation

A file gateway supports a file interface into Amazon Simple Storage Service (Amazon S3) and combines a service and a virtual software appliance. By using this combination, you can store and retrieve objects in Amazon S3 using industry-standard file protocols such as Network File System (NFS) and Server Message

Block (SMB). The software appliance, or gateway, is deployed into your on-premises environment as a virtual machine (VM) running on VMware ESXi, Microsoft Hyper-V, or Linux Kernel-based Virtual Machine (KVM) hyperviso

The gateway provides access to objects in S3 as files or file share mount points. With a file gateway, you can do the following:

- You can store and retrieve files directly using the NFS version 3 or 4.1 protocol.

- You can store and retrieve files directly using the SMB file system version, 2 and 3 protocol.

- You can access your data directly in Amazon S3 from any AWS Cloud application or service.

- You can manage your Amazon S3 data using lifecycle policies, cross-region replication, and versioning. You can think of a file gateway as a file system mount on S3.

AWS Storage Gateway supports the Amazon S3 Standard, Amazon S3 Standard-Infrequent Access, Amazon S3 One Zone-Infrequent Access and Amazon Glacier storage classes. When you create or update a file share, you have the option to select a storage class for your objects. You can either choose the Amazon S3 Standard or any of the infrequent access storage classes such as S3 Standard IA or S3 One Zone IA. Objects stored in any of these storage classes can be transitioned to Amazon Glacier using a Lifecycle Policy.

Although you can write objects directly from a file share to the S3-Standard-IA or S3-One Zone-IA storage class, it is recommended that you use a Lifecycle Policy to transition your objects rather than write directly from the file share, especially if you're expecting to update or delete the object within 30 days of archiving it.

Therefore, the correct answer is: Launch a new file gateway that connects to your on-premises data center using AWS Storage Gateway. Upload the documents to the file gateway and set up a lifecycle policy to move the data into Glacier for data archival.

The option that says: Launch a new tape gateway that connects to your on-premises data center using AWS Storage Gateway. Upload the documents to the tape gateway and set up a lifecycle policy to move the data into Glacier for archival is incorrect because although tape gateways provide cost-effective and durable archive backup data in Amazon Glacier, it does not meet the criteria of being retrievable immediately within minutes. It also doesn't maintain a local cache that provides low latency access to the recently accessed data and reduce data egress charges. Thus, it is still better to set up a file gateway instead.

The option that says: Establish a Direct Connect connection to integrate your on-premises network to your VPC. Upload the documents on Amazon EBS Volumes and use a lifecycle policy to automatically move the EBS snapshots to an S3 bucket, and then later to Glacier for archival is incorrect because EBS Volumes are not as durable compared with S3 and it would be more cost-efficient if you directly store the documents to an S3 bucket. An alternative solution is to use AWS Direct Connect with AWS Storage Gateway to create a connection for high-throughput workload needs, providing a dedicated network connection between your on-premises file gateway and AWS. But this solution is using EBS, hence, this option is still wrong.

The option that says: Use AWS Snowmobile to migrate all of the files from the on-premises network. Upload the documents to an S3 bucket and set up a lifecycle policy to move the data into Glacier for archival is incorrect because Snowmobile is mainly used to migrate the entire data of an on-premises data center to AWS. This is not a suitable approach as the company still has a hybrid cloud architecture which means that they will still use their on-premises data center along with their AWS cloud infrastructure.

References:

https://docs.aws.amazon.com/AmazonS3/latest/dev/object-lifecycle-mgmt.html

https://docs.aws.amazon.com/storagegateway/latest/userguide/StorageGatewayConcepts.html

Question 34:

A media company has an Amazon ECS Cluster, which uses the Fargate launch type, to host its news website. The database credentials should be supplied using environment variables, to comply with strict security compliance. As the Solutions Architect, you have to ensure that the credentials are secure and that they cannot be viewed in plaintext on the cluster itself.

Which of the following is the most suitable solution in this scenario that you can implement with minimal effort?

1. Store the database credentials in the ECS task definition file of the ECS Cluster and encrypt it with KMS. Store the task definition JSON file in a private S3 bucket and ensure that HTTPS is enabled on the bucket to encrypt the data in-flight. Create an IAM role to the ECS task definition script that allows access to the specific S3 bucket and then pass the --cli-input-json parameter when calling the ECS register-task-definition. Reference the task definition JSON file in the S3 bucket which contains the database credentials.
2. In the ECS task definition file of the ECS Cluster, store the database credentials using Docker Secrets to centrally manage these sensitive data and securely transmit it to only those containers that need access to it. Secrets are encrypted during transit and at rest. A given secret is only accessible to those services which have been granted explicit access to it via IAM Role, and only while those service tasks are running.
3. Use the AWS Secrets Manager to store the database credentials and then encrypt them using AWS KMS. Create a resource-based policy for your Amazon ECS task execution role (taskRoleArn) and reference it with your task definition which allows access to both KMS and AWS Secrets

Manager. Within your container definition, specify secrets with the name of the environment variable to set in the container and the full ARN of the Secrets Manager secret which contains the sensitive data, to present to the container.

4. Use the AWS Systems Manager Parameter Store to keep the database credentials and then encrypt them using AWS KMS. Create an IAM Role for your Amazon ECS task execution role (taskRoleArn) and reference it with your task definition, which allows access to both KMS and the Parameter Store. Within your container definition, specify secrets with the name of the environment variable to set in the container and the full ARN of the Systems Manager Parameter Store parameter containing the sensitive data to present to the container.

Answer(s): 4

Explanation

Amazon ECS enables you to inject sensitive data into your containers by storing your sensitive data in either AWS Secrets Manager secrets or AWS Systems Manager Parameter Store parameters and then referencing them in your container definition. This feature is supported by tasks using both the EC2 and Fargate launch types.

Secrets can be exposed to a container in the following ways:

- To inject sensitive data into your containers as environment variables, use the secrets container definition parameter.

- To reference sensitive information in the log configuration of a container, use the secretOptions container definition parameter.

Within your container definition, specify secrets with the name of the environment variable to set in the container and the full ARN of either the Secrets Manager secret or Systems Manager Parameter Store parameter containing the sensitive data to present to the container. The parameter that you reference can be from a different Region than the container using it, but must be from within the same account.

Hence, the correct answer is the option that says: Use the AWS Systems Manager Parameter Store to keep the database credentials and then encrypt them using AWS KMS. Create an IAM Role for your Amazon ECS task execution role (taskRoleArn) and reference it with your task definition, which allows access to both KMS and the Parameter Store. Within your container definition, specify secrets with the name of the environment variable to set in the container and the full ARN of the Systems Manager Parameter Store parameter containing the sensitive data to present to the container.

The option that says: In the ECS task definition file of the ECS Cluster, store the database credentials using Docker Secrets to centrally manage these sensitive data and securely transmit it to only those containers that need access to it. Secrets are encrypted during transit and at rest. A given secret is only accessible to those services which have been granted explicit access to it via IAM Role, and only while those service tasks are running is incorrect because although you can use Docker Secrets to secure the sensitive database credentials, this feature is only applicable in Docker Swarm. In AWS, the recommended way to secure sensitive data is either through the use of Secrets Manager or Systems Manager Parameter Store.

The option that says: Store the database credentials in the ECS task definition file of the ECS Cluster and encrypt it with KMS. Store the task definition JSON file in a private S3 bucket and ensure that HTTPS is enabled on the bucket to encrypt the data in-flight. Create an IAM role to the ECS task definition script that allows access to the specific S3 bucket and then pass the --cli-input-json parameter when calling the ECS register-task-definition. Reference the task definition JSON file in the S3 bucket which contains the database credentials is incorrect because although the solution may work, it is not recommended to store sensitive credentials in S3. This entails a lot of overhead and manual configuration steps which can be simplified by simply using the Secrets Manager or Systems Manager Parameter Store.

The option that says: Use the AWS Secrets Manager to store the database credentials and then encrypt them using AWS KMS. Create a resource-based policy for your Amazon ECS task execution role (taskRoleArn) and reference it with your task definition which allows access to both KMS and AWS Secrets Manager. Within your container definition, specify secrets with the name of the environment variable to set in the container and the full ARN of the Secrets Manager secret which contains the sensitive data, to present to the container is incorrect because although the use of Secrets Manager in securing sensitive data in ECS is valid, using an IAM Role is a more suitable choice over a resource-based policy for the Amazon ECS task execution role.

References:

https://docs.aws.amazon.com/AmazonECS/latest/developerguide/specifying-sensitive-data.html

https://aws.amazon.com/blogs/mt/the-right-way-to-store-secrets-using-parameter-store/

Question 35:

You have launched a new enterprise application with a web server and a database. You are using a large EC2 Instance with one 500 GB EBS volume to host a relational database. Upon checking the performance, it shows that write throughput to the database needs to be improved.

Which of the following is the most suitable configuration to help you achieve this requirement? (Select TWO.)

1. Set up the EC2 instance in a placement group

2. Re-launch the instance with a Paravirtual (PV) AMI and enable Enhanced Networking
3. Set up a standard RAID 0 configuration with two EBS Volumes
4. Use a standard RAID 1 configuration with two EBS Volumes
5. Increase the size of the EC2 Instance

Answer(s): 3, 5

Explanation

The goal here is to increase the write performance of the database hosted in an EC2 instance. You can achieve this by either setting up a standard RAID 0 configuration or simply by increasing the size of the EC2 instance.

Some EC2 instance types can drive more I/O throughput than what you can provision for a single EBS volume. You can join multiple gp2, io1, st1, or sc1 volumes together in a RAID 0 configuration to use the available bandwidth for these instances.

With Amazon EBS, you can use any of the standard RAID configurations that you can use with a traditional bare metal server, as long as that particular RAID configuration is supported by the operating system for your instance. This is because all RAID is accomplished at the software level. For greater I/O performance than you can achieve with a single volume, RAID 0 can stripe multiple volumes together; for on-instance redundancy, RAID 1 can mirror two volumes together.

Take note that HVM AMIs are required to take advantage of enhanced networking and GPU processing. In order to pass through instructions to specialized network and GPU devices, the OS needs to be able to have access to the native hardware platform which the HVM virtualization provides.

Re-launching the instance with a Paravirtual (PV) AMI and enabling Enhanced Networking is incorrect because although the Enhanced Networking feature can provide higher I/O performance and lower CPU utilization to your EC2 instance, you have to use an HVM AMI instead of PV AMI.

Using a standard RAID 1 configuration with two EBS Volumes is incorrect because the main use case for RAID 1 is to provide mirroring, redundancy, and fault-tolerance. RAID 0 is a more suitable option for providing faster read and write operations, compared with RAID 1.

Setting up the EC2 instance in a placement group is incorrect because the placement groups feature is primarily used for inter-instance communication.

References:

https://docs.aws.amazon.com/AWSEC2/latest/UserGuide/raid-config.html

https://docs.aws.amazon.com/AWSEC2/latest/UserGuide/EBSPerformance.html

https://aws.amazon.com/ec2/features/#enhanced-networking

Question 36:

An online shopping platform is hosted on an Auto Scaling group of Spot EC2 instances and uses Amazon Aurora PostgreSQL as its database. There is a requirement to optimize your database workloads in your cluster where you have to direct the write operations of the production traffic to your high-capacity instances and point the reporting queries sent by your internal staff to the low-capacity instances.

Which is the most suitable configuration for your application as well as your Aurora database cluster to achieve this requirement?

1. Do nothing since by default, Aurora will automatically direct the production traffic to your high-capacity instances and the reporting queries to your low-capacity instances.
2. In your application, use the instance endpoint of your Aurora database to handle the incoming production traffic and use the cluster endpoint to handle reporting queries.
3. Configure your application to use the reader endpoint for both production traffic and reporting queries, which will enable your Aurora database to automatically perform load-balancing among all the Aurora Replicas.
4. Create a custom endpoint in Aurora based on the specified criteria for the production traffic and another custom endpoint to handle the reporting queries.

Answer(s): 4

Explanation

Amazon Aurora typically involves a cluster of DB instances instead of a single instance. Each connection is handled by a specific DB instance. When you connect to an Aurora cluster, the host name and port that you specify point to an intermediate handler called an endpoint. Aurora uses the endpoint mechanism to abstract these connections. Thus, you don't have to hardcode all the hostnames or write your own logic for load-balancing and rerouting connections when some DB instances aren't available.

For certain Aurora tasks, different instances or groups of instances perform different roles. For example, the primary instance handles all data definition language (DDL) and data manipulation language (DML) statements. Up to 15 Aurora Replicas handle read-only query traffic.

Using endpoints, you can map each connection to the appropriate instance or group of instances based on your use case. For example, to perform DDL statements you can connect to whichever instance is the primary instance. To perform queries, you can connect to the reader endpoint, with Aurora automatically performing load-balancing among all the Aurora Replicas. For clusters with DB instances of different capacities or configurations, you can connect to custom endpoints associated with different subsets of DB instances. For diagnosis or tuning, you can connect to a specific instance endpoint to examine details about a specific DB instance.

The custom endpoint provides load-balanced database connections based on criteria other than the read-only or read-write capability of the DB instances. For example, you might define a custom endpoint to connect to instances that use a particular AWS instance class or a particular DB parameter group. Then you might tell particular groups of users about this custom endpoint. For example, you might direct internal users to low-capacity instances for report generation or ad hoc (one-time) querying, and direct production traffic to high-capacity instances. Hence, creating a custom endpoint in Aurora based on the specified criteria for the production traffic and another custom endpoint to handle the reporting queries is the correct answer.

Configuring your application to use the reader endpoint for both production traffic and reporting queries, which will enable your Aurora database to automatically perform load-balancing among all the Aurora Replicas is incorrect because although it is true that a reader endpoint enables your Aurora database to automatically perform load-balancing among all the Aurora Replicas, it is quite limited to doing read operations only. You still need to use a custom endpoint to load-balance the database connections based on the specified criteria.

The option that says: In your application, use the instance endpoint of your Aurora database to handle the incoming production traffic and use the cluster endpoint to handle reporting queries is incorrect because a cluster endpoint (also known as a writer endpoint) for an Aurora DB cluster simply connects to the current primary DB instance for that DB cluster. This endpoint can perform write operations in the database such as DDL statements, which is perfect for handling production traffic but not suitable for handling queries for reporting since there will be no write database operations that will be sent. Moreover, the endpoint does not point to lower-capacity or high-capacity instances as per the requirement. A better solution for this is to use a custom endpoint.

The option that says: Do nothing since by default, Aurora will automatically direct the production traffic to your high-capacity instances and the reporting queries to your low-capacity instances is incorrect because Aurora does not do this by default. You have to create custom endpoints in order to accomplish this requirement.

Reference:

https://docs.aws.amazon.com/AmazonRDS/latest/AuroraUserGuide/Aurora.Overview.Endpoints.html

Question 37:

You are working as a Solutions Architect for a technology company which is in the process of migrating their applications to AWS. One of their systems requires a database that can scale globally and can handle frequent schema changes. The application should not have any downtime or performance issues whenever there is a schema change in the database. It should also provide low-latency response to high-traffic queries.

Which is the most suitable database solution to use to achieve this requirement?

1. Amazon DynamoDB
2. An Amazon RDS instance in Multi-AZ Deployments configuration
3. An Amazon Aurora database with Read Replicas
4. Redshift

Answer(s): 1

Explanation

Before we proceed in answering this question, we must first be clear with the actual definition of a "schema". Basically, the english definition of a schema is: a representation of a plan or theory in the form of an outline or model.

Just think of a schema as the "structure" or a "model" of your data in your database. Since the scenario requires that the schema, or the structure of your data, changes frequently, then you have to pick a database which provides a non-rigid and flexible way of adding or removing new types of data. This is a classic example of choosing between a relational database and non-relational (NoSQL) database.

A relational database is known for having a rigid schema, with a lot of constraints and limits as to which (and what type of) data can be inserted or not. It is primarily used for scenarios where you have to support complex queries which fetch data across a number of tables. It is best for scenarios where you have complex table relationships but for use cases where you need to have a flexible schema, this is not a suitable database to use.

For NoSQL, it is not as rigid as a relational database because you can easily add or remove rows or elements in your table/collection entry. It also has a more flexible schema because it can store complex hierarchical data within a single item which, unlike a relational database, does not entail changing multiple related tables. Hence, the best answer to be used here is a NoSQL database, like DynamoDB. When your business requires a low-latency response to high-traffic queries, taking advantage of a NoSQL system generally makes technical and economic sense.

Amazon DynamoDB helps solve the problems that limit the relational system scalability by avoiding them. In DynamoDB, you design your schema specifically to make the most common and important queries as fast and as inexpensive as possible.

Your data structures are tailored to the specific requirements of your business use cases.

Remember that a relational database system does not scale well for the following reasons:

- It normalizes data and stores it on multiple tables that require multiple queries to write to disk.

- It generally incurs the performance costs of an ACID-compliant transaction system.

- It uses expensive joins to reassemble required views of query results.

For DynamoDB, it scales well due to these reasons:

- Its schema flexibility lets DynamoDB store complex hierarchical data within a single item. DynamoDB is not a totally schemaless database since the very definition of a schema is just the model or structure of your data.

- Composite key design lets it store related items close together on the same table.

An Amazon RDS instance in Multi-AZ Deployments configuration and an Amazon Aurora database with Read Replicas are incorrect because both of them are a type of relational database.

Redshift is incorrect because it is primarily used for OLAP systems.

References:

https://docs.aws.amazon.com/amazondynamodb/latest/developerguide/bp-general-nosql-design.html

https://docs.aws.amazon.com/amazondynamodb/latest/developerguide/bp-relational-modeling.html

https://docs.aws.amazon.com/amazondynamodb/latest/developerguide/SQLtoNoSQL.html

Also check the AWS Certified Solutions Architect Official Study Guide: Associate Exam 1st Edition and turn to page 161 which talks about NoSQL Databases.

Question 38:

A Solutions Architect is hosting a website in an Amazon S3 bucket named tutorialsfree. The users load the website using the following URL: http://tutorialsfree.s3-website-us-east-1.amazonaws.com and there is a new requirement to add a JavaScript on the webpages in order to make authenticated HTTP GET requests against the same bucket by using the Amazon S3 API endpoint (tutorialsfree.s3.amazonaws.com). Upon testing, you noticed that the web browser blocks JavaScript from allowing those requests.

Which of the following options is the MOST suitable solution that you should implement for this scenario?

1. Enable Cross-Region Replication (CRR).
2. Enable Cross-Zone Load Balancing.
3. Enable Cross-origin resource sharing (CORS) configuration in the bucket.
4. Enable cross-account access.

Answer(s): 3

Explanation

Cross-origin resource sharing (CORS) defines a way for client web applications that are loaded in one domain to interact with resources in a different domain. With CORS support, you can build rich client-side web applications with Amazon S3 and selectively allow cross-origin access to your Amazon S3 resources.

Suppose that you are hosting a website in an Amazon S3 bucket named your-website and your users load the website endpoint http://your-website.s3-website-us-east-1.amazonaws.com. Now you want to use JavaScript on the webpages that are stored in this bucket to be able to make authenticated GET and PUT requests against the same bucket by using the Amazon S3 API endpoint for the bucket, your-website.s3.amazonaws.com. A browser would normally block JavaScript from allowing those requests, but with CORS you can configure your bucket to explicitly enable cross-origin requests from your-website.s3-website-us-east-1.amazonaws.com.

In this scenario, you can solve the issue by enabling the CORS in the S3 bucket. Hence, enabling Cross-origin resource sharing (CORS) configuration in the bucket is the correct answer.

Enabling cross-account access is incorrect because cross-account access is a feature in IAM and not in Amazon S3.

Enabling Cross-Zone Load Balancing is incorrect because Cross-Zone Load Balancing is only used in ELB and not in S3.

Enabling Cross-Region Replication (CRR) is incorrect because CRR is a bucket-level configuration that enables automatic, asynchronous copying of objects across buckets in different AWS Regions.

References:

http://docs.aws.amazon.com/AmazonS3/latest/dev/cors.html

https://docs.aws.amazon.com/AmazonS3/latest/dev/ManageCorsUsing.html

Question 39:

You are an AWS Solutions Architect designing an online analytics application that uses Redshift Cluster for its data warehouse. Which service will allow you to monitor all API calls to your Redshift instance and can also provide secured data for auditing and compliance purposes?

1. CloudTrail for security logs
2. CloudWatch
3. Redshift Spectrum
4. AWS X-Ray

Answer(s): 1

Explanation

AWS CloudTrail is a service that enables governance, compliance, operational auditing, and risk auditing of your AWS account. With CloudTrail, you can log, continuously monitor, and retain account activity related to actions across your AWS infrastructure.

CloudTrail provides event history of your AWS account activity, including actions taken through the AWS Management Console, AWS SDKs, command line tools, API calls, and other AWS services. This event history simplifies security analysis, resource change tracking, and troubleshooting.

CloudWatch is incorrect because although this is also a monitoring service, it cannot track the API calls to your AWS resources.

AWS X-Ray is incorrect because this is not a suitable service to use to track each API call to your AWS resources. It just helps you debug and analyze your microservices applications with request tracing so you can find the root cause of issues and performance.

Redshift Spectrum is incorrect because this is not a monitoring service but rather a feature of Amazon Redshift that enables you to query and analyze all of your data in Amazon S3 using the open data formats you already use, with no data loading or transformations needed.

Reference:

https://aws.amazon.com/cloudtrail/

Question 40:

A Solutions Architect is working for a company which has multiple VPCs in various AWS regions. The Architect is assigned to set up a logging system which will track all of the changes made to their AWS resources in all regions, including the configurations made in IAM, CloudFront, AWS WAF, and Route 53. In order to pass the compliance requirements, the solution must ensure the security, integrity, and durability of the log data. It should also provide an event history of all API calls made in AWS Management Console and AWS CLI.

Which of the following solutions is the best fit for this scenario?

1. Set up a new CloudWatch trail in a new S3 bucket using the AWS CLI and also pass both the --is-multi-region-trail and --include-global-service-events parameters then encrypt log files using KMS encryption. Apply Multi Factor Authentication (MFA) Delete on the S3 bucket and ensure that only authorized users can access the logs by configuring the bucket policies.
2. Set up a new CloudTrail trail in a new S3 bucket using the AWS CLI and also pass both the --is-multi-region-trail and --no-include-global-service-events parameters then encrypt log files using KMS encryption. Apply Multi Factor Authentication (MFA) Delete on the S3 bucket and ensure that only authorized users can access the logs by configuring the bucket policies.
3. Set up a new CloudWatch trail in a new S3 bucket using the CloudTrail console and also pass the --is-multi-region-trail parameter then encrypt log files using KMS encryption. Apply Multi Factor Authentication (MFA) Delete on the S3 bucket and ensure that only authorized users can access the logs by configuring the bucket policies.
4. Set up a new CloudTrail trail in a new S3 bucket using the AWS CLI and also pass both the --is-multi-region-trail and --include-global-service-events parameters then encrypt log files using KMS encryption. Apply Multi Factor Authentication (MFA) Delete on the S3 bucket and ensure that only authorized users can access the logs by configuring the bucket policies.

Answer(s): 4

Explanation

An event in CloudTrail is the record of an activity in an AWS account. This activity can be an action taken by a user, role, or service that is monitorable by CloudTrail. CloudTrail events provide a history of both API and non-API account activity made through the AWS Management Console, AWS SDKs, command line tools, and other AWS services. There are two types of events that can be logged in CloudTrail: management events and data events. By default, trails log management events, but not data events.

A trail can be applied to all regions or a single region. As a best practice, create a trail that applies to all regions in the AWS partition in which you are working. This is the default setting when you create a trail in the CloudTrail console.

For most services, events are recorded in the region where the action occurred. For global services such as AWS Identity and Access Management (IAM), AWS STS, Amazon CloudFront, and Route 53, events are delivered to any trail that includes global services, and are logged as occurring in US East (N. Virginia) Region.

In this scenario, the company requires a secure and durable logging solution that will track all of the activities of all AWS resources on all regions. CloudTrail can be used for this case with multi-region trail enabled, however, it will only cover the activities of the regional services (EC2, S3, RDS etc.) and not for global services such as IAM, CloudFront, AWS WAF, and Route 53. In order to satisfy the requirement, you have to add the --include-global-service-events parameter in your AWS CLI command.

The option that says: Set up a new CloudTrail trail in a new S3 bucket using the AWS CLI and also pass both the --is-multi-region-trail and --include-global-service-events parameters then encrypt log files using KMS encryption. Apply Multi Factor Authentication (MFA) Delete on the S3 bucket and ensure that only authorized users can access the logs by configuring the bucket policies is correct because it provides security, integrity, and durability to your log data and in addition, it has the -include-global-service-events parameter enabled which will also include activity from global services such as IAM, Route 53, AWS WAF, and CloudFront.

The option that says: Set up a new CloudWatch trail in a new S3 bucket using the AWS CLI and also pass both the --is-multi-region-trail and --include-global-service-events parameters then encrypt log files using KMS encryption. Apply Multi Factor Authentication (MFA) Delete on the S3 bucket and ensure that only authorized users can access the logs by configuring the bucket policies is incorrect because you need to use CloudTrail instead of CloudWatch.

The option that says: Set up a new CloudWatch trail in a new S3 bucket using the CloudTrail console and also pass the --is-multi-region-trail parameter then encrypt log files using KMS encryption. Apply Multi Factor Authentication (MFA) Delete on the S3 bucket and ensure that only authorized users can access the logs by configuring the bucket policies is incorrect because you need to use CloudTrail instead of CloudWatch. In addition, the --include-global-service-events parameter is also missing in this setup.

The option that says: Set up a new CloudTrail trail in a new S3 bucket using the AWS CLI and also pass both the --is-multi-region-trail and --no-include-global-service-events parameters then encrypt log files using KMS encryption. Apply Multi Factor Authentication (MFA) Delete on the S3 bucket and ensure that only authorized users can access the logs by configuring the bucket policies is incorrect because the --is-multi-region-trail is not enough as you also need to add the --include-global-service-events parameter and not --no-include-global-service-events. Plus, you cannot enable the Global Service Events using the CloudTrail console but by using AWS CLI.

References:

https://docs.aws.amazon.com/awscloudtrail/latest/userguide/cloudtrail-concepts.html#cloudtrail-concepts-global-service-events

http://docs.aws.amazon.com/IAM/latest/UserGuide/cloudtrail-integration.html

https://docs.aws.amazon.com/awscloudtrail/latest/userguide/cloudtrail-create-and-update-a-trail-by-using-the-aws-cli.html

Question 41:

A popular social media website uses a CloudFront web distribution to serve their static contents to their millions of users around the globe. They are receiving a number of complaints recently that their users take a lot of time to log into their website. There are also occasions when their users are getting HTTP 504 errors. You are instructed by your manager to significantly reduce the user's login time to further optimize the system.

Which of the following options should you use together to set up a cost-effective solution that can improve your application's performance? (Select TWO.)

1. Customize the content that the CloudFront web distribution delivers to your users using Lambda@Edge, which allows your Lambda functions to execute the authentication process in AWS locations closer to the users.
2. Deploy your application to multiple AWS regions to accommodate your users around the world. Set up a Route 53 record with latency routing policy to route incoming traffic to the region that provides the best latency to the user.
3. Set up an origin failover by creating an origin group with two origins. Specify one as the primary origin and the other as the second origin which CloudFront automatically switches to when the primary origin returns specific HTTP status code failure responses.
4. Configure your origin to add a Cache-Control max-age directive to your objects, and specify the longest practical value for max-age to increase the cache hit ratio of your CloudFront distribution.
5. Use multiple and geographically disperse VPCs to various AWS regions then create a transit VPC to connect all of your resources. In order to handle the requests faster, set up Lambda functions in each region using the AWS Serverless Application Model (SAM) service.

Answer(s): 1, 3

Explanation

Lambda@Edge lets you run Lambda functions to customize the content that CloudFront delivers, executing the functions in AWS locations closer to the viewer. The functions run in response to CloudFront events, without provisioning or managing servers. You can use Lambda functions to change CloudFront requests and responses at the following points:

- After CloudFront receives a request from a viewer (viewer request)

- Before CloudFront forwards the request to the origin (origin request)

- After CloudFront receives the response from the origin (origin response)

- Before CloudFront forwards the response to the viewer (viewer response)

In the given scenario, you can use Lambda@Edge to allow your Lambda functions to customize the content that CloudFront delivers and to execute the authentication process in AWS locations closer to the users. In addition, you can set up an origin failover by creating an origin group with two origins with one as the primary origin and the other as the second origin which CloudFront automatically switches to when the primary origin fails. This will alleviate the occasional HTTP 504 errors that users are experiencing. Therefore, the correct answers are:

- Customize the content that the CloudFront web distribution delivers to your users using Lambda@Edge, which allows your Lambda functions to execute the authentication process in AWS locations closer to the users.

- Set up an origin failover by creating an origin group with two origins. Specify one as the primary origin and the other as the second origin which CloudFront automatically switches to when the primary origin returns specific HTTP status code failure responses.

The option that says: Use multiple and geographically disperse VPCs to various AWS regions then create a transit VPC to connect all of your resources. In order to handle the requests faster, set up Lambda functions in each region using the AWS Serverless Application Model (SAM) service is incorrect because of the same reason provided above. Although setting up multiple VPCs across various regions which are connected with a transit VPC is valid, this solution still entails higher setup and maintenance costs. A more cost-effective option would be to use Lambda@Edge instead.

The option that says: Configure your origin to add a Cache-Control max-age directive to your objects, and specify the longest practical value for max-age to increase the cache hit ratio of your CloudFront distribution is incorrect because improving the cache hit ratio for the CloudFront distribution is irrelevant in this scenario. You can improve your cache performance by increasing the proportion of your viewer requests that are served from CloudFront edge caches instead of going to your origin servers for content. However, take note that the problem in the scenario is the sluggish authentication process of your global users and not just the caching of the static objects.

The option that says: Deploy your application to multiple AWS regions to accommodate your users around the world. Set up a Route 53 record with latency routing policy to route incoming traffic to the region that provides the best latency to the user is incorrect because although this may resolve the performance issue, this solution entails a significant implementation cost since you have to deploy your application to multiple AWS regions. Remember that the scenario asks for a solution that will improve the performance of the application with minimal cost.

References:

https://docs.aws.amazon.com/AmazonCloudFront/latest/DeveloperGuide/high_availability_origin_failover.html

https://docs.aws.amazon.com/lambda/latest/dg/lambda-edge.html

Question 42:

Your cloud architecture is composed of Linux and Windows EC2 instances which process high volumes of financial data 24 hours a day, 7 days a week. To ensure high availability of your systems, you are required to monitor the memory and disk utilization of all of your instances.

Which of the following is the most suitable monitoring solution to implement?

1. Use Amazon Inspector and install the Inspector agent to all of your EC2 instances.
2. Use the default CloudWatch configuration to your EC2 instances where the memory and disk utilization metrics are already available. Install the AWS Systems Manager (SSM) Agent to all of your EC2 instances.
3. Install the CloudWatch agent to all of your EC2 instances which gathers the memory and disk utilization data. View the custom metrics in the Amazon CloudWatch console.
4. Enable the Enhanced Monitoring option in EC2 and install CloudWatch agent to all of your EC2 instances to be able to view the memory and disk utilization in the CloudWatch dashboard.

Answer(s): 3

Explanation

CloudWatch has available Amazon EC2 Metrics for you to use for monitoring CPU utilization, Network utilization, Disk performance, and Disk Reads/Writes. In case that you need to monitor the below items, you need to prepare a custom metric using a Perl or other shell script, as there are no ready to use metrics for these:

Memory utilization

disk swap utilization

disk space utilization

page file utilization

log collection

Take note that there is a multi-platform CloudWatch agent which can be installed on both Linux and Windows-based instances. You can use a single agent to collect both system metrics and log files from Amazon EC2 instances and on-premises servers. This agent supports both Windows Server and Linux and enables you to select the metrics to be collected, including sub-resource metrics such as per-CPU core. It is recommended that you use the new agent instead of the older monitoring scripts to collect metrics and logs.

The option that says: Use the default CloudWatch configuration to your EC2 instances where the memory and disk utilization metrics are already available. Install the AWS Systems Manager (SSM) Agent to all of your EC2 instances is incorrect because, by default, CloudWatch does not automatically provide memory and disk utilization metrics of your instances. You have to set up custom CloudWatch metrics to monitor the memory, disk swap, disk space and page file utilization of your instances.

The option that says: Enable the Enhanced Monitoring option in EC2 and install CloudWatch agent to all of your EC2 instances to be able to view the memory and disk utilization in the CloudWatch dashboard is incorrect because Enhanced Monitoring is a feature of RDS and not of CloudWatch.

Using Amazon Inspector and installing the Inspector agent to all of your EC2 instances is incorrect because Amazon Inspector is an automated security assessment service that helps you test the network accessibility of your Amazon EC2 instances and the security state of your applications running on the instances. It does not provide a custom metric to track the memory and disk utilization of each and every EC2 instance in your VPC.

References:

https://docs.aws.amazon.com/AWSEC2/latest/UserGuide/monitoring_ec2.html

https://docs.aws.amazon.com/AWSEC2/latest/UserGuide/mon-scripts.html#using_put_script

Question 43:

You are working as a Solutions Architect in a new startup that provides storage for high-quality photos which are infrequently accessed by the users. To make the architecture cost-effective, you designed the cloud service to use an S3 One Zone-Infrequent Access (S3 One Zone-IA) storage type for free users and an S3 Standard-Infrequent Access (S3 Standard-IA) storage type for premium users. When your manager found out about this, he asked you about the differences between using S3 One Zone-IA and S3 Standard-IA.

What will you say to your manager? (Select TWO.)

1. Storing data in S3 One Zone-IA costs more than storing it in S3 Standard-IA but provides more durability.
2. S3 One Zone-IA offers lower durability and low throughput compared with Amazon S3 Standard and S3 Standard-IA which is why it has a low per GB storage price and per GB retrieval fee.
3. Unlike other Amazon object storage classes, which store data in a minimum of three Availability Zones (AZs), S3 One Zone-IA stores data in two AZs only. Hence the name, One Zone-IA since the data replication is in one Availability Zone.
4. Storing data in S3 One Zone-IA costs less than storing it in S3 Standard-IA.

5. Unlike other Amazon object storage classes, which store data in a minimum of three Availability Zones (AZs), S3 One Zone-IA stores data in a single AZ.

Answer(s): 4, 5

Explanation

Amazon S3 One Zone-Infrequent Access (S3 One Zone-IA) is an Amazon S3 storage class for data that is accessed less frequently but requires rapid access when needed. Unlike other Amazon object storage classes, which store data in a minimum of three Availability Zones (AZs), S3 One Zone-IA stores data in a single AZ. Because of this, storing data in S3 One Zone-IA costs 20% less than storing it in S3 Standard-IA. S3 One Zone-IA is ideal for customers who want a lower cost option for infrequently accessed data but do not require the availability and resilience of S3 Standard or S3 Standard-IA storage. It's a good choice, for example, for storing secondary backup copies of on-premises data or easily re-creatable data, or for storage used as an S3 Cross-Region Replication target from another AWS Region.

S3 One Zone-IA offers the same high durability, high throughput, and low latency of Amazon S3 Standard and S3 Standard-IA, with a low per GB storage price and per GB retrieval fee. The S3 One Zone-IA storage class is set at the object level and can exist in the same bucket as S3 Standard and S3 Standard-IA, allowing you to use S3 Lifecycle Policies to automatically transition objects between storage classes without any application changes.

Key Features:

Same low latency and high throughput performance of S3 Standard and S3 Standard-IA

Designed for durability of 99.999999999% of objects in a single Availability Zone, but data will be lost in the event of Availability Zone destruction

Designed for 99.5% availability over a given year

Backed with the Amazon S3 Service Level Agreement for availability

Supports SSL for data in transit and encryption of data at rest

Lifecycle management for automatic migration of objects

Remember that since the S3 One Zone-IA stores data in a single AWS Availability Zone, data stored in this storage class will be lost in the event of Availability Zone destruction.

Reference:

https://aws.amazon.com/s3/storage-classes/#Amazon_S3_One_Zone-Infrequent_Access

Question 44:

Your company announced that there would be a surprise IT audit on all of the AWS resources being used in the production environment. During the audit activities, it was noted that you are using a combination of Standard and Scheduled Reserved EC2 instances in your applications. They argued that you should have used Spot EC2 instances instead as it is cheaper than the Reserved Instance.

Which of the following are the characteristics and benefits of using these two types of Reserved EC2 instances, which you can use as justification? (Select TWO.)

1. Standard Reserved Instances can be later exchanged for other Convertible Reserved Instances
2. Reserved Instances doesn't get interrupted unlike Spot instances in the event that there are not enough unused EC2 instances to meet the demand.
3. It can enable you to reserve capacity for your Amazon EC2 instances in multiple Availability Zones and multiple AWS Regions for any duration.
4. You can have capacity reservations that recur on a daily, weekly, or monthly basis, with a specified start time and duration, for a one-year term through Scheduled Reserved Instances
5. It runs in a VPC on hardware that's dedicated to a single customer.

Answer(s): 2, 4

Explanation

Reserved Instances (RIs) provide you with a significant discount (up to 75%) compared to On-Demand instance pricing. You have the flexibility to change families, OS types, and tenancies while benefiting from RI pricing when you use Convertible RIs. One important thing to remember here is that Reserved Instances are not physical instances, but rather a billing discount applied to the use of On-Demand Instances in your account.

When your computing needs change, you can modify your Standard or Convertible Reserved Instances and continue to take advantage of the billing benefit. You can modify the Availability Zone, scope, network platform, or instance size (within the same instance type) of your Reserved Instance. You can also sell your unused instance on the Reserved Instance Marketplace.

The option that says: Reserved Instances don't get interrupted unlike Spot instances in the event that there are not enough unused EC2 instances to meet the demand is correct. Likewise, the option that says: You can have capacity reservations that recur on a daily, weekly, or monthly basis, with a specified start time and duration, for a one-year term through Scheduled Reserved Instances is correct. You reserve the capacity in advance, so that you know it is available when you need it. You pay for the time that the instances are scheduled, even if you do not use them.

The option that says: Standard Reserved Instances can be later exchanged for other Convertible Reserved Instances is incorrect because only Convertible Reserved Instances can be exchanged for other Convertible Reserved Instances.

The option that says: It can enable you to reserve capacity for your Amazon EC2 instances in multiple Availability Zones and multiple AWS Regions for any duration is incorrect because you can reserve capacity to a specific AWS Region (regional Reserved Instance) or specific Availability Zone (zonal Reserved Instance) only. You cannot reserve capacity to multiple AWS Regions in a single RI purchase.

The option that says: It runs in a VPC on hardware that's dedicated to a single customer is incorrect because that is the description of a Dedicated instance and not a Reserved Instance. A Dedicated instance runs in a VPC on hardware that's dedicated to a single customer.

References:

https://docs.aws.amazon.com/AWSEC2/latest/UserGuide/ri-modifying.html

https://aws.amazon.com/ec2/pricing/reserved-instances/

https://docs.aws.amazon.com/AWSEC2/latest/UserGuide/ec2-reserved-instances.html

https://docs.aws.amazon.com/AWSEC2/latest/UserGuide/reserved-instances-types.html

Question 45:

You founded a tech startup that provides online training and software development courses to various students across the globe. Your team has developed an online portal in AWS where the students can log into and access the courses they are subscribed to.

Since you are in the early phases of the startup and the funding is still hard to come by, which service can help you manage the budgets for all your AWS resources?

1. Payment History
2. Cost Explorer
3. Cost Allocation Tags
4. AWS Budgets

Answer(s): 4

Explanation

AWS Budgets gives you the ability to set custom budgets that alert you when your costs or usage exceed (or are forecasted to exceed) your budgeted amount.

Budgets can be tracked at the monthly, quarterly, or yearly level, and you can customize the start and end dates. You can further refine your budget to track costs associated with multiple dimensions, such as AWS service, linked account, tag, and others. Budget alerts can be sent via email and/or Amazon Simple Notification Service (SNS) topic.

You can also use AWS Budgets to set a custom reservation utilization target and receive alerts when your utilization drops below the threshold you define. RI utilization alerts support Amazon EC2, Amazon RDS, Amazon Redshift, and Amazon ElastiCache reservations.

Budgets can be created and tracked from the AWS Budgets dashboard or via the Budgets API.

Cost Explorer is incorrect because it only helps you visualize and manage your AWS costs and usages over time. It offers a set of reports you can view data with for up to the last 13 months, forecast how much you're likely to spend for the next three months, and get recommendations for what Reserved Instances to purchase. You use Cost Explorer to identify areas that need further inquiry and see trends to understand your costs.

Cost Allocation Tags is incorrect because it only eases the organization of your resource costs on your cost allocation report to make it easier for you to categorize and track your AWS costs.

Payment History is incorrect because this option only provides a location where you can view the monthly invoices you receive from AWS. If your account isn't past due, the Payment History page shows only previous invoices and payment status.

Reference:

https://aws.amazon.com/aws-cost-management/aws-budgets/

Question 46:

A Forex trading platform, which frequently processes and stores global financial data every minute, is hosted in your on-premises data center and uses an Oracle database. Due to a recent cooling problem in their data center, the company urgently needs to migrate their infrastructure to AWS to improve the performance of their applications. As the Solutions Architect, you are responsible in ensuring that the database is properly migrated and should remain available in case of database server failure in the future.

Which of the following is the most suitable solution to meet the requirement?

1. Launch an Oracle Real Application Clusters (RAC) in RDS.
2. Create an Oracle database in RDS with Multi-AZ deployments.

3. Migrate your Oracle data to Amazon Aurora by converting the database schema using AWS Schema Conversion Tool and AWS Database Migration Service.
4. Launch an Oracle database instance in RDS with Recovery Manager (RMAN) enabled.

Answer(s): 2

Explanation

Amazon RDS Multi-AZ deployments provide enhanced availability and durability for Database (DB) Instances, making them a natural fit for production database workloads. When you provision a Multi-AZ DB Instance, Amazon RDS automatically creates a primary DB Instance and synchronously replicates the data to a standby instance in a different Availability Zone (AZ). Each AZ runs on its own physically distinct, independent infrastructure, and is engineered to be highly reliable.

In case of an infrastructure failure, Amazon RDS performs an automatic failover to the standby (or to a read replica in the case of Amazon Aurora), so that you can resume database operations as soon as the failover is complete. Since the endpoint for your DB Instance remains the same after a failover, your application can resume database operation without the need for manual administrative intervention.

In this scenario, the best RDS configuration to use is an Oracle database in RDS with Multi-AZ deployments to ensure high availability even if the primary database instance goes down. Hence, creating an Oracle database in RDS with Multi-AZ deployments is the correct answer.

Launching an Oracle database instance in RDS with Recovery Manager (RMAN) enabled and launching an Oracle Real Application Clusters (RAC) in RDS are incorrect because Oracle RMAN and RAC are not supported in RDS.

Migrating your Oracle data to Amazon Aurora by converting the database schema using AWS Schema Conversion Tool and AWS Database Migration Service is incorrect because although this solution is feasible, it takes time to migrate your Oracle database to Aurora which is not acceptable. Based on this option, the Aurora database does not have a Read Replica and is not configured as an Amazon Aurora DB cluster, which could have improved the availability of the database.

References:

https://aws.amazon.com/rds/details/multi-az/

https://docs.aws.amazon.com/AmazonRDS/latest/UserGuide/Concepts.MultiAZ.html

Question 47:

A Docker application, which is running on an Amazon ECS cluster behind a load balancer, is heavily using DynamoDB. You are instructed to improve the database performance by distributing the workload evenly and using the provisioned throughput efficiently.

Which of the following would you consider to implement for your DynamoDB table?

1. Avoid using a composite primary key, which is composed of a partition key and a sort key.
2. Use partition keys with low-cardinality attributes, which have a few number of distinct values for each item.
3. Use partition keys with high-cardinality attributes, which have a large number of distinct values for each item.
4. Reduce the number of partition keys in the DynamoDB table.

Answer(s): 3

Explanation

The partition key portion of a table's primary key determines the logical partitions in which a table's data is stored. This in turn affects the underlying physical partitions. Provisioned I/O capacity for the table is divided evenly among these physical partitions. Therefore a partition key design that doesn't distribute I/O requests evenly can create "hot" partitions that result in throttling and use your provisioned I/O capacity inefficiently.

The optimal usage of a table's provisioned throughput depends not only on the workload patterns of individual items, but also on the partition-key design. This doesn't mean that you must access all partition key values to achieve an efficient throughput level, or even that the percentage of accessed partition key values must be high. It does mean that the more distinct partition key values that your workload accesses, the more those requests will be spread across the partitioned space. In general, you will use your provisioned throughput more efficiently as the ratio of partition key values accessed to the total number of partition key values increases.

One example for this is the use of partition keys with high-cardinality attributes, which have a large number of distinct values for each item.

Reducing the number of partition keys in the DynamoDB table is incorrect because instead of doing this, you should actually add more to improve its performance to distribute the I/O requests evenly and not avoid "hot" partitions.

Using partition keys with low-cardinality attributes, which have a few number of distinct values for each item is incorrect because this is the exact opposite of the correct answer. Remember that the more distinct partition key values your workload accesses, the more those requests will be spread across the partitioned space.

Conversely, the less distinct partition key values, the less evenly spread it would be across the partitioned space, which effectively slows the performance.

The option that says: Avoid using a composite primary key, which is composed of a partition key and a sort key is incorrect because as mentioned, a composite primary key will provide more partition for the table and in turn, improves the performance. Hence, it should be used and not avoided.

References:

https://docs.aws.amazon.com/amazondynamodb/latest/developerguide/bp-partition-key-uniform-load.html

https://aws.amazon.com/blogs/database/choosing-the-right-dynamodb-partition-key/

Question 48:

A Solutions Architect is tasked to host a web application in a new VPC with private and public subnets. In order to do this, the Architect will need to deploy a new MySQL database server and a fleet of EC2 instances to host the application.

In which subnet should the Architect launch the new database server into?

1. Ideally be launched outside the Amazon VPC
2. Either public or private subnet
3. The public subnet
4. The private subnet

Answer(s): 4

Explanation

In an ideal and secure VPC architecture, you launch the web servers or elastic load balancers in the public subnet and the database servers in the private subnet.

The private subnet is correct because it is more secure to launch your database in the private subnet to prevent other external and unauthorized users to access or attack your system.

The public subnet is incorrect because if you launch your database server in the public subnet, it will be publicly accessible all over the Internet which has a higher security risk.

Either public or private subnet is incorrect since only the private subnet is the correct answer if you want to secure your database from external traffic.

The option that says: Ideally be launched outside the Amazon VPC is incorrect as there is no need to launch it outside the VPC. Having it run in a private subnet should address the security and networking concerns of your database.

Reference:

https://docs.aws.amazon.com/AmazonVPC/latest/UserGuide/VPC_Scenario2.ht ml

Question 49:

A popular social network is hosted in AWS and is using a DynamoDB table as its database. There is a requirement to implement a 'follow' feature where users can subscribe to certain updates made by a particular user and be notified via email. Which of the following is the most suitable solution that you should implement to meet the requirement?

1. Enable DynamoDB Stream and create an AWS Lambda trigger, as well as the IAM role which contains all of the permissions that the Lambda function will need at runtime. The data from the stream record will be processed by the Lambda function which will then publish a message to SNS Topic that will notify the subscribers via email.
2. Using the Kinesis Client Library (KCL), write an application that leverages on DynamoDB Streams Kinesis Adapter that will fetch data from the DynamoDB Streams endpoint. When there are updates made by a particular user, notify the subscribers via email using SNS.
3. Set up a DAX cluster to access the source DynamoDB table. Create a new DynamoDB trigger and a Lambda function. For every update made in the user data, the trigger will send data to the Lambda function which will then notify the subscribers via email using SNS.
4. Create a Lambda function that uses DynamoDB Streams Kinesis Adapter which will fetch data from the DynamoDB Streams endpoint. Set up an SNS Topic that will notify the subscribers via email when there is an update made by a particular user.

Answer(s): 1

Explanation

A DynamoDB stream is an ordered flow of information about changes to items in an Amazon DynamoDB table. When you enable a stream on a table, DynamoDB captures information about every modification to data items in the table.

Whenever an application creates, updates, or deletes items in the table, DynamoDB Streams writes a stream record with the primary key attribute(s) of the items that were modified. A stream record contains information about a data modification to a single item in a DynamoDB table. You can configure the stream so that the stream records capture additional information, such as the "before" and "after" images of modified items.

Amazon DynamoDB is integrated with AWS Lambda so that you can create triggers—pieces of code that automatically respond to events in DynamoDB Streams. With triggers, you can build applications that react to data modifications in DynamoDB tables.

If you enable DynamoDB Streams on a table, you can associate the stream ARN with a Lambda function that you write. Immediately after an item in the table is modified, a new record appears in the table's stream. AWS Lambda polls the stream and invokes your Lambda function synchronously when it detects new stream records. The Lambda function can perform any actions you specify, such as sending a notification or initiating a workflow.

Hence, the correct answer in this scenario is the option that says: Enable DynamoDB Stream and create an AWS Lambda trigger, as well as the IAM role which contains all of the permissions that the Lambda function will need at runtime. The data from the stream record will be processed by the Lambda function which will then publish a message to SNS Topic that will notify the subscribers via email.

The option that says: Using the Kinesis Client Library (KCL), write an application that leverages on DynamoDB Streams Kinesis Adapter that will fetch data from the DynamoDB Streams endpoint. When there are updates made by a particular user, notify the subscribers via email using SNS is incorrect because although this is a valid solution, it is missing a vital step which is to enable DynamoDB Streams. With the DynamoDB Streams Kinesis Adapter in place, you can begin developing applications via the KCL interface, with the API calls seamlessly directed at the DynamoDB Streams endpoint. Remember that the DynamoDB Stream feature is not enabled by default.

The option that says: Create a Lambda function that uses DynamoDB Streams Kinesis Adapter which will fetch data from the DynamoDB Streams endpoint. Set up an SNS Topic that will notify the subscribers via email when there is an update made by a particular user is incorrect because just like in the above, you have to manually enable DynamoDB Streams first before you can use its endpoint.

The option that says: Set up a DAX cluster to access the source DynamoDB table. Create a new DynamoDB trigger and a Lambda function. For every update made in the user data, the trigger will send data to the Lambda function which will then notify the subscribers via email using SNS is incorrect because the DynamoDB Accelerator (DAX) feature is primarily used to significantly improve the in-memory read performance of your database, and not to capture the time-ordered sequence of item-level modifications. You should use DynamoDB Streams in this scenario instead.

References:

https://docs.aws.amazon.com/amazondynamodb/latest/developerguide/Streams.html

https://docs.aws.amazon.com/amazondynamodb/latest/developerguide/Streams.Lambda.Tutorial.html

Question 50:

There are a lot of outages in the Availability Zone of your RDS database instance to the point that you have lost access to the database. What could you do to prevent losing access to your database in case that this event happens again?

1. Create a read replica
2. Increase the database instance size
3. Make a snapshot of the database
4. Enabled Multi-AZ failover

Answer(s): 4

Explanation

Amazon RDS Multi-AZ deployments provide enhanced availability and durability for Database (DB) Instances, making them a natural fit for production database workloads. For this scenario, enabling Multi-AZ failover is the correct answer. When you provision a Multi-AZ DB Instance, Amazon RDS automatically creates a primary DB Instance and synchronously replicates the data to a standby instance in a different Availability Zone (AZ). Each AZ runs on its own physically distinct, independent infrastructure, and is engineered to be highly reliable.

In case of an infrastructure failure, Amazon RDS performs an automatic failover to the standby (or to a read replica in the case of Amazon Aurora), so that you can resume database operations as soon as the failover is complete.

Making a snapshot of the database allows you to have a backup of your database, but it does not provide immediate availability in case of AZ failure. So this is incorrect.

Increasing the database instance size is not a solution for this problem. Doing this action addresses the need to upgrade your compute capacity but does not solve the requirement of providing access to your database even in the event of a loss of one of the Availability Zones.

Creating a read replica is incorrect because this simply provides enhanced performance for read-heavy database workloads. Although you can promote a read replica, its asynchronous replication might not provide you the latest version of your database.

Reference:

https://aws.amazon.com/rds/details/multi-az/

Question 51:

You are working as a Solutions Architect in a top software development company in Silicon Valley. The company has multiple applications hosted in their VPC. While you are monitoring the system, you noticed that multiple port scans are coming in from a specific IP address block which are trying to connect to several AWS resources inside your VPC. The internal security team has requested that all offending IP addresses be denied for the next 24 hours for security purposes.

Which of the following is the best method to quickly and temporarily deny access from the specified IP addresses?

1. Configure the firewall in the operating system of the EC2 instances to deny access from the IP address block.
2. Modify the Network Access Control List associated with all public subnets in the VPC to deny access from the IP Address block.
3. Add a rule in the Security Group of the EC2 instances to deny access from the IP Address block.
4. Create a policy in IAM to deny access from the IP Address block.

Answer(s): 2

Explanation

To control the traffic coming in and out of your VPC network, you can use the network access control list (ACL). It is an optional layer of security for your VPC that acts as a firewall for controlling traffic in and out of one or more subnets. This is the best solution among other options as you can easily add and remove the restriction in a matter of minutes.

Creating a policy in IAM to deny access from the IP Address block is incorrect as an IAM policy does not control the inbound and outbound traffic of your VPC.

Adding a rule in the Security Group of the EC2 instances to deny access from the IP Address block is incorrect as although a Security Group acts as a firewall, it will only control both inbound and outbound traffic at the instance level and not on the whole VPC.

Configuring the firewall in the operating system of the EC2 instances to deny access from the IP address block is incorrect because adding a firewall in the underlying operating system of the EC2 instance is not enough; the attacker can just connect to other AWS resources since the network access control list still allows them to do so.

Reference:

http://docs.aws.amazon.com/AmazonVPC/latest/UserGuide/VPC_ACLs.html

Question 52:

You are working for a large financial company as an IT consultant. Your role is to help their development team to build a highly available web application using stateless web servers. In this scenario, which AWS services are suitable for storing session state data? (Select TWO.)

1. Glacier
2. Redshift Spectrum
3. ElastiCache
4. RDS
5. DynamoDB

Answer(s): 3, 5

Explanation

DynamoDB and ElastiCache are the correct answers. You can store session state data on both DynamoDB and ElastiCache. These AWS services provide high-performance storage of key-value pairs which can be used to build a highly available web application.

Redshift Spectrum is incorrect since this is a data warehousing solution where you can directly query data from your data warehouse. Redshift is not suitable for storing session state, but more on analytics and OLAP processes.

RDS is incorrect as well since this is a relational database solution of AWS. This relational storage type might not be the best fit for session states, and it might not provide the performance you need compared to DynamoDB for the same cost.

S3 Glacier is incorrect as well since this is a low-cost cloud storage service for data archiving and long-term backup. The archival and retrieval speeds of Glacier is too slow for handling session states.

References:

https://aws.amazon.com/caching/database-caching/

https://aws.amazon.com/caching/session-management/

Question 53:

You have a requirement to make sure that an On-Demand EC2 instance can only be accessed from this IP address (110.238.98.71) via an SSH connection. Which configuration below will satisfy this requirement?

1. Security Group Inbound Rule: Protocol – UDP, Port Range – 22, Source 110.238.98.71/32

2. Security Group Inbound Rule: Protocol – TCP. Port Range – 22, Source 110.238.98.71/0
3. Security Group Inbound Rule: Protocol – TCP. Port Range – 22, Source 110.238.98.71/32
4. Security Group Inbound Rule: Protocol – UDP, Port Range – 22, Source 110.238.98.71/0

Answer(s): 3

Explanation

The SSH protocol uses TCP and port 22. Hence, Protocol – UDP, Port Range – 22, Source 110.238.98.71/32 and Protocol – UDP, Port Range – 22, Source 110.238.98.71/0 are incorrect as they are using UDP.

The following two options: Protocol – TCP, Port Range – 22, Source 110.238.98.71/32 and Protocol – TCP, Port Range – 22, Source 110.238.98.71/0 have one major difference and that is their CIDR block.

The requirement is to only allow the individual IP of the client and not the entire network. Therefore, the proper CIDR notation should be used. The /32 denotes one IP address and the /0 refers to the entire network. That is why Protocol – TCP, Port Range – 22, Source 110.238.98.71/0 is incorrect as it allowed the entire network instead of a single IP.

Reference:

https://docs.aws.amazon.com/AWSEC2/latest/UserGuide/using-network-security.html#security-group-rules

Question 54:

The company that you are working for has a highly available architecture consisting of an elastic load balancer and several EC2 instances configured with auto-scaling in three Availability Zones. You want to monitor your EC2 instances based on a particular metric, which is not readily available in CloudWatch.

Which of the following is a custom metric in CloudWatch which you have to manually set up?

1. Memory Utilization of an EC2 instance
2. Disk Reads activity of an EC2 instance
3. Network packets out of an EC2 instance
4. CPU Utilization of an EC2 instance

Answer(s): 1

Explanation

CloudWatch has available Amazon EC2 Metrics for you to use for monitoring. CPU Utilization identifies the processing power required to run an application upon a selected instance. Network Utilization identifies the volume of incoming and outgoing network traffic to a single instance. Disk Reads metric is used to determine the volume of the data the application reads from the hard disk of the instance. This can be used to determine the speed of the application. However, there are certain metrics that are not readily available in CloudWatch such as memory utilization, disk space utilization, and many others which can be collected by setting up a custom metric.

You need to prepare a custom metric using CloudWatch Monitoring Scripts which is written in Perl. You can also install CloudWatch Agent to collect more system-level metrics from Amazon EC2 instances. Here's the list of custom metrics that you can set up:

- Memory utilization

- Disk swap utilization

- Disk space utilization

- Page file utilization

- Log collection

CPU Utilization of an EC2 instance, Disk Reads activity of an EC2 instance, and Network packets out of an EC2 instance are all incorrect because these metrics are readily available in CloudWatch by default.

References:

https://docs.aws.amazon.com/AWSEC2/latest/UserGuide/monitoring_ec2.html

https://docs.aws.amazon.com/AWSEC2/latest/UserGuide/mon-scripts.html#using_put_script

Question 55:

A pharmaceutical company has resources hosted on both their on-premises network and in AWS cloud. They want all of their Software Architects to access resources on both environments using their on-premises credentials, which is stored in Active Directory.

In this scenario, which of the following can be used to fulfill this requirement?

1. Set up SAML 2.0-Based Federation by using a Web Identity Federation.

2. Set up SAML 2.0-Based Federation by using a Microsoft Active Directory Federation Service (AD FS).
3. Use Amazon VPC
4. Use IAM users

Answer(s): 2

Explanation

Since the company is using Microsoft Active Directory which implements Security Assertion Markup Language (SAML), you can set up a SAML-Based Federation for API Access to your AWS cloud. In this way, you can easily connect to AWS using the login credentials of your on-premises network.

AWS supports identity federation with SAML 2.0, an open standard that many identity providers (IdPs) use. This feature enables federated single sign-on (SSO), so users can log into the AWS Management Console or call the AWS APIs without you having to create an IAM user for everyone in your organization. By using SAML, you can simplify the process of configuring federation with AWS, because you can use the IdP's service instead of writing custom identity proxy code.

Before you can use SAML 2.0-based federation as described in the preceding scenario and diagram, you must configure your organization's IdP and your AWS account to trust each other. The general process for configuring this trust is described in the following steps. Inside your organization, you must have an IdP that supports SAML 2.0, like Microsoft Active Directory Federation Service (AD FS, part of Windows Server), Shibboleth, or another compatible SAML 2.0 provider.

Hence, the correct answer is: Set up SAML 2.0-Based Federation by using a Microsoft Active Directory Federation Service (AD FS).

Setting up SAML 2.0-Based Federation by using a Web Identity Federation is incorrect because this is primarily used to let users sign in via a well-known external identity provider (IdP), such as Login with Amazon, Facebook, Google. It does not utilize Active Directory.

Using IAM users is incorrect because the situation requires you to use the existing credentials stored in their Active Directory, and not user accounts that will be generated by IAM.

Using Amazon VPC is incorrect because this only lets you provision a logically isolated section of the AWS Cloud where you can launch AWS resources in a virtual network that you define. This has nothing to do with user authentication or Active Directory.

References:

http://docs.aws.amazon.com/IAM/latest/UserGuide/id_roles_providers_saml.html

https://docs.aws.amazon.com/IAM/latest/UserGuide/id_roles_providers.html

Question 56:

A popular mobile game uses CloudFront, Lambda, and DynamoDB for its backend services. The player data is persisted on a DynamoDB table and the static assets are distributed by CloudFront. However, there are a lot of complaints that saving and retrieving player information is taking a lot of time.

To improve the game's performance, which AWS service can you use to reduce DynamoDB response times from milliseconds to microseconds?

1. Amazon ElastiCache
2. Amazon DynamoDB Accelerator (DAX)
3. AWS Device Farm
4. DynamoDB Auto Scaling

Answer(s): 2

Explanation

Amazon DynamoDB Accelerator (DAX) is a fully managed, highly available, in-memory cache that can reduce Amazon DynamoDB response times from milliseconds to microseconds, even at millions of requests per second.

Amazon ElastiCache is incorrect because although you may use ElastiCache as your database cache, it will not reduce the DynamoDB response time from milliseconds to microseconds as compared with DynamoDB DAX.

AWS Device Farm is incorrect because this is an app testing service that lets you test and interact with your Android, iOS, and web apps on many devices at once, or reproduce issues on a device in real time.

DynamoDB Auto Scaling is incorrect because this is primarily used to automate capacity management for your tables and global secondary indexes.

References:

https://aws.amazon.com/dynamodb/dax

https://aws.amazon.com/device-farm

Question 57:

A global IT company with offices around the world has multiple AWS accounts. To improve efficiency and drive costs down, the Chief Information Officer (CIO) wants to set up a solution that centrally manages their AWS resources. This will allow them to procure AWS resources centrally and share resources such as AWS Transit

Gateways, AWS License Manager configurations, or Amazon Route 53 Resolver rules across their various accounts.

As the Solutions Architect, which combination of options should you implement in this scenario? (Select TWO.)

1. Consolidate all of the company's accounts using AWS ParallelCluster.
2. Use AWS Control Tower to easily and securely share your resources with your AWS accounts.
3. Use the AWS Resource Access Manager (RAM) service to easily and securely share your resources with your AWS accounts.
4. Consolidate all of the company's accounts using AWS Organizations.
5. Use the AWS Identity and Access Management service to set up cross-account access that will easily and securely share your resources with your AWS accounts.

Answer(s): 3, 4

Explanation

AWS Resource Access Manager (RAM) is a service that enables you to easily and securely share AWS resources with any AWS account or within your AWS Organization. You can share AWS Transit Gateways, Subnets, AWS License Manager configurations, and Amazon Route 53 Resolver rules resources with RAM.

Many organizations use multiple accounts to create administrative or billing isolation, and limit the impact of errors. RAM eliminates the need to create duplicate resources in multiple accounts, reducing the operational overhead of managing those resources in every single account you own. You can create resources centrally in a multi-account environment, and use RAM to share those resources across accounts in three simple steps: create a Resource Share, specify resources, and specify accounts. RAM is available to you at no additional charge.

You can procure AWS resources centrally, and use RAM to share resources such as subnets or License Manager configurations with other accounts. This eliminates the need to provision duplicate resources in every account in a multi-account environment, reducing the operational overhead of managing those resources in every account.

AWS Organizations is an account management service that lets you consolidate multiple AWS accounts into an organization that you create and centrally manage. With Organizations, you can create member accounts and invite existing accounts to join your organization. You can organize those accounts into groups and attach policy-based controls.

Hence, the correct combination of options in this scenario is:

- Consolidate all of the company's accounts using AWS Organizations.

- Use the AWS Resource Access Manager (RAM) service to easily and securely share your resources with your AWS accounts.

The option that says: Use the AWS Identity and Access Management service to set up cross-account access that will easily and securely share your resources with your AWS accounts is incorrect because although you can delegate access to resources that are in different AWS accounts using IAM, this process is extremely tedious and entails a lot of operational overhead since you have to manually set up cross-account access to each and every AWS account of the company. A better solution is to use AWS Resources Access Manager instead.

The option that says: Use AWS Control Tower to easily and securely share your resources with your AWS accounts is incorrect because AWS Control Tower simply offers the easiest way to set up and govern a new, secure, multi-account AWS environment. This is not the most suitable service to use to securely share your resources across AWS accounts or within your Organization. You have to use AWS Resources Access Manager (RAM) instead.

The option that says: Consolidate all of the company's accounts using AWS ParallelCluster is incorrect because AWS ParallelCluster is simply an AWS-supported open-source cluster management tool that makes it easy for you to deploy and manage High-Performance Computing (HPC) clusters on AWS. In this particular scenario, it is more appropriate to use AWS Organizations to consolidate all of your AWS accounts.

References:

https://aws.amazon.com/ram/

https://docs.aws.amazon.com/ram/latest/userguide/shareable.html

Question 58:

A telecommunications company is planning to give AWS Console access to developers. Company policy mandates the use of identity federation and role-based access control. Currently, the roles are already assigned using groups in the corporate Active Directory.

In this scenario, what combination of the following services can provide developers access to the AWS console? (Select TWO.)

1. AWS Directory Service Simple AD
2. AWS Directory Service AD Connector
3. Lambda
4. IAM Groups
5. IAM Roles

Answer(s): 2, 5

Explanation

Considering that the company is using a corporate Active Directory, it is best to use AWS Directory Service AD Connector for easier integration. In addition, since the roles are already assigned using groups in the corporate Active Directory, it would be better to also use IAM Roles. Take note that you can assign an IAM Role to the users or groups from your Active Directory once it is integrated with your VPC via the AWS Directory Service AD Connector.

AWS Directory Service provides multiple ways to use Amazon Cloud Directory and Microsoft Active Directory (AD) with other AWS services. Directories store information about users, groups, and devices, and administrators use them to manage access to information and resources. AWS Directory Service provides multiple directory choices for customers who want to use existing Microsoft AD or Lightweight Directory Access Protocol (LDAP)–aware applications in the cloud. It also offers those same choices to developers who need a directory to manage users, groups, devices, and access.

AWS Directory Service Simple AD is incorrect because this just provides a subset of the features offered by AWS Managed Microsoft AD, including the ability to manage user accounts and group memberships, create and apply group policies, securely connect to Amazon EC2 instances, and provide Kerberos-based single sign-on (SSO). In this scenario, the more suitable component to use is the AD Connector since it is a directory gateway with which you can redirect directory requests to your on-premises Microsoft Active Directory.

IAM Groups is incorrect because this is just a collection of IAM users. Groups let you specify permissions for multiple users, which can make it easier to manage the permissions for those users. In this scenario, the more suitable one to use is IAM Roles in order for permissions to create AWS Directory Service resources.

Lambda is incorrect because this is primarily used for serverless computing.

Reference:

https://aws.amazon.com/blogs/security/how-to-connect-your-on-premises-active-directory-to-aws-using-ad-connector/

Here is a video tutorial on AWS Directory Service:

https://youtu.be/4XeqotTYBtY

Question 59:

You are designing a banking portal which uses Amazon ElastiCache for Redis as its distributed session management component. Since the other Cloud Engineers in your department have access to your ElastiCache cluster, you have to secure the session data in the portal by requiring them to enter a password before they are granted permission to execute Redis commands.

As the Solutions Architect, which of the following should you do to meet the above requirement?

1. Set up an IAM Policy and MFA which requires the Cloud Engineers to enter their IAM credentials and token before they can access the ElastiCache cluster.
2. Set up a Redis replication group and enable the AtRestEncryptionEnabled parameter.
3. Enable the in-transit encryption for Redis replication groups.
4. Authenticate the users using Redis AUTH by creating a new Redis Cluster with both the --transit-encryption-enabled and --auth-token parameters enabled.

Answer(s): 4

Explanation

Using Redis AUTH command can improve data security by requiring the user to enter a password before they are granted permission to execute Redis commands on a password-protected Redis server. Hence, the correct answer is: Authenticate the users using Redis AUTH by creating a new Redis Cluster with both the --transit-encryption-enabled and --auth-token parameters enabled.

To require that users enter a password on a password-protected Redis server, include the parameter --auth-token with the correct password when you create your replication group or cluster and on all subsequent commands to the replication group or cluster.

Setting up an IAM Policy and MFA which requires the Cloud Engineers to enter their IAM credentials and token before they can access the ElastiCache cluster is incorrect because this is not possible in IAM. You have to use the Redis AUTH option instead.

Setting up a Redis replication group and enabling the AtRestEncryptionEnabled parameter is incorrect because the Redis At-Rest Encryption feature only secures the data inside the in-memory data store. You have to use Redis AUTH option instead.

Enabling the in-transit encryption for Redis replication groups is incorrect because although in-transit encryption is part of the solution, it is missing the most important thing which is the Redis AUTH option.

References:

https://docs.aws.amazon.com/AmazonElastiCache/latest/red-ug/auth.html

https://docs.aws.amazon.com/AmazonElastiCache/latest/red-ug/encryption.html

Question 60:

In the VPC that you are managing, it has one EC2 instance that has its data stored in an instance store. The instance was shut down by a 2nd level support staff over the weekend to save costs. When you arrived in the office the next Monday, you noticed that all data are lost and are no longer available on the EC2 instance.

What might be the cause of this?

1. The EC2 instance has been hacked.
2. The EC2 instance was using an instance store hence, data will be erased when the instance is stopped or terminated.
3. AWS automatically erased the data due to a virus found on the EC2 instance.
4. The EC2 instance was using EBS-backed root volumes hence, the data will be erased when the instance is shut down or stopped.

Answer(s): 2

Explanation

Since you are using an EC2 instance with an Instance store, its data is ephemeral which means that it will be erased once the instance is stopped or terminated. You may argue that the instance was only shut down but remember that the Operating system shutdown commands always terminate an instance store-backed instance. That is why the right answer is the option that says: The EC2 instance was using an instance store hence, data will be erased when the instance is stopped or terminated.

The data in an instance store persists only during the lifetime of its associated instance. If an instance reboots (intentionally or unintentionally), data in the instance store persists. However, data in the instance store is lost under any of the following circumstances:

- The underlying disk drive fails

- The instance stops

- The instance terminates

Therefore, do not rely on instance store for valuable, long-term data. Instead, use more durable data storage such as Amazon S3, Amazon EBS, or Amazon EFS. When you stop or terminate an instance, every block of storage in the instance store is reset. Hence, your data cannot be accessed through the instance store of another instance.

If you create an AMI from an instance, the data on its instance store volumes aren't preserved and aren't present on the instance store volumes of the instances that you launch from the AMI. You can specify instance store volumes for an instance only when you launch it. You can't detach an instance store volume from one instance and attach it to a different instance.

The option that says: The EC2 instance was using EBS-backed root volumes hence, the data will be erased when the instance is shut down or stopped is incorrect because the data will persist if you use an EBS-backed root volume.

The option that says: AWS automatically erased the data due to a virus found on the EC2 instance is incorrect because based on the AWS Shared Responsibility model, AWS will only manage the underlying resources that the services are using and not your actual data. Hence, it is highly unlikely that AWS will automatically erase your data due to a virus.

The option that says: The EC2 instance has been hacked is incorrect because although it is remotely possible that someone got hold of your AWS security credentials and deletes your data, this reason is still far fetched and quite unlikely to happen. Based on the given scenario, the stopping of the instance is one key attribute which we can link to its use of Instance Store volumes.

References:

https://docs.aws.amazon.com/AWSEC2/latest/UserGuide/ec2-instance-lifecycle.html

https://docs.aws.amazon.com/AWSEC2/latest/UserGuide/Storage.html

Question 61:

A financial application is composed of an Auto Scaling group of EC2 instances, an Application Load Balancer, and a MySQL RDS instance in a Multi-AZ Deployments configuration. To protect the confidential data of your customers, you have to ensure that your RDS database can only be accessed using the profile credentials specific to your EC2 instances via an authentication token.

As the Solutions Architect of the company, which of the following should you do to meet the above requirement?

1. Create an IAM Role and assign it to your EC2 instances which will grant exclusive access to your RDS instance.
2. Enable the IAM DB Authentication.
3. Use a combination of IAM and STS to restrict access to your RDS instance via a temporary token.
4. Configure SSL in your application to encrypt the database connection to RDS.

Answer(s): 2

Explanation

You can authenticate to your DB instance using AWS Identity and Access Management (IAM) database authentication. IAM database authentication works with MySQL and PostgreSQL. With this authentication method, you don't need to use a password when you connect to a DB instance. Instead, you use an authentication token.

An authentication token is a unique string of characters that Amazon RDS generates on request. Authentication tokens are generated using AWS Signature Version 4. Each token has a lifetime of 15 minutes. You don't need to store user credentials in the database, because authentication is managed externally using IAM. You can also still use standard database authentication.

IAM database authentication provides the following benefits:

Network traffic to and from the database is encrypted using Secure Sockets Layer (SSL).

You can use IAM to centrally manage access to your database resources, instead of managing access individually on each DB instance.

For applications running on Amazon EC2, you can use profile credentials specific to your EC2 instance to access your database instead of a password, for greater security

Hence, enabling IAM DB Authentication is the correct answer based on the above reference.

Configuring SSL in your application to encrypt the database connection to RDS is incorrect because an SSL connection is not using an authentication token from IAM. Although configuring SSL to your application can improve the security of your data in flight, it is still not a suitable option to use in this scenario.

Creating an IAM Role and assigning it to your EC2 instances which will grant exclusive access to your RDS instance is incorrect because although you can create and assign an IAM Role to your EC2 instances, you still need to configure your RDS to use IAM DB Authentication.

Using a combination of IAM and STS to restrict access to your RDS instance via a temporary token is incorrect because you have to use IAM DB Authentication for this scenario, and not a combination of an IAM and STS. Although STS is used to send temporary tokens for authentication, this is not a compatible use case for RDS.

Reference:

https://docs.aws.amazon.com/AmazonRDS/latest/UserGuide/UsingWithRDS.IA
MDBAuth.html

Question 62:

A traffic monitoring and reporting application uses Kinesis to accept real-time data. In order to process and store the data, they used Amazon Kinesis Data Firehose to load the streaming data to various AWS resources.

Which of the following services can you load streaming data into?

1. Amazon Redshift Spectrum
2. Amazon Elasticsearch Service
3. Amazon S3 Select
4. Amazon Athena

Answer(s): 2

Explanation

Amazon Kinesis Data Firehose is the easiest way to load streaming data into data stores and analytics tools. It can capture, transform, and load streaming data into Amazon S3, Amazon Redshift, Amazon Elasticsearch Service, and Splunk, enabling near real-time analytics with existing business intelligence tools and dashboards you're already using today.

It is a fully managed service that automatically scales to match the throughput of your data and requires no ongoing administration. It can also batch, compress, and encrypt the data before loading it, minimizing the amount of storage used at the destination and increasing security.

Amazon S3 Select and Amazon Redshift Spectrum are incorrect because Amazon S3 Select is just a feature of Amazon S3. Likewise, Redshift Spectrum is also just a feature of Amazon Redshift. Although Amazon Kinesis Data Firehose can load streaming data to both Amazon S3 and Amazon Redshift, it does not directly load the data to S3 Select and Redshift Spectrum.

S3 Select is an Amazon S3 feature that makes it easy to retrieve specific data from the contents of an object using simple SQL expressions without having to retrieve the entire object. Amazon Redshift Spectrum is a feature of Amazon Redshift that enables you to run queries against exabytes of unstructured data in Amazon S3 with no loading or ETL required.

Amazon Athena is incorrect because Amazon Kinesis Data Firehose cannot load streaming data to Athena.

Reference:

https://aws.amazon.com/kinesis/data-firehose/

Question 63:

You have a new e-commerce web application written in Angular framework which is deployed to a fleet of EC2 instances behind an Application Load Balancer. You configured the load balancer to perform health checks on these EC2 instances.

What will happen if one of these EC2 instances failed the health checks?

1. The Application Load Balancer stops sending traffic to the instance that failed its health check.
2. The EC2 instance gets quarantined by the Application Load Balancer for root cause analysis.
3. The EC2 instance gets terminated automatically by the Application Load Balancer.
4. The EC2 instance is replaced automatically by the Application Load Balancer.

Answer(s): 1

Explanation

In case that one of the EC2 instances failed a health check, the Application Load Balancer stops sending traffic to that instance.

Your Application Load Balancer periodically sends requests to its registered targets to test their status. These tests are called health checks. Each load balancer node routes requests only to the healthy targets in the enabled Availability Zones for the load balancer. Each load balancer node checks the health of each target, using the health check settings for the target group with which the target is registered. After your target is registered, it must pass one health check to be considered healthy. After each health check is completed, the load balancer node closes the connection that was established for the health check.

Reference:

http://docs.aws.amazon.com/elasticloadbalancing/latest/classic/elb-healthchecks.html

Question 64:

You are building a new data analytics application in AWS which will be deployed in an Auto Scaling group of On-Demand EC2 instances and a MongoDB database. It is expected that the database will have high-throughput workloads performing small, random I/O operations. As the Solutions Architect, you are required to properly set up and launch the required resources in AWS.

Which of the following is the most suitable EBS type to use for your database?

1. Provisioned IOPS SSD (io1)
2. Cold HDD (sc1)
3. General Purpose SSD (gp2)
4. Throughput Optimized HDD (st1)

Answer(s): 1

Explanation

On a given volume configuration, certain I/O characteristics drive the performance behavior for your EBS volumes. SSD-backed volumes, such as General Purpose SSD (gp2) and Provisioned IOPS SSD (io1), deliver consistent performance whether an I/O operation is random or sequential. HDD-backed volumes like Throughput Optimized HDD (st1) and Cold HDD (sc1) deliver optimal performance only when I/O operations are large and sequential.

In the exam, always consider the difference between SSD and HDD as shown on the table below. This will allow you to easily eliminate specific EBS-types in the options which are not SSD or not HDD, depending on whether the question asks for a storage type which has small, random I/O operations or large, sequential I/O operations.

Provisioned IOPS SSD (io1) volumes are designed to meet the needs of I/O-intensive workloads, particularly database workloads, that are sensitive to storage performance and consistency. Unlike gp2, which uses a bucket and credit model to calculate performance, an io1 volume allows you to specify a consistent IOPS rate when you create the volume, and Amazon EBS delivers within 10 percent of the provisioned IOPS performance 99.9 percent of the time over a given year.

General Purpose SSD (gp2) is incorrect because although General Purpose is a type of SSD that can handle small, random I/O operations, the Provisioned IOPS SSD volumes are much more suitable to meet the needs of I/O-intensive database workloads such as MongoDB, Oracle, MySQL, and many others.

Throughput Optimized HDD (st1) and Cold HDD (sc1) are incorrect because HDD volumes (such as Throughput Optimized HDD and Cold HDD volumes) are more suitable for workloads with large, sequential I/O operations instead of small, random I/O operations.

Reference:

https://docs.aws.amazon.com/AWSEC2/latest/UserGuide/EBSVolumeTypes.html#EBSVolumeTypes_piops

https://docs.aws.amazon.com/AWSEC2/latest/UserGuide/ebs-io-characteristics.html

Question 65:

A multi-tiered application hosted in your on-premises data center is scheduled to be migrated to AWS. The application has a message broker service which uses industry standard messaging APIs and protocols that must be migrated as well, without rewriting the messaging code in your application.

Which of the following is the most suitable service that you should use to move your messaging service to AWS?

1. Amazon MQ
2. Amazon SWF
3. Amazon SNS
4. Amazon SQS

Answer(s): 1

Explanation

Amazon MQ, Amazon SQS, and Amazon SNS are messaging services that are suitable for anyone from startups to enterprises. If you're using messaging with existing applications and want to move your messaging service to the cloud quickly and easily, it is recommended that you consider Amazon MQ. It supports industry-standard APIs and protocols so you can switch from any standards-based message broker to Amazon MQ without rewriting the messaging code in your applications.

Hence, Amazon MQ is the correct answer.

If you are building brand new applications in the cloud, then it is highly recommended that you consider Amazon SQS and Amazon SNS. Amazon SQS and SNS are lightweight, fully managed message queue and topic services that scale almost infinitely and provide simple, easy-to-use APIs. You can use Amazon SQS and SNS to decouple and scale microservices, distributed systems, and serverless applications, and improve reliability.

Amazon SQS is incorrect because although this is a fully managed message queuing service, it does not support an extensive list of industry-standard messaging APIs and protocol, unlike Amazon MQ. Moreover, using Amazon SQS requires you to do additional changes in the messaging code of applications to make it compatible.

Amazon SNS is incorrect because SNS is more suitable as a pub/sub messaging service instead of a message broker service.

Amazon SWF is incorrect because this is a fully-managed state tracker and task coordinator service and not a messaging service, unlike Amazon MQ, AmazonSQS and Amazon SNS.

References:

https://aws.amazon.com/amazon-mq/faqs/

https://docs.aws.amazon.com/AWSSimpleQueueService/latest/SQSDeveloperGuid
e/welcome.html#sqs-difference-from-amazon-mq-sns

PRACTICE TEST 2

AWS CERTIFIED SOLUTIONS ARCHITECT ASSOCIATE

AWS CERTIFIED SOLUTIONS ARCHITECT ASSOCIATE PRACTICE TEST 2

Question 1:

You have set up a VPC with public subnet and an Internet gateway. You set up an EC2 instance with a public IP as well. However, you are still not able to connect to the instance via the Internet. You checked its associated security group and it seems okay.

What should you do to ensure you can connect to the EC2 instance from the Internet?

1. Set an Elastic IP Address to the EC2 instance.
2. (Incorrect)
3. Check the CloudWatch logs as there must be some issue in the EC2 instance.
4. Check the main route table and ensure that the right route entry to the Internet Gateway (IGW) is configured.
5. Set a Secondary Private IP Address to the EC2 instance.

Answer(s): 4

Explanation

The route table entries enable EC2 instances in the subnet to use IPv4 to communicate with other instances in the VPC, and to communicate directly over the Internet. A subnet that's associated with a route table that has a route to an Internet gateway is known as a public subnet.

If you could not connect to your EC2 instance even if there is already an Internet Gateway in your VPC and there is no issue in the security group, then you must check if the entries in the route table are properly configured.

Setting an Elastic IP Address to the EC2 instance is incorrect since you already have a public IP address for your EC2 instance, and doesn't require an EIP anymore.

Setting a Secondary Private IP Address to the EC2 instance is incorrect because having a secondary private IP address is only used within the VPC, not when connecting to the outside Internet.

Checking the CloudWatch logs as there must be some issue in the EC2 instance is incorrect because it is better to go through your setup and make sure that you didn't miss a step, such as adding a route in the route table, before you check the actual CloudWatch logs to see if an instance has an issue.

Reference:

http://docs.aws.amazon.com/AmazonVPC/latest/UserGuide/VPC_Scenario1.html

Question 2:

An online events registration system is hosted in AWS and uses ECS to host its front-end tier and a Multi-AZ RDS for its database tier, which also has a standby replica. What are the events that will make Amazon RDS automatically perform a failover to the standby replica? (Select TWO.)

1. Storage failure on primary
2. Compute unit failure on secondary DB instance
3. In the event of Read Replica failure
4. Loss of availability in primary Availability Zone
5. Storage failure on secondary DB instance

Answer(s): 1, 4

Explanation

Amazon RDS provides high availability and failover support for DB instances using Multi-AZ deployments. Amazon RDS uses several different technologies to provide failover support. Multi-AZ deployments for Oracle, PostgreSQL, MySQL, and MariaDB DB instances use Amazon's failover technology. SQL Server DB instances use SQL Server Database Mirroring (DBM).

In a Multi-AZ deployment, Amazon RDS automatically provisions and maintains a synchronous standby replica in a different Availability Zone. The primary DB instance is synchronously replicated across Availability Zones to a standby replica to provide data redundancy, eliminate I/O freezes, and minimize latency spikes during system backups. Running a DB instance with high availability can enhance availability during planned system maintenance, and help protect your databases against DB instance failure and Availability Zone disruption.

Amazon RDS detects and automatically recovers from the most common failure scenarios for Multi-AZ deployments so that you can resume database operations as quickly as possible without administrative intervention.

The high-availability feature is not a scaling solution for read-only scenarios; you cannot use a standby replica to serve read traffic. To service read-only traffic, you should use a Read Replica.

Amazon RDS automatically performs a failover in the event of any of the following:

Loss of availability in primary Availability Zone

Loss of network connectivity to primary

Compute unit failure on primary

Storage failure on primary

The following options are incorrect because all these scenarios do not affect the primary database. Automatic failover only occurs if the primary database is the one that is affected.

- Storage failure on secondary DB instance

- In the event of Read Replica failure

- Compute unit failure on secondary DB instance

References:

https://aws.amazon.com/rds/details/multi-az/

https://docs.aws.amazon.com/AmazonRDS/latest/UserGuide/Concepts.MultiAZ.html

Question 3:

You are an IT Consultant for an advertising company that is currently working on a proof of concept project that automatically provides SEO analytics for their clients. Your company has a VPC in AWS that operates in dual-stack mode in which IPv4 and IPv6 communication is allowed. You deployed the application to an Auto Scaling group of EC2 instances with an Application Load Balancer in front that evenly distributes the incoming traffic. You are ready to go live but you need to point your domain name (sample.com) to the Application Load Balancer.

In Route 53, which record types will you use to point the DNS name of the Application Load Balancer? (Select TWO.)

1. Alias with a type "CNAME" record set
2. Alias with a type "A" record set
3. Alias with a type "AAAA" record set
4. Alias with a type of "MX" record set
5. Non-Alias with a type "A" record set

Answer(s): 2, 3

Explanation

Alias with a type "AAAA" record set and Alias with a type "A" record set are correct. To route domain traffic to an ELB load balancer, use Amazon Route 53 to create an alias record that points to your load balancer. An alias record is a Route 53 extension to DNS. It's similar to a CNAME record, but you can create an alias record both for the root domain, such as sample.com, and for subdomains, such as portal.to samplecom. (You can create CNAME records only for subdomains.) To enable IPv6 resolution, you would need to create a second resource record, sample.com ALIAS AAAA -> myelb.us-west-2.elb.amazonnaws.com, this is assuming your Elastic Load Balancer has IPv6 support.

Non-Alias with a type "A" record set is incorrect because you only use Non-Alias with a type "A" record set for IP addresses.

Alias with a type "CNAME" record set is incorrect because you can't create a CNAME record at the zone apex. For example, if you register the DNS name sample.com, the zone apex is sample.com.

Alias with a type of "MX" record set is incorrect because an MX record is primarily used for mail servers. It includes a priority number and a domain name, for example: 10 mailserver. sample.com.

Reference:

https://docs.aws.amazon.com/Route53/latest/DeveloperGuide/routing-to-elb-load-balancer.html

https://docs.aws.amazon.com/Route53/latest/DeveloperGuide/resource-record-sets-choosing-alias-non-alias.html

Question 4:

A media company hosts large volumes of archive data that are about 250 TB in size on their internal servers. They have decided to move these data to S3 because of its durability and redundancy. The company currently has a 100 Mbps dedicated line connecting their head office to the Internet.

Which of the following is the FASTEST and the MOST cost-effective way to import all these data to Amazon S3?

1. Use AWS Snowmobile to transfer the data over to S3.
2. Establish an AWS Direct Connect connection then transfer the data over to S3.
3. Order multiple AWS Snowball devices to upload the files to Amazon S3.
4. Upload it directly to S3

Answer(s): 3

Explanation

AWS Snowball is a petabyte-scale data transport solution that uses secure appliances to transfer large amounts of data into and out of the AWS cloud. Using Snowball addresses common challenges with large-scale data transfers including high network costs, long transfer times, and security concerns. Transferring data with Snowball is simple, fast, secure, and can be as little as one-fifth the cost of high-speed Internet.

Snowball is a strong choice for data transfer if you need to more securely and quickly transfer terabytes to many petabytes of data to AWS. Snowball can also be the right choice if you don't want to make expensive upgrades to your network infrastructure, if you frequently experience large backlogs of data, if you're located in a physically isolated environment, or if you're in an area where high-speed Internet connections are not available or cost-prohibitive.

As a rule of thumb, if it takes more than one week to upload your data to AWS using the spare capacity of your existing Internet connection, then you should consider using Snowball. For example, if you have a 100 Mb connection that you can solely dedicate to transferring your data and need to transfer 100 TB of data, it takes more than 100 days to complete data transfer over that connection. You can make the same transfer by using multiple Snowballs in about a week.

(xyx)Hence, ordering multiple AWS Snowball devices to upload the files to Amazon S3 is the correct answer.

Uploading it directly to S3 is incorrect since this would take too long to finish due to the slow Internet connection of the company.

Establishing an AWS Direct Connect connection then transferring the data over to S3 is incorrect since provisioning a line for Direct Connect would take too much time and might not give you the fastest data transfer solution. In addition, the scenario didn't warrant an establishment of a dedicated connection from your on-premises data center to AWS. The primary goal is to just do a one-time migration of data to AWS which can be accomplished by using AWS Snowball devices.

Using AWS Snowmobile to transfer the data over to S3 is incorrect because Snowmobile is more suitable if you need to move extremely large amounts of data to AWS or need to transfer up to 100PB of data. This will be transported on a 45-foot long ruggedized shipping container, pulled by a semi-trailer truck. Take note that you only need to migrate 250 TB of data, hence, this is not the most suitable and cost-effective solution.

References:

https://aws.amazon.com/snowball/

https://aws.amazon.com/snowball/faqs/

Question 5:

As a Network Architect developing a food ordering application, you need to retrieve the instance ID, public keys, and public IP address of the EC2 server you made for tagging and grouping the attributes into your internal application running on-premises.

Which EC2 feature will help you achieve your requirements?

1. Instance user data
2. Instance metadata
3. Amazon Machine Image
4. Resource tags

Answer(s): 2

Explanation

Instance metadata is the data about your instance that you can use to configure or manage the running instance. You can get the instance ID, public keys, public IP address and many other information from the instance metadata by firing a URL command in your instance to this URL:

http://169.254.169.254/latest/meta-data/

Instance user data is incorrect because this is mainly used to perform common automated configuration tasks and run scripts after the instance starts.

Resource tags is incorrect because these are labels that you assign to an AWS resource. Each tag consists of a key and an optional value, both of which you define.

Amazon Machine Image is incorrect because this mainly provides the information required to launch an instance, which is a virtual server in the cloud.

Reference:

http://docs.aws.amazon.com/AWSEC2/latest/UserGuide/ec2-instance-metadata.htm

Question 6:

You are a Solutions Architect working with a company that uses Chef Configuration management in their datacenter. Which service is designed to let the customer leverage existing Chef recipes in AWS?

1. AWS Elastic Beanstalk
2. Amazon Simple Workflow Service
3. AWS CloudFormation
4. AWS OpsWorks

Answer(s): 4

Explanation

AWS OpsWorks is a configuration management service that provides managed instances of Chef and Puppet. Chef and Puppet are automation platforms that allow you to use code to automate the configurations of your servers. OpsWorks lets you use Chef and Puppet to automate how servers are configured, deployed, and managed across your Amazon EC2 instances or on-premises compute environments. OpsWorks has three offerings - AWS Opsworks for Chef Automate, AWS OpsWorks for Puppet Enterprise, and AWS OpsWorks Stacks.

Amazon Simple Workflow Service is incorrect because AWS SWF is a fully-managed state tracker and task coordinator in the Cloud. It does not let you leverage Chef recipes.

AWS Elastic Beanstalk is incorrect because this handles an application's deployment details of capacity provisioning, load balancing, auto-scaling, and application health monitoring. It does not let you leverage Chef recipes just like Amazon SWF.

AWS CloudFormation is incorrect because this is a service that lets you create a collection of related AWS resources and provision them in a predictable fashion using infrastructure as code. It does not let you leverage Chef recipes just like Amazon SWF and AWS Elastic Beanstalk.

Reference:

https://aws.amazon.com/opsworks/

Question 7:

You are developing a meal planning application that provides meal recommendations for the week as well as the food consumption of your users. Your application resides on an EC2 instance which requires access to various AWS services for its day-to-day operations.

Which of the following is the best way to allow your EC2 instance to access your S3 bucket and other AWS services?

1. Create a role in IAM and assign it to the EC2 instance.
2. Add the API Credentials in the Security Group and assign it to the EC2 instance.
3. Store the API credentials in a bastion host.
4. Store the API credentials in the EC2 instance.

Answer(s): 1

Explanation

The best practice in handling API Credentials is to create a new role in the Identity Access Management (IAM) service and then assign it to a specific EC2 instance. In this way, you have a secure and centralized way of storing and managing your credentials.

Storing the API credentials in the EC2 instance, adding the API Credentials in the Security Group and assigning it to the EC2 instance, and storing the API credentials in a bastion host are incorrect because it is not secure to store nor use the API credentials from an EC2 instance. You should use IAM service instead.

Reference:

http://docs.aws.amazon.com/AWSEC2/latest/UserGuide/iam-roles-for-amazon-ec2.html

Question 8:

You have a static corporate website hosted in a standard S3 bucket and a new web domain name which was registered using Route 53. You are instructed by your manager to integrate these two services in order to successfully launch their corporate website.

What are the prerequisites when routing traffic using Amazon Route 53 to a website that is hosted in an Amazon S3 Bucket? (Select TWO.)

1. A registered domain name
2. The S3 bucket name must be the same as the domain name
3. The S3 bucket must be in the same region as the hosted zone
4. The record set must be of type "MX"
5. The Cross-Origin Resource Sharing (CORS) option should be enabled in the S3 bucket

Answer(s): 1, 2

Explanation

Here are the prerequisites for routing traffic to a website that is hosted in an Amazon S3 Bucket:

- An S3 bucket that is configured to host a static website. The bucket must have the same name as your domain or subdomain. For example, if you want to use the subdomain portal. Sample.com, the name of the bucket must be portal. sample.com.

- A registered domain name. You can use Route 53 as your domain registrar, or you can use a different registrar.

- Route 53 as the DNS service for the domain. If you register your domain name by using Route 53, we automatically configure Route 53 as the DNS service for the domain.

The option that says: The record set must be of type "MX" is incorrect since an MX record specifies the mail server responsible for accepting email messages on behalf of a domain name. This is not what is being asked by the question.

The option that says: The S3 bucket must be in the same region as the hosted zone is incorrect. There is no constraint that the S3 bucket must be in the same region as the hosted zone, in order for the Route 53 service to route traffic into it.

The option that says: The Cross-Origin Resource Sharing (CORS) option should be enabled in the S3 bucket is incorrect because you only need to enable Cross-Origin Resource Sharing (CORS) when your client web application on one domain interacts with the resources in a different domain.

Reference:

https://docs.aws.amazon.com/Route53/latest/DeveloperGuide/RoutingToS3Bucket.html

Question 9:

Your client is an insurance company that utilizes SAP HANA for their day-to-day ERP operations. Since you can't migrate this database due to customer preferences, you need to integrate it with your current AWS workload in your VPC in which you are required to establish a site-to-site VPN connection.

What needs to be configured outside of the VPC for you to have a successful site-to-site VPN connection?

1. A dedicated NAT instance in a public subnet
2. An EIP to the Virtual Private Gateway
3. The main route table in your VPC to route traffic through a NAT instance
4. An Internet-routable IP address (static) of the customer gateway's external interface for the on-premises network

Answer(s): 4

Explanation

By default, instances that you launch into a virtual private cloud (VPC) can't communicate with your own network. You can enable access to your network from your VPC by attaching a virtual private gateway to the VPC, creating a custom route table, updating your security group rules, and creating an AWS managed VPN connection.

Although the term VPN connection is a general term, in the Amazon VPC documentation, a VPN connection refers to the connection between your VPC and your own network. AWS supports Internet Protocol security (IPsec) VPN connections.

A customer gateway is a physical device or software application on your side of the VPN connection.

To create a VPN connection, you must create a customer gateway resource in AWS, which provides information to AWS about your customer gateway device. Next, you have to set up an Internet-routable IP address (static) of the customer gateway's external interface.

The following diagram illustrates single VPN connections. The VPC has an attached virtual private gateway, and your remote network includes a customer gateway, which you must configure to enable the VPN connection. You set up the routing so that any traffic from the VPC bound for your network is routed to the virtual private gateway.

A dedicated NAT instance in a public subnet and the main route table in your VPC to route traffic through a NAT instance are incorrect since you don't need a NAT instance for you to be able to create a VPN connection.

An EIP to the Virtual Private Gateway is incorrect since you do not attach an EIP to a VPG.

References:

https://docs.aws.amazon.com/AmazonVPC/latest/UserGuide/VPC_VPN.html

https://docs.aws.amazon.com/vpc/latest/userguide/SetUpVPNConnections.html

How to create a VPN with Amazon VPC:

https://www.youtube.com/watch?v=pf0J6oPCIbE

Question 10:

One of your EC2 instances is reporting an unhealthy system status check. The operations team is looking for an easier way to monitor and repair these instances instead of fixing them manually.

How will you automate the monitoring and repair of the system status check failure in an AWS environment?

1. Buy and implement a third party monitoring tool.
2. Write a python script that queries the EC2 API for each instance status check

3. Create CloudWatch alarms that stop and start the instance based on status check alarms.
4. Write a shell script that periodically shuts down and starts instances based on certain stats.

Answer(s): 3

Explanation

Using Amazon CloudWatch alarm actions, you can create alarms that automatically stop, terminate, reboot, or recover your EC2 instances. You can use the stop or terminate actions to help you save money when you no longer need an instance to be running. You can use the reboot and recover actions to automatically reboot those instances or recover them onto new hardware if a system impairment occurs.

Writing a python script that queries the EC2 API for each instance status check, writing a shell script that periodically shuts down and starts instances based on certain stats, and buying and implementing a third party monitoring tool are all incorrect because it is unnecessary to go through such lengths when CloudWatch Alarms already has such a feature for you, offered at a low cost.

Reference:

https://docs.aws.amazon.com/AmazonCloudWatch/latest/monitoring/UsingAlarmActions.html

Question 11:

You are a Solutions Architect working for a large insurance company that deployed their production environment on a custom Virtual Private Cloud in AWS with a default configuration. The VPC consists of two private subnets and one public subnet. Inside the public subnet is a group of EC2 instances which are created by an Auto Scaling group and all of the instances are in the same Security Group. Your development team has created a new application which will be accessed by mobile devices via a custom port. This application has been deployed to the production environment and you need to open this port globally to the Internet.

Which of the following is the correct procedure to meet this requirement?

1. Open the custom port on the Network Access Control List of your VPC. Your EC2 instances will be able to use this port after a reboot.
2. Open the custom port on the Network Access Control List of your VPC. Your EC2 instances will be able to use this port immediately.
3. Open the custom port on the Security Group. Your EC2 instances will be able to use this port after 60 minutes.
4. Open the custom port on the Security Group. Your EC2 instances will be able to use this port immediately.

Answer(s): 4

Explanation

To allow the custom port, you have to change the Inbound Rules in your Security Group to allow traffic coming from the mobile devices. Security Groups usually control the list of ports that are allowed to be used by your EC2 instances and the NACLs control which network or list of IP addresses can connect to your whole VPC.

When you create a security group, it has no inbound rules. Therefore, no inbound traffic originating from another host to your instance is allowed until you add inbound rules to the security group. By default, a security group includes an outbound rule that allows all outbound traffic. You can remove the rule and add outbound rules that allow specific outbound traffic only. If your security group has no outbound rules, no outbound traffic originating from your instance is allowed.

The option that says: Open the custom port on the Security Group. Your EC2 instances will be able to use this port after 60 minutes and Open the custom port on the Network Access Control List of your VPC. Your EC2 instances will be able to use this port after a reboot are both incorrect because any changes to the Security Groups or Network Access Control Lists are applied immediately and not after 60 minutes or after the instance reboot.

The option that says: Open the custom port on the Network Access Control List of your VPC. Your EC2 instances will be able to use this port immediately is incorrect because the scenario says that VPC is using a default configuration. Since by default, Network ACL allows all inbound and outbound IPv4 traffic, then there is no point of explicitly allowing the port in the Network ACL. Security Groups, on the other hand, does not allow incoming traffic by default, unlike Network ACL.

Reference:

http://docs.aws.amazon.com/AmazonVPC/latest/UserGuide/VPC_SecurityGroups.html

Question 12:

An accounting application uses an RDS database configured with Multi-AZ deployments to improve availability. What would happen to RDS if the primary database instance fails?

1. A new database instance is created in the standby Availability Zone.
2. The primary database instance will reboot.
3. The canonical name record (CNAME) is switched from the primary to standby instance.

4. The IP address of the primary DB instance is switched to the standby DB instance.

Answer(s): 3

Explanation

In Amazon RDS, failover is automatically handled so that you can resume database operations as quickly as possible without administrative intervention in the event that your primary database instance went down. When failing over, Amazon RDS simply flips the canonical name record (CNAME) for your DB instance to point at the standby, which is in turn promoted to become the new primary.

The option that says: The IP address of the primary DB instance is switched to the standby DB instance is incorrect since IP addresses are per subnet, and subnets cannot span multiple AZs.

The option that says: The primary database instance will reboot is incorrect since in the event of a failure, there is no database to reboot with.

The option that says: A new database instance is created in the standby Availability Zone is incorrect since with multi-AZ enabled, you already have a standby database in another AZ.

References:

https://aws.amazon.com/rds/details/multi-az/

https://aws.amazon.com/rds/faqs/

Question 13:

You have a cryptocurrency exchange portal which is hosted in an Auto Scaling group of EC2 instances behind an Application Load Balancer, and are deployed across multiple AWS regions. Your users can be found all around the globe, but the majority are from Japan and Sweden. Because of the compliance requirements in these two locations, you want your Japanese users to connect to the servers in the ap-northeast-1 Asia Pacific (Tokyo) region, while your Swedish users should be connected to the servers in the eu-west-1 EU (Ireland) region.

Which of the following services would allow you to easily fulfill this requirement?

1. Use Route 53 Weighted Routing policy.
2. Set up a new CloudFront web distribution with the geo-restriction feature enabled.
3. Set up an Application Load Balancers that will automatically route the traffic to the proper AWS region.
4. Use Route 53 Geolocation Routing policy.

Answer(s): 4

Explanation

Geolocation routing lets you choose the resources that serve your traffic based on the geographic location of your users, meaning the location that DNS queries originate from. For example, you might want all queries from Europe to be routed to an ELB load balancer in the Frankfurt region.

When you use geolocation routing, you can localize your content and present some or all of your website in the language of your users. You can also use geolocation routing to restrict distribution of content to only the locations in which you have distribution rights. Another possible use is for balancing load across endpoints in a predictable, easy-to-manage way, so that each user location is consistently routed to the same endpoint.

Setting up an Application Load Balancers that will automatically route the traffic to the proper AWS region is incorrect because Elastic Load Balancers distribute traffic among EC2 instances across multiple Availability Zones but not across AWS regions.

Setting up a new CloudFront web distribution with the geo-restriction feature enabled is incorrect because the CloudFront geo-restriction feature is primarily used to prevent users in specific geographic locations from accessing content that you're distributing through a CloudFront web distribution. It does not let you choose the resources that serve your traffic based on the geographic location of your users, unlike the Geolocation routing policy in Route 53.

Using Route 53 Weighted Routing policy is incorrect because this is not a suitable solution to meet the requirements of this scenario. It just lets you associate multiple resources with a single domain name (sample com) or subdomain name (forums. sample com) and choose how much traffic is routed to each resource. You have to use a Geolocation routing policy instead.

References:

https://docs.aws.amazon.com/Route53/latest/DeveloperGuide/routing-policy.html

https://aws.amazon.com/premiumsupport/knowledge-center/geolocation-routing-policy

Question 14:

As part of the Business Continuity Plan of your company, your IT Director instructed you to set up an automated backup of all of the EBS Volumes for your EC2 instances as soon as possible.

What is the fastest and most cost-effective solution to automatically back up all of your EBS Volumes?

1. Use an EBS-cycle policy in Amazon S3 to automatically back up the EBS volumes.
2. For an automated solution, create a scheduled job that calls the "create-snapshot" command via the AWS CLI to take a snapshot of production EBS volumes periodically.
3. Use Amazon Data Lifecycle Manager (Amazon DLM) to automate the creation of EBS snapshots.
4. Set your Amazon Storage Gateway with EBS volumes as the data source and store the backups in your on-premises servers through the storage gateway.

Answer(s): 3

Explanation

You can use Amazon Data Lifecycle Manager (Amazon DLM) to automate the creation, retention, and deletion of snapshots taken to back up your Amazon EBS volumes. Automating snapshot management helps you to:

- Protect valuable data by enforcing a regular backup schedule.

- Retain backups as required by auditors or internal compliance.

- Reduce storage costs by deleting outdated backups.

Combined with the monitoring features of Amazon CloudWatch Events and AWS CloudTrail, Amazon DLM provides a complete backup solution for EBS volumes at no additional cost.

Hence, using Amazon Data Lifecycle Manager (Amazon DLM) to automate the creation of EBS snapshots is the correct answer as it is the fastest and most cost-effective solution that provides an automated way of backing up your EBS volumes.

The option that says: For an automated solution, create a scheduled job that calls the "create-snapshot" command via the AWS CLI to take a snapshot of production EBS volumes periodically is incorrect because even though this is a valid solution, you would still need additional time to create a scheduled job that calls the "create-snapshot" command. It would be better to use Amazon Data Lifecycle Manager (Amazon DLM) instead as this provides you the fastest solution which enables you to automate the creation, retention, and deletion of the EBS snapshots without having to write custom shell scripts or creating scheduled jobs.

Setting your Amazon Storage Gateway with EBS volumes as the data source and storing the backups in your on-premises servers through the storage gateway is incorrect as the Amazon Storage Gateway is used only for creating a backup of data from your on-premises server and not from the Amazon Virtual Private Cloud.

Using an EBS-cycle policy in Amazon S3 to automatically back up the EBS volumes is incorrect as there is no such thing as EBS-cycle policy in Amazon S3.

References:

https://docs.aws.amazon.com/AWSEC2/latest/UserGuide/snapshot-lifecycle.html

http://docs.aws.amazon.com/AWSEC2/latest/UserGuide/ebs-creating-snapshot.html

Question 15:

You are working for a central bank as the Principal AWS Solutions Architect. Due to compliance requirements and security concerns, you are tasked to implement strict access to the central bank's AWS resources using the AWS Identity and Access Management service.

Which of the following can you manage in the IAM dashboard? (Select TWO.)

1. Cost Allocation Reports
2. Security Groups
3. Identity providers
4. Groups
5. Network Access Control List

Answer(s): 3, 4

Explanation

AWS Identity and Access Management (IAM) is a web service for securely controlling access to AWS services. With IAM, you can centrally manage users, security credentials such as access keys, and permissions that control which AWS resources users and applications can access.

Groups is correct because an IAM group is a collection of IAM users. Groups let you specify permissions for multiple users, which can make it easier to manage the permissions for those users.

Identity providers is correct as you can manage identity providers using IAM Dashboard instead of creating IAM users in your AWS account. With an identity provider (IdP), you can manage your user identities outside of AWS and give these external user identities permission to use AWS resources in your account.

Cost Allocation Reports is incorrect because these are under AWS Billing and Cost Management.

Security Groups is incorrect because this can be managed in the EC2 console and not in the IAM dashboard.

Network Access Control List is incorrect because this is an optional layer of security for your VPC that acts as a firewall for controlling traffic in and out of one or more subnets while security groups act as virtual firewall for your instance to control inbound and outbound traffic, both of which cannot be managed in the IAM dashboard.

Reference:

https://docs.aws.amazon.com/IAM/latest/UserGuide/introduction.html

Here is a short video tutorial on IAM Roles:

https://youtu.be/wY7FOFaPNuE

Question 16:

A startup company has a serverless architecture that uses AWS Lambda, API Gateway, and DynamoDB. They received an urgent feature request from their client last month and now, it is ready to be pushed to production. The company is using AWS CodeDeploy as their deployment service.

Which of the following configuration types will allow you to specify the percentage of traffic shifted to your updated Lambda function version before the remaining traffic is shifted in the second increment?

1. Linear
2. Canary
3. Blue/Green
4. All-at-once

Answer(s): 2

Explanation

If you're using the AWS Lambda compute platform, you must choose one of the following deployment configuration types to specify how traffic is shifted from the original AWS Lambda function version to the new AWS Lambda function version:

Canary: Traffic is shifted in two increments. You can choose from predefined canary options that specify the percentage of traffic shifted to your updated Lambda function version in the first increment and the interval, in minutes, before the remaining traffic is shifted in the second increment.

Linear: Traffic is shifted in equal increments with an equal number of minutes between each increment. You can choose from predefined linear options that specify the percentage of traffic shifted in each increment and the number of minutes between each increment.

All-at-once: All traffic is shifted from the original Lambda function to the updated Lambda function version at once.

Blue/Green is incorrect because this is not a predefined deployment type configuration for an AWS Lambda Compute Platform. You can only choose Canary, Linear, and All-at-once.

Linear is incorrect because this type of deployment shifts the traffic in equal increments with an equal number of minutes between each increment. You can't specify the percentage of traffic shifted to your updated Lambda function version before the remaining traffic is shifted in the second increment, unlike Canary.

All-at-once is incorrect because there are no increments for this type of deployment. All traffic is shifted from the original Lambda function to the updated Lambda function version at once.

References:

https://docs.aws.amazon.com/codedeploy/latest/userguide/welcome.html#blue-green-lambda-compute-type

https://docs.aws.amazon.com/codedeploy/latest/userguide/deployment-configurations.html#deployment-configurations-predefined-lambda

Question 17:

You are building a transcription service for a company in which a fleet of EC2 worker instances processes an uploaded audio file and generates a text file as an output. You must store both of these frequently accessed files in the same durable storage until the text file is retrieved by the uploader. Due to an expected surge in demand, you have to ensure that the storage is scalable and can be retrieved within minutes.

Which storage option in AWS can you use in this situation, which is both cost-efficient and scalable?

1. Multiple instance stores
2. Amazon S3 Glacier Deep Archive
3. Multiple Amazon EBS volume with snapshots
4. A single Amazon S3 bucket

Answer(s): 4

Explanation

In this scenario, the best option is to use Amazon S3. It's a simple storage service that offers a highly-scalable, reliable, and low-latency data storage infrastructure at very low costs.

Multiple Amazon EBS volume with snapshots and Multiple instance stores are incorrect because these services do not provide durable storage.

Amazon S3 Glacier Deep Archive is incorrect because this is mainly used for data archives with data retrieval times that can take more than 12 hours. Hence, it is not suitable for the transcription service where the data are stored and frequently accessed.

Reference:

https://aws.amazon.com/s3/faqs/

Question 18:

A start-up company has an EC2 instance that is hosting a web application. The volume of users is expected to grow in the coming months and hence, you need to add more elasticity and scalability in your AWS architecture to cope with the demand.

Which of the following options can satisfy the above requirement for the given scenario? (Select TWO.)

1. Set up two EC2 instances deployed using Launch Templates and integrated with AWS Glue.
2. Set up an AWS WAF behind your EC2 Instance.
3. Set up two EC2 instances and then put them behind an Elastic Load balancer (ELB).
4. Set up an S3 Cache in front of the EC2 instance.
5. Set up two EC2 instances and use Route 53 to route traffic based on a Weighted Routing Policy.

Answer(s): 3, 5

Explanation

Using an Elastic Load Balancer is an ideal solution for adding elasticity to your application. Alternatively, you can also create a policy in Route 53, such as a Weighted routing policy, to evenly distribute the traffic to 2 or more EC2 instances. Hence, setting up two EC2 instances and then put them behind an Elastic Load balancer (ELB) and setting up two EC2 instances and using Route 53 to route traffic based on a Weighted Routing Policy are the correct answers.

Setting up an S3 Cache in front of the EC2 instance is incorrect because doing so does not provide elasticity and scalability to your EC2 instances.

Setting up an AWS WAF behind your EC2 Instance is incorrect because AWS WAF is a web application firewall that helps protect your web applications from common web exploits. This service is more on providing security to your applications.

Setting up two EC2 instances deployed using Launch Templates and integrated with AWS Glue is incorrect because AWS Glue is a fully managed extract, transform, and load (ETL) service that makes it easy for customers to prepare and load their data for analytics. It does not provide scalability or elasticity to your instances.

References:

https://aws.amazon.com/elasticloadbalancing

http://docs.aws.amazon.com/Route53/latest/DeveloperGuide/Welcome.html

Question 19:

A company is hosting its web application in an Auto Scaling group of EC2 instances behind an Application Load Balancer. Recently, the Solutions Architect identified a series of SQL injection attempts and cross-site scripting attacks to the application, which had adversely affected their production data.

Which of the following should the Architect implement to mitigate this kind of attack?

1. Use Amazon GuardDuty to prevent any further SQL injection and cross-site scripting attacks in your application.
2. Set up security rules that block SQL injection and cross-site scripting attacks in AWS Web Application Firewall (WAF). Associate the rules to the Application Load Balancer.
3. Using AWS Firewall Manager, set up security rules that block SQL injection and cross-site scripting attacks. Associate the rules to the Application Load Balancer.
4. Block all the IP addresses where the SQL injection and cross-site scripting attacks originated using the Network Access Control List.

Answer(s): 2

Explanation

AWS WAF is a web application firewall that lets you monitor the HTTP and HTTPS requests that are forwarded to an Amazon API Gateway API, Amazon CloudFront or an Application Load Balancer. AWS WAF also lets you control access to your content. Based on conditions that you specify, such as the IP addresses that requests originate from or the values of query strings, API Gateway, CloudFront or an Application Load Balancer responds to requests either with the requested content or with an HTTP 403 status code (Forbidden). You also can configure CloudFront to return a custom error page when a request is blocked.

At the simplest level, AWS WAF lets you choose one of the following behaviors:

Allow all requests except the ones that you specify – This is useful when you want CloudFront or an Application Load Balancer to serve content for a public website, but you also want to block requests from attackers.

Block all requests except the ones that you specify – This is useful when you want to serve content for a restricted website whose users are readily identifiable by properties in web requests, such as the IP addresses that they use to browse to the website.

Count the requests that match the properties that you specify – When you want to allow or block requests based on new properties in web requests, you first can configure AWS WAF to count the requests that match those properties without allowing or blocking those requests. This lets you confirm that you didn't accidentally configure AWS WAF to block all the traffic to your website. When you're confident that you specified the correct properties, you can change the behavior to allow or block requests.

Hence, the correct answer in this scenario is: Set up security rules that block SQL injection and cross-site scripting attacks in AWS Web Application Firewall (WAF). Associate the rules to the Application Load Balancer.

Using Amazon GuardDuty to prevent any further SQL injection and cross-site scripting attacks in your application is incorrect because Amazon GuardDuty is just a threat detection service that continuously monitors for malicious activity and unauthorized behavior to protect your AWS accounts and workloads.

Using AWS Firewall Manager to set up security rules that block SQL injection and cross-site scripting attacks, then associating the rules to the Application Load Balancer is incorrect because the AWS Firewall Manager just simplifies your AWS WAF and AWS Shield Advanced administration and maintenance tasks across multiple accounts and resources.

Blocking all the IP addresses where the SQL injection and cross-site scripting attacks originated using the Network Access Control List is incorrect because this is an optional layer of security for your VPC that acts as a firewall for controlling traffic in and out of one or more subnets. NACLs are not effective in blocking SQL injection and cross-site scripting attacks

References:

https://aws.amazon.com/waf/

https://docs.aws.amazon.com/waf/latest/developerguide/what-is-aws-waf.html

Question 20:

To protect your enterprise applications against unauthorized access, you configured multiple rules for your Network ACLs in your VPC. How are the access rules evaluated?

1. Network ACL Rules are evaluated by rule number, from highest to lowest and are executed immediately when a matching allow/deny rule is found.
2. By default, all Network ACL Rules are evaluated before any traffic is allowed or denied.
3. Network ACL Rules are evaluated by rule number, from lowest to highest, and executed after all rules are checked for conflicting allow/deny rules.
4. Network ACL Rules are evaluated by rule number, from lowest to highest, and executed immediately when a matching allow/deny rule is found.

Answer(s): 4

Explanation

A network access control list (ACL) is an optional layer of security for your VPC that acts as a firewall for controlling traffic in and out of one or more subnets. You might set up network ACLs with rules similar to your security groups in order to add an additional layer of security to your VPC.

Network ACL Rules are evaluated by rule number, from lowest to highest, and executed immediately when a matching allow/deny rule is found.

The option that says: Network ACL Rules are evaluated by rule number, from highest to lowest and are executed immediately when a matching allow/deny rule is found is incorrect since rules are evaluated from lowest to highest, not the other way around.

The option that says: By default, all Network ACL Rules are evaluated before any traffic is allowed or denied is incorrect because the Network ACL Rules are evaluated by rule number, from lowest to highest, and executed immediately when a matching allow/deny rule is found.

The option that says: Network ACL Rules are evaluated by rule number, from lowest to highest, and executed after all rules are checked for conflicting allow/deny rules is incorrect since rules are executed immediately when a match is found and not after all rules are checked for conflicting allow/deny rules.

Reference:

http://docs.aws.amazon.com/AmazonVPC/latest/UserGuide/VPC_ACLs.html

Question 21:

As a Junior Software Engineer, you are developing a hotel reservations application and are given the task of improving the database aspect of the app. You found out that RDS does not satisfy the needs of your application because it does not scale as easily compared with DynamoDB. You need to demonstrate to your Senior Software Engineer the advantages of using DynamoDB over RDS.

What are the valid use cases for Amazon DynamoDB? (Select TWO.)

1. Managing web sessions.
2. Storing large amounts of infrequently accessed data.
3. Storing BLOB data.
4. Running a database with a well-defined schema and enforces referential integrity in relationships between tables.
5. Storing metadata for Amazon S3 objects.

Answer(s): 1, 5

Explanation

DynamoDB is a NoSQL database that supports key-value and document data structures. A key-value store is a database service that provides support for storing, querying, and updating collections of objects that are identified using a key and values that contain the actual content being stored. Meanwhile, a document data store provides support for storing, querying, and updating items in a document format such as JSON, XML, and HTML.

Managing web sessions is correct because the DynamoDB Time-to-Live (TTL) mechanism enables you to manage web sessions of your application easily. It lets you set a specific timestamp to delete expired items from your tables. Once the timestamp expires, the corresponding item is marked as expired and is subsequently deleted from the table. By using this functionality, you do not have to track expired data and delete it manually. TTL can help you reduce storage usage and reduce the cost of storing data that is no longer relevant.

Storing metadata for Amazon S3 objects is correct because the Amazon DynamoDB stores structured data indexed by primary key and allow low latency read and write access to items ranging from 1 byte up to 400KB. Amazon S3 stores unstructured blobs and is suited for storing large objects up to 5 TB. In order to optimize your costs across AWS services, large objects or infrequently accessed data sets should be stored in Amazon S3, while smaller data elements or file pointers (possibly to Amazon S3 objects) are best saved in Amazon DynamoDB.

To speed up access to relevant data, you can pair Amazon S3 with a search engine such as Amazon CloudSearch or a database such as Amazon DynamoDB or Amazon RDS. In these scenarios, Amazon S3 stores the actual information, and the search engine or database serves as the repository for associated metadata such as the object name, size, keywords, and so on. Metadata in the database can easily be indexed and queried, making it very efficient to locate an object's reference by using a search engine or a database query. This result can be used to pinpoint and retrieve the object itself from Amazon S3.

The option that says: Running a database with a well-defined schema and enforces referential integrity in relationships between tables is incorrect since DynamoDB is a NoSQL database solution and not a relational database. RDS is more suitable for a relational model that normalizes data into tables that are composed of rows and columns. An RDS database enforces referential integrity in relationships between tables, unlike a DynamoDB table.

Storing large amounts of infrequently accessed data is incorrect because DynamoDB is not meant to store large amounts of infrequently accessed data, due to factors like sizing, scaling, and cost. Amazon Glacier would be a better option for this scenario.

Storing BLOB data is incorrect because BLOB data is too large a chunk of data to be put into a NoSQL database such as DynamoDB.

References:

https://aws.amazon.com/dynamodb/faqs/

https://d1.awsstatic.com/whitepapers/Storage/AWS%20Storage%20Services%20W hitepaper-v9.pdf#page=9

https://aws.amazon.com/nosql/

Question 22:

A start-up company that offers an intuitive financial data analytics service has consulted you about their AWS architecture. They have a fleet of Amazon EC2 worker instances that process financial data and then outputs reports which are used by their clients. You must store the generated report files in a durable storage. The number of files to be stored can grow over time as the start-up company is expanding rapidly overseas and hence, they also need a way to distribute the reports faster to clients located across the globe.

Which of the following is a cost-efficient and scalable storage option that you should use for this scenario?

1. Use multiple EC2 instance stores for data storage and ElastiCache as the CDN.
2. Use Amazon Glacier as the data storage and ElastiCache as the CDN.
3. Use Amazon Redshift as the data storage and CloudFront as the CDN.
4. Use Amazon S3 as the data storage and CloudFront as the CDN.

Answer(s): 4

Explanation

A Content Delivery Network (CDN) is a critical component of nearly any modern web application. It used to be that CDN merely improved the delivery of content by replicating commonly requested files (static content) across a globally distributed set of caching servers. However, CDNs have become much more useful over time.

For caching, a CDN will reduce the load on an application origin and improve the experience of the requestor by delivering a local copy of the content from a nearby cache edge, or Point of Presence (PoP). The application origin is off the hook for opening the connection and delivering the content directly as the CDN takes care of the heavy lifting. The end result is that the application origins don't need to scale to meet demands for static content.

Amazon CloudFront is a fast content delivery network (CDN) service that securely delivers data, videos, applications, and APIs to customers globally with low latency, high transfer speeds, all within a developer-friendly environment. CloudFront is integrated with AWS – both physical locations that are directly connected to the AWS global infrastructure, as well as other AWS services.

Amazon S3 offers a highly durable, scalable, and secure destination for backing up and archiving your critical data. This is the correct option as the start-up company is looking for a durable storage to store the audio and text files. In addition, ElastiCache is only used for caching and not specifically as a Global Content Delivery Network (CDN).

Using Amazon Redshift as the data storage and CloudFront as the CDN is incorrect as Amazon Redshift is usually used as a Data Warehouse.

Using Amazon S3 Glacier as the data storage and ElastiCache as the CDN is incorrect as Amazon S3 Glacier is usually used for data archives.

Using multiple EC2 instance stores for data storage and ElastiCache as the CDN is incorrect as data stored in an instance store is not durable.

References:

https://aws.amazon.com/s3/

https://aws.amazon.com/caching/cdn/

Question 23:

You work for an Intelligence Agency as its Principal Consultant developing a missile tracking application, which is hosted on both development and production AWS accounts. Alice, the Intelligence agency's Junior Developer, only has access to the development account. She has received security clearance to access the agency's production account but the access is only temporary and only write access to EC2 and S3 is allowed.

Which of the following allows you to issue short-lived access tokens that acts as temporary security credentials to allow access to your AWS resources?

1. Use AWS SSO

2. Use AWS STS
3. Use AWS Cognito to issue JSON Web Tokens (JWT)
4. All of the given options are correct.

Answer(s): 2

Explanation

AWS Security Token Service (AWS STS) is the service that you can use to create and provide trusted users with temporary security credentials that can control access to your AWS resources. Temporary security credentials work almost identically to the long-term access key credentials that your IAM users can use.

In this diagram, IAM user Alice in the Dev account (the role-assuming account) needs to access the Prod account (the role-owning account). Here's how it works:

Alice in the Dev account assumes an IAM role (WriteAccess) in the Prod account by calling AssumeRole.

STS returns a set of temporary security credentials.

Alice uses the temporary security credentials to access services and resources in the Prod account. Alice could, for example, make calls to Amazon S3 and Amazon EC2, which are granted by the WriteAccess role.

Using AWS Cognito to issue JSON Web Tokens (JWT) is incorrect because the Amazon Cognito service is primarily used for user authentication and not for providing access to your AWS resources. A JSON Web Token (JWT) is meant to be used for user authentication and session management.

Using AWS SSO is incorrect because although the AWS SSO service uses STS, it does not issue short-lived credentials by itself. AWS Single Sign-On (SSO) is a cloud SSO service that makes it easy to centrally manage SSO access to multiple AWS accounts and business applications.

The option that says All of the given options are correct is incorrect as only STS has the ability to provide temporary security credentials.

Reference:

https://docs.aws.amazon.com/IAM/latest/UserGuide/id_credentials_temp.html

Question 24:

Your company is running a multi-tier web application farm in a virtual private cloud (VPC) that is not connected to their corporate network. They are connecting to the VPC over the Internet to manage the fleet of Amazon EC2 instances running in both the public and private subnets. You have added a bastion host with Microsoft Remote Desktop Protocol (RDP) access to the application instance security groups, but the company wants to further limit administrative access to all of the instances in the VPC.

Which of the following bastion host deployment options will meet this requirement?

1. Deploy a Windows Bastion host with an Elastic IP address in the private subnet, and restrict RDP access to the bastion from only the corporate public IP addresses.
2. Deploy a Windows Bastion host on the corporate network that has RDP access to all EC2 instances in the VPC.
3. Deploy a Windows Bastion host with an Elastic IP address in the public subnet and allow RDP access to bastion only from the corporate IP addresses.
4. Deploy a Windows Bastion host with an Elastic IP address in the public subnet and allow SSH access to the bastion from anywhere.

Answer(s): 3

Explanation

The correct answer is to deploy a Windows Bastion host with an Elastic IP address in the public subnet and allow RDP access to bastion only from the corporate IP addresses.

A bastion host is a special purpose computer on a network specifically designed and configured to withstand attacks. If you have a bastion host in AWS, it is basically just an EC2 instance. It should be in a public subnet with either a public or Elastic IP address with sufficient RDP or SSH access defined in the security group. Users log on to the bastion host via SSH or RDP and then use that session to manage other hosts in the private subnets.

Deploying a Windows Bastion host on the corporate network that has RDP access to all EC2 instances in the VPC is incorrect since you do not deploy the Bastion host to your corporate network. It should be in the public subnet of a VPC.

Deploying a Windows Bastion host with an Elastic IP address in the private subnet, and restricting RDP access to the bastion from only the corporate public IP addresses is incorrect since it should be deployed in a public subnet, not a private subnet.

Deploying a Windows Bastion host with an Elastic IP address in the public subnet and allowing SSH access to the bastion from anywhere is incorrect. Since it is a Windows bastion, you should allow RDP access and not SSH as this is mainly used for Linux-based systems.

Reference:

https://docs.aws.amazon.com/quickstart/latest/linux-bastion/architecture.html

Question 25:

Your customer is building an internal application that serves as a repository for images uploaded by a couple of users. Whenever a user uploads an image, it would be sent to Kinesis for processing before it is stored in an S3 bucket. Afterwards, if the upload was successful, the application will return a prompt telling the user that the upload is successful. The entire processing typically takes about 5 minutes to finish.

Which of the following options will allow you to asynchronously process the request to the application in the most cost-effective manner?

1. Use a combination of Lambda and Step Functions to orchestrate service components and asynchronously process the requests.
2. Use a combination of SQS to queue the requests and then asynchronously process them using On-Demand EC2 Instances.
3. Create a Lambda function that will asynchronously process the requests.
4. Use a combination of SNS to buffer the requests and then asynchronously process them using On-Demand EC2 Instances.

Answer(s): 3

Explanation

AWS Lambda supports synchronous and asynchronous invocation of a Lambda function. You can control the invocation type only when you invoke a Lambda function. When you use an AWS service as a trigger, the invocation type is predetermined for each service. You have no control over the invocation type that these event sources use when they invoke your Lambda function. Since the processing only takes 5 minutes, Lambda is also a cost-effective choice.

Using a combination of Lambda and Step Functions to orchestrate service components and asynchronously process the requests is incorrect because the AWS Step Functions service lets you coordinate multiple AWS services into serverless workflows so you can build and update apps quickly. Although this can be a valid solution, it is not cost-effective since the application does not have a lot of components to orchestrate. Lambda functions can effectively meet the requirements in this scenario without using Step Functions. This service is not as cost-effective as Lambda.

Using a combination of SQS to queue the requests and then asynchronously processing them using On-Demand EC2 Instances and Using a combination of SNS to buffer the requests and then asynchronously processing them using On-Demand EC2 Instances are both incorrect as using On-Demand EC2 instances is not cost-effective. It is better to use a Lambda function instead.

References:

https://docs.aws.amazon.com/lambda/latest/dg/welcome.html

116

https://docs.aws.amazon.com/lambda/latest/dg/lambda-invocation.html

Check out this AWS Lambda Cheat Sheet:

Question 26:

In Elastic Load Balancing, there are various security features that you can use such as Server Order Preference, Predefined Security Policy, Perfect Forward Secrecy and many others. Perfect Forward Secrecy is a feature that provides additional safeguards against the eavesdropping of encrypted data through the use of a unique random session key. This prevents the decoding of captured data, even if the secret long-term key is compromised.

Perfect Forward Secrecy is used to offer SSL/TLS cipher suites for which two AWS services?

1. CloudTrail and CloudWatch
2. EC2 and S3
3. CloudFront and Elastic Load Balancing
4. Trusted Advisor and GovCloud

Answer(s): 3

Explanation

Perfect Forward Secrecy is a feature that provides additional safeguards against the eavesdropping of encrypted data, through the use of a unique random session key. This prevents the decoding of captured data, even if the secret long-term key is compromised.

CloudFront and Elastic Load Balancing are the two AWS services that support Perfect Forward Secrecy. Hence, the correct answer is: CloudFront and Elastic Load Balancing.

EC2 and S3, CloudTrail and CloudWatch, and Trusted Advisor and GovCloud are incorrect since these services do not use Perfect Forward Secrecy. SSL/TLS is commonly used when you have sensitive data travelling through the public network.

References:

https://aws.amazon.com/about-aws/whats-new/2014/02/19/elastic-load-balancing-perfect-forward-secrecy-and-more-new-security-features/

https://d1.awsstatic.com/whitepapers/Security/Secure_content_delivery_with_CloudFront_whitepaper.pdf

Question 27:

You are an AWS Network Engineer working for a utility provider where you are managing a monolithic application with an EC2 instance using a Windows AMI. The legacy application must maintain the same private IP address and MAC address in order for it to work. You want to implement a cost-effective and highly available architecture for your application by launching a standby EC2 instance that is an exact replica of the Windows server. If the primary instance terminates, you can attach the ENI to the standby secondary instance, which allows the traffic flow to resume within a few seconds.

When it comes to the ENI attachment to an EC2 instance, what does 'warm attach' refer to?

1. Attaching an ENI to an instance when it is idle.
2. Attaching an ENI to an instance when it is stopped.
3. Attaching an ENI to an instance when it is running.
4. Attaching an ENI to an instance during the launch process.

Answer(s): 2

Explanation

You can create a network interface, attach it to an instance, detach it from an instance, and attach it to another instance. The attributes of a network interface follow it as it's attached or detached from an instance and reattached to another instance. When you move a network interface from one instance to another, network traffic is redirected to the new instance.

If one of your instances serving a particular function fails, its network interface can be attached to a replacement or hot standby instance pre-configured for the same role in order to rapidly recover the service. For example, you can use a network interface as your primary or secondary network interface to a critical service such as a database instance or a NAT instance.

If the instance fails, you (or more likely, the code running on your behalf) can attach the network interface to a hot standby instance. Because the interface maintains its private IP addresses, Elastic IP addresses, and MAC address, network traffic begins flowing to the standby instance as soon as you attach the network interface to the replacement instance. Users experience a brief loss of connectivity between the time the instance fails and the time that the network interface is attached to the standby instance, but no changes to the VPC route table or your DNS server are required.

An elastic network interface (ENI) is a logical networking component in a VPC that represents a virtual network card. You can attach a network interface to an EC2 instance in the following ways:

When it's running (hot attach)

When it's stopped (warm attach)

When the instance is being launched (cold attach).

Therefore, attaching an ENI to an instance when it is stopped is the correct answer.

Attaching an ENI to an instance during the launch process is incorrect because this describes a "cold attach" scenario.

Attaching an ENI to an instance when it is running is incorrect because this describes a "hot attach" scenario.

Attaching an ENI to an instance when it is idle is incorrect because there is no specific name for attaching an ENI to an idle EC2 instance.

References:

http://docs.aws.amazon.com/AWSEC2/latest/UserGuide/using-eni.html#attach_eni_launch

https://aws.amazon.com/premiumsupport/knowledge-center/vpc-detach-or-delete-eni/

Question 28:

A music publishing company is building a multitier web application that requires a key-value store which will save the document models. Each model is composed of band ID, album ID, song ID, composer ID, lyrics, and other data. The web tier will be hosted in an Amazon ECS cluster with AWS Fargate launch type.

Which of the following is the MOST suitable setup for the database-tier?

1. Use Amazon WorkDocs to store the document models.
2. Launch an Amazon Aurora Serverless database.
3. Launch a DynamoDB table.
4. Launch an Amazon RDS database with Read Replicas.

Answer(s): 3

Explanation

Amazon DynamoDB is a fast and flexible NoSQL database service for all applications that need consistent, single-digit millisecond latency at any scale. It is a fully managed cloud database and supports both document and key-value store models. Its flexible data model, reliable performance, and automatic scaling of throughput capacity makes it a great fit for mobile, web, gaming, ad tech, IoT, and many other applications.

Hence, the correct answer is: Launch a DynamoDB table.

The option that says: Launch an Amazon RDS database with Read Replicas is incorrect because this is a relational database. This is not suitable to be used as a key-value store. A better option is to use DynamoDB as it supports both document and key-value store models.

The option that says: Use Amazon WorkDocs to store the document models is incorrect because Amazon WorkDocs simply enables you to share content, provide rich feedback, and collaboratively edit documents. It is not a key-value store like DynamoDB.

The option that says: Launch an Amazon Aurora Serverless database is incorrect because this type of database is not suitable to be used as a key-value store. Amazon Aurora Serverless is an on-demand, auto-scaling configuration for Amazon Aurora where the database will automatically start-up, shut down, and scale capacity up or down based on your application's needs. It enables you to run your database in the cloud without managing any database instances. It's a simple, cost-effective option for infrequent, intermittent, or unpredictable workloads and not as a key-value store.

References:

https://aws.amazon.com/dynamodb/

https://aws.amazon.com/nosql/key-value/

Question 29:

You are working as a Solutions Architect for an investment bank and your Chief Technical Officer intends to migrate all of your applications to AWS. You are looking for block storage to store all of your data and have decided to go with EBS volumes. Your boss is worried that EBS volumes are not appropriate for your workloads due to compliance requirements, downtime scenarios, and IOPS performance.

Which of the following are valid points in proving that EBS is the best service to use for your migration? (Select TWO.)

1. When you create an EBS volume in an Availability Zone, it is automatically replicated on a separate AWS region to prevent data loss due to a failure of any single hardware component.
2. EBS volumes support live configuration changes while in production which means that you can modify the volume type, volume size, and IOPS capacity without service interruptions.
3. EBS volumes can be attached to any EC2 Instance in any Availability Zone.
4. An EBS volume is off-instance storage that can persist independently from the life of an instance.
5. Amazon EBS provides the ability to create snapshots (backups) of any EBS volume and write a copy of the data in the volume to Amazon RDS, where it is stored redundantly in multiple Availability Zones

Answer(s): 2, 4

Explanation

An Amazon EBS volume is a durable, block-level storage device that you can attach to a single EC2 instance. You can use EBS volumes as primary storage for data that requires frequent updates, such as the system drive for an instance or storage for a database application. You can also use them for throughput-intensive applications that perform continuous disk scans. EBS volumes persist independently from the running life of an EC2 instance.

Here is a list of important information about EBS Volumes:

- When you create an EBS volume in an Availability Zone, it is automatically replicated within that zone to prevent data loss due to a failure of any single hardware component.

- An EBS volume can only be attached to one EC2 instance at a time.

- After you create a volume, you can attach it to any EC2 instance in the same Availability Zone

- An EBS volume is off-instance storage that can persist independently from the life of an instance. You can specify not to terminate the EBS volume when you terminate the EC2 instance during instance creation.

- EBS volumes support live configuration changes while in production which means that you can modify the volume type, volume size, and IOPS capacity without service interruptions.

- Amazon EBS encryption uses 256-bit Advanced Encryption Standard algorithms (AES-256)

- EBS Volumes offer 99.999% SLA.

The option that says: When you create an EBS volume in an Availability Zone, it is automatically replicated on a separate AWS region to prevent data loss due to a failure of any single hardware component is incorrect because when you create an EBS volume in an Availability Zone, it is automatically replicated within that zone only, and not on a separate AWS region, to prevent data loss due to a failure of any single hardware component.

The option that says: EBS volumes can be attached to any EC2 Instance in any Availability Zone is incorrect as EBS volumes can only be attached to an EC2 instance in the same Availability Zone.

The option that says: Amazon EBS provides the ability to create snapshots (backups) of any EBS volume and write a copy of the data in the volume to Amazon RDS, where it is stored redundantly in multiple Availability Zones is almost correct. But instead of storing the volume to Amazon RDS, the EBS Volume snapshots are actually sent to Amazon S3.

References:

http://docs.aws.amazon.com/AWSEC2/latest/UserGuide/EBSVolumes.html

https://aws.amazon.com/ebs/features/

Here is a short video tutorial on EBS:

https://youtu.be/ljYH5lHQdxo

Question 30:

You run a website which accepts high-quality photos and turns them into a downloadable video montage. The website offers a free account and a premium account that guarantees faster processing. All requests by both free and premium members go through a single SQS queue and then processed by a group of EC2 instances which generate the videos. You need to ensure that the premium users who paid for the service have higher priority than your free members.

How do you re-design your architecture to address this requirement?

1. Create an SQS queue for free members and another one for premium members. Configure your EC2 instances to consume messages from the premium queue first and if it is empty, poll from the free members' SQS queue.
2. For the requests made by premium members, set a higher priority in the SQS queue so it will be processed first compared to the requests made by free members.
3. Use Amazon Kinesis to process the photos and generate the video montage in real time.
4. Use Amazon S3 to store and process the photos and then generate the video montage afterwards.

Answer(s): 1

Explanation

In this scenario, it is best to create 2 separate SQS queues for each type of members. The SQS queues for the premium members can be polled first by the EC2 Instances and once completed, the messages from the free members can be processed next.

The option that says: For the requests made by premium members, set a higher priority in the SQS queue so it will be processed first compared to the requests made by free members is incorrect as you cannot set a priority to individual items in the SQS queue.

Using Amazon Kinesis to process the photos and generate the video montage in real time is incorrect as Amazon Kinesis is used to process streaming data and it is not applicable in this scenario.

Using Amazon S3 to store and process the photos and then generating the video montage afterwards is incorrect as Amazon S3 is used for durable storage and not for processing data.

Reference:

https://docs.aws.amazon.com/AWSSimpleQueueService/latest/SQSDeveloperGuid e/sqs-best-practices.html

Question 31:

An application is hosted in AWS Fargate and uses RDS database in Multi-AZ Deployments configuration with several Read Replicas. A Solutions Architect was instructed to ensure that all of their database credentials, API keys, and other secrets are encrypted and rotated on a regular basis to improve data security. The application should also use the latest version of the encrypted credentials when connecting to the RDS database.

Which of the following is the MOST appropriate solution to secure the credentials?

1. Store the database credentials, API keys, and other secrets in AWS KMS.
2. Use AWS Secrets Manager to store and encrypt the database credentials, API keys, and other secrets. Enable automatic rotation for all of the credentials.
3. Store the database credentials, API keys, and other secrets to AWS ACM.
4. Store the database credentials, API keys, and other secrets to Systems Manager Parameter Store each with a SecureString data type. The credentials are automatically rotated by default.

Answer(s): 2

Explanation

AWS Secrets Manager is an AWS service that makes it easier for you to manage secrets. Secrets can be database credentials, passwords, third-party API keys, and even arbitrary text. You can store and control access to these secrets centrally by using the Secrets Manager console, the Secrets Manager command line interface (CLI), or the Secrets Manager API and SDKs.

In the past, when you created a custom application that retrieves information from a database, you typically had to embed the credentials (the secret) for accessing the database directly in the application. When it came time to rotate the credentials, you had to do much more than just create new credentials. You had to invest time to update the application to use the new credentials. Then you had to distribute the updated application. If you had multiple applications that shared credentials and you missed updating one of them, the application would break. Because of this risk, many customers have chosen not to regularly rotate their credentials, which effectively substitutes one risk for another.

Secrets Manager enables you to replace hardcoded credentials in your code (including passwords), with an API call to Secrets Manager to retrieve the secret programmatically. This helps ensure that the secret can't be compromised by someone examining your code, because the secret simply isn't there. Also, you can configure Secrets Manager to automatically rotate the secret for you according to a schedule that you specify. This enables you to replace long-term secrets with short-term ones, which helps to significantly reduce the risk of compromise.

Hence, the most appropriate solution for this scenario is: Use AWS Secrets Manager to store and encrypt the database credentials, API keys, and other secrets. Enable automatic rotation for all of the credentials.

The option that says: Store the database credentials, API keys, and other secrets to Systems Manager Parameter Store each with a SecureString data type. The credentials are automatically rotated by default is incorrect because Systems Manager Parameter Store doesn't rotate its parameters by default.

The option that says: Store the database credentials, API keys, and other secrets to AWS ACM is incorrect because it is just a managed private CA service that helps you easily and securely manage the lifecycle of your private certificates to allow SSL communication to your application. This is not a suitable service to store database or any other confidential credentials.

The option that says: Store the database credentials, API keys, and other secrets in AWS KMS is incorrect because this only makes it easy for you to create and manage encryption keys and control the use of encryption across a wide range of AWS services. This is primarily used for encryption and not for hosting your credentials.

References:

https://aws.amazon.com/secrets-manager/

https://aws.amazon.com/blogs/security/how-to-securely-provide-database-credentials-to-lambda-functions-by-using-aws-secrets-manager/

Question 32:

You are working for an advertising company as their Senior Solutions Architect handling the S3 storage data. Your company has terabytes of data sitting on AWS S3 standard storage class, which accumulates significant operational costs. The management wants to cut down on the cost of their cloud infrastructure so you were instructed to switch to Glacier to lessen the cost per GB storage.

The Amazon Glacier storage service is primarily used for which use case? (Select TWO.)

1. Storing infrequently accessed data

2. Used for active database storage
3. Storing Data archives
4. Storing cached session data
5. Used as a data warehouse

Answer(s): 1, 3

Explanation

Amazon S3 Glacier is an extremely low-cost storage service that provides secure, durable, and flexible storage for data backup and archival. Amazon Glacier is designed to store data that is infrequently accessed. Amazon Glacier enables customers to offload the administrative burdens of operating and scaling storage to AWS so that they don't have to worry about capacity planning, hardware provisioning, data replication, hardware failure detection and repair, or time-consuming hardware migrations.

Storing cached session data is incorrect because this is the main use case for ElastiCache and not Amazon Glacier.

The option that says: Used for active database storage is incorrect because you should use RDS or DynamoDB for your active database storage as S3, in general, is used for storing your data or files.

The option that says: Used as a data warehouse is incorrect because storing it for data warehousing is the main use case of Amazon Redshift. It does not meet the requirement of being able to archive your infrequently accessed data. You can use S3 standard instead for frequently accessed data or Glacier for infrequently accessed data and archiving.

It is advisable to transition the standard data to infrequent access first then transition it to Amazon Glacier. You can specify in the lifecycle rule the time it will sit in standard tier and infrequent access. You can also delete the objects after a certain amount of time.

In transitioning S3 standard to Glacier you need to tell S3 which objects are to be archived to the new Glacier storage option, and under what conditions. You do this by setting up a lifecycle rule using the following elements:

A prefix to specify which objects in the bucket are subject to the policy.

A relative or absolute time specifier and a time period for transitioning objects to Glacier. The time periods are interpreted with respect to the object's creation date. They can be relative (migrate items that are older than a certain number of days) or absolute (migrate items on a specific date)

An object age at which the object will be deleted from S3. This is measured from the original PUT of the object into the service, and the clock is not reset by a transition to Glacier.

You can create a lifecycle rule in the AWS Management Console.

Reference:

https://aws.amazon.com/glacier/faqs/

Question 33:

A software company has resources hosted in AWS and on-premises servers. You have been requested to create a decoupled architecture for applications which make use of both resources.

Which of the following options are valid? (Select TWO.)

1. Use Amazon Simple Decoupling Service to utilize both on-premises servers and EC2 instances for your decoupled application
2. Use SWF to utilize both on-premises servers and EC2 instances for your decoupled application
3. Use DynamoDB to utilize both on-premises servers and EC2 instances for your decoupled application
4. Use SQS to utilize both on-premises servers and EC2 instances for your decoupled application
5. Use RDS to utilize both on-premises servers and EC2 instances for your decoupled application

Answer(s): 2, 4

Explanation

Amazon Simple Queue Service (SQS) and Amazon Simple Workflow Service (SWF) are the services that you can use for creating a decoupled architecture in AWS. Decoupled architecture is a type of computing architecture that enables computing components or layers to execute independently while still interfacing with each other.

Amazon SQS offers reliable, highly-scalable hosted queues for storing messages while they travel between applications or microservices. Amazon SQS lets you move data between distributed application components and helps you decouple these components. Amazon SWF is a web service that makes it easy to coordinate work across distributed application components.

Using RDS to utilize both on-premises servers and EC2 instances for your decoupled application and using DynamoDB to utilize both on-premises servers and EC2 instances for your decoupled application are incorrect as RDS and DynamoDB are database services.

Using Amazon Simple Decoupling Service to utilize both on-premises servers and EC2 instances for your decoupled application is incorrect because there is no such thing as Amazon Simple Decoupling Service.

References:

https://aws.amazon.com/sqs/

http://docs.aws.amazon.com/amazonswf/latest/developerguide/swf-welcome.html

Question 34:

You are a Solutions Architect of a media company and you are instructed to migrate an on-premises web application architecture to AWS. During your design process, you have to give consideration to current on-premises security and determine which security attributes you are responsible for on AWS.

Which of the following does AWS provide for you as part of the shared responsibility model?

1. Customer Data
2. Physical network infrastructure
3. Instance security
4. User access to the AWS environment

Answer(s): 2

Explanation

Security and Compliance is a shared responsibility between AWS and the customer. This shared model can help relieve customer's operational burden as AWS operates, manages and controls the components from the host operating system and virtualization layer down to the physical security of the facilities in which the service operates. The customer assumes responsibility and management of the guest operating system (including updates and security patches), other associated application software as well as the configuration of the AWS provided security group firewall.

Customers should carefully consider the services they choose as their responsibilities vary depending on the services used, the integration of those services into their IT environment, and applicable laws and regulations. The nature of this shared responsibility also provides the flexibility and customer control that permits the deployment. As shown in the chart below, this differentiation of responsibility is commonly referred to as Security "of" the Cloud versus Security "in" the Cloud.

Customer Data is incorrect since providing you customer data would be a breach in security protocols and data privacy laws.

Instance security is incorrect because it is your responsibility to set up the security tools AWS has provided you to secure your instances in your cloud environment.

User access to the AWS environment is incorrect since it is your responsibility to delegate user access to your cloud environment.

Refer to this diagram for a better understanding of the shared responsibility model.

References:

https://aws.amazon.com/compliance/shared-responsibility-model/

Question 35:

You are a Solutions Architect of a multi-national gaming company which develops video games for PS4, Xbox One and Nintendo Switch consoles, plus a number of mobile games for Android and iOS. Due to the wide range of their products and services, you proposed that they use API Gateway.

What are the key features of API Gateway that you can tell your client? (Select TWO.)

1. It automatically provides a query language for your APIs similar to GraphQL.
2. Enables you to run applications requiring high levels of inter-node communications at scale on AWS through its custom-built operating system (OS) bypass hardware interface.
3. You pay only for the API calls you receive and the amount of data transferred out.
4. Provides you with static anycast IP addresses that serve as a fixed entry point to your applications hosted in one or more AWS Regions.
5. Enables you to build RESTful APIs and WebSocket APIs that are optimized for serverless workloads.

Answer(s): 3, 5

Explanation

Amazon API Gateway is a fully managed service that makes it easy for developers to create, publish, maintain, monitor, and secure APIs at any scale. With a few clicks in the AWS Management Console, you can create an API that acts as a "front door" for applications to access data, business logic, or functionality from your back-end services, such as workloads running on Amazon Elastic Compute Cloud (Amazon EC2), code running on AWS Lambda, or any web application. Since it can use AWS Lambda, you can run your APIs without servers.

Amazon API Gateway handles all the tasks involved in accepting and processing up to hundreds of thousands of concurrent API calls, including traffic management, authorization and access control, monitoring, and API version management. Amazon API Gateway has no minimum fees or startup costs. You pay only for the API calls you receive and the amount of data transferred out.

Hence, the correct answers are:

- Enables you to build RESTful APIs and WebSocket APIs that are optimized for serverless workloads

- You pay only for the API calls you receive and the amount of data transferred out.

The option that says: It automatically provides a query language for your APIs similar to GraphQL is incorrect because this is not provided by API Gateway.

The option that says: Provides you with static anycast IP addresses that serve as a fixed entry point to your applications hosted in one or more AWS Regions is incorrect because this is a capability of AWS Global Accelerator and not API Gateway.

The option that says: Enables you to run applications requiring high levels of inter-node communications at scale on AWS through its custom-built operating system (OS) bypass hardware interface is incorrect because this is a capability of Elastic Fabric Adapter and not API Gateway.

References:

https://aws.amazon.com/api-gateway/

https://aws.amazon.com/api-gateway/features/

Question 36:

You are working for a commercial bank as an AWS Infrastructure Engineer handling the forex trading application of the bank. You have an Auto Scaling group of EC2 instances that allow your company to cope up with the current demand of traffic and achieve cost-efficiency. You want the Auto Scaling group to behave in such a way that it will follow a predefined set of parameters before it scales down the number of EC2 instances, which protects your system from unintended slowdown or unavailability.

Which of the following statements are true regarding the cooldown period? (Select TWO.)

1. It ensures that the Auto Scaling group launches or terminates additional EC2 instances without any downtime.
2. It ensures that before the Auto Scaling group scales out, the EC2 instances have an ample time to cooldown.

3. It ensures that the Auto Scaling group does not launch or terminate additional EC2 instances before the previous scaling activity takes effect.
4. Its default value is 300 seconds.
5. Its default value is 600 seconds.

Answer(s): 3, 4

Explanation

In Auto Scaling, the following statements are correct regarding the cooldown period:

It ensures that the Auto Scaling group does not launch or terminate additional EC2 instances before the previous scaling activity takes effect.

Its default value is 300 seconds.

It is a configurable setting for your Auto Scaling group.

The following options are incorrect:

- It ensures that before the Auto Scaling group scales out, the EC2 instances have an ample time to cooldown.

- It ensures that the Auto Scaling group launches or terminates additional EC2 instances without any downtime.

- Its default value is 600 seconds.

These statements are inaccurate and don't depict what the word "cooldown" actually means for Auto Scaling. The cooldown period is a configurable setting for your Auto Scaling group that helps to ensure that it doesn't launch or terminate additional instances before the previous scaling activity takes effect. After the Auto Scaling group dynamically scales using a simple scaling policy, it waits for the cooldown period to complete before resuming scaling activities.

The figure below demonstrates the scaling cooldown:

Reference:

http://docs.aws.amazon.com/autoscaling/latest/userguide/as-instance-termination.html

Question 37:

A company is planning to launch an application which requires a data warehouse that will be used for their infrequently accessed data. You need to use an EBS Volume that can handle large, sequential I/O operations.

Which of the following is the most cost-effective storage type that you should use to meet the requirement?

1. Cold HDD (sc1)
2. Provisioned IOPS SSD (io1)
3. EBS General Purpose SSD (gp2)
4. Throughput Optimized HDD (st1)

Answer(s): 1

Explanation

Cold HDD volumes provide low-cost magnetic storage that defines performance in terms of throughput rather than IOPS. With a lower throughput limit than Throughput Optimized HDD, this is a good fit ideal for large, sequential cold-data workloads. If you require infrequent access to your data and are looking to save costs, Cold HDD provides inexpensive block storage. Take note that bootable Cold HDD volumes are not supported.

Cold HDD provides the lowest cost HDD volume and is designed for less frequently accessed workloads. Hence, Cold HDD (sc1) is the correct answer.

In the exam, always consider the difference between SSD and HDD as shown on the table below. This will allow you to easily eliminate specific EBS-types in the options which are not SSD or not HDD, depending on whether the question asks for a storage type which has small, random I/O operations or large, sequential I/O operations.

EBS General Purpose SSD (gp2) is incorrect because a General purpose SSD volume costs more and it is mainly used for a wide variety of workloads. It is recommended to be used as system boot volumes, virtual desktops, low-latency interactive apps, and many more.

Provisioned IOPS SSD (io1) is incorrect because this costs more than Cold HDD and thus, not cost-effective for this scenario. It provides the highest performance SSD volume for mission-critical low-latency or high-throughput workloads, which is not needed in the scenario.

Throughput Optimized HDD (st1) is incorrect because this is primarily used for frequently accessed, throughput-intensive workloads. In this scenario, Cold HDD perfectly fits the requirement as it is used for their infrequently accessed data and provides the lowest cost, unlike Throughput Optimized HDD.

References:

https://aws.amazon.com/ebs/details/

https://docs.aws.amazon.com/AWSEC2/latest/UserGuide/EBSVolumeTypes.html

Question 38:

You are working for a University as their AWS Consultant. They want to have a disaster recovery strategy in AWS for mission-critical applications after suffering a disastrous outage wherein they lost student and employee records. They don't want this to happen again but at the same time want to minimize the monthly costs. You are instructed to set up a minimal version of the application that is always available in case of any outages. The DR site should only run the most critical core elements of your system in AWS to save cost which can be rapidly upgraded to a full-scale production environment in the event of system outages.

Which of the following disaster recovery architectures is the most cost-effective type to use in this scenario?

1. Multi Site
2. Pilot Light
3. Backup & Restore
4. Warm Standby

Answer(s): 2

Explanation

The correct answer is Pilot Light.

The term pilot light is often used to describe a DR scenario in which a minimal version of an environment is always running in the cloud. The idea of the pilot light is an analogy that comes from the gas heater. In a gas heater, a small flame that's always on can quickly ignite the entire furnace to heat up a house. This scenario is similar to a backup-and-restore scenario.

For example, with AWS you can maintain a pilot light by configuring and running the most critical core elements of your system in AWS. When the time comes for recovery, you can rapidly provision a full-scale production environment around the critical core.

Backup & Restore is incorrect because you are running mission-critical applications, and the speed of recovery from backup and restore solution might not meet your RTO and RPO.

Warm Standby is incorrect. Warm standby is a method of redundancy in which the scaled-down secondary system runs in the background of the primary system. Doing so would not optimize your savings as much as running a pilot light recovery since some of your services are always running in the background.

Multi Site is incorrect as well. Multi-site is the most expensive solution out of disaster recovery solutions. You are trying to save monthly costs so this should be the least probable choice for you.

References:

https://www.slideshare.net/AmazonWebServices/disaster-recovery-options-with-aws

RPO and RTO Explained:

https://youtu.be/rD3nBaS3OG4

Question 39:

One member of your DevOps team consulted you about a connectivity problem in one of your Amazon EC2 instances. The application architecture is initially set up with four EC2 instances, each with an EIP address that all belong to a public non-default subnet. You launched another instance to handle the increasing workload of your application. The EC2 instances also belong to the same security group. Everything works well as expected except for one of the EC2 instances which is not able to send nor receive traffic over the Internet.

Which of the following is the MOST likely reason for this issue?

1. The EC2 instance does not have a private IP address associated with it.
2. The EC2 instance is running in an Availability Zone that is not connected to an Internet gateway.
3. The route table is not properly configured to allow traffic to and from the Internet through the Internet gateway.
4. The EC2 instance does not have a public IP address associated with it.

Answer(s): 4

Explanation

IP addresses enable resources in your VPC to communicate with each other, and with resources over the Internet. Amazon EC2 and Amazon VPC support the IPv4 and IPv6 addressing protocols.

By default, Amazon EC2 and Amazon VPC use the IPv4 addressing protocol. When you create a VPC, you must assign it an IPv4 CIDR block (a range of private IPv4 addresses). Private IPv4 addresses are not reachable over the Internet. To connect to your instance over the Internet, or to enable communication between your instances and other AWS services that have public endpoints, you can assign a globally-unique public IPv4 address to your instance.

You can optionally associate an IPv6 CIDR block with your VPC and subnets, and assign IPv6 addresses from that block to the resources in your VPC. IPv6 addresses are public and reachable over the Internet.

All subnets have a modifiable attribute that determines whether a network interface created in that subnet is assigned a public IPv4 address and, if applicable, an IPv6 address. This includes the primary network interface (eth0) that's created for an instance when you launch an instance in that subnet. Regardless of the subnet attribute, you can still override this setting for a specific instance during launch.

By default, nondefault subnets have the IPv4 public addressing attribute set to false, and default subnets have this attribute set to true. An exception is a nondefault subnet created by the Amazon EC2 launch instance wizard — the wizard sets the attribute to true. You can modify this attribute using the Amazon VPC console.

In this scenario, there are 5 EC2 instances that belong to the same security group that should be able to connect to the Internet. The main route table is properly configured but there is a problem connecting to one instance. Since the other four instances are working fine, we can assume that the security group and the route table are correctly configured. One possible reason for this issue is that the problematic instance does not have a public or an EIP address.

Take note as well that the four EC2 instances all belong to a public non-default subnet. Which means that a new EC2 instance will not have a public IP address by default since the since IPv4 public addressing attribute is initially set to false.

Hence, the correct answer is the option that says: The EC2 instance does not have a public IP address associated with it.

The option that says: The route table is not properly configured to allow traffic to and from the Internet through the Internet gateway is incorrect because the other three instances, which are associated with the same route table and security group, do not have any issues.

The option that says: The EC2 instance is running in an Availability Zone that is not connected to an Internet gateway is incorrect because there is no relationship between the Availability Zone and the Internet Gateway (IGW) that may have caused the issue.

References:

http://docs.aws.amazon.com/AmazonVPC/latest/UserGuide/VPC_Scenario1.html

https://docs.aws.amazon.com/vpc/latest/userguide/vpc-ip-addressing.html#vpc-ip-addressing-subnet

Question 40:

A corporate and investment bank has recently decided to adopt a hybrid cloud architecture for their Trade Finance web application which uses an Oracle database with Oracle Real Application Clusters (RAC) configuration. Since Oracle RAC is not supported in RDS, they decided to launch their database in a large On-Demand EC2 instance instead, with multiple EBS Volumes attached. As a Solutions Architect, you are responsible to ensure the security, availability, scalability, and disaster recovery of the whole architecture.

In this scenario, which of the following will enable you to take backups of your EBS volumes that are being used by the Oracle database?

1. Use Disk Mirroring, which is also known as RAID 1, that replicates data to two or more disks/EBS Volumes.
2. Launch the EBS Volumes to a Placement Group which will automatically back up your data.
3. EBS-backed EC2 instances.
4. Create snapshots of the EBS Volumes.

Answer(s): 4

Explanation

Creating snapshots of the EBS Volumes is correct. You can back up the data on your Amazon EBS volumes to Amazon S3 by taking point-in-time snapshots. Snapshots are incremental backups, which means that only the blocks on the device that have changed after your most recent snapshot are saved.

This minimizes the time required to create the snapshot and saves on storage costs by not duplicating data. When you delete a snapshot, only the data unique to that snapshot is removed. Each snapshot contains all of the information needed to restore your data (from the moment the snapshot was taken) to a new EBS volume.

EBS-backed EC2 instances is incorrect since running an EBS-backed EC2 instance does not relate to your problem as you are already running a few of them in the first place.

Using Disk Mirroring, which is also known as RAID 1, that replicates data to two or more disks/EBS Volumes is incorrect. Disk mirroring is not an efficient and cost-optimized solution for your problem. You should use EBS snapshots instead.

Launching the EBS Volumes to a Placement Group which will automatically back up your data is incorrect. A placement group is a logical grouping of instances within a single Availability Zone (AZ) that allows low-latency communication between instances. Hence, this is not an efficient way to back up data.

Reference:

https://docs.aws.amazon.com/AWSEC2/latest/UserGuide/EBSSnapshots.html

Question 41:

Your fellow AWS Engineer has created a new Standard-class S3 bucket to store financial reports that are not frequently accessed but should be immediately available when an auditor requests for it. To save costs, you changed the storage class of the S3 bucket from Standard to Infrequent Access storage class.

In Amazon S3 Standard - Infrequent Access storage class, which of the following statements are true? (Select TWO.)

1. It is designed for data that is accessed less frequently.
2. It provides high latency and low throughput performance
3. It is the best storage option to store noncritical and reproducible data
4. Ideal to use for data archiving.
5. It is designed for data that requires rapid access when needed.

Answer(s): 1, 5

Explanation

Amazon S3 Standard - Infrequent Access (Standard - IA) is an Amazon S3 storage class for data that is accessed less frequently, but requires rapid access when needed. Standard - IA offers the high durability, throughput, and low latency of Amazon S3 Standard, with a low per GB storage price and per GB retrieval fee.

This combination of low cost and high performance make Standard - IA ideal for long-term storage, backups, and as a data store for disaster recovery. The Standard - IA storage class is set at the object level and can exist in the same bucket as Standard, allowing you to use lifecycle policies to automatically transition objects between storage classes without any application changes.

Key Features:

- Same low latency and high throughput performance of Standard

- Designed for durability of 99.999999999% of objects

- Designed for 99.9% availability over a given year

- Backed with the Amazon S3 Service Level Agreement for availability

- Supports SSL encryption of data in transit and at rest

- Lifecycle management for automatic migration of objects

The option that says: It is the best storage option to store noncritical and reproducible data is incorrect as it actually refers to Amazon S3 - Reduced Redundancy Storage (RRS). In addition, RRS will be completely deprecated soon and AWS recommends to use S3 IA One-Zone instead.

The option that says: It provides high latency and low throughput performance is incorrect as it should be "low latency" and "high throughput" instead. S3 automatically scales performance to meet user demands.

The option that says: Ideal to use for data archiving is incorrect because this statement refers to Amazon S3 Glacier. Glacier is a secure, durable, and extremely low-cost cloud storage service for data archiving and long-term backup.

Reference:

https://aws.amazon.com/s3/storage-classes/

Question 42:

You are building a cloud infrastructure where you have EC2 instances that require access to various AWS services such as S3 and Redshift. You will also need to provision access to system administrators so they can deploy and test their changes.

Which configuration should be used to ensure that the access to your resources are secured and not compromised? (Select TWO.)

1. Store the AWS Access Keys in the EC2 instance.
2. Assign an IAM role to the Amazon EC2 instance.
3. Store the AWS Access Keys in ACM.
4. Assign an IAM user for each Amazon EC2 Instance.
5. Enable Multi-Factor Authentication.

Answer(s): 2, 5

Explanation

In this scenario, the correct answers are:

- Enable Multi-Factor Authentication

- Assign an IAM role to the Amazon EC2 instance

Always remember that you should associate IAM roles to EC2 instances and not an IAM user, for the purpose of accessing other AWS services. IAM roles are designed so that your applications can securely make API requests from your instances, without requiring you to manage the security credentials that the applications use. Instead of creating and distributing your AWS credentials, you can delegate permission to make API requests using IAM roles.

AWS Multi-Factor Authentication (MFA) is a simple best practice that adds an extra layer of protection on top of your user name and password. With MFA enabled, when a user signs in to an AWS website, they will be prompted for their user name and password (the first factor—what they know), as well as for an authentication code from their AWS MFA device (the second factor—what they have). Taken together, these multiple factors provide increased security for your AWS account settings and resources. You can enable MFA for your AWS account and for individual IAM users you have created under your account. MFA can also be used to control access to AWS service APIs.

Storing the AWS Access Keys in the EC2 instance is incorrect because this is not recommended by AWS, as it can be compromised. Instead of storing access keys on an EC2 instance for use by applications that run on the instance and make AWS API

137

requests, you can use an IAM role to provide temporary access keys for these applications.

Assigning an IAM user for each Amazon EC2 Instance is incorrect because there is no need to create an IAM user for this scenario since IAM roles already provide greater flexibility and easier management.

Storing the AWS Access Keys in ACM is incorrect because ACM is just a service that lets you easily provision, manage, and deploy public and private SSL/TLS certificates for use with AWS services and your internal connected resources. It is not used as a secure storage for your access keys.

References:

https://aws.amazon.com/iam/details/mfa/

https://docs.aws.amazon.com/AWSEC2/latest/UserGuide/iam-roles-for-amazon-ec2.html

Here's a short video tutorial on how to enable MFA for your AWS user account:

https://youtu.be/A3AObXBJ4Lw

Question 43:

A company has a requirement to move 80 TB data warehouse to the cloud. It would take 2 months to transfer the data given their current bandwidth allocation.

Which is the most cost-effective service that would allow you to quickly upload their data into AWS?

1. AWS Snowmobile
2. AWS Direct Connect
3. Amazon S3 Multipart Upload
4. AWS Snowball Edge

Answer(s): 4

Explanation

AWS Snowball Edge is a type of Snowball device with on-board storage and compute power for select AWS capabilities. Snowball Edge can undertake local processing and edge-computing workloads in addition to transferring data between your local environment and the AWS Cloud.

Each Snowball Edge device can transport data at speeds faster than the internet. This transport is done by shipping the data in the appliances through a regional carrier. The appliances are rugged shipping containers, complete with E Ink shipping labels. The AWS Snowball Edge device differs from the standard Snowball because it can bring the power of the AWS Cloud to your on-premises location, with local storage and compute functionality.

Snowball Edge devices have three options for device configurations – storage optimized, compute optimized, and with GPU.

Hence, the correct answer is: AWS Snowball Edge.

AWS Snowmobile is incorrect because this is an Exabyte-scale data transfer service used to move extremely large amounts of data to AWS. It is not suitable for transferring a small amount of data, like 80 TB in this scenario. You can transfer up to 100PB per Snowmobile, a 45-foot long ruggedized shipping container, pulled by a semi-trailer truck. A more cost-effective solution here is to order a Snowball Edge device instead.

AWS Direct Connect is incorrect because it is primarily used to establish a dedicated network connection from your premises network to AWS. This is not suitable for one-time data transfer tasks, like what is depicted in the scenario.

Amazon S3 Multipart Upload is incorrect because this feature simply enables you to upload large objects in multiple parts. It still uses the same Internet connection of the company, which means that the transfer will still take time due to its current bandwidth allocation.

References:

https://docs.aws.amazon.com/snowball/latest/ug/whatissnowball.html

https://docs.aws.amazon.com/snowball/latest/ug/device-differences.html

Here is a quick introduction on AWS Snowball Edge:

https://youtu.be/bxSD1Nha2k8

Using AWS Snowball Edge and AWS DMS for Database Migration:

https://youtu.be/6Hw--HE8ILg

Question 44:

You are instructed by your manager to set up a bastion host in your Amazon VPC and it should only be accessed from the corporate data center via SSH. What is the best way for you to achieve this?

1. Create a large EC2 instance with a security group which only allows access on port 22 using your own pre-configured password.
2. Create a small EC2 instance with a security group which only allows access on port 22 using your own pre-configured password.
3. Create a large EC2 instance with a security group which only allows access on port 22 via the IP address of the corporate data center. Use a private key (.pem) file to connect to the bastion host.

4. Create a small EC2 instance with a security group which only allows access on port 22 via the IP address of the corporate data center. Use a private key (.pem) file to connect to the bastion host.

Answer(s): 4

Explanation

The best way to implement a bastion host is to create a small EC2 instance which should only have a security group from a particular IP address for maximum security. This will block any SSH Brute Force attacks on your bastion host. It is also recommended to use a small instance rather than a large one because this host will only act as a jump server to connect to other instances in your VPC and nothing else.

Therefore, there is no point of allocating a large instance simply because it doesn't need that much computing power to process SSH (port 22) or RDP (port 3389) connections. It is possible to use SSH with an ordinary user ID and a pre-configured password as credentials but it is more secure to use public key pairs for SSH authentication for better security.

Hence, the right answer for this scenario is the option that says: Create a small EC2 instance with a security group which only allows access on port 22 via the IP address of the corporate data center. Use a private key (.pem) file to connect to the bastion host.

Creating a large EC2 instance with a security group which only allows access on port 22 using your own pre-configured password and creating a small EC2 instance with a security group which only allows access on port 22 using your own pre-configured password are incorrect because even though you have your own pre-configured password, the SSH connection can still be accessed by anyone over the Internet, which poses as a security vulnerability.

The option that says: Create a large EC2 instance with a security group which only allows access on port 22 via the IP address of the corporate data center. Use a private key (.pem) file to connect to the bastion host is incorrect because you don't need a large instance for a bastion host as it does not require much CPU resources.

References:

https://docs.aws.amazon.com/quickstart/latest/linux-bastion/architecture.html

https://aws.amazon.com/blogs/security/how-to-record-ssh-sessions-established-through-a-bastion-host/

Question 45:

A media company has two VPCs: VPC-1 and VPC-2 with peering connection between each other. VPC-1 only contains private subnets while VPC-2 only contains public subnets. The company uses a single AWS Direct Connect connection and a virtual interface to connect their on-premises network with VPC-1.

Which of the following options increase the fault tolerance of the connection to VPC-1? (Select TWO.)

1. Establish a hardware VPN over the Internet between VPC-2 and the on-premises network.
2. Use the AWS VPN CloudHub to create a new AWS Direct Connect connection and private virtual interface in the same region as VPC-2.
3. Establish another AWS Direct Connect connection and private virtual interface in the same AWS region as VPC-1.
4. Establish a hardware VPN over the Internet between VPC-1 and the on-premises network.
5. Establish a new AWS Direct Connect connection and private virtual interface in the same region as VPC-2.

Answer(s): 3, 4

Explanation

In this scenario, you have two VPCs which have peering connections with each other. Note that a VPC peering connection does not support edge to edge routing. This means that if either VPC in a peering relationship has one of the following connections, you cannot extend the peering relationship to that connection:

- A VPN connection or an AWS Direct Connect connection to a corporate network

- An Internet connection through an Internet gateway

- An Internet connection in a private subnet through a NAT device

- A gateway VPC endpoint to an AWS service; for example, an endpoint to Amazon S3.

- (IPv6) A ClassicLink connection. You can enable IPv4 communication between a linked EC2-Classic instance and instances in a VPC on the other side of a VPC peering connection. However, IPv6 is not supported in EC2-Classic, so you cannot extend this connection for IPv6 communication.

For example, if VPC A and VPC B are peered, and VPC A has any of these connections, then instances in VPC B cannot use the connection to access resources on the other side of the connection. Similarly, resources on the other side of a connection cannot use the connection to access VPC B.

Hence, this means that you cannot use VPC-2 to extend the peering relationship that exists between VPC-1 and the on-premises network. For example, traffic from the corporate network can't directly access VPC-1 by using the VPN connection or the AWS Direct Connect connection to VPC-2, which is why the following options are incorrect:

- Use the AWS VPN CloudHub to create a new AWS Direct Connect connection and private virtual interface in the same region as VPC-2.

- Establish a hardware VPN over the Internet between VPC-2 and the on-premises network.

- Establish a new AWS Direct Connect connection and private virtual interface in the same region as VPC-2.

You can do the following to provide a highly available, fault-tolerant network connection:

- Establish a hardware VPN over the Internet between the VPC and the on-premises network.

- Establish another AWS Direct Connect connection and private virtual interface in the same AWS region.

References:

https://docs.aws.amazon.com/vpc/latest/peering/invalid-peering-configurations.html#edge-to-edge-vgw

https://aws.amazon.com/premiumsupport/knowledge-center/configure-vpn-backup-dx/

https://aws.amazon.com/answers/networking/aws-multiple-data-center-ha-network-connectivity/

Question 46:

You have two On-Demand EC2 instances inside your Virtual Private Cloud in the same Availability Zone but are deployed to different subnets. One EC2 instance is running a database and the other EC2 instance a web application that connects with the database. You want to ensure that these two instances can communicate with each other for your system to work properly.

What are the things you have to check so that these EC2 instances can communicate inside the VPC? (Select TWO.)

1. Ensure that the EC2 instances are in the same Placement Group.
2. Check if both instances are the same instance class.
3. Check if the default route is set to a NAT instance or Internet Gateway (IGW) for them to communicate.
4. Check the Network ACL if it allows communication between the two subnets.
5. Check if all security groups are set to allow the application host to communicate to the database on the right port and protocol.

Answer(s): 4, 5

Explanation

First, the Network ACL should be properly set to allow communication between the two subnets. The security group should also be properly configured so that your web server can communicate with the database server. Hence, these are the correct answers:

Check if all security groups are set to allow the application host to communicate to the database on the right port and protocol.

Check the Network ACL if it allows communication between the two subnets.

The option that says: Check if both instances are the same instance class is incorrect because the EC2 instances do not need to be of the same class in order to communicate with each other.

The option that says: Check if the default route is set to a NAT instance or Internet Gateway (IGW) for them to communicate is incorrect because an Internet gateway is primarily used to communicate to the Internet.

The option that says: Ensure that the EC2 instances are in the same Placement Group is incorrect because Placement Group is mainly used to provide low-latency network performance necessary for tightly-coupled node-to-node communication.

Reference:

http://docs.aws.amazon.com/AmazonVPC/latest/UserGuide/VPC_Subnets.html

Question 47:

Your company has a top priority requirement to monitor a few database metrics and then afterwards, send email notifications to the Operations team in case there is an issue. Which AWS services can accomplish this requirement? (Select TWO.)

1. Amazon Simple Email Service
2. Amazon CloudWatch
3. Amazon Simple Notification Service (SNS)
4. Amazon Simple Queue Service (SQS)
5. Amazon EC2 Instance with a running Berkeley Internet Name Domain (BIND) Server.

Answer(s): 2, 3

Explanation

Amazon CloudWatch and Amazon Simple Notification Service (SNS) are correct. In this requirement, you can use Amazon CloudWatch to monitor the database and then Amazon SNS to send the emails to the Operations team. Take note that you should use SNS instead of SES (Simple Email Service) when you want to monitor your EC2 instances.

CloudWatch collects monitoring and operational data in the form of logs, metrics, and events, providing you with a unified view of AWS resources, applications, and services that run on AWS, and on-premises servers.

SNS is a highly available, durable, secure, fully managed pub/sub messaging service that enables you to decouple microservices, distributed systems, and serverless applications.

Amazon Simple Email Service is incorrect. SES is a cloud-based email sending service designed to send notification and transactional emails.

Amazon Simple Queue Service (SQS) is incorrect. SQS is a fully-managed message queuing service. It does not monitor applications nor send email notifications unlike SES.

Amazon EC2 Instance with a running Berkeley Internet Name Domain (BIND) Server is incorrect because BIND is primarily used as a Domain Name System (DNS) web service. This is only applicable if you have a private hosted zone in your AWS account. It does not monitor applications nor send email notifications.

References:

https://aws.amazon.com/cloudwatch/

https://aws.amazon.com/sns/

Question 48:

For data privacy, a healthcare company has been asked to comply with the Health Insurance Portability and Accountability Act (HIPAA). They have been told that all of the data being backed up or stored on Amazon S3 must be encrypted.

What is the best option to do this? (Select TWO.)

1. Before sending the data to Amazon S3 over HTTPS, encrypt the data locally first using your own encryption keys.
2. Enable Server-Side Encryption on an S3 bucket to make use of AES-128 encryption.
3. Store the data in encrypted EBS snapshots.

4. Store the data on EBS volumes with encryption enabled instead of using Amazon S3.
5. Enable Server-Side Encryption on an S3 bucket to make use of AES-256 encryption.

Answer(s): 1, 5

Explanation

Server-side encryption is about data encryption at rest—that is, Amazon S3 encrypts your data at the object level as it writes it to disks in its data centers and decrypts it for you when you access it. As long as you authenticate your request and you have access permissions, there is no difference in the way you access encrypted or unencrypted objects. For example, if you share your objects using a pre-signed URL, that URL works the same way for both encrypted and unencrypted objects.

You have three mutually exclusive options depending on how you choose to manage the encryption keys:

Use Server-Side Encryption with Amazon S3-Managed Keys (SSE-S3)

Use Server-Side Encryption with AWS KMS-Managed Keys (SSE-KMS)

Use Server-Side Encryption with Customer-Provided Keys (SSE-C)

The options that say: Before sending the data to Amazon S3 over HTTPS, encrypt the data locally first using your own encryption keys and Enable Server-Side Encryption on an S3 bucket to make use of AES-256 encryption are correct because these options are using client-side encryption and Amazon S3-Managed Keys (SSE-S3) respectively. Client-side encryption is the act of encrypting data before sending it to Amazon S3 while SSE-S3 uses AES-256 encryption.

Storing the data on EBS volumes with encryption enabled instead of using Amazon S3 and storing the data in encrypted EBS snapshots are incorrect because both options use EBS encryption and not S3.

Enabling Server-Side Encryption on an S3 bucket to make use of AES-128 encryption is incorrect as S3 doesn't provide AES-128 encryption, only AES-256.

References:

http://docs.aws.amazon.com/AmazonS3/latest/dev/UsingEncryption.html

https://docs.aws.amazon.com/AmazonS3/latest/dev/UsingClientSideEncryption.html

Question 49:

You have built a web application that checks for new items in an S3 bucket once every hour. If new items exist, a message is added to an SQS queue. You have a fleet of EC2 instances which retrieve messages from the SQS queue, process the file, and finally, send you and the user an email confirmation that the item has been successfully processed. Your officemate uploaded one test file to the S3 bucket and after a couple of hours, you noticed that you and your officemate have 50 emails from your application with the same message.

Which of the following is most likely the root cause why the application has sent you and the user multiple emails?

1. By default, SQS automatically deletes the messages that were processed by the consumers. It might be possible that your officemate has submitted the request 50 times which is why you received a lot of emails.
2. There is a bug in the application.
3. The sqsSendEmailMessage attribute of the SQS queue is configured to 50.
4. Your application does not issue a delete command to the SQS queue after processing the message, which is why this message went back to the queue and was processed multiple times.

Answer(s): 4

Explanation

In this scenario, the main culprit is that your application does not issue a delete command to the SQS queue after processing the message, which is why this message went back to the queue and was processed multiple times.

The option that says: The sqsSendEmailMessage attribute of the SQS queue is configured to 50 is incorrect as there is no sqsSendEmailMessage attribute in SQS.

The option that says: There is a bug in the application is a valid answer but since the scenario did not mention that the EC2 instances deleted the processed messages, the most likely cause of the problem is that the application does not issue a delete command to the SQS queue as mentioned above.

The option that says: By default, SQS automatically deletes the messages that were processed by the consumers. It might be possible that your officemate has submitted the request 50 times which is why you received a lot of emails is incorrect as SQS does not automatically delete the messages.

Reference:

https://aws.amazon.com/sqs/faqs/

Question 50:

You are working for a litigation firm as the Data Engineer for their case history application. You need to keep track of all the cases your firm has handled. The static assets like .jpg, .png, and .pdf files are stored in S3 for cost efficiency and high durability. As these files are critical to your business, you want to keep track of what's happening in your S3 bucket. You found out that S3 has an event notification whenever a delete or write operation happens within the S3 bucket.

What are the possible Event Notification destinations available for S3 buckets? (Select TWO.)

1. Lambda function
2. SQS
3. SWF
4. SES
5. Kinesis

Answer(s): 1, 2

Explanation

The Amazon S3 notification feature enables you to receive notifications when certain events happen in your bucket. To enable notifications, you must first add a notification configuration identifying the events you want Amazon S3 to publish, and the destinations where you want Amazon S3 to send the event notifications.

Amazon S3 supports the following destinations where it can publish events:

Amazon Simple Notification Service (Amazon SNS) topic - A web service that coordinates and manages the delivery or sending of messages to subscribing endpoints or clients.

Amazon Simple Queue Service (Amazon SQS) queue - Offers reliable and scalable hosted queues for storing messages as they travel between computer.

AWS Lambda - AWS Lambda is a compute service where you can upload your code and the service can run the code on your behalf using the AWS infrastructure. You package up and upload your custom code to AWS Lambda when you create a Lambda function

Kinesis is incorrect because this is used to collect, process, and analyze real-time, streaming data so you can get timely insights and react quickly to new information, and not used for event notifications. You have to use SNS, SQS or Lambda.

SES is incorrect because this is mainly used for sending emails designed to help digital marketers and application developers send marketing, notification, and transactional emails, and not for sending event notifications from S3. You have to use SNS, SQS or Lambda.

SWF is incorrect because this is mainly used to build applications that use Amazon's cloud to coordinate work across distributed components and not used as a way to trigger event notifications from S3. You have to use SNS, SQS or Lambda.

Here's what you need to do in order to start using this new feature with your application:

Create the queue, topic, or Lambda function (which I'll call the target for brevity) if necessary.

Grant S3 permission to publish to the target or invoke the Lambda function. For SNS or SQS, you do this by applying an appropriate policy to the topic or the queue. For Lambda, you must create and supply an IAM role, then associate it with the Lambda function.

Arrange for your application to be invoked in response to activity on the target. As you will see in a moment, you have several options here.

Set the bucket's Notification Configuration to point to the target.

Reference:

https://docs.aws.amazon.com/AmazonS3/latest/dev/NotificationHowTo.html

Question 51:

You have a data analytics application that updates a real-time, foreign exchange dashboard and another separate application that archives data to Amazon Redshift. Both applications are configured to consume data from the same stream concurrently and independently by using Amazon Kinesis Data Streams. However, you noticed that there are a lot of occurrences where a shard iterator expires unexpectedly. Upon checking, you found out that the DynamoDB table used by Kinesis does not have enough capacity to store the lease data.

Which of the following is the most suitable solution to rectify this issue?

1. Use Amazon Kinesis Data Analytics to properly support the data analytics application instead of Kinesis Data Stream.
2. Upgrade the storage capacity of the DynamoDB table.
3. Enable In-Memory Acceleration with DynamoDB Accelerator (DAX).
4. Increase the write capacity assigned to the shard table.

Answer(s): 4

Explanation

A new shard iterator is returned by every GetRecords request (as NextShardIterator), which you then use in the next GetRecords request (as ShardIterator). Typically, this shard iterator does not expire before you use it. However, you may find that shard iterators expire because you have not called GetRecords for more than 5 minutes, or because you've performed a restart of your consumer application.

If the shard iterator expires immediately before you can use it, this might indicate that the DynamoDB table used by Kinesis does not have enough capacity to store the lease data. This situation is more likely to happen if you have a large number of shards. To solve this problem, increase the write capacity assigned to the shard table.

Hence, increasing the write capacity assigned to the shard table is the correct answer.

Upgrading the storage capacity of the DynamoDB table is incorrect because DynamoDB is a fully managed service which automatically scales its storage, without setting it up manually. The scenario refers to the write capacity of the shard table when it says that the DynamoDB table used by Kinesis does not have enough capacity to store the lease data.

Enabling In-Memory Acceleration with DynamoDB Accelerator (DAX) is incorrect because the DAX feature is primarily used for read performance improvement of your DynamoDB table from milliseconds response time to microseconds. It does not have any relationship with Amazon Kinesis Data Stream in this scenario.

Using Amazon Kinesis Data Analytics to properly support the data analytics application instead of Kinesis Data Stream is incorrect because although Amazon Kinesis Data Analytics can support a data analytics application, it is still not a suitable solution for this issue. You simply need to increase the write capacity assigned to the shard table in order to rectify the problem which is why switching to Amazon Kinesis Data Analytics is not necessary.

Reference:

https://docs.aws.amazon.com/streams/latest/dev/kinesis-record-processor-ddb.html

https://docs.aws.amazon.com/streams/latest/dev/troubleshooting-consumers.html

Question 52:

You have a new, dynamic web app written in MEAN stack that is going to be launched in the next month. There is a probability that the traffic will be quite high in the first couple of weeks. In the event of a load failure, how can you set up DNS failover to a static website?

1. Enable failover to an application hosted in an on-premises data center.
2. Use Route 53 with the failover option to a static S3 website bucket or CloudFront distribution.
3. Duplicate the exact application architecture in another region and configure DNS weight-based routing.
4. Add more servers in case the application fails.

Answer(s): 2

Explanation

For this scenario, using Route 53 with the failover option to a static S3 website bucket or CloudFront distribution is correct. You can create a new Route 53 with the failover option to a static S3 website bucket or CloudFront distribution as an alternative.

Duplicating the exact application architecture in another region and configuring DNS weight-based routing is incorrect because running a duplicate system is not a cost-effective solution. Remember that you are trying to build a failover mechanism for your web app, not a distributed setup.

Enabling failover to an application hosted in an on-premises data center is incorrect because, although you can set up failover to your on-premises data center, you are not maximizing the AWS environment such as using Route 53 failover.

Adding more servers in case the application fails is incorrect because this is not the best way to handle a failover event. If you add more servers only in case the application fails, then there would be a period of downtime in which your application is unavailable. Since there are no running servers on that period, your application will be unavailable for a certain period of time until your new server is up and running.

Reference:

https://aws.amazon.com/premiumsupport/knowledge-center/fail-over-s3-r53/

http://docs.aws.amazon.com/Route53/latest/DeveloperGuide/dns-failover.html

Question 53:

A web application, which is used by your clients around the world, is hosted in an Auto Scaling group of EC2 instances behind a Classic Load Balancer. You need to secure your application by allowing multiple domains to serve SSL traffic over the same IP address.

Which of the following should you do to meet the above requirement?

1. It is not possible to allow multiple domains to serve SSL traffic over the same IP address in AWS
2. Generate an SSL certificate with AWS Certificate Manager and create a CloudFront web distribution. Associate the certificate with your web distribution and enable the support for Server Name Indication (SNI).
3. Use an Elastic IP and upload multiple 3rd party certificates in your Classic Load Balancer using the AWS Certificate Manager.
4. Use Server Name Indication (SNI) on your Classic Load Balancer by adding multiple SSL certificates to allow multiple domains to serve SSL traffic.

Answer(s): 2

Explanation

SNI Custom SSL relies on the SNI extension of the Transport Layer Security protocol, which allows multiple domains to serve SSL traffic over the same IP address by including the hostname which the viewers are trying to connect to.

Amazon CloudFront delivers your content from each edge location and offers the same security as the Dedicated IP Custom SSL feature. SNI Custom SSL works with most modern browsers, including Chrome version 6 and later (running on Windows XP and later or OS X 10.5.7 and later), Safari version 3 and later (running on Windows Vista and later or Mac OS X 10.5.6. and later), Firefox 2.0 and later, and Internet Explorer 7 and later (running on Windows Vista and later).

Some users may not be able to access your content because some older browsers do not support SNI and will not be able to establish a connection with CloudFront to load the HTTPS version of your content. If you need to support non-SNI compliant browsers for HTTPS content, it is recommended to use the Dedicated IP Custom SSL feature.

Using Server Name Indication (SNI) on your Classic Load Balancer by adding multiple SSL certificates to allow multiple domains to serve SSL traffic is incorrect because a Classic Load Balancer does not support Server Name Indication (SNI). You have to use an Application Load Balancer instead or a CloudFront web distribution to allow the SNI feature.

Using an Elastic IP and uploading multiple 3rd party certificates in your Classic Load Balancer using the AWS Certificate Manager is incorrect because just like in the above, a Classic Load Balancer does not support Server Name Indication (SNI) and the use of an Elastic IP is not a suitable solution to allow multiple domains to serve SSL traffic. You have to use Server Name Indication (SNI).

The option that says: It is not possible to allow multiple domains to serve SSL traffic over the same IP address in AWS is incorrect because AWS does support the use of Server Name Indication (SNI).

References:

https://aws.amazon.com/about-aws/whats-new/2014/03/05/amazon-cloudront-announces-sni-custom-ssl/

https://aws.amazon.com/blogs/security/how-to-help-achieve-mobile-app-transport-security-compliance-by-using-amazon-cloudfront-and-aws-certificate-manager/

Question 54:

A media company is setting up an ECS batch architecture for its image processing application. It will be hosted in an Amazon ECS Cluster with two ECS tasks that will handle image uploads from the users and image processing. The first ECS task will process the user requests, store the image in an S3 input bucket, and push a message to a queue. The second task reads from the queue, parses the message containing the object name, and then downloads the object. Once the image is processed and transformed, it will upload the objects to the S3 output bucket. To complete the architecture, the Solutions Architect must create a queue and the necessary IAM permissions for the ECS tasks.

Which of the following should the Architect do next?

1. Launch a new Amazon SQS queue and configure the second ECS task to read from it. Create an IAM role that the ECS tasks can assume in order to get access to the S3 buckets and SQS queue. Declare the IAM Role (taskRoleArn) in the task definition.
2. Launch a new Amazon MQ queue and configure the second ECS task to read from it. Create an IAM role that the ECS tasks can assume in order to get access to the S3 buckets and Amazon MQ queue. Set the (EnableTaskIAMRole) option to true in the task definition.
3. Launch a new Amazon Kinesis Data Firehose and configure the second ECS task to read from it. Create an IAM role that the ECS tasks can assume in order to get access to the S3 buckets and Kinesis Data Firehose. Specify the ARN of the IAM Role in the (taskDefinitionArn) field of the task definition.
4. Launch a new Amazon AppStream 2.0 queue and configure the second ECS task to read from it. Create an IAM role that the ECS tasks can assume in order to get access to the S3 buckets and AppStream 2.0 queue. Declare the IAM Role (taskRoleArn) in the task definition.

Answer(s): 1

Explanation

Docker containers are particularly suited for batch job workloads. Batch jobs are often short-lived and embarrassingly parallel. You can package your batch processing application into a Docker image so that you can deploy it anywhere, such as in an Amazon ECS task.

Amazon ECS supports batch jobs. You can use Amazon ECS Run Task action to run one or more tasks once. The Run Task action starts the ECS task on an instance that meets the task's requirements including CPU, memory, and ports.

For example, you can set up an ECS Batch architecture for an image processing application. You can set up an AWS CloudFormation template that creates an Amazon S3 bucket, an Amazon SQS queue, an Amazon CloudWatch alarm, an ECS cluster, and an ECS task definition. Objects uploaded to the input S3 bucket trigger an event that sends object details to the SQS queue. The ECS task deploys a Docker container that reads from that queue, parses the message containing the object name and then downloads the object. Once transformed it will upload the objects to the S3 output bucket.

By using the SQS queue as the location for all object details, you can take advantage of its scalability and reliability as the queue will automatically scale based on the incoming messages and message retention can be configured. The ECS Cluster will then be able to scale services up or down based on the number of messages in the queue.

You have to create an IAM Role that the ECS task assumes in order to get access to the S3 buckets and SQS queue. Note that the permissions of the IAM role don't specify the S3 bucket ARN for the incoming bucket. This is to avoid a circular dependency issue in the CloudFormation template. You should always make sure to assign the least amount of privileges needed to an IAM role.

Hence, the correct answer is: Launch a new Amazon SQS queue and configure the second ECS task to read from it. Create an IAM role that the ECS tasks can assume in order to get access to the S3 buckets and SQS queue. Declare the IAM Role (taskRoleArn) in the task definition.

The option that says: Launch a new Amazon AppStream 2.0 queue and configure the second ECS task to read from it. Create an IAM role that the ECS tasks can assume in order to get access to the S3 buckets and AppStream 2.0 queue. Declare the IAM Role (taskRoleArn) in the task definition is incorrect because Amazon AppStream 2.0 is a fully managed application streaming service and can't be used as a queue. You have to use Amazon SQS instead.

The option that says: Launch a new Amazon Kinesis Data Firehose and configure the second ECS task to read from it. Create an IAM role that the ECS tasks can assume in order to get access to the S3 buckets and Kinesis Data Firehose. Specify the ARN of the IAM Role in the (taskDefinitionArn) field of the task definition is incorrect because Amazon Kinesis Data Firehose is a fully managed service for delivering real-time streaming data. Although it can stream data to an S3 bucket, it is not suitable to be used as a queue for a batch application in this scenario. In addition, the ARN of the IAM Role should be declared in the taskRoleArn and not in the taskDefinitionArn field.

The option that says: Launch a new Amazon MQ queue and configure the second ECS task to read from it. Create an IAM role that the ECS tasks can assume in order to get access to the S3 buckets and Amazon MQ queue. Set the (EnableTaskIAMRole) option to true in the task definition is incorrect because Amazon MQ is primarily used as a managed message broker service and not a queue. The EnableTaskIAMRole option is only applicable for Windows-based ECS Tasks that require extra configuration.

References:

https://github.com/aws-samples/ecs-refarch-batch-processing

https://docs.aws.amazon.com/AmazonECS/latest/developerguide/common_use_c
ases.html

https://aws.amazon.com/ecs/faqs/

Question 55:

A digital media company shares static content to its premium users around the world and also to their partners who syndicate their media files. The company is looking for ways to reduce its server costs and securely deliver their data to their customers globally with low latency.

Which combination of services should be used to provide the MOST suitable and cost-effective architecture? (Select TWO.)

1. Amazon S3
2. AWS Global Accelerator
3. Amazon CloudFront
4. AWS Lambda
5. AWS Fargate

Answer(s): 1, 3

Explanation

Amazon CloudFront is a fast content delivery network (CDN) service that securely delivers data, videos, applications, and APIs to customers globally with low latency, high transfer speeds, all within a developer-friendly environment.

CloudFront is integrated with AWS – both physical locations that are directly connected to the AWS global infrastructure, as well as other AWS services. CloudFront works seamlessly with services including AWS Shield for DDoS mitigation, Amazon S3, Elastic Load Balancing or Amazon EC2 as origins for your applications, and Lambda@Edge to run custom code closer to customers' users and to customize the user experience. Lastly, if you use AWS origins such as Amazon S3, Amazon EC2 or Elastic Load Balancing, you don't pay for any data transferred between these services and CloudFront.

 Amazon S3 is object storage built to store and retrieve any amount of data from anywhere on the Internet. It's a simple storage service that offers an extremely durable, highly available, and infinitely scalable data storage infrastructure at very low costs.

AWS Global Accelerator and Amazon CloudFront are separate services that use the AWS global network and its edge locations around the world. CloudFront improves performance for both cacheable content (such as images and videos) and dynamic content (such as API acceleration and dynamic site delivery). Global Accelerator improves performance for a wide range of applications over TCP or UDP by proxying packets at the edge to applications running in one or more AWS Regions. Global Accelerator is a good fit for non-HTTP use cases, such as gaming (UDP), IoT (MQTT), or Voice over IP, as well as for HTTP use cases that specifically require static IP addresses or deterministic, fast regional failover. Both services integrate with AWS Shield for DDoS protection.

Hence, the correct options are Amazon CloudFront and Amazon S3.

AWS Fargate is incorrect because this service is just a serverless compute engine for containers that work with both Amazon Elastic Container Service (ECS) and Amazon Elastic Kubernetes Service (EKS). Although this service is more cost-effective than its server-based counterpart, Amazon S3 still costs way less than Fargate, especially for storing static content.

AWS Lambda is incorrect because this simply lets you run your code serverless, without provisioning or managing servers. Although this is also a cost-effective service since you have to pay only for the compute time you consume, you can't use this to store static content or as a Content Delivery Network (CDN). A better combination is Amazon CloudFront and Amazon S3.

AWS Global Accelerator is incorrect because this service is more suitable for non-HTTP use cases, such as gaming (UDP), IoT (MQTT), or Voice over IP, as well as for HTTP use cases that specifically require static IP addresses or deterministic, fast regional failover. Moreover, there is no direct way that you can integrate AWS Global Accelerator with Amazon S3. It's more suitable to use Amazon CloudFront instead in this scenario.

References:

https://aws.amazon.com/premiumsupport/knowledge-center/cloudfront-serve-static-website/

https://aws.amazon.com/blogs/networking-and-content-delivery/amazon-s3-amazon-cloudfront-a-match-made-in-the-cloud/

https://aws.amazon.com/global-accelerator/faqs/

Question 56:

You are helping out a new DevOps Engineer to design her first architecture in AWS. She is planning to develop a highly available and fault-tolerant architecture which is composed of an Elastic Load Balancer and an Auto Scaling group of EC2 instances deployed across multiple Availability Zones. This will be used by an online accounting application which requires path-based routing, host-based routing, and bi-directional communication channels using WebSockets.

Which is the most suitable type of Elastic Load Balancer that you should recommend for her to use?

1. Either a Classic Load Balancer or a Network Load Balancer
2. Network Load Balancer
3. Application Load Balancer
4. Classic Load Balancer

Answer(s): 3

Explanation

Elastic Load Balancing supports three types of load balancers. You can select the appropriate load balancer based on your application needs.

If you need flexible application management and TLS termination then we recommend that you use Application Load Balancer. If extreme performance and static IP is needed for your application then we recommend that you use Network Load Balancer. If your application is built within the EC2 Classic network then you should use Classic Load Balancer.

An Application Load Balancer functions at the application layer, the seventh layer of the Open Systems Interconnection (OSI) model. After the load balancer receives a request, it evaluates the listener rules in priority order to determine which rule to apply, and then selects a target from the target group for the rule action. You can configure listener rules to route requests to different target groups based on the content of the application traffic. Routing is performed independently for each target group, even when a target is registered with multiple target groups.

Application Load Balancers support path-based routing, host-based routing and support for containerized applications hence, Application Load Balancer is the correct answer.

Network Load Balancer, Classic Load Balancer, and either a Classic Load Balancer or a Network Load Balancer are all incorrect as none of these support path-based routing and host-based routing, unlike an Application Load Balancer.

References:

https://docs.aws.amazon.com/elasticloadbalancing/latest/application/introduction.html#application-load-balancer-benefits

https://aws.amazon.com/elasticloadbalancing/faqs/

Here is a deep dive on Elastic Load Balancing and Best Practices:

https://youtu.be/VIgAT7vjol8

Question 57:

A company has an enterprise web application hosted in an AWS Fargate cluster with an Amazon FSx for Lustre filesystem for its high performance computing workloads. A warm standby environment is running in another AWS region for disaster recovery. A Solutions Architect was assigned to design a system that will automatically route the live traffic to the disaster recovery (DR) environment only in the event that the primary application stack experiences an outage.

What should the Architect do to satisfy this requirement?

1. Set up a Weighted routing policy configuration in Route 53 by adding health checks on both the primary stack and the DR environment. Configure the network access control list and the route table to allow Route 53 to send requests to the endpoints specified in the health checks. Enable the Evaluate Target Health option by setting it to Yes.
2. Set up a failover routing policy configuration in Route 53 by adding a health check on the primary service endpoint. Configure Route 53 to direct the DNS queries to the secondary record when the primary resource is unhealthy. Configure the network access control list and the route table to allow Route 53 to send requests to the endpoints specified in the health checks. Enable the Evaluate Target Health option by setting it to Yes.
3. Set up a CloudWatch Alarm to monitor the primary Route 53 DNS endpoint and create a custom Lambda function. Execute the ChangeResourceRecordSets API call using the function to initiate the failover to the secondary DNS record.
4. Set up a CloudWatch Events rule to monitor the primary Route 53 DNS endpoint and create a custom Lambda function. Execute the ChangeResourceRecordSets API call using the function to initiate the failover to the secondary DNS record.

Answer(s): 2

Explanation

Use an active-passive failover configuration when you want a primary resource or group of resources to be available majority of the time and you want a secondary resource or group of resources to be on standby in case all the primary resources become unavailable. When responding to queries, Route 53 includes only the healthy primary resources. If all the primary resources are unhealthy, Route 53 begins to include only the healthy secondary resources in response to DNS queries.

To create an active-passive failover configuration with one primary record and one secondary record, you just create the records and specify Failover for the routing policy. When the primary resource is healthy, Route 53 responds to DNS queries using the primary record. When the primary resource is unhealthy, Route 53 responds to DNS queries using the secondary record.

You can configure a health check that monitors an endpoint that you specify either by IP address or by domain name. At regular intervals that you specify, Route 53 submits automated requests over the Internet to your application, server, or other resource to verify that it's reachable, available, and functional. Optionally, you can configure the health check to make requests similar to those that your users make, such as requesting a web page from a specific URL.

When Route 53 checks the health of an endpoint, it sends an HTTP, HTTPS, or TCP request to the IP address and port that you specified when you created the health check. For a health check to succeed, your router and firewall rules must allow inbound traffic from the IP addresses that the Route 53 health checkers use.

Hence, the correct answer is: Set up a failover routing policy configuration in Route 53 by adding a health check on the primary service endpoint. Configure Route 53 to direct the DNS queries to the secondary record when the primary resource is unhealthy. Configure the network access control list and the route table to allow Route 53 to send requests to the endpoints specified in the health checks. Enable the Evaluate Target Health option by setting it to Yes.

The option that says: Set up a Weighted routing policy configuration in Route 53 by adding health checks on both the primary stack and the DR environment. Configure the network access control list and the route table to allow Route 53 to send requests to the endpoints specified in the health checks. Enable the Evaluate Target Health option by setting it to Yes is incorrect because Weighted routing simply lets you associate multiple resources with a single domain name (sample.com) or subdomain name (blog. sample.com) and choose how much traffic is routed to each resource. This can be useful for a variety of purposes, including load balancing and testing new versions of software, but not for a failover configuration. Remember that the scenario says that the solution should automatically route the live traffic to the disaster recovery (DR) environment only in the event that the primary application stack experiences an outage. This configuration is incorrectly distributing the traffic on both the primary and DR environment.

The option that says: Set up a CloudWatch Alarm to monitor the primary Route 53 DNS endpoint and create a custom Lambda function. Execute the ChangeResourceRecordSets API call using the function to initiate the failover to the secondary DNS record is incorrect because setting up a CloudWatch Alarm and using the Route 53 API is not applicable nor useful at all in this scenario. Remember that CloudWatch Alam is primarily used for monitoring CloudWatch metrics. You have to use a Failover routing policy instead.

The option that says: Set up a CloudWatch Events rule to monitor the primary Route 53 DNS endpoint and create a custom Lambda function. Execute theChangeResourceRecordSets API call using the function to initiate the failover to the secondary DNS record is incorrect because the Amazon CloudWatch Events service is commonly used to deliver a near real-time stream of system events that describe changes in some Amazon Web Services (AWS) resources. There is no direct way for CloudWatch Events to monitor the status of your Route 53 endpoints. You have to configure a health check and a failover configuration in Route 53 instead to satisfy the requirement in this scenario.

References:

https://docs.aws.amazon.com/Route53/latest/DeveloperGuide/dns-failover-types.html

https://docs.aws.amazon.com/Route53/latest/DeveloperGuide/health-checks-types.html

https://docs.aws.amazon.com/Route53/latest/DeveloperGuide/dns-failover-router-firewall-rules.html

Question 58:

Your company just recently adopted a hybrid architecture that integrates their on-premises data center to their AWS cloud. You are assigned to configure the VPC as well as to implement the required IAM users, IAM roles, IAM groups and IAM policies.

In this scenario, what is a best practice when creating IAM policies?

1. Use the principle of least privilege which means granting only the permissions required to perform a task.
2. Determine what users need to do and then craft policies for them that let the users perform those tasks including additional administrative operations.
3. Use the principle of least privilege which means granting only the least number of people with full root access.
4. Grant all permissions to any EC2 user.

Answer(s): 1

Explanation

One of the best practices in Amazon IAM is to grant least privilege.

When you create IAM policies, follow the standard security advice of granting least privilege—that is, granting only the permissions required to perform a task. Determine what users need to do and then craft policies for them that let the users perform only those tasks. Therefore, using the principle of least privilege which means granting only the permissions required to perform a task is the correct answer.

Start with a minimum set of permissions and grant additional permissions as necessary.

Defining the right set of permissions requires some understanding of the user's objectives. Determine what is required for the specific task, what actions a particular service supports, and what permissions are required in order to perform those actions.

Granting all permissions to any EC2 user is incorrect since you don't want your users to gain access to everything and perform unnecessary actions. Doing so is not a good security practice.

Using the principle of least privilege which means granting only the least number of people with full root access is incorrect because this is not the correct definition of what the principle of least privilege is.

Determining what users need to do and then craft policies for them that let the users perform those tasks including additional administrative operations is incorrect as well since there are some users who you should not give administrative access to. You should follow the principle of least privilege when providing permissions and accesses to your resources.

Reference:

https://docs.aws.amazon.com/IAM/latest/UserGuide/best-practices.html#use-groups-for-permissions

Question 59:

You are working for an online hotel booking firm with terabytes of customer data coming from your websites and applications. There is an annual corporate meeting where you need to present the booking behavior and acquire new insights from your customers' data. You are looking for a service to perform super-fast analytics on massive data sets in near real-time.

Which of the following services gives you the ability to store huge amounts of data and perform quick and flexible queries on it?

1. ElastiCache
2. Redshift
3. DynamoDB
4. RDS

Answer(s): 2

Explanation

Amazon Redshift is a fast, scalable data warehouse that makes it simple and cost-effective to analyze all your data across your data warehouse and data lake. Redshift delivers ten times faster performance than other data warehouses by using machine learning, massively parallel query execution, and columnar storage on high-performance disk.

DynamoDB is incorrect. DynamoDB is a NoSQL database which is based on key-value pairs used for fast processing of small data that dynamically grows and changes. But if you need to scan large amounts of data (ie a lot of keys all in one query), the performance will not be optimal.

ElastiCache is incorrect because this is used to increase the performance, speed and redundancy with which applications can retrieve data by providing an in-memory database caching system, and not for database analytical processes.

RDS is incorrect because this is mainly used for On-Line Transaction Processing (OLTP) applications and not for Online Analytics Processing (OLAP).

References:

https://docs.aws.amazon.com/redshift/latest/mgmt/welcome.html

https://docs.aws.amazon.com/redshift/latest/gsg/getting-started.html

Question 60:

You are working as a Solutions Architect for a leading commercial bank which has recently adopted a hybrid cloud architecture. You have to ensure that the required data security is in place on all of their AWS resources to meet the strict financial regulatory requirements.

In the AWS Shared Responsibility Model, which security aspects are the responsibilities of the customer? (Select TWO.)

1. OS Patching of an EC2 instance
2. Managing the underlying network infrastructure
3. IAM Policies and Credentials Management
4. Physical security of hardware
5. Virtualization infrastructure

Answer(s): 1, 3

Explanation

Security and Compliance is a shared responsibility between AWS and the customer. This shared model can help relieve customer's operational burden as AWS operates, manages and controls the components from the host operating system and virtualization layer down to the physical security of the facilities in which the service operates. The customer assumes responsibility and management of the guest operating system (including updates and security patches), other associated application software as well as the configuration of the AWS provided security group firewall.

Customers should carefully consider the services they choose as their responsibilities vary depending on the services used, the integration of those services into their IT environment, and applicable laws and regulations. The nature of this shared responsibility also provides the flexibility and customer control that permits the deployment. This differentiation of responsibility is commonly referred to as Security "of" the Cloud versus Security "in" the Cloud.

The shared responsibility model for infrastructure services, such as Amazon Elastic Compute Cloud (Amazon EC2) for example, specifies that AWS manages the security of the following assets:

Facilities

Physical security of hardware

Network infrastructure

Virtualization infrastructure

You as the customer are responsible for the security of the following assets:

Amazon Machine Images (AMIs)

Operating systems

Applications

Data in transit

Data at rest

Data stores

Credentials

Policies and configuration

For a better understanding about this topic, refer to the AWS Security Best Practices whitepaper on the reference link below and also the Shared Responsibility Model diagram:

References:

https://d0.awsstatic.com/whitepapers/aws-security-best-practices.pdf

https://aws.amazon.com/compliance/shared-responsibility-model/

Question 61:

You work for a leading university as an AWS Infrastructure Engineer and also as a professor to aspiring AWS architects. As a way to familiarize your students with AWS, you gave them a project to host their applications to an EC2 instance. One of your students created an instance to host their online enrollment system project but is having a hard time connecting to their newly created EC2 instance. Your students have explored all of the troubleshooting guides by AWS and narrowed it down to login issues.

Which of the following can you use to log into an EC2 instance?

1. Key Pairs
2. Custom EC2 password
3. EC2 Connection Strings
4. Access Keys

Answer(s): 1

Explanation

Amazon EC2 uses public–key cryptography to encrypt and decrypt login information. Public–key cryptography uses a public key to encrypt a piece of data, such as a password, then the recipient uses the private key to decrypt the data. The public and private keys are known as a key pair.

To log in to your instance, you must create a key pair, specify the name of the key pair when you launch the instance, and provide the private key when you connect to the instance. On a Linux instance, the public key content is placed in an entry within ~/.ssh/authorized_keys. This is done at boot time and enables you to securely access your instance using the private key instead of a password.

Custom EC2 password and EC2 Connection Strings are incorrect as both do not exist.

Access Keys is incorrect as these are used for API calls and not for logging in to EC2.

Reference:

http://docs.aws.amazon.com/AWSEC2/latest/UserGuide/ec2-key-pairs.html

Question 62:

You developed a web application and deployed it on a fleet of EC2 instances, which is using Amazon SQS. The requests are saved as messages in the SQS queue which is configured with the maximum message retention period. However, after thirteen days of operation, the web application suddenly crashed and there are 10,000 unprocessed messages that are still waiting in the queue. Since you developed the application, you can easily resolve the issue but you need to send a communication to the users on the issue.

What information will you provide and what will happen to the unprocessed messages?

1. Tell the users that unfortunately, they have to resubmit all of the requests since the queue would not be able to process the 10,000 messages together.
2. Tell the users that the application will be operational shortly however, requests sent over three days ago will need to be resubmitted.
3. Tell the users that the application will be operational shortly and all received requests will be processed after the web application is restarted.
4. Tell the users that unfortunately, they have to resubmit all the requests again.

Answer(s): 3

Explanation

In this scenario, it is stated that the SQS queue is configured with the maximum message retention period. The maximum message retention in SQS is 14 days that is why the option that says: Tell the users that the application will be operational shortly and all received requests will be processed after the web application is restarted is the correct answer i.e. there will be no missing messages.

The options that say: Tell the users that unfortunately, they have to resubmit all the requests again and Tell the users that the application will be operational shortly, however, requests sent over three days ago will need to be resubmitted are incorrect as there are no missing messages in the queue thus, there is no need to resubmit any previous requests.

The option that says: Tell the users that unfortunately, they have to resubmit all of the requests since the queue would not be able to process the 10,000 messages together is incorrect as the queue can contain an unlimited number of messages, not just 10,000 messages.

In Amazon SQS, you can configure the message retention period to a value from 1 minute to 14 days. The default is 4 days. Once the message retention limit is reached, your messages are automatically deleted.

A single Amazon SQS message queue can contain an unlimited number of messages. However, there is a 120,000 limit for the number of inflight messages for a standard queue and 20,000 for a FIFO queue. Messages are inflight after they have been received from the queue by a consuming component, but have not yet been deleted from the queue.

Reference:

https://aws.amazon.com/sqs/

Question 63:

A San Francisco-based tech startup is building a cross-platform mobile app that can notify the user with upcoming astronomical events such as eclipses, blue moon, novae or a meteor shower. Your mobile app authenticates with the Identity Provider (IdP) using the provider's SDK and Amazon Cognito. Once the end user is authenticated with the IdP, the OAuth or OpenID Connect token returned from the IdP is passed by your app to Amazon Cognito.

Which of the following is returned for the user to provide a set of temporary, limited-privilege AWS credentials?

1. Cognito ID
2. Cognito API
3. Cognito Key Pair
4. Cognito SDK

Answer(s): 1

Explanation

You can use Amazon Cognito to deliver temporary, limited-privilege credentials to your application so that your users can access AWS resources. Amazon Cognito identity pools support both authenticated and unauthenticated identities. You can retrieve a unique Amazon Cognito identifier (identity ID) for your end user immediately if you're allowing unauthenticated users or after you've set the login tokens in the credentials provider if you're authenticating users.

That is why the correct answer for this question is Cognito ID.

Cognito SDK is incorrect because this is not a unique Amazon Cognito identifier but a software development kit that is available in various programming languages.

Cognito Key Pair is incorrect because this is not a unique Amazon Cognito identifier but a cryptography key.

Cognito API is incorrect because this is not a unique Amazon Cognito identifier and is primarily used as an Application Programming Interface.

Reference:

http://docs.aws.amazon.com/cognito/latest/developerguide/getting-credentials.html

Question 64:

You are working as a Cloud Consultant for a government agency with a mandate of improving traffic planning, maintenance of roadways and preventing accidents. There is a need to manage traffic infrastructure in real time, alert traffic engineers and emergency response teams when problems are detected, and automatically change traffic signals to get emergency personnel to accident scenes faster by using sensors and smart devices.

Which AWS service will allow the developers of the agency to connect the said devices to your cloud-based applications?

1. Container service
2. CloudFormation
3. Elastic Beanstalk
4. AWS IoT Core

Answer(s): 4

Explanation

AWS IoT Core is a managed cloud service that lets connected devices easily and securely interact with cloud applications and other devices. AWS IoT Core provides secure communication and data processing across different kinds of connected devices and locations so you can easily build IoT applications.

CloudFormation is incorrect because this is mainly used for creating and managing the architecture and not for handling connected devices. You have to use AWS IoT Core instead.

Elastic Beanstalk is incorrect because this is mainly used as a substitute to Infrastructure-as-a-Service with Platform-as-a-Service, which reduces management complexity without restricting choice or control and not for handling connected devices.

Container service is incorrect because this is mainly used for creating and managing docker instances and not for handling devices.

References:

https://aws.amazon.com/iot-core/

https://aws.amazon.com/iot/

Question 65:

The operations team of your company asked you for a way to monitor the health of your production EC2 instances in AWS. You told them to use the CloudWatch service.

Which of the following metrics is not available by default in CloudWatch?

1. Disk Read operations
2. CPU Usage
3. Network In and Out
4. Memory Usage

Answer(s): 4

Explanation

Memory Usage is a metric not available by default in CloudWatch. You need to add a custom metric for it to work.

Reference:

http://docs.aws.amazon.com/AWSEC2/latest/UserGuide/mon-scripts.html

PRACTICE
TEST
3

AWS CERTIFIED SOLUTIONS ARCHITECT ASSOCIATE

AWS CERTIFIED SOLUTIONS ARCHITECT ASSOCIATE PRACTICE TEST 3

Question 1:

Your company has an e-commerce application that saves the transaction logs to an S3 bucket. You are instructed by the CTO to configure the application to keep the transaction logs for one month for troubleshooting purposes, and then afterwards, purge the logs. What should you do to accomplish this requirement?

1. Enable CORS on the Amazon S3 bucket which will enable the automatic monthly deletion of data
2. Add a new bucket policy on the Amazon S3 bucket.
3. (Incorrect)
4. Configure the lifecycle configuration rules on the Amazon S3 bucket to purge the transaction logs after a month
5. Create a new IAM policy for the Amazon S3 bucket that automatically deletes the logs after a month

Answer(s): 4

Explanation

In this scenario, the best way to accomplish the requirement is to simply configure the lifecycle configuration rules on the Amazon S3 bucket to purge the transaction logs after a month.

Lifecycle configuration enables you to specify the lifecycle management of objects in a bucket. The configuration is a set of one or more rules, where each rule defines an action for Amazon S3 to apply to a group of objects. These actions can be classified as follows:

Transition actions – In which you define when objects transition to another storage class. For example, you may choose to transition objects to the STANDARD_IA (IA, for infrequent access) storage class 30 days after creation, or archive objects to the GLACIER storage class one year after creation.

Expiration actions – In which you specify when the objects expire. Then Amazon S3 deletes the expired objects on your behalf.

Adding a new bucket policy on the Amazon S3 bucket is incorrect as it does not provide a solution to any of your needs in this scenario. You add a bucket policy to a bucket to grant other AWS accounts or IAM users access permissions for the bucket and the objects in it.

Creating a new IAM policy for the Amazon S3 bucket that automatically deletes the logs after a month is incorrect because IAM policies are primarily used to specify what actions are allowed or denied on your S3 buckets. You cannot configure an IAM policy to automatically purge logs for you in any way.

Enabling CORS on the Amazon S3 bucket which will enable the automatic monthly deletion of data is incorrect. CORS allows client web applications that are loaded in one domain to interact with resources in a different domain.

Reference:

https://docs.aws.amazon.com/AmazonS3/latest/dev/object-lifecycle-mgmt.html

Question 2:

You are working for a large financial firm and you are instructed to set up a Linux bastion host. It will allow access to the Amazon EC2 instances running in their VPC. For security purposes, only the clients connecting from the corporate external public IP address 175.45.116.100 should have SSH access to the host.

Which is the best option that can meet the customer's requirement?

1. Network ACL Inbound Rule: Protocol – TCP, Port Range-22, Source 175.45.116.100/0
2. Security Group Inbound Rule: Protocol – TCP. Port Range – 22, Source 175.45.116.100/32
3. Network ACL Inbound Rule: Protocol – UDP, Port Range – 22, Source 175.45.116.100/32
4. Security Group Inbound Rule: Protocol – UDP, Port Range – 22, Source 175.45.116.100/32

Answer(s): 2

Explanation

A bastion host is a special purpose computer on a network specifically designed and configured to withstand attacks. The computer generally hosts a single application, for example a proxy server, and all other services are removed or limited to reduce the threat to the computer.

When setting up a bastion host in AWS, you should only allow the individual IP of the client and not the entire network. Therefore, in the Source, the proper CIDR notation should be used. The /32 denotes one IP address and the /0 refers to the entire network.

The option that says: Security Group Inbound Rule: Protocol – UDP, Port Range – 22, Source 175.45.116.100/32 is incorrect since the SSH protocol uses TCP and port 22, and not UDP.

The option that says: Network ACL Inbound Rule: Protocol – UDP, Port Range – 22, Source 175.45.116.100/32 is incorrect since the SSH protocol uses TCP and port 22, and not UDP. Aside from that, network ACLs act as a firewall for your whole VPC subnet, while security groups operate on an instance level. Since you are securing an EC2 instance, you should be using security groups.

The option that says: Network ACL Inbound Rule: Protocol – TCP, Port Range-22, Source 175.45.116.100/0 is incorrect as it allowed the entire network instead of a single IP to gain access to the host.

Reference:

http://docs.aws.amazon.com/AWSEC2/latest/UserGuide/ec2-instance-metadata.html

Question 3:

You are working for an investment bank as their IT Consultant. You are working with their IT team to handle the launch of their digital wallet system. The applications will run on multiple EBS-backed EC2 instances which will store the logs, transactions, and billing statements of the user in an S3 bucket. Due to tight security and compliance requirements, you are exploring options on how to safely store sensitive data on the EBS volumes and S3.

Which of the below options should be carried out when storing sensitive data on AWS? (Select TWO.)

1. Enable Amazon S3 Server-Side or use Client-Side Encryption
2. Enable EBS Encryption
3. Use AWS Shield and WAF
4. Create an EBS Snapshot
5. Migrate the EC2 instances from the public to private subnet.

Answer(s): 1, 2

Explanation

Enabling EBS Encryption and enabling Amazon S3 Server-Side or use Client-Side Encryption are correct. Amazon EBS encryption offers a simple encryption solution for your EBS volumes without the need to build, maintain, and secure your own key management infrastructure.

In Amazon S3, data protection refers to protecting data while in-transit (as it travels to and from Amazon S3) and at rest (while it is stored on disks in Amazon S3 data centers). You can protect data in transit by using SSL or by using client-side encryption. You have the following options to protect data at rest in Amazon S3.

Use Server-Side Encryption – You request Amazon S3 to encrypt your object before saving it on disks in its data centers and decrypt it when you download the objects.

Use Client-Side Encryption – You can encrypt data client-side and upload the encrypted data to Amazon S3. In this case, you manage the encryption process, the encryption keys, and related tools.

Creating an EBS Snapshot is incorrect because this is a backup solution of EBS. It does not provide security of data inside EBS volumes when executed.

Migrating the EC2 instances from the public to private subnet is incorrect because the data you want to secure are those in EBS volumes and S3 buckets. Moving your EC2 instance to a private subnet involves a different matter of security practice, which does not achieve what you want in this scenario.

Using AWS Shield and WAF is incorrect because these protect you from common security threats for your web applications. However, what you are trying to achieve is securing and encrypting your data inside EBS and S3.

References:

http://docs.aws.amazon.com/AWSEC2/latest/UserGuide/EBSEncryption.html

http://docs.aws.amazon.com/AmazonS3/latest/dev/UsingEncryption.html

Question 4:

You are a Solutions Architect in your company where you are tasked to set up a cloud infrastructure. In the planning, it was discussed that you will need two EC2 instances which should continuously run for three years. The CPU utilization of the EC2 instances is also expected to be stable and predictable.

Which is the most cost-efficient Amazon EC2 Pricing type that is most appropriate for this scenario?

1. Reserved Instances
2. On-Demand instances
3. Dedicated Hosts
4. Spot instances

Answer(s): 1

Explanation

Reserved Instances provide you with a significant discount (up to 75%) compared to On-Demand instance pricing. In addition, when Reserved Instances are assigned to a specific Availability Zone, they provide a capacity reservation, giving you additional confidence in your ability to launch instances when you need them.

For applications that have steady state or predictable usage, Reserved Instances can provide significant savings compared to using On-Demand instances.

Reserved Instances are recommended for:

- Applications with steady state usage

- Applications that may require reserved capacity

- Customers that can commit to using EC2 over a 1 or 3 year term to reduce their total computing costs

References:

https://aws.amazon.com/ec2/pricing/

https://aws.amazon.com/ec2/pricing/reserved-instances/

Question 5:

An online stocks trading application that stores financial data in an S3 bucket has a lifecycle policy that moves older data to Glacier every month. There is a strict compliance requirement where a surprise audit can happen at anytime and you should be able to retrieve the required data in under 15 minutes under all circumstances. Your manager instructed you to ensure that retrieval capacity is available when you need it and should handle up to 150 MB/s of retrieval throughput.

Which of the following should you do to meet the above requirement? (Select TWO.)

1. Use Bulk Retrieval to access the financial data.
2. Specify a range, or portion, of the financial data archive to retrieve.
3. Retrieve the data using Amazon Glacier Select.
4. Purchase provisioned retrieval capacity.
5. Use Expedited Retrieval to access the financial data.

Answer(s): 4, 5

Explanation

Expedited retrievals allow you to quickly access your data when occasional urgent requests for a subset of archives are required. For all but the largest archives (250 MB+), data accessed using Expedited retrievals are typically made available within 1–5 minutes. Provisioned Capacity ensures that retrieval capacity for Expedited retrievals is available when you need it.

To make an Expedited, Standard, or Bulk retrieval, set the Tier parameter in the Initiate Job (POST jobs) REST API request to the option you want, or the equivalent in the AWS CLI or AWS SDKs. If you have purchased provisioned capacity, then all expedited retrievals are automatically served through your provisioned capacity.

Provisioned capacity ensures that your retrieval capacity for expedited retrievals is available when you need it. Each unit of capacity provides that at least three expedited retrievals can be performed every five minutes and provides up to 150 MB/s of retrieval throughput. You should purchase provisioned retrieval capacity if your workload requires highly reliable and predictable access to a subset of your data in minutes. Without provisioned capacity Expedited retrievals are accepted, except for rare situations of unusually high demand. However, if you require access to Expedited retrievals under all circumstances, you must purchase provisioned retrieval capacity.

Retrieving the data using Amazon Glacier Select is incorrect because this is not an archive retrieval option and is primarily used to perform filtering operations using simple Structured Query Language (SQL) statements directly on your data archive in Glacier.

Using Bulk Retrieval to access the financial data is incorrect because bulk retrievals typically complete within 5–12 hours hence, this does not satisfy the requirement of retrieving the data within 15 minutes. The provisioned capacity option is also not compatible with Bulk retrievals.

Specifying a range, or portion, of the financial data archive to retrieve is incorrect because using ranged archive retrievals is not enough to meet the requirement of retrieving the whole archive in the given timeframe. In addition, it does not provide additional retrieval capacity which is what the provisioned capacity option can offer.

References:

https://docs.aws.amazon.com/amazonglacier/latest/dev/downloading-an-archive-two-steps.html

https://docs.aws.amazon.com/amazonglacier/latest/dev/glacier-select.html

Question 6:

You are working as an IT Consultant for a large investment bank that generates large financial datasets with millions of rows. The data must be stored in a columnar fashion to reduce the number of disk I/O requests and reduce the amount of data needed to load from the disk. The bank has an existing third-party business intelligence application which will connect to the storage service and then generate daily and monthly financial reports for its clients around the globe.

In this scenario, which is the best storage service to use to meet the requirement?

1. Amazon Redshift
2. Amazon Aurora
3. Amazon RDS

4. DynamoDB

Answer(s): 1

Explanation

Amazon Redshift is a fast, scalable data warehouse that makes it simple and cost-effective to analyze all your data across your data warehouse and data lake. Redshift delivers ten times faster performance than other data warehouses by using machine learning, massively parallel query execution, and columnar storage on high-performance disk.

In this scenario, there is a requirement to have a storage service which will be used by a business intelligence application and where the data must be stored in a columnar fashion. Business Intelligence reporting systems is a type of Online Analytical Processing (OLAP) which Redshift is known to support. In addition, Redshift also provides columnar storage unlike the other options. Hence, the correct answer in this scenario is Amazon Redshift.

References:

https://docs.aws.amazon.com/redshift/latest/dg/c_columnar_storage_disk_mem_mgmnt.html

https://aws.amazon.com/redshift/

Here is a case study on finding the most suitable analytical tool - Kinesis vs EMR vs Athena vs Redshift:

https://youtu.be/wEOm6aiN4ww

Question 7:

A data analytics company is setting up an innovative checkout-free grocery store. Their Solutions Architect developed a real-time monitoring application that uses smart sensors to collect the items that the customers are getting from the grocery's refrigerators and shelves then automatically deduct it from their accounts. The company wants to analyze the items that are frequently being bought and store the results in S3 for durable storage to determine the purchase behavior of its customers.

What service must be used to easily capture, transform, and load streaming data into Amazon S3, Amazon Elasticsearch Service, and Splunk?

1. Amazon SQS
2. Amazon Kinesis
3. Amazon Redshift
4. Amazon Kinesis Data Firehose

Answer(s): 4

Explanation

Amazon Kinesis Data Firehose is the easiest way to load streaming data into data stores and analytics tools. It can capture, transform, and load streaming data into Amazon S3, Amazon Redshift, Amazon Elasticsearch Service, and Splunk, enabling near real-time analytics with existing business intelligence tools and dashboards you are already using today.

It is a fully managed service that automatically scales to match the throughput of your data and requires no ongoing administration. It can also batch, compress, and encrypt the data before loading it, minimizing the amount of storage used at the destination and increasing security.

In the diagram below, you gather the data from your smart refrigerators and use Kinesis Data firehouse to prepare and load the data. S3 will be used as a method of durably storing the data for analytics and the eventual ingestion of data for output using analytical tools.

You can use Amazon Kinesis Data Firehose in conjunction with Amazon Kinesis Data Streams if you need to implement real-time processing of streaming big data. Kinesis Data Streams provides ordering of records, as well as the ability to read and/or replay records in the same order to multiple Amazon Kinesis Applications. The Amazon Kinesis Client Library (KCL) delivers all records for a given partition key to the same record processor, making it easier to build multiple applications reading from the same Amazon Kinesis data stream (for example, to perform counting, aggregation, and filtering).

Amazon Simple Queue Service (Amazon SQS) is different from Amazon Kinesis Data Firehose. SQS offers a reliable, highly scalable hosted queue for storing messages as they travel between computers. Amazon SQS lets you easily move data between distributed application components and helps you build applications in which messages are processed independently (with message-level ack/fail semantics), such as automated workflows. Amazon Firehose Data Firehose is primarily used to load streaming data into data stores and analytics tools.

Hence, the correct answer is: Amazon Kinesis Data Firehose.

Amazon Kinesis is incorrect because this is the streaming data platform of AWS and has four distinct services under it: Kinesis Data Firehose, Kinesis Data Streams, Kinesis Video Streams, and Amazon Kinesis Data Analytics. For the specific use case just as asked in the scenario, use Kinesis Data Firehose.

Amazon Redshift is incorrect because this is mainly used for data warehousing making it simple and cost-effective to analyze your data across your data warehouse and data lake. It does not meet the requirement of being able to load and stream data into data stores for analytics. You have to use Kinesis Data Firehose instead.

Amazon SQS is incorrect because you can't capture, transform, and load streaming data into Amazon S3, Amazon Elasticsearch Service, and Splunk using this service. You have to use Kinesis Data Firehose instead.

References:

https://aws.amazon.com/kinesis/data-firehose/

https://aws.amazon.com/kinesis/data-streams/faqs/

Question 8:

Your company is in a hurry of deploying their new web application written in NodeJS to AWS. As the Solutions Architect of the company, you were assigned to do the deployment without worrying about the underlying infrastructure that runs the application. Which service will you use to easily deploy and manage your new web application in AWS?

1. AWS CodeCommit
2. Amazon CloudFront
3. AWS CloudFormation
4. AWS Elastic Beanstalk

Answer(s): 4

Explanation

With Elastic Beanstalk, you can quickly deploy and manage applications in the AWS Cloud without worrying about the infrastructure that runs those applications. AWS Elastic Beanstalk reduces management complexity without restricting choice or control. You simply upload your application, and Elastic Beanstalk automatically handles the details of capacity provisioning, load balancing, scaling, and application health monitoring.

Amazon CloudFront is incorrect because this is a fast content delivery network (CDN) service that securely delivers data, videos, applications, and APIs to customers globally with low latency and high transfer speeds. It does not provide any deployment capability for your custom applications unlike Elastic Beanstalk.

AWS CloudFormation is incorrect because although this service provides deployment capabilities, you will still have to design a custom template that contains the required AWS resources for your application needs. Hence, this will require more time to complete instead of just directly using Elastic Beanstalk.

AWS CodeCommit is incorrect because although you can upload your NodeJS code in AWS CloudCommit, this service is just a fully-managed source control service that hosts secure Git-based repositories and hence, it does not provide a way to deploy or manage your applications in AWS.

Reference:

https://docs.aws.amazon.com/elasticbeanstalk/latest/dg/Welcome.html

Question 9:

You are working as a Solutions Architect for an aerospace manufacturer which heavily uses AWS. They are running a prototype high performance computing (HPC) cluster that spans multiple EC2 instances across multiple Availability Zones, which processes various wind simulation models. Currently, you are experiencing a slowdown in your applications and upon further investigation, it was discovered that it was due to latency issues.

Which is the MOST suitable solution that you should implement to provide low-latency network performance necessary for tightly-coupled node-to-node communication of your HPC cluster?

1. Use EC2 Dedicated Instances.
2. Set up a cluster placement group within a single Availability Zone in the same AWS Region.
3. Set up AWS Direct Connect connections across multiple Availability Zones for increased bandwidth throughput and more consistent network experience.
4. Set up a spread placement group across multiple Availability Zones in multiple AWS Regions.

Answer(s): 2

Explanation

When you launch a new EC2 instance, the EC2 service attempts to place the instance in such a way that all of your instances are spread out across underlying hardware to minimize correlated failures. You can use placement groups to influence the placement of a group of interdependent instances to meet the needs of your workload. Depending on the type of workload, you can create a placement group using one of the following placement strategies:

Cluster – packs instances close together inside an Availability Zone. This strategy enables workloads to achieve the low-latency network performance necessary for tightly-coupled node-to-node communication that is typical of HPC applications.

Partition – spreads your instances across logical partitions such that groups of instances in one partition do not share the underlying hardware with groups of instances in different partitions. This strategy is typically used by large distributed and replicated workloads, such as Hadoop, Cassandra, and Kafka.

Spread – strictly places a small group of instances across distinct underlying hardware to reduce correlated failures.

Cluster placement groups are recommended for applications that benefit from low network latency, high network throughput, or both. They are also recommended when the majority of the network traffic is between the instances in the group. To provide the lowest latency and the highest packet-per-second network performance for your placement group, choose an instance type that supports enhanced networking.

Partition placement groups can be used to deploy large distributed and replicated workloads, such as HDFS, HBase, and Cassandra, across distinct racks. When you launch instances into a partition placement group, Amazon EC2 tries to distribute the instances evenly across the number of partitions that you specify. You can also launch instances into a specific partition to have more control over where the instances are placed.

Spread placement groups are recommended for applications that have a small number of critical instances that should be kept separate from each other. Launching instances in a spread placement group reduces the risk of simultaneous failures that might occur when instances share the same racks. Spread placement groups provide access to distinct racks, and are therefore suitable for mixing instance types or launching instances over time. A spread placement group can span multiple Availability Zones in the same Region. You can have a maximum of seven running instances per Availability Zone per group.

Hence, the correct answer is: Set up a cluster placement group within a single Availability Zone in the same AWS Region.

The option that says: Set up a spread placement group across multiple Availability Zones in multiple AWS Regions is incorrect because although using a placement group is valid for this particular scenario, you can only set up a placement group in a single AWS Region only. A spread placement group can span multiple Availability Zones in the same Region.

The option that says: Set up AWS Direct Connect connections across multiple Availability Zones for increased bandwidth throughput and more consistent network experience is incorrect because this is primarily used for hybrid architectures. It bypasses the public Internet and establishes a secure, dedicated connection from your on-premises data center into AWS, and not used for having low latency within your AWS network.

The option that says: Use EC2 Dedicated Instances is incorrect because these are EC2 instances that run in a VPC on hardware that is dedicated to a single customer and are physically isolated at the host hardware level from instances that belong to other AWS accounts. It is not used for reducing latency.

References:

http://docs.aws.amazon.com/AWSEC2/latest/UserGuide/placement-groups.html

https://aws.amazon.com/hpc/

Question 10:

You are working as a Solutions Architect for a leading airline company where you are building a decoupled application in AWS using EC2, Auto Scaling group, S3 and SQS. You designed the architecture in such a way that the EC2 instances will consume the message from the SQS queue and will automatically scale up or down based on the number of messages in the queue.

In this scenario, which of the following statements is false about SQS?

1. FIFO queues provide exactly-once processing.
2. Standard queues provide at-least-once delivery, which means that each message is delivered at least once.
3. Standard queues preserve the order of messages.
4. Amazon SQS can help you build a distributed application with decoupled components.

Answer(s): 3

Explanation

All of the answers are correct except for the option that says: Standard queues preserve the order of messages. Only FIFO queues can preserve the order of messages and not standard queues.

Reference:

https://aws.amazon.com/sqs/faqs/

Question 11:

A Solutions Architect working for a startup is designing a High Performance Computing (HPC) application which is publicly accessible for their customers. The startup founders want to mitigate distributed denial-of-service (DDoS) attacks on their application.

Which of the following options are not suitable to be implemented in this scenario? (Select TWO.)

1. Use Dedicated EC2 instances to ensure that each instance has the maximum performance possible.

2. Use an Application Load Balancer with Auto Scaling groups for your EC2 instances then restrict direct Internet traffic to your Amazon RDS database by deploying to a private subnet.
3. Use AWS Shield and AWS WAF.
4. Add multiple Elastic Fabric Adapters (EFA) to each EC2 instance to increase the network bandwidth.
5. Use an Amazon CloudFront service for distributing both static and dynamic content.

Answer(s): 1, 4

Explanation

Take note that the question asks about the viable mitigation techniques that are NOT suitable to prevent Distributed Denial of Service (DDoS) attack.

A Denial of Service (DoS) attack is an attack that can make your website or application unavailable to end users. To achieve this, attackers use a variety of techniques that consume network or other resources, disrupting access for legitimate end users.

To protect your system from DDoS attack, you can do the following:

- Use an Amazon CloudFront service for distributing both static and dynamic content.

- Use an Application Load Balancer with Auto Scaling groups for your EC2 instances then restrict direct Internet traffic to your Amazon RDS database by deploying to a private subnet.

- Set up alerts in Amazon CloudWatch to look for high Network In and CPU utilization metrics.

Services that are available within AWS Regions, like Elastic Load Balancing and Amazon Elastic Compute Cloud (EC2), allow you to build Distributed Denial of Service resiliency and scale to handle unexpected volumes of traffic within a given region. Services that are available in AWS edge locations, like Amazon CloudFront, AWS WAF, Amazon Route53, and Amazon API Gateway, allow you to take advantage of a global network of edge locations that can provide your application with greater fault tolerance and increased scale for managing larger volumes of traffic.

In addition, you can also use AWS Shield and AWS WAF to fortify your cloud network. AWS Shield is a managed DDoS protection service that is available in two tiers: Standard and Advanced. AWS Shield Standard applies always-on detection and inline mitigation techniques, such as deterministic packet filtering and priority-based traffic shaping, to minimize application downtime and latency.

AWS WAF is a web application firewall that helps protect web applications from common web exploits that could affect application availability, compromise security, or consume excessive resources. You can use AWS WAF to define customizable web security rules that control which traffic accesses your web applications. If you use AWS Shield Advanced, you can use AWS WAF at no extra cost for those protected resources and can engage the DRT to create WAF rules.

Using Dedicated EC2 instances to ensure that each instance has the maximum performance possible is not a viable mitigation technique because Dedicated EC2 instances are just an instance billing option. Although it may ensure that each instance gives the maximum performance, that by itself is not enough to mitigate a DDoS attack.

Adding multiple Elastic Fabric Adapters (EFA) to each EC2 instance to increase the network bandwidth is also not a viable option as this is mainly done for performance improvement, and not for DDoS attack mitigation. Moreover, you can attach only one EFA per EC2 instance. An Elastic Fabric Adapter (EFA) is a network device that you can attach to your Amazon EC2 instance to accelerate High-Performance Computing (HPC) and machine learning applications.

The following options are valid mitigation techniques that can be used to prevent DDoS:

- Use an Amazon CloudFront service for distributing both static and dynamic content.

- Use an Application Load Balancer with Auto Scaling groups for your EC2 instances then restrict direct Internet traffic to your Amazon RDS database by deploying to a private subnet.

- Use AWS Shield and AWS WAF.

References:

https://aws.amazon.com/answers/networking/aws-ddos-attack-mitigation/

https://d0.awsstatic.com/whitepapers/DDoS_White_Paper_June2015.pdf

Best practices on DDoS Attack Mitigation:

https://youtu.be/HnoZS5jj7pk/

Question 12:

Your web application is relying entirely on slower disk-based databases, causing it to perform slowly. To improve its performance, you integrated an in-memory data store to your web application using ElastiCache. How does Amazon ElastiCache improve database performance?

1. It reduces the load on your database by routing read queries from your applications to the Read Replica.
2. It securely delivers data to customers globally with low latency and high transfer speeds.

3. By caching database query results.
4. It provides an in-memory cache that delivers up to 10x performance improvement from milliseconds to microseconds or even at millions of requests per second.

Answer(s): 3

Explanation

ElastiCache improves the performance of your database through caching query results.

The primary purpose of an in-memory key-value store is to provide ultra-fast (submillisecond latency) and inexpensive access to copies of data. Most data stores have areas of data that are frequently accessed but seldom updated. Additionally, querying a database is always slower and more expensive than locating a key in a key-value pair cache. Some database queries are especially expensive to perform, for example, queries that involve joins across multiple tables or queries with intensive calculations.

By caching such query results, you pay the price of the query once and then are able to quickly retrieve the data multiple times without having to re-execute the query.

The option that says: It securely delivers data to customers globally with low latency and high transfer speeds is incorrect because this option describes what CloudFront does and not ElastiCache.

The option that says: It provides an in-memory cache that delivers up to 10x performance improvement from milliseconds to microseconds or even at millions of requests per second is incorrect because this option describes what Amazon DynamoDB Accelerator (DAX) does and not ElastiCache. Amazon DynamoDB Accelerator (DAX) is a fully managed, highly available, in-memory cache for DynamoDB. Amazon ElastiCache cannot provide a performance improvement from milliseconds to microseconds, let alone millions of requests per second like DAX can.

The option that says: It reduces the load on your database by routing read queries from your applications to the Read Replica is incorrect because this option describes what an RDS Read Replica does and not ElastiCache. Amazon RDS Read Replicas enable you to create one or more read-only copies of your database instance within the same AWS Region or in a different AWS Region.

References:

https://aws.amazon.com/elasticache/

https://docs.aws.amazon.com/AmazonElastiCache/latest/red-ug/elasticache-use-cases.html

Question 13:

You are working for a large financial firm in the country. They have an AWS environment which contains several Reserved EC2 instances hosted in a web application that has been decommissioned last week. To save cost, you need to stop incurring charges for the Reserved instances as soon as possible.

What cost-effective steps will you take in this circumstance? (Select TWO.)

1. Go to the AWS Reserved Instance Marketplace and sell the Reserved instances.
2. Contact AWS to cancel your AWS subscription.
3. Go to the Amazon.com online shopping website and sell the Reserved instances.
4. Stop the Reserved instances as soon as possible.
5. Terminate the Reserved instances as soon as possible to avoid getting billed at the on-demand price when it expires.

Answer(s): 1, 5

Explanation

The correct options are:

- Go to the AWS Reserved Instance Marketplace and sell the Reserved instances.

- Terminate the Reserved instances as soon as possible to avoid getting billed at the on-demand price when it expires.

The Reserved Instance Marketplace is a platform that supports the sale of third-party and AWS customers' unused Standard Reserved Instances, which vary in terms of lengths and pricing options. For example, you may want to sell Reserved Instances after moving instances to a new AWS region, changing to a new instance type, ending projects before the term expiration, when your business needs change, or if you have unneeded capacity.

Stopping the Reserved instances as soon as possible is incorrect because a stopped instance can still be restarted. Take note that when a Reserved Instance expires, any instances that were covered by the Reserved Instance are billed at the on-demand price which costs significantly higher. Since the application is already decommissioned, there is no point of keeping the unused instances. It is also possible that there are associated Elastic IP addresses, which will incur charges if they are associated with stopped instances

Contacting AWS to cancel your AWS subscription is incorrect as you don't need to close down your AWS account.

Going to the Amazon.com online shopping website and selling the Reserved instances is incorrect as you have to use AWS Reserved Instance Marketplace to sell your instances.

References:

https://docs.aws.amazon.com/AWSEC2/latest/UserGuide/ri-market-general.html

https://docs.aws.amazon.com/AWSEC2/latest/UserGuide/ec2-instance-lifecycle.html

Question 14:

In Amazon EC2, you can manage your instances from the moment you launch them up to their termination. You can flexibly control your computing costs by changing the EC2 instance state. Which of the following statements is true regarding EC2 billing? (Select TWO.)

1. You will be billed when your On-Demand instance is preparing to hibernate with a stopping state.
2. You will not be billed for any instance usage while an instance is not in the running state.
3. You will be billed when your Spot instance is preparing to stop with a stopping state.
4. You will be billed when your Reserved instance is in terminated state.
5. You will be billed when your On-Demand instance is in pending state.

Answer(s): 1, 4

Explanation

By working with Amazon EC2 to manage your instances from the moment you launch them through their termination, you ensure that your customers have the best possible experience with the applications or sites that you host on your instances. The following illustration represents the transitions between instance states. Notice that you can't stop and start an instance store-backed instance:

Below are the valid EC2 lifecycle instance states:

pending - The instance is preparing to enter the running state. An instance enters the pending state when it launches for the first time, or when it is restarted after being in the stopped state.

running - The instance is running and ready for use.

stopping - The instance is preparing to be stopped. Take note that you will not billed if it is preparing to stop however, you will still be billed if it is just preparing to hibernate.

stopped - The instance is shut down and cannot be used. The instance can be restarted at any time.

shutting-down - The instance is preparing to be terminated.

terminated - The instance has been permanently deleted and cannot be restarted. Take note that Reserved Instances that applied to terminated instances are still billed until the end of their term according to their payment option.

The option that says: You will be billed when your On-Demand instance is preparing to hibernate with a stopping state is correct because when the instance state is stopping, you will not billed if it is preparing to stop however, you will still be billed if it is just preparing to hibernate.

The option that says: You will be billed when your Reserved instance is in terminated state is correct because Reserved Instances that applied to terminated instances are still billed until the end of their term according to their payment option. I actually raised a pull-request to Amazon team about the billing conditions for Reserved Instances, which has been approved and reflected on your official AWS Documentation: https://github.com/awsdocs/amazon-ec2-user-guide/pull/45

The option that says: You will be billed when your On-Demand instance is in pending state is incorrect because you will not be billed if your instance is in pending state.

The option that says: You will be billed when your Spot instance is preparing to stop with a stopping state is incorrect because you will not be billed if your instance is preparing to stop with a stopping state.

The option that says: You will not be billed for any instance usage while an instance is not in the running state is incorrect because the statement is not entirely true. You can still be billed if your instance is preparing to hibernate with a stopping state.

References:

https://github.com/awsdocs/amazon-ec2-user-guide/pull/45

http://docs.aws.amazon.com/AWSEC2/latest/UserGuide/ec2-instance-lifecycle.html

Question 15:

You are working for a tech company that uses a lot of EBS volumes in their EC2 instances. An incident occurred that requires you to delete the EBS volumes and then re-create them again.

What step should you do before you delete the EBS volumes?

1. Store a snapshot of the volume.
2. Download the content to an EC2 instance.
3. Create a copy of the EBS volume using the CopyEBSVolume command.
4. Back up the data into a physical disk.

Answer(s): 1

Explanation

You can back up the data on your Amazon EBS volumes to Amazon S3 by taking point-in-time snapshots. Snapshots are incremental backups, which means that only the blocks on the device that have changed after your most recent snapshot are saved.

When you no longer need an Amazon EBS volume, you can delete it. After deletion, its data is gone and the volume can't be attached to any instance. However, before deletion, you can store a snapshot of the volume, which you can use to re-create the volume later.

Creating a copy of the EBS volume using the CopyEBSVolume command is incorrect as there is no such thing as CopyEBSVolume command.

Downloading the content to an EC2 instance and backing up the data into a physical disk are both incorrect as these actions take a lot of time. The best and easiest way is to create a snapshot.

Reference:

http://docs.aws.amazon.com/AWSEC2/latest/UserGuide/ebs-deleting-volume.html

Question 16:

You were recently promoted to a technical lead role in your DevOps team. Your company has an existing VPC which is quite unutilized for the past few months. The business manager instructed you to integrate your on-premises data center and your VPC. You explained the list of tasks that you'll be doing and mentioned about a Virtual Private Network (VPN) connection. The business manager is not tech-savvy but he is interested to know what a VPN is and its benefits.

What is one of the major advantages of having a VPN in AWS?

1. It provides a cost-effective, hybrid connection from your VPC to your on-premises data centers which bypasses the public Internet.
2. It allows you to connect your AWS cloud resources to your on-premises data center using secure and private sessions with IP Security (IPSec) or Transport Layer Security (TLS) tunnels.
3. It enables you to establish a private and dedicated network connection between your network and your VPC
4. It provides a networking connection between two VPCs which enables you to route traffic between them using private IPv4 addresses or IPv6 addresses.

Answer(s): 2

Explanation

Amazon VPC offers you the flexibility to fully manage both sides of your Amazon VPC connectivity by creating a VPN connection between your remote network and a software VPN appliance running in your Amazon VPC network. This option is recommended if you must manage both ends of the VPN connection either for compliance purposes or for leveraging gateway devices that are not currently supported by Amazon VPC's VPN solution.

You can create an IPsec VPN connection between your VPC and your remote network. On the AWS side of the VPN connection, a virtual private gateway provides two VPN endpoints (tunnels) for automatic failover. You configure your customer gateway on the remote side of the VPN connection. If you have more than one remote network (for example, multiple branch offices), you can create multiple AWS managed VPN connections via your virtual private gateway to enable communication between these networks.

With AWS Site-to-Site VPN, you can connect to an Amazon VPC in the cloud the same way you connect to your branches. AWS Site-to-Site VPN establishes secure and private sessions with IP Security (IPSec) and Transport Layer Security (TLS) tunnels.

Hence, the correct answer is the option that says: It allows you to connect your AWS cloud resources to your on-premises data center using secure and private sessions with IP Security (IPSec) or Transport Layer Security (TLS) tunnels since one of the main advantages of having a VPN connection is that you will be able to connect your Amazon VPC to other remote networks securely.

The option that says: It provides a cost-effective, hybrid connection from your VPC to your on-premises data centers which bypasses the public Internet is incorrect because although it is true that a VPN provides a cost-effective, hybrid connection from your VPC to your on-premises data centers, it certainly does not bypass the public Internet. A VPN connection actually goes through the public Internet, unlike the AWS Direct Connect connection which has a direct and dedicated connection to your on-premises network.

The option that says: It provides a networking connection between two VPCs which enables you to route traffic between them using private IPv4 addresses or IPv6 addresses is incorrect because this actually describes VPC Peering and not a VPN connection.

The option that says: It enables you to establish a private and dedicated network connection between your network and your VPC is incorrect because this is the advantage of an AWS Direct Connect connection and not a VPN.

References:

http://docs.aws.amazon.com/AmazonVPC/latest/UserGuide/vpn-connections.html

https://docs.aws.amazon.com/whitepapers/latest/aws-vpc-connectivity-options/software-vpn-network-to-amazon.html

Question 17:

You installed sensors to track the number of visitors that goes to the park. The data is sent everyday to an Amazon Kinesis stream with default settings for processing, in which a consumer is configured to process the data every other day. You noticed that your S3 bucket is not receiving all of the data that is being sent to the Kinesis stream. You checked the sensors if they are properly sending the data to Amazon Kinesis and verified that the data is indeed sent everyday.

What could be the reason for this?

1. There is a problem in the sensors. They probably had some intermittent connection hence, the data is not sent to the stream.
2. By default, the data records are only accessible for 24 hours from the time they are added to a Kinesis stream.
3. By default, Amazon S3 stores the data for 1 day and moves it to Amazon Glacier.
4. Your AWS account was hacked and someone has deleted some data in your Kinesis stream.

Answer(s): 2

Explanation

Kinesis Data Streams supports changes to the data record retention period of your stream. A Kinesis data stream is an ordered sequence of data records meant to be written to and read from in real-time. Data records are therefore stored in shards in your stream temporarily.

The time period from when a record is added to when it is no longer accessible is called the retention period. A Kinesis data stream stores records from 24 hours by default to a maximum of 168 hours.

This is the reason why there are missing data in your S3 bucket. To fix this, you can either configure your sensors to send the data everyday instead of every other day or alternatively, you can increase the retention period of your Kinesis data stream.

The option that says: There is a problem in the sensors. They probably had some intermittent connection hence, the data is not sent to the stream is incorrect. You already verified that the sensors are working as they should be hence, this is not the root cause of the issue.

The option that says: By default, Amazon S3 stores the data for 1 day and moves it to Amazon Glacier is incorrect because by default, Amazon S3 does not store the data for 1 day and moves it to Amazon Glacier.

The option that says: Your AWS account was hacked and someone has deleted some data in your Kinesis stream is incorrect because although this could be a possibility, you should verify first if there are other more probable reasons for the missing data in your S3 bucket. Be sure to follow and apply security best practices as well to prevent being hacked by someone. By default, the data records are only accessible for 24 hours from the time they are added to a Kinesis stream, which depicts the root cause of this issue.

Reference:

http://docs.aws.amazon.com/streams/latest/dev/kinesis-extended-retention.html

Question 18:

A large insurance company has an AWS account that contains three VPCs (DEV, UAT and PROD) in the same region. UAT is peered to both PROD and DEV using a VPC peering connection. All VPCs have non-overlapping CIDR blocks. The company wants to push minor code releases from Dev to Prod to speed up time to market.

Which of the following options helps the company accomplish this?

1. Create a new entry to PROD in the DEV route table using the VPC peering connection as the target.
2. Change the DEV and PROD VPCs to have overlapping CIDR blocks to be able to connect them.
3. Create a new VPC peering connection between PROD and DEV with the appropriate routes.
4. Do nothing. Since these two VPCs are already connected via UAT, they already have a connection to each other.

Answer(s): 3

Explanation

A VPC peering connection is a networking connection between two VPCs that enables you to route traffic between them privately. Instances in either VPC can communicate with each other as if they are within the same network. You can create a VPC peering connection between your own VPCs, with a VPC in another AWS account, or with a VPC in a different AWS Region.

AWS uses the existing infrastructure of a VPC to create a VPC peering connection; it is neither a gateway nor a VPN connection and does not rely on a separate piece of physical hardware. There is no single point of failure for communication or a bandwidth bottleneck.

Creating a new entry to PROD in the DEV route table using the VPC peering connection as the target is incorrect because even if you configure the route tables, the two VPCs will still be disconnected until you set up a VPC peering connection between them.

Changing the DEV and PROD VPCs to have overlapping CIDR blocks to be able to connect them is incorrect because you cannot peer two VPCs with overlapping CIDR blocks.

The option that says: Do nothing. Since these two VPCs are already connected via UAT, they already have a connection to each other is incorrect as transitive VPC peering is not allowed hence, even though DEV and PROD are both connected in UAT, these two VPCs do not have a direct connection to each other.

Reference:

https://docs.aws.amazon.com/AmazonVPC/latest/UserGuide/vpc-peering.html

Here is a quick introduction to VPC Peering:

https://youtu.be/i1A1eH8vLtk

Question 19:

You are the Solutions Architect for your company's AWS account of approximately 300 IAM users. They have a new company policy that will change the access of 100 of the IAM users to have a particular sort of access to Amazon S3 buckets.

What will you do to avoid the time-consuming task of applying the policy at the individual user?

1. Create a new IAM group and then add the users that require access to the S3 bucket. Afterwards, apply the policy to IAM group.
2. Create a new IAM role and add each user to the IAM role.
3. Create a new policy and apply it to multiple IAM users using a shell script.
4. Create a new S3 bucket access policy with unlimited access for each IAM user.

Answer(s): 1

Explanation

In this scenario, the best option is to group the set of users in an IAM Group and then apply a policy with the required access to the Amazon S3 bucket. This will enable you to easily add, remove, and manage the users instead of manually adding a policy to each and every 100 IAM users.

Creating a new policy and applying it to multiple IAM users using a shell script is incorrect because you need a new IAM Group for this scenario and not assign a policy to each user via a shell script. This method can save you time but afterwards, it will be difficult to manage all 100 users that are not contained in an IAM Group.

Creating a new S3 bucket access policy with unlimited access for each IAM user is incorrect because you need a new IAM Group and the method is also time-consuming.

Creating a new IAM role and adding each user to the IAM role is incorrect because you need to use an IAM Group and not an IAM role.

Reference:

http://docs.aws.amazon.com/IAM/latest/UserGuide/id_groups.html

Question 20:

In your VPC, you have a Classic Load Balancer distributing traffic to 2 running EC2 instances in ap-southeast-1a AZ and 8 EC2 instances in ap-southeast-1b AZ. However, you noticed that half of your incoming traffic goes to ap-southeast-1a AZ which over-utilize its 2 instances but underutilize the other 8 instances in the other AZ.

What could be the most likely cause of this problem?

1. The security group of the EC2 instances does not allow HTTP traffic.
2. The Classic Load Balancer listener is not set to port 22.
3. The Classic Load Balancer listener is not set to port 80.
4. Cross-Zone Load Balancing is disabled.

Answer(s): 4

Explanation

Cross-zone load balancing reduces the need to maintain equivalent numbers of instances in each enabled Availability Zone, and improves your application's ability to handle the loss of one or more instances.

When you create a Classic Load Balancer, the default for cross-zone load balancing depends on how you create the load balancer. With the API or CLI, cross-zone load balancing is disabled by default. With the AWS Management Console, the option to enable cross-zone load balancing is selected by default. After you create a Classic Load Balancer, you can enable or disable cross-zone load balancing at any time.

The following diagrams demonstrate the effect of cross-zone load balancing. There are two enabled Availability Zones, with 2 targets in Availability Zone A and 8 targets in Availability Zone B. Clients send requests, and Amazon Route 53 responds to each request with the IP address of one of the load balancer nodes. This distributes traffic such that each load balancer node receives 50% of the traffic from the clients. Each load balancer node distributes its share of the traffic across the registered targets in its scope.

If cross-zone load balancing is enabled, each of the 10 targets receives 10% of the traffic. This is because each load balancer node can route its 50% of the client traffic to all 10 targets.

If cross-zone load balancing is disabled, each of the 2 targets in Availability Zone A receives 25% of the traffic and each of the 8 targets in Availability Zone B receives 6.25% of the traffic. This is because each load balancer node can route its 50% of the client traffic only to targets in its Availability Zone.

References:

https://docs.aws.amazon.com/elasticloadbalancing/latest/userguide/how-elastic-load-balancing-works.html#cross-zone-load-balancing

http://docs.aws.amazon.com/elasticloadbalancing/latest/classic/enable-disable-crosszone-lb.html

Question 21:

A manufacturing company has EC2 instances running in AWS. The EC2 instances are configured with Auto Scaling. There are a lot of requests being lost because of too much load on the servers. The Auto Scaling is launching new EC2 instances to take the load accordingly yet, there are still some requests that are being lost.

Which of the following is the MOST suitable solution that you should implement to avoid losing recently submitted requests?

1. Set up Amazon Aurora Serverless for on-demand, auto-scaling configuration of your EC2 Instances and also enable Amazon Aurora Parallel Query feature for faster analytical queries over your current data.
2. Use an Amazon SQS queue to decouple the application components and scale-out the EC2 instances based upon the ApproximateNumberOfMessages metric in Amazon CloudWatch.
3. Replace the Auto Scaling group with a cluster placement group to achieve a low-latency network performance necessary for tightly-coupled node-to-node communication.
4. Use larger instances for your application with an attached Elastic Fabric Adapter (EFA).

Answer(s): 2

Explanation

Amazon Simple Queue Service (SQS) is a fully managed message queuing service that makes it easy to decouple and scale microservices, distributed systems, and serverless applications. Building applications from individual components that each perform a discrete function improves scalability and reliability, and is best practice design for modern applications. SQS makes it simple and cost-effective to decouple and coordinate the components of a cloud application. Using SQS, you can send, store, and receive messages between software components at any volume, without losing messages or requiring other services to be always available.

The number of messages in your Amazon SQS queue does not solely define the number of instances needed. In fact, the number of instances in the fleet can be driven by multiple factors, including how long it takes to process a message and the acceptable amount of latency (queue delay).

The solution is to use a backlog per instance metric with the target value being the acceptable backlog per instance to maintain. You can calculate these numbers as follows:

Backlog per instance: To determine your backlog per instance, start with the Amazon SQS metric ApproximateNumberOfMessages to determine the length of the SQS queue (number of messages available for retrieval from the queue). Divide that number by the fleet's running capacity, which for an Auto Scaling group is the number of instances in the InService state, to get the backlog per instance.

Acceptable backlog per instance: To determine your target value, first calculate what your application can accept in terms of latency. Then, take the acceptable latency value and divide it by the average time that an EC2 instance takes to process a message.

To illustrate with an example, let's say that the current ApproximateNumberOfMessages is 1500 and the fleet's running capacity is 10. If the average processing time is 0.1 seconds for each message and the longest acceptable latency is 10 seconds then the acceptable backlog per instance is 10 / 0.1, which equals 100. This means that 100 is the target value for your target tracking policy. Because the backlog per instance is currently at 150 (1500 / 10), your fleet scales out by five instances to maintain proportion to the target value.

Hence, the correct answer is: Use an Amazon SQS queue to decouple the application components and scale-out the EC2 instances based upon the ApproximateNumberOfMessages metric in Amazon CloudWatch.

Replacing the Auto Scaling group with a cluster placement group to achieve a low-latency network performance necessary for tightly-coupled node-to-node communication is incorrect because although it is true that a cluster placement group allows you to achieve a low-latency network performance, you still need to use Auto Scaling for your architecture to add more EC2 instances.

Using larger instances for your application with an attached Elastic Fabric Adapter (EFA) is incorrect because using a larger EC2 instance would not prevent data from being lost in case of a larger spike. You can take advantage of the durability and elasticity of SQS to keep the messages available for consumption by your instances. Elastic Fabric Adapter (EFA) is simply a network interface for Amazon EC2 instances that enables customers to run applications requiring high levels of inter-node communications at scale on AWS.

Setting up Amazon Aurora Serverless for on-demand, auto-scaling configuration of your EC2 Instances and also enabling Amazon Aurora Parallel Query feature for faster analytical queries over your current data is incorrect because although the Amazon Aurora Parallel Query feature provides faster analytical queries over your current data, Amazon Aurora Serverless is an on-demand, auto-scaling configuration for your database, and NOT for your EC2 instances. This is actually an auto-scaling configuration for your Amazon Aurora database and not for your compute services.

References:

https://aws.amazon.com/sqs/

https://docs.aws.amazon.com/AWSSimpleQueueService/latest/SQSDeveloperGuide/welcome.html

https://docs.aws.amazon.com/autoscaling/ec2/userguide/as-using-sqs-queue.html

Question 22:

A leading media company has an application hosted in an EBS-backed EC2 instance which uses Simple Workflow Service (SWF) to handle its sequential background jobs. The application works well in production and your manager asked you to also implement the same solution to other areas of their business.

In which other scenarios can you use both Simple Workflow Service (SWF) and Amazon EC2 as a solution? (Select TWO.)

1. For a distributed session management for your mobile application.
2. For web applications that require content delivery networks.
3. Orchestrating the execution of distributed business processes.
4. For applications that require a message queue.
5. Managing a multi-step and multi-decision checkout process of an e-commerce mobile app.

Answer(s): 3, 5

Explanation

You can use a combination of EC2 and SWF for the following scenarios:

Managing a multi-step and multi-decision checkout process of an e-commerce mobile app.

Orchestrating the execution of distributed business processes

Amazon Simple Workflow Service (SWF) is a web service that makes it easy to coordinate work across distributed application components. Amazon SWF enables applications for a range of use cases, including media processing, web application back-ends, business process workflows, and analytics pipelines, to be designed as a coordination of tasks. Tasks represent invocations of various processing steps in an application which can be performed by executable code, web service calls, human actions, and scripts.

The option that says: For a distributed session management for your mobile application is incorrect as Elasticache is the best option for distributed session management.

The option that says: For applications that require a message queue is incorrect as SQS is the best service to use as a message queue.

The option that says: For web applications that require content delivery networks is incorrect as CloudFront is the best option for applications that require a global content delivery network.

References:

https://aws.amazon.com/swf/

https://aws.amazon.com/ec2/

Question 23:

You are working for an insurance firm as their Senior Solutions Architect. The firm has an application which processes thousands of customer data stored in an Amazon MySQL database with Multi-AZ deployments configuration for high availability in case of downtime. For the past few days, you noticed an increasing trend of read and write operations, which is increasing the latency of the queries to your database. You are planning to use the standby database instance to balance the read and write operations from the primary instance.

When running your primary Amazon RDS Instance as a Multi-AZ deployment, can you use the standby instance for read and write operations?

1. No
2. Yes
3. Only with Microsoft SQL Server-based RDS
4. Only for Oracle RDS instances

Answer(s): 1

Explanation

The answer is No. The standby instance will not perform any read and write operations while the primary instance is running.

Multi-AZ deployments for the MySQL, MariaDB, Oracle, and PostgreSQL engines utilize synchronous physical replication to keep data on the standby up-to-date with the primary. Multi-AZ deployments for the SQL Server engine use synchronous logical replication to achieve the same result, employing SQL Server-native Mirroring technology. Both approaches safeguard your data in the event of a DB Instance failure or loss of an Availability Zone.

If a storage volume on your primary instance fails in a Multi-AZ deployment, Amazon RDS automatically initiates a failover to the up-to-date standby (or to a replica in the case of Amazon Aurora). Compare this to a Single-AZ deployment: in case of a Single-AZ database failure, a user-initiated point-in-time-restore operation will be required. This operation can take several hours to complete, and any data updates that occurred after the latest restorable time (typically within the last five minutes) will not be available.

The rest of the options are incorrect because regardless of the database engine, you cannot use a standby database for read and write operations.

Reference:

https://aws.amazon.com/rds/details/multi-az/

Question 24:

A company is deploying a Microsoft SharePoint Server environment on AWS using CloudFormation. The Solutions Architect needs to install and configure the architecture that is composed of Microsoft Active Directory (AD) domain controllers, Microsoft SQL Server 2012, multiple Amazon EC2 instances to host the Microsoft SharePoint Server and many other dependencies. The Architect needs to ensure that the required components are properly running before the stack creation proceeds.

Which of the following should the Architect do to meet this requirement?

1. Configure the DependsOn attribute in the CloudFormation template. Send a success signal after the applications are installed and configured using the cfn-init helper script.
2. Configure the UpdateReplacePolicy attribute in the CloudFormation template. Send a success signal after the applications are installed and configured using the cfn-signal helper script.

3. Configure a UpdatePolicy attribute to the instance in the CloudFormation template. Send a success signal after the applications are installed and configured using the cfn-signal helper script.
4. Configure a CreationPolicy attribute to the instance in the CloudFormation template. Send a success signal after the applications are installed and configured using the cfn-signal helper script.

Answer(s): 4

Explanation

You can associate the CreationPolicy attribute with a resource to prevent its status from reaching create complete until AWS CloudFormation receives a specified number of success signals or the timeout period is exceeded. To signal a resource, you can use the cfn-signal helper script or SignalResource API. AWS CloudFormation publishes valid signals to the stack events so that you track the number of signals sent.

The creation policy is invoked only when AWS CloudFormation creates the associated resource. Currently, the only AWS CloudFormation resources that support creation policies are AWS::AutoScaling::AutoScalingGroup, AWS::EC2::Instance, and AWS::CloudFormation::WaitCondition.

Use the CreationPolicy attribute when you want to wait on resource configuration actions before stack creation proceeds. For example, if you install and configure software applications on an EC2 instance, you might want those applications to be running before proceeding. In such cases, you can add a CreationPolicy attribute to the instance, and then send a success signal to the instance after the applications are installed and configured.

Hence, the option that says: Configure a CreationPolicy attribute to the instance in the CloudFormation template. Send a success signal after the applications are installed and configured using the cfn-signal helper script is correct.

The option that says: Configure the DependsOn attribute in the CloudFormation template. Send a success signal after the applications are installed and configured using the cfn-init helper script is incorrect because the cfn-init helper script is not suitable to be used to signal another resource. You have to use cfn-signal instead. And although you can use the DependsOn attribute to ensure the creation of a specific resource follows another, it is still better to use the CreationPolicy attribute instead as it ensures that the applications are properly running before the stack creation proceeds.

The option that says: Configure a UpdatePolicy attribute to the instance in the CloudFormation template. Send a success signal after the applications are installed and configured using the cfn-signal helper script is incorrect because the UpdatePolicy attribute is primarily used for updating resources and for stack update rollback operations.

The option that says: Configure the UpdateReplacePolicy attribute in the CloudFormation template. Send a success signal after the applications are installed and configured using the cfn-signal helper script is incorrect because the UpdateReplacePolicy attribute is primarily used to retain or in some cases, back up the existing physical instance of a resource when it is replaced during a stack update operation.

References:

https://docs.aws.amazon.com/AWSCloudFormation/latest/UserGuide/aws-attribute-creationpolicy.html

https://docs.aws.amazon.com/AWSCloudFormation/latest/UserGuide/deploying.applications.html#deployment-walkthrough-cfn-signal

https://aws.amazon.com/blogs/devops/use-a-creationpolicy-to-wait-for-on-instance-configurations/

Question 25:

Your customer has clients all across the globe that access product files stored in several S3 buckets, which are behind each of their own CloudFront web distributions. They currently want to deliver their content to a specific client, and they need to make sure that only that client can access the data. Currently, all of their clients can access their S3 buckets directly using an S3 URL or through their CloudFront distribution. The Solutions Architect must serve the private content via CloudFront only, to secure the distribution of files.

Which combination of actions should you implement to meet the above requirements? (Select TWO.)

1. Use AWS App Mesh to ensure that only their client can access the files.
2. Use AWS Cloud Map to ensure that only their client can access the files.
3. Use S3 pre-signed URLs to ensure that only their client can access the files. Remove permission to use Amazon S3 URLs to read the files for anyone else.
4. Restrict access to files in the origin by creating an origin access identity (OAI) and give it permission to read the files in the bucket.
5. Require the users to access the private content by using special CloudFront signed URLs or signed cookies.

Answer(s): 4, 5

Explanation

Many companies that distribute content over the Internet want to restrict access to documents, business data, media streams, or content that is intended for selected users, for example, users who have paid a fee. To securely serve this private content by using CloudFront, you can do the following:

- Require that your users access your private content by using special CloudFront signed URLs or signed cookies.

- Require that your users access your Amazon S3 content by using CloudFront URLs, not Amazon S3 URLs. Requiring CloudFront URLs isn't necessary, but it is recommended to prevent users from bypassing the restrictions that you specify in signed URLs or signed cookies. You can do this by setting up an origin access identity (OAI) for your Amazon S3 bucket. You can also configure the custom headers for a private HTTP server or an Amazon S3 bucket configured as a website endpoint.

All objects and buckets by default are private. The pre-signed URLs are useful if you want your user/customer to be able to upload a specific object to your bucket, but you don't require them to have AWS security credentials or permissions. You can generate a pre-signed URL programmatically using the AWS SDK for Java or the AWS SDK for .NET. If you are using Microsoft Visual Studio, you can also use AWS Explorer to generate a pre-signed object URL without writing any code. Anyone who receives a valid pre-signed URL can then programmatically upload an object.

 Hence, the correct answers are:

- Restrict access to files in the origin by creating an origin access identity (OAI) and give it permission to read the files in the bucket.

- Require the users to access the private content by using special CloudFront signed URLs or signed cookies.

The option that says: Use AWS App Mesh to ensure that only their client can access the files is incorrect because AWS App Mesh is just a service mesh that provides application-level networking to make it easy for your services to communicate with each other across multiple types of compute infrastructure.

The option that says: Use AWS Cloud Map to ensure that only their client can access the files is incorrect because AWS Cloud Map is simply a cloud resource discovery service that enables you to name your application resources with custom names and automatically update the locations of your dynamically changing resources.

The option that says: Use S3 pre-signed URLs to ensure that only their client can access the files. Remove permission to use Amazon S3 URLs to read the files for anyone else is incorrect. Although this could be a valid solution, it doesn't satisfy the requirement to serve the private content via CloudFront only, to secure the distribution of files. A better solution is to set up an origin access identity (OAI) then use Signed URL or Signed Cookies in your CloudFront web distribution.

References:

https://docs.aws.amazon.com/AmazonCloudFront/latest/DeveloperGuide/Private
Content.html

https://docs.aws.amazon.com/AmazonS3/latest/dev/PresignedUrlUploadObject.ht
ml

Question 26:

A travel company has a suite of web applications hosted in an Auto Scaling group of On-Demand EC2 instances behind an Application Load Balancer that handles traffic from various web domains such as i-love-manila.com, i-love-boracay.com, i-love-cebu.com and many others. To improve security and lessen the overall cost, you are instructed to secure the system by allowing multiple domains to serve SSL traffic without the need to reauthenticate and reprovision your certificate everytime you add a new domain. This migration from HTTP to HTTPS will help improve their SEO and Google search ranking.

Which of the following is the most cost-effective solution to meet the above requirement?

1. Upload all SSL certificates of the domains in the ALB using the console and bind multiple certificates to the same secure listener on your load balancer. ALB will automatically choose the optimal TLS certificate for each client using Server Name Indication (SNI).
2. Use a wildcard certificate to handle multiple sub-domains and different domains.
3. Create a new CloudFront web distribution and configure it to serve HTTPS requests using dedicated IP addresses in order to associate your alternate domain names with a dedicated IP address in each CloudFront edge location.
4. Add a Subject Alternative Name (SAN) for each additional domain to your certificate.

Answer(s): 1

Explanation

SNI Custom SSL relies on the SNI extension of the Transport Layer Security protocol, which allows multiple domains to serve SSL traffic over the same IP address by including the hostname which the viewers are trying to connect to.

You can host multiple TLS secured applications, each with its own TLS certificate, behind a single load balancer. In order to use SNI, all you need to do is bind multiple certificates to the same secure listener on your load balancer. ALB will automatically choose the optimal TLS certificate for each client. These features are provided at no additional charge.

To meet the requirements in the scenario, you can upload all SSL certificates of the domains in the ALB using the console and bind multiple certificates to the same secure listener on your load balancer. ALB will automatically choose the optimal TLS certificate for each client using Server Name Indication (SNI).

Hence, the correct answer is the option that says: Upload all SSL certificates of the domains in the ALB using the console and bind multiple certificates to the same secure listener on your load balancer. ALB will automatically choose the optimal TLS certificate for each client using Server Name Indication (SNI).

Using a wildcard certificate to handle multiple sub-domains and different domains is incorrect because a wildcard certificate can only handle multiple sub-domains but not different domains.

Adding a Subject Alternative Name (SAN) for each additional domain to your certificate is incorrect because although using SAN is correct, you will still have to reauthenticate and reprovision your certificate every time you add a new domain. One of the requirements in the scenario is that you should not have to reauthenticate and reprovision your certificate hence, this solution is incorrect.

The option that says: Create a new CloudFront web distribution and configure it to serve HTTPS requests using dedicated IP addresses in order to associate your alternate domain names with a dedicated IP address in each CloudFront edge location is incorrect because although it is valid to use dedicated IP addresses to meet this requirement, this solution is not cost-effective. Remember that if you configure CloudFront to serve HTTPS requests using dedicated IP addresses, you incur an additional monthly charge. The charge begins when you associate your SSL/TLS certificate with your CloudFront distribution. You can just simply upload the certificates to the ALB and use SNI to handle multiple domains in a cost-effective manner.

References:

https://aws.amazon.com/blogs/aws/new-application-load-balancer-sni/

https://docs.aws.amazon.com/AmazonCloudFront/latest/DeveloperGuide/cnames-https-dedicated-ip-or-sni.html#cnames-https-dedicated-ip

https://docs.aws.amazon.com/elasticloadbalancing/latest/application/create-https-listener.html

Question 27:

A company is storing its financial reports and regulatory documents in an Amazon S3 bucket. To comply with the IT audit, they tasked their Solutions Architect to track all new objects added to the bucket as well as the removed ones. It should also track whether a versioned object is permanently deleted. The Architect must configure Amazon S3 to publish notifications for these events to a queue for post-processing and to an Amazon SNS topic that will notify the Operations team.

Which of the following is the MOST suitable solution that the Architect should implement?

1. Create a new Amazon SNS topic and Amazon MQ. Add an S3 event notification configuration on the bucket to publish s3:ObjectAdded:* and s3:ObjectRemoved:* event types to SQS and SNS.
2. Create a new Amazon SNS topic and Amazon MQ. Add an S3 event notification configuration on the bucket to publish s3:ObjectCreated:* and ObjectRemoved:DeleteMarkerCreated event types to SQS and SNS.
3. Create a new Amazon SNS topic and Amazon SQS queue. Add an S3 event notification configuration on the bucket to publish s3:ObjectCreated:* and s3:ObjectRemoved:Delete event types to SQS and SNS.
4. Create a new Amazon SNS topic and Amazon SQS queue. Add an S3 event notification configuration on the bucket to publish s3:ObjectCreated:* and ObjectRemoved:DeleteMarkerCreated event types to SQS and SNS.

Answer(s): 3

Explanation

The Amazon S3 notification feature enables you to receive notifications when certain events happen in your bucket. To enable notifications, you must first add a notification configuration that identifies the events you want Amazon S3 to publish and the destinations where you want Amazon S3 to send the notifications. You store this configuration in the notification subresource that is associated with a bucket. Amazon S3 provides an API for you to manage this subresource.

Amazon S3 event notifications typically deliver events in seconds but can sometimes take a minute or longer. If two writes are made to a single non-versioned object at the same time, it is possible that only a single event notification will be sent. If you want to ensure that an event notification is sent for every successful write, you can enable versioning on your bucket. With versioning, every successful write will create a new version of your object and will also send an event notification.

Amazon S3 can publish notifications for the following events:

1. New object created events

2. Object removal events

3. Restore object events

4. Reduced Redundancy Storage (RRS) object lost events

5. Replication events

Amazon S3 supports the following destinations where it can publish events:

1. Amazon Simple Notification Service (Amazon SNS) topic

2. Amazon Simple Queue Service (Amazon SQS) queue

3. AWS Lambda

If your notification ends up writing to the bucket that triggers the notification, this could cause an execution loop. For example, if the bucket triggers a Lambda function each time an object is uploaded and the function uploads an object to the bucket, then the function indirectly triggers itself. To avoid this, use two buckets, or configure the trigger to only apply to a prefix used for incoming objects.

Hence, the correct answers is: Create a new Amazon SNS topic and Amazon SQS queue. Add an S3 event notification configuration on the bucket to publish s3:ObjectCreated:* and s3:ObjectRemoved:Delete event types to SQS and SNS.

The option that says: Create a new Amazon SNS topic and Amazon MQ. Add an S3 event notification configuration on the bucket to publish s3:ObjectAdded:* and s3:ObjectRemoved:* event types to SQS and SNS is incorrect because there is no s3:ObjectAdded:* type in Amazon S3. You should add an S3 event notification configuration on the bucket to publish events of the s3:ObjectCreated:* type instead. Moreover, Amazon S3 does not support Amazon MQ as a destination to publish events.

The option that says: Create a new Amazon SNS topic and Amazon SQS queue. Add an S3 event notification configuration on the bucket to publish s3:ObjectCreated:* and ObjectRemoved:DeleteMarkerCreated event types to SQS and SNS is incorrect because the s3:ObjectRemoved:DeleteMarkerCreated type is only triggered when a delete marker is created for a versioned object and not when an object is deleted or a versioned object is permanently deleted.

The option that says: Create a new Amazon SNS topic and Amazon MQ. Add an S3 event notification configuration on the bucket to publish s3:ObjectCreated:* and ObjectRemoved:DeleteMarkerCreated event types to SQS and SNS is incorrect because Amazon S3 does public event messages to Amazon MQ. You should use an Amazon SQS instead. In addition, the s3:ObjectRemoved:DeleteMarkerCreated type is only triggered when a delete marker is created for a versioned object. Remember that the scenario asked to publish events when an object is deleted or a versioned object is permanently deleted.

References:

https://docs.aws.amazon.com/AmazonS3/latest/dev/NotificationHowTo.html

https://docs.aws.amazon.com/AmazonS3/latest/dev/ways-to-add-notification-config-to-bucket.html

https://aws.amazon.com/blogs/aws/s3-event-notification/

Question 28:

A VPC has a non-default subnet which has four On-Demand EC2 instances that can be accessed over the Internet. Using the AWS CLI, you launched a fifth instance that uses the same subnet, Amazon Machine Image (AMI), and security group which are being used by the other instances. Upon testing, you are not able to access the new instance.

Which of the following is the most suitable solution to solve this problem?

1. Set up a NAT gateway to allow access to the fifth EC2 instance.
2. Include the fifth EC2 instance to the Placement Group of the other four EC2 instances and enable Enhanced Networking.
3. Associate an Elastic IP address to the fifth EC2 instance.
4. Enable AWS Transfer for SFTP to allow the incoming traffic to the fifth EC2 Instance.

Answer(s): 3

Explanation

By default, a "default subnet" of your VPC is actually a public subnet, because the main route table sends the subnet's traffic that is destined for the internet to the internet gateway. You can make a default subnet into a private subnet by removing the route from the destination 0.0.0.0/0 to the internet gateway. However, if you do this, any EC2 instance running in that subnet can't access the internet.

Instances that you launch into a default subnet receive both a public IPv4 address and a private IPv4 address, and both public and private DNS hostnames. Instances that you launch into a nondefault subnet in a default VPC don't receive a public IPv4 address or a DNS hostname. You can change your subnet's default public IP addressing behavior

By default, nondefault subnets have the IPv4 public addressing attribute set to false, and default subnets have this attribute set to true. An exception is a nondefault subnet created by the Amazon EC2 launch instance wizard — the wizard sets the attribute to true.

In this scenario, it is possible that the fifth EC2 instance launched in a nondefault subnet doesn't have a public IP address or an Elastic IP address, just like the first 4 instances.

Associating an Elastic IP address to the fifth EC2 instance is correct because the fifth instance does not have a public IP address since it was deployed on a nondefault subnet. The other 4 instances are accessible over the Internet because they each have an Elastic IP address attached, unlike the last instance which only has a private IP address. An Elastic IP address is a public IPv4 address, which is reachable from the Internet. If your instance does not have a public IPv4 address, you can associate an Elastic IP address with your instance to enable communication with the Internet.

Including the fifth EC2 instance to the Placement Group of the other four EC2 instances and enabling Enhanced Networking is incorrect because Placement Groups is primarily used to determine how your instances are placed on the underlying hardware while Enhanced Networking, on the other hand, is for providing high-performance networking capabilities using single root I/O virtualization (SR-IOV) on supported EC2 instance types.

Setting up a NAT gateway to allow access to the fifth EC2 instance is incorrect because you do not need a NAT Gateway nor a NAT instance in this scenario considering that the instances are already in public subnet. Remember that a NAT Gateway or a NAT instance is primarily used to enable instances in a private subnet to connect to the Internet or other AWS services, but prevent the Internet from initiating a connection with those instances.

Enabling AWS Transfer for SFTP to allow the incoming traffic to the fifth EC2 Instance instance is incorrect because AWS Transfer for SFTP (AWS SFTP) is simply a fully managed AWS service that enables you to transfer files over Secure File Transfer Protocol (SFTP), into and out of Amazon Simple Storage Service (Amazon S3) storage. This service is not related to EC2 instances at all.

References:

https://docs.aws.amazon.com/vpc/latest/userguide/default-vpc.html

https://docs.aws.amazon.com/transfer/latest/userguide/what-is-aws-transfer-for-sftp.html

https://docs.aws.amazon.com/AWSEC2/latest/UserGuide/elastic-ip-addresses-eip.html

Question 29:

A company is using a custom shell script to automate the deployment and management of their EC2 instances. The script is using various AWS CLI commands such as revoke-security-group-ingress, revoke-security-group-egress, run-scheduled-instances and many others.

In the shell script, what does the revoke-security-group-ingress command do?

1. Removes one or more security groups from a rule.
2. Removes one or more security groups from an Amazon EC2 instance.
3. Removes one or more ingress rules from a security group.
4. Removes one or more egress rules from a security group.

Answer(s): 3

Explanation

The revoke-security-group-ingress command removes one or more ingress rules from a security group.

Each rule consists of the protocol and the CIDR range or source security group. For the TCP and UDP protocols, you must also specify the destination port or range of ports. For the ICMP protocol, you must also specify the ICMP type and code. If the security group rule has a description, you do not have to specify the description to revoke the rule.

Rule changes are propagated to instances within the security group as quickly as possible. However, a small delay might occur. This example removes TCP port 22 access for the 203.0.113.0/24 address range from the security group named MySecurityGroup. If the command succeeds, no output is returned.

Command:

aws ec2 revoke-security-group-ingress --group-name MySecurityGroup --protocol tcp --port 22 --cidr 203.0.113.0/24

References:

https://docs.aws.amazon.com/cli/latest/reference/ec2/revoke-security-group-ingress.html

https://docs.aws.amazon.com/vpc/latest/userguide/VPC_SecurityGroups.html

Question 30:

A new online banking platform has been re-designed to have a microservices architecture in which complex applications are decomposed into smaller, independent services. The new platform is using Docker considering that application containers are optimal for running small, decoupled services. The new solution should remove the need to provision and manage servers, let you specify and pay for resources per application, and improve security through application isolation by design.

Which of the following is the MOST suitable service to use to migrate this new platform to AWS?

1. AWS Fargate
2. Amazon EFS
3. Amazon EKS
4. Amazon EBS

Answer(s): 1

Explanation

AWS Fargate is a serverless compute engine for containers that works with both Amazon Elastic Container Service (ECS) and Amazon Elastic Kubernetes Service (EKS). Fargate makes it easy for you to focus on building your applications. Fargate removes the need to provision and manage servers, lets you specify and pay for resources per application, and improves security through application isolation by design.

Fargate allocates the right amount of compute, eliminating the need to choose instances and scale cluster capacity. You only pay for the resources required to run your containers, so there is no over-provisioning and paying for additional servers. Fargate runs each task or pod in its own kernel providing the tasks and pods their own isolated compute environment. This enables your application to have workload isolation and improved security by design. This is why customers such as Vanguard, Accenture, Foursquare, and Ancestry have chosen to run their mission critical applications on Fargate.

Hence, the correct answer is: AWS Fargate.

Amazon EKS is incorrect because this is more suitable to run the Kubernetes management infrastructure and not Docker. It does not remove the need to provision and manage servers nor let you specify and pay for resources per application, unlike AWS Fargate.

Amazon EFS is incorrect because this is a file system for Linux-based workloads for use with AWS Cloud services and on-premises resources.

Amazon EBS is incorrect because this is primarily used to provide persistent block storage volumes for use with Amazon EC2 instances in the AWS Cloud.

References:

https://aws.amazon.com/fargate/

https://docs.aws.amazon.com/AmazonECS/latest/developerguide/ECS_GetStarted_Fargate.html

Question 31:

You are a new Solutions Architect in your company. Upon checking the existing Inbound Rules of your Network ACL, you saw this configuration:

If a computer with an IP address of 110.238.109.37 sends a request to your VPC, what will happen?

1. Initially, it will be allowed and then after a while, the connection will be denied.
2. It will be denied.
3. It will be allowed.
4. Initially, it will be denied and then after a while, the connection will be allowed.

Answer(s): 3

Explanation

Rules are evaluated starting with the lowest numbered rule. As soon as a rule matches traffic, it's applied immediately regardless of any higher-numbered rule that may contradict it.

We have 3 rules here:

1. Rule 100 permits all traffic from any source.

2. Rule 101 denies all traffic coming from 110.238.109.37

3. The Default Rule (*) denies all traffic from any source.

The Rule 100 will first be evaluated. If there is a match, then it will allow the request. Otherwise, it will then go to Rule 101 to repeat the same process until it goes to the default rule. In this case, when there is a request from 110.238.109.37, it will go through Rule 100 first. As Rule 100 says it will permit all traffic from any source, it will allow this request and will not further evaluate Rule 101 (which denies 110.238.109.37) nor the default rule.

Reference:

http://docs.aws.amazon.com/AmazonVPC/latest/UserGuide/VPC_ACLs.html

Question 32:

You are a Solutions Architect for a major TV network. They have a web application running on eight Amazon T3 EC2 instances, consuming about 55% of resources on each instance. You are using Auto Scaling to make sure that eight instances are running at all times. The number of requests that this application processes are consistent and do not experience spikes. Your manager instructed you to ensure high availability of this web application at all times to avoid any loss of revenue. You want the load to be distributed evenly between all instances. You also want to use the same Amazon Machine Image (AMI) for all EC2 instances.

How will you be able to achieve this?

1. Deploy four EC2 instances with Auto Scaling in one Availability Zone and four in another availability zone in the same region behind an Amazon Elastic Load Balancer.
2. Deploy eight EC2 instances with Auto Scaling in one Availability Zone behind an Amazon Elastic Load Balancer.
3. Deploy two EC2 instances with Auto Scaling in four regions behind an Amazon Elastic Load Balancer.
4. Deploy four EC2 instances with Auto Scaling in one region and four in another region behind an Amazon Elastic Load Balancer.

Answer(s): 1

Explanation

The best option to take is to deploy four EC2 instances in one Availability Zone and four in another availability zone in the same region behind an Amazon Elastic Load Balancer. In this way, if one availability zone goes down, there is still another available zone that can accommodate traffic.

When the first AZ goes down, the second AZ will only have an initial 4 EC2 instances. This will eventually be scaled up to 8 instances since the solution is using Auto Scaling.

The 110% compute capacity for the 4 servers might cause some degradation of the service, but not a total outage since there are still some instances that handle the requests. Depending on your scale-up configuration in your Auto Scaling group, the additional 4 EC2 instances can be launched in a matter of minutes.

T3 instances also have a Burstable Performance capability to burst or go beyond the current compute capacity of the instance to higher performance as required by your workload. So your 4 servers will be able to manage 110% compute capacity for a short period of time. This is the power of cloud computing versus our on-premises network architecture. It provides elasticity and unparalleled scalability.

Take note that Auto Scaling will launch additional EC2 instances to the remaining Availability Zone/s in the event of an Availability Zone outage in the region. Hence, the correct answer is the option that says: Deploy four EC2 instances with Auto Scaling in one Availability Zone and four in another availability zone in the same region behind an Amazon Elastic Load Balancer.

The option that says: Deploy eight EC2 instances with Auto Scaling in one Availability Zone behind an Amazon Elastic Load Balancer is incorrect because this architecture is not highly available. If that Availability Zone goes down then your web application will be unreachable.

The options that say: Deploy four EC2 instances with Auto Scaling in one region and four in another region behind an Amazon Elastic Load Balancer and Deploy two EC2 instances with Auto Scaling in four regions behind an Amazon Elastic Load Balancer are incorrect because the ELB is designed to only run in one region and not across multiple regions.

References:

https://aws.amazon.com/elasticloadbalancing/

https://docs.aws.amazon.com/AWSEC2/latest/UserGuide/ec2-increase-availability.html

Question 33:

You are working as a Solutions Architect for a tech company where you are instructed to build a web architecture using On-Demand EC2 instances and a database in AWS. However, due to budget constraints, the company instructed you to choose a database service in which they no longer need to worry about database management tasks such as hardware or software provisioning, setup, configuration, scaling and backups.

Which database service in AWS is best to use in this scenario?

1. Redshift
2. RDS
3. Amazon ElastiCache
4. DynamoDB

Answer(s): 4

Explanation

Basically, a database service in which you no longer need to worry about database management tasks such as hardware or software provisioning, setup and configuration is called a fully managed database. This means that AWS fully manages all of the database management tasks and the underlying host server. The main differentiator here is the keyword "scaling" in the question. In RDS, you still have to manually scale up your resources and create Read Replicas to improve scalability while in DynamoDB, this is automatically done.

DynamoDB is the best option to use in this scenario. It is a fully managed non-relational database service – you simply create a database table, set your target utilization for Auto Scaling, and let the service handle the rest. You no longer need to worry about database management tasks such as hardware or software provisioning, setup and configuration, software patching, operating a reliable, distributed database cluster, or partitioning data over multiple instances as you scale. DynamoDB also lets you backup and restore all your tables for data archival, helping you meet your corporate and governmental regulatory requirements.

RDS is incorrect because this is just a "managed" service and not "fully managed". This means that you still have to handle the backups and other administrative tasks such as when the automated OS patching will take place.

Amazon ElastiCache is incorrect because although ElastiCache is fully managed, it is not a database service but an In-Memory Data Store.

Redshift is incorrect because although this is fully managed, it is not a database service but a Data Warehouse.

References:

https://aws.amazon.com/dynamodb/

https://aws.amazon.com/products/databases/

Question 34:

You are a Solutions Architect working for an aerospace engineering company which recently adopted a hybrid cloud infrastructure with AWS. One of your tasks is to launch a VPC with both public and private subnets for their EC2 instances as well as their database instances respectively.

Which of the following statements are true regarding Amazon VPC subnets? (Select TWO.)

1. Each subnet maps to a single Availability Zone.
2. EC2 instances in a private subnet can communicate with the Internet only if they have an Elastic IP.
3. Each subnet spans to 2 Availability Zones.
4. The allowed block size in VPC is between a /16 netmask (65,536 IP addresses) and /27 netmask (16 IP addresses).
5. Every subnet that you create is automatically associated with the main route table for the VPC.

Answer(s): 1, 5

Explanation

A VPC spans all the Availability Zones in the region. After creating a VPC, you can add one or more subnets in each Availability Zone. When you create a subnet, you specify the CIDR block for the subnet, which is a subset of the VPC CIDR block. Each subnet must reside entirely within one Availability Zone and cannot span zones. Availability Zones are distinct locations that are engineered to be isolated from failures in other Availability Zones. By launching instances in separate Availability Zones, you can protect your applications from the failure of a single location.

Below are the important points you have to remember about subnets:

- Each subnet maps to a single Availability Zone.

- Every subnet that you create is automatically associated with the main route table for the VPC.

- If a subnet's traffic is routed to an Internet gateway, the subnet is known as a public subnet.

The option that says: EC2 instances in a private subnet can communicate with the Internet only if they have an Elastic IP is incorrect because EC2 instances in a private subnet can communicate with the Internet not just by having an Elastic IP, but also with a public IP address via a NAT Instance or a NAT Gateway. Take note that there is a distinction between private and public IP addresses. To enable communication with the Internet, a public IPv4 address is mapped to the primary private IPv4 address through network address translation (NAT).

The option that says: The allowed block size in VPC is between a /16 netmask (65,536 IP addresses) and /27 netmask (16 IP addresses) is incorrect because the allowed block size in VPC is between a /16 netmask (65,536 IP addresses) and /28 netmask (16 IP addresses) and not /27 netmask. For you to easily remember this, /27 netmask is equivalent to exactly 27 IP addresses but keep in mind that the limit is until /28 netmask.

The option that says: Each subnet spans to 2 Availability Zones is incorrect because each subnet must reside entirely within one Availability Zone and cannot span zones.

References:

https://docs.aws.amazon.com/AmazonVPC/latest/UserGuide/VPC_Subnets.html

https://docs.aws.amazon.com/vpc/latest/userguide/vpc-ip-addressing.html

Question 35:

Your company has recently deployed a new web application which uses a serverless-based architecture in AWS. Your manager instructed you to implement CloudWatch metrics to monitor your systems more effectively. You know that Lambda automatically monitors functions on your behalf and reports metrics through Amazon CloudWatch.

In this scenario, what types of data do these metrics monitor? (Select TWO.)

1. IteratorSize
2. Invocations
3. DeadLetterErrors
4. ReservedConcurrentExecutions
5. ApproximateAgeOfOldestMessage

Answer(s): 2, 3

Explanation

AWS Lambda automatically monitors functions on your behalf, reporting metrics through Amazon CloudWatch. These metrics include total invocation requests, latency, and error rates. The throttles, Dead Letter Queues errors and Iterator age for stream-based invocations are also monitored.

You can monitor metrics for Lambda and view logs by using the Lambda console, the CloudWatch console, the AWS CLI, or the CloudWatch API.

ReservedConcurrentExecutions is incorrect because CloudWatch does not monitor Lambda's reserved concurrent executions. You can view it through the Lambda console or via CLI manually.

IteratorSize and ApproximateAgeOfOldestMessage are incorrect because these two are not Lambda metrics.

References:

https://docs.aws.amazon.com/lambda/latest/dg/monitoring-functions-access-metrics.html

https://docs.aws.amazon.com/lambda/latest/dg/monitoring-functions-metrics.html

Question 36:

You are automating the creation of EC2 instances in your VPC. Hence, you wrote a python script to trigger the Amazon EC2 API to request 50 EC2 instances in a single Availability Zone. However, you noticed that after 20 successful requests, subsequent requests failed.

What could be a reason for this issue and how would you resolve it?

1. By default, AWS allows you to provision a maximum of 20 instances per region. Select a different region and retry the failed request.
2. There is a vCPU-based On-Demand Instance limit per region which is why subsequent requests failed. Just submit the limit increase form to AWS and retry the failed requests once approved.
3. By default, AWS allows you to provision a maximum of 20 instances per Availability Zone. Select a different Availability Zone and retry the failed request.
4. There was an issue with the Amazon EC2 API. Just resend the requests and these will be provisioned successfully.

Answer(s): 2

Explanation

You are limited to running On-Demand Instances per your vCPU-based On-Demand Instance limit, purchasing 20 Reserved Instances, and requesting Spot Instances per your dynamic Spot limit per region. New AWS accounts may start with limits that are lower than the limits described here.

If you need more instances, complete the Amazon EC2 limit increase request form with your use case, and your limit increase will be considered. Limit increases are tied to the region they were requested for.

Hence, the correct answer is: There is a vCPU-based On-Demand Instance limit per region which is why subsequent requests failed. Just submit the limit increase form to AWS and retry the failed requests once approved.

The option that says: There was an issue with the Amazon EC2 API. Just resend the requests and these will be provisioned successfully is incorrect because you are limited to running On-Demand Instances per your vCPU-based On-Demand Instance limit. There is also a limit of purchasing 20 Reserved Instances, and requesting Spot Instances per your dynamic Spot limit per region hence, there is no problem with the EC2 API.

The option that says: By default, AWS allows you to provision a maximum of 20 instances per region. Select a different region and retry the failed request is incorrect. There is no need to select a different region since this limit can be increased after submitting a request form to AWS.

The option that says: By default, AWS allows you to provision a maximum of 20 instances per Availability Zone. Select a different Availability Zone and retry the failed request is incorrect because the vCPU-based On-Demand Instance limit is set per region and not per Availability Zone. This can be increased after submitting a request form to AWS.

References:

https://docs.aws.amazon.com/general/latest/gr/aws_service_limits.html#limits_ec2

https://aws.amazon.com/ec2/faqs/#How_many_instances_can_I_run_in_Amazon_EC2

Question 37:

Your IT Manager instructed you to set up a bastion host in the cheapest, most secure way, and that you should be the only person that can access it via SSH.

Which of the following steps would satisfy your IT Manager's request?

1. Set up a large EC2 instance and a security group which only allows access on port 22
2. Set up a small EC2 instance and a security group which only allows access on port 22
3. Set up a large EC2 instance and a security group which only allows access on port 22 via your IP address
4. Set up a small EC2 instance and a security group which only allows access on port 22 via your IP address

Answer(s): 4

Explanation

A bastion host is a server whose purpose is to provide access to a private network from an external network, such as the Internet. Because of its exposure to potential attack, a bastion host must minimize the chances of penetration.

To create a bastion host, you can create a new EC2 instance which should only have a security group from a particular IP address for maximum security. Since the cost is also considered in the question, you should choose a small instance for your host. By default, t2.micro instance is used by AWS but you can change these settings during deployment.

Setting up a large EC2 instance and a security group which only allows access on port 22 via your IP address is incorrect because you don't need to provision a large EC2 instance to run a single bastion host. At the same time, you are looking for the cheapest solution possible.

The options that say: Set up a large EC2 instance and a security group which only allows access on port 22 and Set up a small EC2 instance and a security group which only allows access on port 22 are both incorrect because you did not set your specific IP address to the security group rules, which possibly means that you publicly allow traffic from all sources in your security group. This is wrong as you should only be the one to have access to the bastion host.

References:

https://docs.aws.amazon.com/quickstart/latest/linux-bastion/architecture.html

https://aws.amazon.com/blogs/security/how-to-record-ssh-sessions-established-through-a-bastion-host/

Question 38:

A company is hosting EC2 instances that are on non-production environment and processing non-priority batch loads, which can be interrupted at any time.

What is the best instance purchasing option which can be applied to your EC2 instances in this case?

1. Spot Instances
2. On-Demand Instances
3. Scheduled Reserved Instances
4. Reserved Instances

Answer(s): 1

Explanation

Amazon EC2 Spot instances are spare compute capacity in the AWS cloud available to you at steep discounts compared to On-Demand prices. It can be interrupted by AWS EC2 with two minutes of notification when the EC2 needs the capacity back.

To use Spot Instances, you create a Spot Instance request that includes the number of instances, the instance type, the Availability Zone, and the maximum price that you are willing to pay per instance hour. If your maximum price exceeds the current Spot price, Amazon EC2 fulfills your request immediately if capacity is available. Otherwise, Amazon EC2 waits until your request can be fulfilled or until you cancel the request.

References:

http://docs.aws.amazon.com/AWSEC2/latest/UserGuide/using-spot-instances.html

https://aws.amazon.com/ec2/spot/

Question 39:

A company is using multiple AWS accounts that are consolidated using AWS Organizations. They want to copy several S3 objects to another S3 bucket that belonged to a different AWS account which they also own. The Solutions Architect was instructed to set up the necessary permissions for this task and to ensure that the destination account owns the copied objects and not the account it was sent from.

How can the Architect accomplish this requirement?

1. Set up cross-origin resource sharing (CORS) in S3 by creating a bucket policy that allows an IAM user or role to copy objects from the source bucket in one account to the destination bucket in the other account.
2. Configure cross-account permissions in S3 by creating an IAM customer managed policy that allows an IAM user or role to copy objects from the source bucket in one account to the destination bucket in the other account. Then attach the policy to the IAM user or role that you want to use to copy objects between accounts.
3. Enable the Requester Pays feature in the source S3 bucket. The fees would be waived through Consolidated Billing since both AWS accounts are part of AWS Organizations.
4. Connect the two S3 buckets from two different AWS accounts to Amazon WorkDocs. Set up cross-account access to integrate the two S3 buckets. Use the Amazon WorkDocs console to copy the objects from one account to the other with modified object ownership assigned to the destination account.

Answer(s): 2

Explanation

By default, an S3 object is owned by the account that uploaded the object. That's why granting the destination account the permissions to perform the cross-account copy makes sure that the destination owns the copied objects. You can also change the ownership of an object by changing its access control list (ACL) to bucket-owner-full-control.

However, object ACLs can be difficult to manage for multiple objects, so it's a best practice to grant programmatic cross-account permissions to the destination account. Object ownership is important for managing permissions using a bucket policy. For a bucket policy to apply to an object in the bucket, the object must be owned by the account that owns the bucket. You can also manage object permissions using the object's ACL. However, object ACLs can be difficult to manage for multiple objects, so it's a best practice to use the bucket policy as a centralized method for setting permissions.

To be sure that a destination account owns an S3 object copied from another account, grant the destination account the permissions to perform the cross-account copy. Follow these steps to configure cross-account permissions to copy objects from a source bucket in Account A to a destination bucket in Account B:

- Attach a bucket policy to the source bucket in Account A.

- Attach an AWS Identity and Access Management (IAM) policy to a user or role in Account B.

- Use the IAM user or role in Account B to perform the cross-account copy.

Hence, the correct answer is: Configure cross-account permissions in S3 by creating an IAM customer managed policy that allows an IAM user or role to copy objects from the source bucket in one account to the destination bucket in the other account. Then attach the policy to the IAM user or role that you want to use to copy objects between accounts.

The option that says: Enable the Requester Pays feature in the source S3 bucket. The fees would be waived through Consolidated Billing since both AWS accounts are part of AWS Organizations is incorrect because the Requester Pays feature is primarily used if you want the requester, instead of the bucket owner, to pay the cost of the data transfer request and download from the S3 bucket. This solution lacks the necessary IAM Permissions to satisfy the requirement. The most suitable solution here is to configure cross-account permissions in S3.

The option that says: Set up cross-origin resource sharing (CORS) in S3 by creating a bucket policy that allows an IAM user or role to copy objects from the source bucket in one account to the destination bucket in the other account is incorrect because CORS simply defines a way for client web applications that are loaded in one domain to interact with resources in a different domain, and not on a different AWS account.

The option that says: Connect the two S3 buckets from two different AWS accounts to Amazon WorkDocs. Set up cross-account access to integrate the two S3 buckets. Use the Amazon WorkDocs console to copy the objects from one account to the other with modified object ownership assigned to the destination account is incorrect because Amazon WorkDocs is commonly used to easily collaborate, share content, provide rich feedback, and collaboratively edit documents with other users. There is no direct way for you to integrate WorkDocs and an Amazon S3 bucket owned by a different AWS account. A better solution here is to use cross-account permissions in S3 to meet the requirement.

References:

https://docs.aws.amazon.com/AmazonS3/latest/dev/example-walkthroughs-managing-access-example2.html

https://aws.amazon.com/premiumsupport/knowledge-center/copy-s3-objects-account/

https://aws.amazon.com/premiumsupport/knowledge-center/cross-account-access-s3/

Question 40:

You are a new Solutions Architect in a large insurance firm. To maintain compliance with HIPAA laws, all data being backed up or stored on Amazon S3 needs to be encrypted at rest. In this scenario, what is the best method of encryption for your data, assuming S3 is being used for storing financial-related data? (Select TWO.)

1. Store the data on EBS volumes with encryption enabled instead of using Amazon S3
2. Use AWS Shield to protect your data at rest
3. Store the data in encrypted EBS snapshots
4. Encrypt the data using your own encryption keys then copy the data to Amazon S3 over HTTPS endpoints.
5. Enable SSE on an S3 bucket to make use of AES-256 encryption

Answer(s): 4, 5

Explanation

Data protection refers to protecting data while in-transit (as it travels to and from Amazon S3) and at rest (while it is stored on disks in Amazon S3 data centers). You can protect data in transit by using SSL or by using client-side encryption. You have the following options for protecting data at rest in Amazon S3.

Use Server-Side Encryption – You request Amazon S3 to encrypt your object before saving it on disks in its data centers and decrypt it when you download the objects.

Use Client-Side Encryption – You can encrypt data client-side and upload the encrypted data to Amazon S3. In this case, you manage the encryption process, the encryption keys, and related tools.

Hence, the following options are the correct answers:

- Enable SSE on an S3 bucket to make use of AES-256 encryption

- Encrypt the data using your own encryption keys then copy the data to Amazon S3 over HTTPS endpoints. This refers to using a Server-Side Encryption with Customer-Provided Keys (SSE-C).

Storing the data in encrypted EBS snapshots and storing the data on EBS volumes with encryption enabled instead of using Amazon S3 are both incorrect because all these options are for protecting your data in your EBS volumes. Note that an S3 bucket does not use EBS volumes to store your data.

Using AWS Shield to protect your data at rest is incorrect because AWS Shield is mainly used to protect your entire VPC against DDoS attacks.

References:

https://docs.aws.amazon.com/AmazonS3/latest/dev/serv-side-encryption.html

https://docs.aws.amazon.com/AmazonS3/latest/dev/UsingClientSideEncryption.html

Question 41:

You are a new Solutions Architect in your department and you have created 7 CloudFormation templates. Each template has been defined for a specific purpose.

What determines the cost of using these new CloudFormation templates?

1. It depends on the region where you will deploy.
2. $2.50 per template per month
3. The length of time it takes to build the architecture with CloudFormation
4. CloudFormation templates are free but you are charged for the underlying resources it builds.

Answer(s): 4

Explanation

There is no additional charge for AWS CloudFormation. You pay for AWS resources (such as Amazon EC2 instances, Elastic Load Balancing load balancers, etc.) created using AWS CloudFormation in the same manner as if you created them manually. You only pay for what you use, as you use it; there are no minimum fees and no required upfront commitments.

The option that says: $2.50 per template per month is incorrect. There is no cost for creating CloudFormation templates. Costs are calculated from the AWS resources that are provisioned from that CloudFormation template.

The option that says: The length of time it takes to build the architecture with CloudFormation is incorrect. There is no cost for the time it takes to execute CloudFormation templates. Costs are calculated from the AWS resources that are provisioned from that CloudFormation template.

The option that says: It depends on the region where you will deploy is incorrect. Costs per region are not calculated based on the CloudFormation template, but rather on the regions where resources are provisioned during the building of the environment using the CloudFormation template.

Reference:

https://aws.amazon.com/cloudformation/pricing/

Question 42:

The media company that you are working for has a video transcoding application running on Amazon EC2. Each EC2 instance polls a queue to find out which video should be transcoded, and then runs a transcoding process. If this process is interrupted, the video will be transcoded by another instance based on the queuing system. This application has a large backlog of videos which need to be transcoded. Your manager would like to reduce this backlog by adding more EC2 instances, however, these instances are only needed until the backlog is reduced.

In this scenario, which type of Amazon EC2 instance is the most cost-effective type to use?

1. Dedicated instances
2. Spot instances
3. On-demand instances
4. Reserved instances

Answer(s): 2

Explanation

You require an instance that will be used not as a primary server but as a spare compute resource to augment the transcoding process of your application. These instances should also be terminated once the backlog has been significantly reduced. In addition, the scenario mentions that if the current process is interrupted, the video can be transcoded by another instance based on the queuing system. This means that the application can gracefully handle an unexpected termination of an EC2 instance, like in the event of a Spot instance termination when the Spot price is greater than your set maximum price. Hence, an Amazon EC2 Spot instance is the best and cost-effective option for this scenario.

Amazon EC2 Spot instances are spare compute capacity in the AWS cloud available to you at steep discounts compared to On-Demand prices. EC2 Spot enables you to optimize your costs on the AWS cloud and scale your application's throughput up to 10X for the same budget. By simply selecting Spot when launching EC2 instances, you can save up-to 90% on On-Demand prices. The only difference between On-Demand instances and Spot Instances is that Spot instances can be interrupted by EC2 with two minutes of notification when the EC2 needs the capacity back.

You can specify whether Amazon EC2 should hibernate, stop, or terminate Spot Instances when they are interrupted. You can choose the interruption behavior that meets your needs.

Take note that there is no "bid price" anymore for Spot EC2 instances since March 2018. You simply have to set your maximum price instead.

Reserved instances and Dedicated instances are incorrect as both do not act as spare compute capacity.

On-demand instances is a valid option but a Spot instance is much cheaper than On-Demand.

References:

https://docs.aws.amazon.com/AWSEC2/latest/UserGuide/spot-interruptions.html

http://docs.aws.amazon.com/AWSEC2/latest/UserGuide/how-spot-instances-work.html

https://aws.amazon.com/blogs/compute/new-amazon-ec2-spot-pricing

Question 43:

Your manager has asked you to deploy a mobile application that can collect votes for a popular singing competition. Millions of users from around the world will submit votes using their mobile phones. These votes must be collected and stored in a highly scalable and highly available data store which will be queried for real-time ranking.

Which of the following combination of services should you use to meet this requirement?

1. Amazon Aurora and Amazon Cognito
2. Amazon DynamoDB and AWS AppSync
3. Amazon Relational Database Service (RDS) and Amazon MQ
4. Amazon Redshift and AWS Mobile Hub

Answer(s): 2

Explanation

When the word durability pops out, the first service that should come to your mind is Amazon S3. Since this service is not available in the answer options, we can look at the other data store available which is Amazon DynamoDB.

DynamoDB is durable, scalable, and highly available data store which can be used for real-time tabulation. You can also use AppSync with DynamoDB to make it easy for you to build collaborative apps that keep shared data updated in real time. You just specify the data for your app with simple code statements and AWS AppSync manages everything needed to keep the app data updated in real time. This will allow your app to access data in Amazon DynamoDB, trigger AWS Lambda functions, or run Amazon Elasticsearch queries and combine data from these services to provide the exact data you need for your app.

Amazon Redshift and AWS Mobile Hub are incorrect as Amazon Redshift is mainly used as a data warehouse and for online analytic processing (OLAP). Although this service can be used for this scenario, DynamoDB is still the top choice given its better durability and scalability.

Amazon Relational Database Service (RDS) and Amazon MQ and Amazon Aurora and Amazon Cognito are possible answers in this scenario, however, DynamoDB is much more suitable for simple mobile apps which do not have complicated data relationships compared with enterprise web applications. The scenario says that the mobile app will be used from around the world, which is why you need a data storage service which can be supported globally. It would be a management overhead to implement multi-region deployment for your RDS and Aurora database instances compared to using the Global table feature of DynamoDB.

References:

https://aws.amazon.com/dynamodb/faqs/

https://aws.amazon.com/appsync/

Here is a deep dive on Amazon DynamoDB Design Patterns:

https://youtu.be/HaEPXoXVf2k

Question 44:

You are working as a Cloud Engineer for a top aerospace engineering firm. One of your tasks is to set up a document storage system using S3 for all of the engineering files. In Amazon S3, which of the following statements are true? (Select TWO.)

1. You can only store ZIP or TAR files in S3.

2. S3 is an object storage service that provides file system access semantics (such as strong consistency and file locking), and concurrently-accessible storage.
3. The total volume of data and number of objects you can store are unlimited.
4. The largest object that can be uploaded in a single PUT is 5 GB.
5. The largest object that can be uploaded in a single PUT is 5 TB.

Answer(s): 3, 4

Explanation

The correct answers are:

- The total volume of data and number of objects you can store are unlimited.

- The largest object that can be uploaded in a single PUT is 5 GB.

The option that says: The largest object that can be uploaded in a single PUT is 5 TB is incorrect as the largest object that can be uploaded in a single PUT is 5 GB and not 5 TB. Remember that the upload limit depends on whether you upload an object using a single PUT operation or via Multipart Upload. The largest object that can be uploaded in a single PUT is 5 GB. Please take note the phrase "... in a single PUT". If you are using the multipart upload API, then the limit is 5 TB.

The option that says: S3 is an object storage service that provides file system access semantics (such as strong consistency and file locking), and concurrently-accessible storage is incorrect because although S3 is indeed an object storage service, it does not provide file system access semantics. EFS provides this feature but not S3.

The option that says: You can only store ZIP or TAR files in S3 is incorrect as you can store virtually any kind of data in any format in S3.

References:

https://aws.amazon.com/s3/faqs/

https://docs.amazon.com/AmazonS3/latest/dev/UploadingObjects.html

Question 45:

A music company is storing data on Amazon Simple Storage Service (S3). The company's security policy requires that data are encrypted at rest. Which of the following methods can achieve this? (Select TWO.)

1. Use Amazon S3 bucket policies to restrict access to the data at rest.
2. Use SSL to encrypt the data while in transit to Amazon S3.

3. Encrypt the data on the client-side before ingesting to Amazon S3 using their own master key.
4. Use Amazon S3 server-side encryption with EC2 key pair.
5. Use Amazon S3 server-side encryption with customer-provided keys.

Answer(s): 3, 5

Explanation

Data protection refers to protecting data while in-transit (as it travels to and from Amazon S3) and at rest (while it is stored on disks in Amazon S3 data centers). You can protect data in transit by using SSL or by using client-side encryption. You have the following options for protecting data at rest in Amazon S3:

Use Server-Side Encryption – You request Amazon S3 to encrypt your object before saving it on disks in its data centers and decrypt it when you download the objects.

Use Server-Side Encryption with Amazon S3-Managed Keys (SSE-S3)

Use Server-Side Encryption with AWS KMS-Managed Keys (SSE-KMS)

Use Server-Side Encryption with Customer-Provided Keys (SSE-C)

Use Client-Side Encryption – You can encrypt data client-side and upload the encrypted data to Amazon S3. In this case, you manage the encryption process, the encryption keys, and related tools.

Use Client-Side Encryption with AWS KMS–Managed Customer Master Key (CMK)

Use Client-Side Encryption Using a Client-Side Master Key

Reference:

http://docs.aws.amazon.com/AmazonS3/latest/dev/UsingEncryption.html

Question 46:

You are setting up the cloud architecture for an international money transfer service to be deployed in AWS which will have thousands of users around the globe. The service should be available 24/7 to avoid any business disruption and should be resilient enough to handle the outage of an entire AWS region. To meet this requirement, you have deployed your AWS resources to multiple AWS Regions. You need to use Route 53 and configure it to set all of your resources to be available all the time as much as possible. When a resource becomes unavailable, your Route 53 should detect that it's unhealthy and stop including it when responding to queries.

Which of the following is the most fault tolerant routing configuration that you should use in this scenario?

1. Configure an Active-Active Failover with Weighted routing policy.
2. Configure an Active-Active Failover with One Primary and One Secondary Resource.
3. Configure an Active-Passive Failover with Weighted Records.
4. Configure an Active-Passive Failover with Multiple Primary and Secondary Resources.

Answer(s): 1

Explanation

You can use Route 53 health checking to configure active-active and active-passive failover configurations. You configure active-active failover using any routing policy (or combination of routing policies) other than failover, and you configure active-passive failover using the failover routing policy.

Active-Active Failover

Use this failover configuration when you want all of your resources to be available the majority of the time. When a resource becomes unavailable, Route 53 can detect that it's unhealthy and stop including it when responding to queries.

In active-active failover, all the records that have the same name, the same type (such as A or AAAA), and the same routing policy (such as weighted or latency) are active unless Route 53 considers them unhealthy. Route 53 can respond to a DNS query using any healthy record.

Active-Passive Failover

Use an active-passive failover configuration when you want a primary resource or group of resources to be available the majority of the time and you want a secondary resource or group of resources to be on standby in case all the primary resources become unavailable. When responding to queries, Route 53 includes only the healthy primary resources. If all the primary resources are unhealthy, Route 53 begins to include only the healthy secondary resources in response to DNS queries.

Configuring an Active-Passive Failover with Weighted Records and configuring an Active-Passive Failover with Multiple Primary and Secondary Resources are incorrect because an Active-Passive Failover is mainly used when you want a primary resource or group of resources to be available most of the time and you want a secondary resource or group of resources to be on standby in case all the primary resources become unavailable. In this scenario, all of your resources should be available all the time as much as possible which is why you have to use an Active-Active Failover instead.

Configuring an Active-Active Failover with One Primary and One Secondary Resource is incorrect because you cannot set up an Active-Active Failover with One Primary and One Secondary Resource. Remember that an Active-Active Failover uses all available resources all the time without a primary nor a secondary resource.

References:

https://docs.aws.amazon.com/Route53/latest/DeveloperGuide/dns-failover-types.html

https://docs.aws.amazon.com/Route53/latest/DeveloperGuide/routing-policy.html

https://docs.aws.amazon.com/Route53/latest/DeveloperGuide/dns-failover-configuring.html

Question 47:

You are working for a FinTech startup as their AWS Solutions Architect. You deployed an application on different EC2 instances with Elastic IP addresses attached for easy DNS resolution and configuration. These servers are only accessed from 8 AM to 6 PM and can be stopped from 6 PM to 8 AM for cost efficiency using Lambda with the script that automates this based on tags.

Which of the following will occur when an EC2-VPC instance with an associated Elastic IP is stopped and started? (Select TWO.)

1. The Elastic IP address is disassociated with the instance.
2. The ENI (Elastic Network Interface) is detached.
3. The underlying host for the instance is possibly changed.
4. There will be no changes.
5. All data on the attached instance-store devices will be lost.

Answer(s): 3, 5

Explanation

This question did not mention the specific type of EC2 instance however, it says that it will be stopped and started. Since only EBS-backed instances can be stopped and restarted, it is implied that the instance is EBS-backed. Remember that an instance store-backed instance can only be rebooted or terminated and its data will be erased if the EC2 instance is terminated.

If you stopped an EBS-backed EC2 instance, the volume is preserved but the data in any attached Instance store volumes will be erased. Keep in mind that an EC2 instance has an underlying physical host computer. If the instance is stopped, AWS usually moves the instance to a new host computer. Your instance may stay on the same host computer if there are no problems with the host computer. In addition, its Elastic IP address is disassociated from the instance if it is an EC2-Classic instance. Otherwise, if it is an EC2-VPC instance, the Elastic IP address remains associated.

Take note that an EBS-backed EC2 instance can have attached Instance Store volumes. This is the reason why there is an option that mentions the Instance Store volume, which is placed to test your understanding of this specific storage type. You can launch an EBS-backed EC2 instance and attach several Instance Store volumes but remember that there are some EC2 Instance types that don't support this kind of set up:

References:

http://docs.aws.amazon.com/AWSEC2/latest/UserGuide/ec2-instance-lifecycle.html

https://docs.aws.amazon.com/AWSEC2/latest/UserGuide/ComponentsAMIs.html#storage-for-the-root-device

Question 48:

You have a VPC that has a CIDR block of 10.31.0.0/27 which is connected to your on-premises data center. There was a requirement to create a Lambda function that will process massive amounts of cryptocurrency transactions every minute and then store the results to EFS. After you set up the serverless architecture and connected Lambda function to your VPC, you noticed that there is an increase in invocation errors with EC2 error types such as EC2ThrottledException on certain times of the day.

Which of the following are the possible causes of this issue? (Select TWO.)

1. Your VPC does not have sufficient subnet ENIs or subnet IPs.
2. Your VPC does not have a NAT gateway.
3. You only specified one subnet in your Lambda function configuration. That single subnet runs out of available IP addresses and there is no other subnet or Availability Zone which can handle the peak load.
4. The associated security group of your function does not allow outbound connections.
5. The attached IAM execution role of your function does not have the necessary permissions to access the resources of your VPC.

Answer(s): 1, 3

Explanation

You can configure a function to connect to a virtual private cloud (VPC) in your account. Use Amazon Virtual Private Cloud (Amazon VPC) to create a private network for resources such as databases, cache instances, or internal services. Connect your function to the VPC to access private resources during execution.

AWS Lambda runs your function code securely within a VPC by default. However, to enable your Lambda function to access resources inside your private VPC, you must provide additional VPC-specific configuration information that includes VPC subnet IDs and security group IDs. AWS Lambda uses this information to set up elastic network interfaces (ENIs) that enable your function to connect securely to other resources within your private VPC.

Lambda functions cannot connect directly to a VPC with dedicated instance tenancy. To connect to resources in a dedicated VPC, peer it to a second VPC with default tenancy.

Your Lambda function automatically scales based on the number of events it processes. If your Lambda function accesses a VPC, you must make sure that your VPC has sufficient ENI capacity to support the scale requirements of your Lambda function. It is also recommended that you specify at least one subnet in each Availability Zone in your Lambda function configuration.

By specifying subnets in each of the Availability Zones, your Lambda function can run in another Availability Zone if one goes down or runs out of IP addresses. If your VPC does not have sufficient ENIs or subnet IPs, your Lambda function will not scale as requests increase, and you will see an increase in invocation errors with EC2 error types like EC2ThrottledException. For asynchronous invocation, if you see an increase in errors without corresponding CloudWatch Logs, invoke the Lambda function synchronously in the console to get the error responses.

Hence, the correct answers for this scenario are:

- You only specified one subnet in your Lambda function configuration. That single subnet runs out of available IP addresses and there is no other subnet or Availability Zone which can handle the peak load.

- Your VPC does not have sufficient subnet ENIs or subnet IPs.

The option that says: Your VPC does not have a NAT gateway is incorrect because an issue in the NAT Gateway is unlikely to cause a request throttling issue or produce an EC2ThrottledException error in Lambda. Take note that the scenario says that the issue is happening only on certain times of the day, which means that the issue is only intermittent and the function works at other times. We can also conclude that an availability issue is not an issue since the application is already using a highly available NAT Gateway and not just a NAT instance.

The option that says: The associated security group of your function does not allow outbound connections is incorrect because if the associated security group does not allow outbound connections then the Lambda function will not work at all in the first place. Remember that the scenario says that the issue only happens intermittently. In addition, Internet traffic restrictions do not usually produce EC2ThrottledException errors.

The option that says: The attached IAM execution role of your function does not have the necessary permissions to access the resources of your VPC is incorrect because just as what is explained above, the issue is intermittent and thus, the IAM execution role of the function does have the necessary permissions to access the resources of the VPC since it works at those specific times. In case that the issue is indeed caused by a permission problem, then an EC2AccessDeniedException the error would most likely be returned and not an EC2ThrottledException error.

References:

https://docs.aws.amazon.com/lambda/latest/dg/vpc.html

https://aws.amazon.com/premiumsupport/knowledge-center/internet-access-lambda-function/

https://aws.amazon.com/premiumsupport/knowledge-center/lambda-troubleshoot-invoke-error-502-500/

Question 49:

You are working for a large telecommunications company where you need to run analytics against all combined log files from your Application Load Balancer as part of the regulatory requirements.

Which AWS services can be used together to collect logs and then easily perform log analysis?

1. Amazon DynamoDB for storing and EC2 for analyzing the logs.
2. Amazon S3 for storing the ELB log files and an EC2 instance for analyzing the log files using a custom-built application.
3. Amazon S3 for storing ELB log files and Amazon EMR for analyzing the log files.
4. Amazon EC2 with EBS volumes for storing and analyzing the log files.

Answer(s): 3

Explanation

In this scenario, it is best to use a combination of Amazon S3 and Amazon EMR: Amazon S3 for storing ELB log files and Amazon EMR for analyzing the log files. Access logging in the ELB is stored in Amazon S3 which means that the following are valid options:

- Amazon S3 for storing the ELB log files and an EC2 instance for analyzing the log files using a custom-built application.

- Amazon S3 for storing ELB log files and Amazon EMR for analyzing the log files.

However, log analysis can be automatically provided by Amazon EMR, which is more economical than building a custom-built log analysis application and hosting it in EC2. Hence, the option that says: Amazon S3 for storing ELB log files and Amazon EMR for analyzing the log files is the best answer between the two.

Access logging is an optional feature of Elastic Load Balancing that is disabled by default. After you enable access logging for your load balancer, Elastic Load Balancing captures the logs and stores them in the Amazon S3 bucket that you specify as compressed files. You can disable access logging at any time.

Amazon EMR provides a managed Hadoop framework that makes it easy, fast, and cost-effective to process vast amounts of data across dynamically scalable Amazon EC2 instances. It securely and reliably handles a broad set of big data use cases, including log analysis, web indexing, data transformations (ETL), machine learning, financial analysis, scientific simulation, and bioinformatics. You can also run other popular distributed frameworks such as Apache Spark, HBase, Presto, and Flink in Amazon EMR, and interact with data in other AWS data stores such as Amazon S3 and Amazon DynamoDB.

The option that says: Amazon DynamoDB for storing and EC2 for analyzing the logs is incorrect because DynamoDB is a noSQL database solution of AWS. It would be inefficient to store logs in DynamoDB while using EC2 to analyze them.

The option that says: Amazon EC2 with EBS volumes for storing and analyzing the log files is incorrect because using EC2 with EBS would be costly, and EBS might not provide the most durable storage for your logs, unlike S3.

The option that says: Amazon S3 for storing the ELB log files and an EC2 instance for analyzing the log files using a custom-built application is incorrect because using EC2 to analyze logs would be inefficient and expensive since you will have to program the analyzer yourself.

References:

https://aws.amazon.com/emr/

https://docs.aws.amazon.com/elasticloadbalancing/latest/application/load-balancer-access-logs.html

Question 50:

You are unable to connect to your new EC2 instance via SSH from your home computer, which you have recently deployed. However, you were able to successfully access other existing instances in your VPC without any issues.

Which of the following should you check and possibly correct to restore connectivity?

1. Configure the Security Group of the EC2 instance to permit ingress traffic over port 3389 from your IP.
2. Configure the Security Group of the EC2 instance to permit ingress traffic over port 22 from your IP.
3. Configure the Network Access Control List of your VPC to permit ingress traffic over port 22 from your IP.

4.   Use Amazon Data Lifecycle Manager.

Answer(s): 2

Explanation

When connecting to your EC2 instance via SSH, you need to ensure that port 22 is allowed on the security group of your EC2 instance.

A security group acts as a virtual firewall that controls the traffic for one or more instances. When you launch an instance, you associate one or more security groups with the instance. You add rules to each security group that allow traffic to or from its associated instances. You can modify the rules for a security group at any time; the new rules are automatically applied to all instances that are associated with the security group.

Using Amazon Data Lifecycle Manager is incorrect because this is primarily used to manage the lifecycle of your AWS resources and not to allow certain traffic to go through.

Configuring the Network Access Control List of your VPC to permit ingress traffic over port 22 from your IP is incorrect because this is not necessary in this scenario as it was specified that you were able to connect to other EC2 instances. In addition, Network ACL is much suitable to control the traffic that goes in and out of your entire VPC and not just on one EC2 instance.

Configure the Security Group of the EC2 instance to permit ingress traffic over port 3389 from your IP is incorrect because this is relevant to RDP and not SSH.

Reference:

http://docs.aws.amazon.com/AWSEC2/latest/UserGuide/using-network-security.html

Question 51:

You are working for a large IT consultancy company as a Solutions Architect. One of your clients is launching a file sharing web application in AWS which requires a durable storage service for hosting their static contents such as PDFs, Word Documents, high resolution images and many others.

Which type of storage service should you use to meet this requirement?

1.   Amazon EBS volume
2.   Amazon RDS instance
3.   Amazon EC2 instance store
4.   Amazon S3

Answer(s): 4

Explanation

Amazon S3 is storage for the Internet. It's a simple storage service that offers software developers a durable, highly-scalable, reliable, and low-latency data storage infrastructure at very low costs. Amazon S3 provides customers with a highly durable storage infrastructure. Versioning offers an additional level of protection by providing a means of recovery when customers accidentally overwrite or delete objects. Remember that the scenario requires a durable storage for static content. These two keywords are actually referring to S3, since it is highly durable and suitable for storing static content.

Hence, Amazon S3 is the correct answer.

Amazon EBS volume is incorrect because this is not as durable compared with S3. In addition, it is best to store the static contents in S3 rather than EBS.

Amazon EC2 instance store is incorrect because it is definitely not suitable - the data it holds will be wiped out immediately once the EC2 instance is restarted.

Amazon RDS instance is incorrect because an RDS instance is just a database and not suitable for storing static content. By default, RDS is not durable, unless you launch it to be in Multi-AZ deployments configuration.

Reference:

https://aws.amazon.com/s3/faqs/

https://d1.awsstatic.com/whitepapers/Storage/AWS%20Storage%20Services%20W
hitepaper-v9.pdf#page=24

Question 52:

A document sharing website is using AWS as its cloud infrastructure. Free users can upload a total of 5 GB data while premium users can upload as much as 5 TB. Their application uploads the user files, which can have a max file size of 1 TB, to an S3 Bucket.

In this scenario, what is the best way for the application to upload the large files in S3?

1. Use a single PUT request to upload the large file
2. Use AWS Snowball
3. Use Multipart Upload
4. Use AWS Import/Export

Answer(s): 3

Explanation

The total volume of data and number of objects you can store are unlimited. Individual Amazon S3 objects can range in size from a minimum of 0 bytes to a maximum of 5 terabytes. The largest object that can be uploaded in a single PUT is 5 gigabytes. For objects larger than 100 megabytes, customers should consider using the Multipart Upload capability.

The Multipart upload API enables you to upload large objects in parts. You can use this API to upload new large objects or make a copy of an existing object. Multipart uploading is a three-step process: you initiate the upload, you upload the object parts, and after you have uploaded all the parts, you complete the multipart upload. Upon receiving the complete multipart upload request, Amazon S3 constructs the object from the uploaded parts and you can then access the object just as you would any other object in your bucket.

Using a single PUT request to upload the large file is incorrect because the largest file size you can upload using a single PUT request is 5 GB. Files larger than this will fail to be uploaded.

Using AWS Snowball is incorrect because this is a migration tool that lets you transfer large amounts of data from your on-premises data center to AWS S3 and vice versa. This tool is not suitable for the given scenario. And when you provision Snowball, the device gets transported to you, and not to your customers. Therefore, you bear the responsibility of securing the device.

Using AWS Import/Export is incorrect because Import/Export is similar to AWS Snowball in such a way that it is meant to be used as a migration tool, and not for multiple customer consumption such as in the given scenario.

References:

https://docs.aws.amazon.com/AmazonS3/latest/dev/mpuoverview.html

https://aws.amazon.com/s3/faqs/

Question 53:

You are working for a Social Media Analytics company as its head data analyst. You want to collect gigabytes of data per second from websites and social media feeds to gain insights from data generated by its offerings and continuously improve the user experience. To meet this design requirement, you have developed an application hosted on an Auto Scaling group of Spot EC2 instances which processes the data and stores the results to DynamoDB and Redshift.

Which AWS service can you use to collect and process large streams of data records in real time?

1. Amazon Redshift
2. Amazon SWF
3. Amazon Kinesis Data Streams
4. Amazon S3

Answer(s): 3

Explanation

Amazon Kinesis Data Streams is used to collect and process large streams of data records in real time. You can use Kinesis Data Streams for rapid and continuous data intake and aggregation. The type of data used includes IT infrastructure log data, application logs, social media, market data feeds, and web clickstream data. Because the response time for the data intake and processing is in real time, the processing is typically lightweight.

The following diagram illustrates the high-level architecture of Kinesis Data Streams. The producers continually push data to Kinesis Data Streams, and the consumers process the data in real time. Consumers (such as a custom application running on Amazon EC2 or an Amazon Kinesis Data Firehose delivery stream) can store their results using an AWS service such as Amazon DynamoDB, Amazon Redshift, or Amazon S3.

Amazon S3 is incorrect because this is mainly used for object storage of frequently and infrequently accessed files with high durability. It does not meet the requirement of being able to collect and process large streams of data in real time. You have to use Kinesis data streams instead.

Amazon Redshift is incorrect because this is mainly used for data warehousing making it simple and cost-effective to analyze your data across your data warehouse and data lake. Again, it does not meet the requirement of being able to collect and process large streams of data real time.

Amazon SWF is incorrect because this is mainly used to build applications that use Amazon's cloud to coordinate work across distributed components and not used as a way to process large streams of data records.

Reference:

https://docs.aws.amazon.com/streams/latest/dev/introduction.html

Question 54:

A tech startup is launching an on-demand food delivery platform using Amazon ECS cluster with an AWS Fargate serverless compute engine and Amazon Aurora. It is expected that the database read queries will significantly increase in the coming weeks ahead. A Solutions Architect recently launched two Read Replicas to the database cluster to improve the platform's scalability.

Which of the following is the MOST suitable configuration that the Architect should implement to load balance all of the incoming read requests equally to the two Read Replicas?

1. Enable Amazon Aurora Parallel Query.
2. Use the built-in Reader endpoint of the Amazon Aurora database.
3. Use the built-in Cluster endpoint of the Amazon Aurora database.
4. Create a new Network Load Balancer to evenly distribute the read queries to the Read Replicas of the Amazon Aurora database.

Answer(s): 2

Explanation

Amazon Aurora typically involves a cluster of DB instances instead of a single instance. Each connection is handled by a specific DB instance. When you connect to an Aurora cluster, the hostname and port that you specify point to an intermediate handler called an endpoint. Aurora uses the endpoint mechanism to abstract these connections. Thus, you don't have to hardcode all the hostnames or write your own logic for load-balancing and rerouting connections when some DB instances aren't available.

For certain Aurora tasks, different instances or groups of instances perform different roles. For example, the primary instance handles all data definition language (DDL) and data manipulation language (DML) statements. Up to 15 Aurora Replicas handle read-only query traffic.

Using endpoints, you can map each connection to the appropriate instance or group of instances based on your use case. For example, to perform DDL statements you can connect to whichever instance is the primary instance. To perform queries, you can connect to the reader endpoint, with Aurora automatically performing load-balancing among all the Aurora Replicas. For clusters with DB instances of different capacities or configurations, you can connect to custom endpoints associated with different subsets of DB instances. For diagnosis or tuning, you can connect to a specific instance endpoint to examine details about a specific DB instance.

A reader endpoint for an Aurora DB cluster provides load-balancing support for read-only connections to the DB cluster. Use the reader endpoint for read operations, such as queries. By processing those statements on the read-only Aurora Replicas, this endpoint reduces the overhead on the primary instance. It also helps the cluster to scale the capacity to handle simultaneous SELECT queries, proportional to the number of Aurora Replicas in the cluster. Each Aurora DB cluster has one reader endpoint.

If the cluster contains one or more Aurora Replicas, the reader endpoint load-balances each connection request among the Aurora Replicas. In that case, you can only perform read-only statements such as SELECT in that session. If the cluster only contains a primary instance and no Aurora Replicas, the reader endpoint connects to the primary instance. In that case, you can perform write operations through the endpoint.

Hence, the correct answer is to use the built-in Reader endpoint of the Amazon Aurora database.

The option that says: Use the built-in Cluster endpoint of the Amazon Aurora database is incorrect because a cluster endpoint (also known as a writer endpoint) simply connects to the current primary DB instance for that DB cluster. This endpoint can perform write operations in the database such as DDL statements, which is perfect for handling production traffic but not suitable for handling queries for reporting since there will be no write database operations that will be sent.

The option that says: Enable Amazon Aurora Parallel Query is incorrect because this feature simply enables Amazon Aurora to push down and distribute the computational load of a single query across thousands of CPUs in Aurora's storage layer. Take note that it does not load balance all of the incoming read requests equally to the two Read Replicas. With Parallel Query, query processing is pushed down to the Aurora storage layer. The query gains a large amount of computing power, and it needs to transfer far less data over the network. In the meantime, the Aurora database instance can continue serving transactions with much less interruption. This way, you can run transactional and analytical workloads alongside each other in the same Aurora database, while maintaining high performance.

The option that says: Create a new Network Load Balancer to evenly distribute the read queries to the Read Replicas of the Amazon Aurora database is incorrect because a Network Load Balancer is not the suitable service/component to use for this requirement since an NLB is primarily used to distribute traffic to servers, not Read Replicas. You have to use the built-in Reader endpoint of the Amazon Aurora database instead.

References:

https://docs.aws.amazon.com/AmazonRDS/latest/AuroraUserGuide/Aurora.Overview.Endpoints.html

https://docs.aws.amazon.com/AmazonRDS/latest/AuroraUserGuide/Aurora.Overview.html

https://aws.amazon.com/rds/aurora/parallel-query/

Question 55:

You have an On-Demand EC2 instance located in a subnet in AWS which hosts a web application. The security group attached to this EC2 instance has the following Inbound Rules:

Larger image

The Route table attached to the VPC is shown below. You can establish an SSH connection into the EC2 instance from the internet. However, you are not able to connect to the web server using your Chrome browser.

Larger image

Which of the below steps would resolve the issue?

1. In the Security Group, add an Inbound HTTP rule.
2. In the Security Group, remove the SSH rule.
3. In the Route table, add this new route entry: 10.0.0.0/27 -> local
4. In the Route table, add this new route entry: 0.0.0.0 -> igw-b51618cc

Answer(s): 1

Explanation

The scenario is that you can already connect to the EC2 instance via SSH. This means that there is no problem in the Route Table of your VPC. To fix this issue, you simply need to update your Security Group and add an Inbound rule to allow HTTP traffic.

The option that says: In the Security Group, remove the SSH rule is incorrect as doing so will not solve the issue. It will just disable SSH traffic that is already available.

The options that say: In the Route table, add this new route entry: 0.0.0.0 -> igw-b51618cc and In the Route table, add this new route entry: 10.0.0.0/27 -> local are incorrect as there is no need to change the Route Tables.

Reference:

http://docs.aws.amazon.com/AmazonVPC/latest/UserGuide/VPC_SecurityGroups.html

Question 56:

You are a new Solutions Architect working for a financial company. Your manager wants to have the ability to automatically transfer obsolete data from their S3 bucket to a low cost storage system in AWS.

What is the best solution you can provide to them?

1. Use Lifecycle Policies in S3 to move obsolete data to Glacier.
2. Use Amazon SQS.
3. Use an EC2 instance and a scheduled job to transfer the obsolete data from their S3 location to Amazon S3 Glacier.
4. Use Amazon SWF.

Answer(s): 1

Explanation

In this scenario, you can use lifecycle policies in S3 to automatically move obsolete data to Glacier.

Lifecycle configuration in Amazon S3 enables you to specify the lifecycle management of objects in a bucket. The configuration is a set of one or more rules, where each rule defines an action for Amazon S3 to apply to a group of objects. These actions can be classified as follows:

Transition actions – In which you define when objects transition to another storage class. For example, you may choose to transition objects to the STANDARD_IA (IA, for infrequent access) storage class 30 days after creation, or archive objects to the GLACIER storage class one year after creation.

Expiration actions – In which you specify when the objects expire. Then Amazon S3 deletes the expired objects on your behalf.

Using an EC2 instance and a scheduled job to transfer the obsolete data from their S3 location to Amazon S3 Glacier is incorrect because you don't need to create a scheduled job in EC2 as you can just simply use the lifecycle policy in S3.

Using Amazon SQS and Amazon SWF are incorrect as SQS and SWF are not storage services.

References:

http://docs.aws.amazon.com/AmazonS3/latest/dev/object-lifecycle-mgmt.html
https://aws.amazon.com/blogs/aws/archive-s3-to-glacier/

Question 57:

A global online sports betting company has its popular web application hosted in AWS. They are planning to develop a new online portal for their new business venture and they hired you to implement the cloud architecture for a new online portal that will accept bets globally for world sports. You started to design the system with a relational database that runs on a single EC2 instance, which requires a single EBS volume that can support up to 30,000 IOPS.

In this scenario, which Amazon EBS volume type can you use that will meet the performance requirements of this new online portal?

1. EBS Provisioned IOPS SSD (io1)
2. EBS Throughput Optimized HDD (st1)
3. EBS Cold HDD (sc1)
4. EBS General Purpose SSD (gp2)

Answer(s): 1

Explanation

The scenario requires a storage type for a relational database with a high IOPS performance. For these scenarios, SSD volumes are more suitable to use instead of HDD volumes. Remember that the dominant performance attribute of SSD is IOPS while HDD is Throughput.

In the exam, always consider the difference between SSD and HDD as shown on the table below. This will allow you to easily eliminate specific EBS-types in the options which are not SSD or not HDD, depending on whether the question asks for a storage type which has small, random I/O operations or large, sequential I/O operations.

Since the requirement is 30,000 IOPS, you have to use an EBS type of Provisioned IOPS SSD. This provides sustained performance for mission-critical low-latency workloads. Hence, EBS Provisioned IOPS SSD (io1) is the correct answer.

EBS Throughput Optimized HDD (st1) and EBS Cold HDD (sc1) are incorrect because these are HDD volumes which are more suitable for large streaming workloads rather than transactional database workloads.

EBS General Purpose SSD (gp2) is incorrect because although a General Purpose SSD volume can be used for this scenario, it does not provide the high IOPS required by the application, unlike the Provisioned IOPS SSD volume.

Reference:

https://aws.amazon.com/ebs/details/

Question 58:

You are working for a startup company that has resources deployed on the AWS Cloud. Your company is now going through a set of scheduled audits by an external auditing firm for compliance.

Which of the following services available in AWS can be utilized to help ensure the right information are present for auditing purposes?

1. Amazon VPC
2. AWS CloudTrail
3. Amazon EC2
4. Amazon CloudWatch

Answer(s): 2

Explanation

AWS CloudTrail is a service that enables governance, compliance, operational auditing, and risk auditing of your AWS account. With CloudTrail, you can log, continuously monitor, and retain account activity related to actions across your AWS infrastructure. CloudTrail provides event history of your AWS account activity, including actions taken through the AWS Management Console, AWS SDKs, command line tools, and other AWS services. This event history simplifies security analysis, resource change tracking, and troubleshooting.

CloudTrail provides visibility into user activity by recording actions taken on your account. CloudTrail records important information about each action, including who made the request, the services used, the actions performed, parameters for the actions, and the response elements returned by the AWS service. This information helps you to track changes made to your AWS resources and troubleshoot operational issues. CloudTrail makes it easier to ensure compliance with internal policies and regulatory standards.

Amazon VPC is incorrect because a VPC is a logically isolated section of the AWS Cloud where you can launch AWS resources in a virtual network that you define. It does not provide you the auditing information that were asked for in this scenario.

Amazon EC2 is incorrect because EC2 is a service that provides secure, resizable compute capacity in the cloud and does not provide the needed information in this scenario just like the option above.

Amazon CloudWatch is incorrect because this is a monitoring tool for your AWS resources. Like the above options, it does not provide the needed information to satisfy the requirement in the scenario.

Reference:

https://aws.amazon.com/cloudtrail/

Question 59:

You currently have an Augment Reality (AR) mobile game which has a serverless backend. It is using a DynamoDB table which was launched using the AWS CLI to store all the user data and information gathered from the players and a Lambda function to pull the data from DynamoDB. The game is being used by millions of users each day to read and store data.

How would you design the application to improve its overall performance and make it more scalable while keeping the costs low? (Select TWO.)

1. Use AWS SSO and Cognito to authenticate users and have them directly access DynamoDB using single-sign on. Manually set the provisioned read and write capacity to a higher RCU and WCU.
2. Use API Gateway in conjunction with Lambda and turn on the caching on frequently accessed data and enable DynamoDB global replication.
3. Enable DynamoDB Accelerator (DAX) and ensure that the Auto Scaling is enabled and increase the maximum provisioned read and write capacity.
4. Since Auto Scaling is enabled by default, the provisioned read and write capacity will adjust automatically. Also enable DynamoDB Accelerator (DAX) to improve the performance from milliseconds to microseconds.
5. Configure CloudFront with DynamoDB as the origin; cache frequently accessed data on client device using ElastiCache.

Answer(s): 2, 3

Explanation

Amazon DynamoDB Accelerator (DAX) is a fully managed, highly available, in-memory cache for DynamoDB that delivers up to a 10x performance improvement – from milliseconds to microseconds – even at millions of requests per second. DAX does all the heavy lifting required to add in-memory acceleration to your DynamoDB tables, without requiring developers to manage cache invalidation, data population, or cluster management.

Amazon API Gateway lets you create an API that acts as a "front door" for applications to access data, business logic, or functionality from your back-end services, such as code running on AWS Lambda. Amazon API Gateway handles all of the tasks involved in accepting and processing up to hundreds of thousands of concurrent API calls, including traffic management, authorization and access control, monitoring, and API version management. Amazon API Gateway has no minimum fees or startup costs.

AWS Lambda scales your functions automatically on your behalf. Every time an event notification is received for your function, AWS Lambda quickly locates free capacity within its compute fleet and runs your code. Since your code is stateless, AWS Lambda can start as many copies of your function as needed without lengthy deployment and configuration delays.

The option that says: Configure CloudFront with DynamoDB as the origin; cache frequently accessed data on client device using ElastiCache is incorrect because although CloudFront delivers content faster to your users using edge locations, you still cannot integrate DynamoDB table with CloudFront as these two are incompatible.

The option that says: Use AWS SSO and Cognito to authenticate users and have them directly access DynamoDB using single-sign on. Manually set the provisioned read and write capacity to a higher RCU and WCU is incorrect because AWS Single Sign-On (SSO) is a cloud SSO service that just makes it easy to centrally manage SSO access to multiple AWS accounts and business applications. This will not be of much help on the scalability and performance of the application. It is costly to manually set the provisioned read and write capacity to a higher RCU and WCU because this capacity will run round the clock and will still be the same even if the incoming traffic is stable and there is no need to scale.

The option that says: Since Auto Scaling is enabled by default, the provisioned read and write capacity will adjust automatically. Also enable DynamoDB Accelerator (DAX) to improve the performance from milliseconds to microseconds is incorrect because, by default, Auto Scaling is not enabled in a DynamoDB table which is created using the AWS CLI.

References:

https://aws.amazon.com/lambda/faqs/

https://aws.amazon.com/api-gateway/faqs/

https://aws.amazon.com/dynamodb/dax/

Question 60:

An Architect is managing a data analytics application which exclusively uses Amazon S3 as its data storage. For the past few weeks, the application works as expected until a new change was implemented to increase the rate at which the application updates its data. There have been reports that outdated data intermittently appears when the application accesses objects from S3 bucket. The development team investigated the application logic and didn't find any issues.

Which of the following is the MOST likely cause of this issue?

1. The data analytics application is designed to fetch parts of objects from the S3 bucket using a range header.
2. The data analytics application is designed to use atomic updates across object keys.
3. The data analytics application is designed to update its data with an object-locking mechanism.
4. The data analytics application is designed to fetch objects from the S3 bucket using parallel requests.

Answer(s): 4

Explanation

Amazon S3 provides read-after-write consistency for PUTS of new objects in your S3 bucket in all regions with one caveat: if you make a HEAD or GET request to the key name (to find if the object exists) before creating the object, Amazon S3 provides eventual consistency for read-after-write. Amazon S3 offers eventual consistency for overwrite PUTS and DELETES in all regions.

Updates to a single key are atomic. For example, if you PUT to an existing key, a subsequent read might return the old data or the updated data, but it will never return corrupted or partial data. This usually happens if your application is using parallel requests on the same object.

Amazon S3 achieves high availability by replicating data across multiple servers within Amazon's data centers. If a PUT request is successful, your data is safely stored. However, information about the changes must replicate across Amazon S3, which can take some time, and so you might observe the following behaviors:

- A process writes a new object to Amazon S3 and immediately lists keys within its bucket. Until the change is fully propagated, the object might not appear in the list.

- A process replaces an existing object and immediately attempts to read it. Until the change is fully propagated, Amazon S3 might return the prior data.

- A process deletes an existing object and immediately attempts to read it. Until the deletion is fully propagated, Amazon S3 might return the deleted data.

- A process deletes an existing object and immediately lists keys within its bucket. Until the deletion is fully propagated, Amazon S3 might list the deleted object.

Amazon S3's support for parallel requests means you can scale your S3 performance by the factor of your compute cluster, without making any customizations to your application. Amazon S3 does not currently support Object Locking. If two PUT requests are simultaneously made to the same key, the request with the latest timestamp wins. If this is an issue, you will need to build an object-locking mechanism into your application.

Updates are key-based; there is no way to make atomic updates across keys. For example, you cannot make the update of one key dependent on the update of another key unless you design this functionality into your application.

Hence, the correct answer is the option that says: The data analytics application is designed to fetch objects from the S3 bucket using parallel requests.

The option that says: The data analytics application is designed to fetch parts of objects from the S3 bucket using a range header is incorrect because using a Range header is primarily used to retrieve an object in parts and is unlikely the root cause on why the application is intermittently getting old data. Using the Range HTTP header in a GET request, you can retrieve a specific range of bytes in an object stored in Amazon S3. With this, you can resume fetching other parts of the object whenever your application is ready. This resumable download is useful when you need only portions of your object data. It is also useful where network connectivity is poor and you need to react to failures.

The option that says: The data analytics application is designed to use atomic updates across object keys is incorrect because the update operations are key-based which means that there is no way to make atomic updates across keys. Hence, this is not the root cause of this issue.

The option that says: The data analytics application is designed to update its data with an object-locking mechanism is incorrect because an object-locking mechanism will actually safeguard the application from the issue of getting obsolete data and not the other way around. Moreover, Amazon S3 does not currently support Object Locking for concurrent updates. Take note that this is different from the Amazon S3 Object Lock feature which prevents an object from being deleted or overwritten for a fixed amount of time or indefinitely. The scenario mentioned here is about two or more clients that are concurrently accessing and updating the same object at the same time. An "Object-locking" mechanism is a system that "locks" the very first update request to the S3 object and blocks any concurrent update requests to the same object.

References:

https://docs.aws.amazon.com/AmazonS3/latest/dev/Introduction.html

https://docs.aws.amazon.com/AmazonS3/latest/API/RESTObjectGET.html

Question 61:

Due to the large volume of query requests, the database performance of an online reporting application significantly slowed down. The Solutions Architect is trying to convince her client to use Amazon RDS Read Replica for their application instead of setting up a Multi-AZ Deployments configuration.

What are two benefits of using Read Replicas over Multi-AZ that the Architect should point out? (Select TWO.)

1. It elastically scales out beyond the capacity constraints of a single DB instance for read-heavy database workloads.
2. Provides synchronous replication and automatic failover in the case of Availability Zone service failures.
3. Provides asynchronous replication and improves the performance of the primary database by taking read-heavy database workloads from it.
4. Allows both read and write operations on the read replica to complement the primary database.
5. It enhances the read performance of your primary database by increasing its IOPS and accelerates its query processing via AWS Global Accelerator.

Answer(s): 1, 3

Explanation

Amazon RDS Read Replicas provide enhanced performance and durability for database (DB) instances. This feature makes it easy to elastically scale out beyond the capacity constraints of a single DB instance for read-heavy database workloads.

You can create one or more replicas of a given source DB Instance and serve high-volume application read traffic from multiple copies of your data, thereby increasing aggregate read throughput. Read replicas can also be promoted when needed to become standalone DB instances.

For the MySQL, MariaDB, PostgreSQL, and Oracle database engines, Amazon RDS creates a second DB instance using a snapshot of the source DB instance. It then uses the engines' native asynchronous replication to update the read replica whenever there is a change to the source DB instance. The read replica operates as a DB instance that allows only read-only connections; applications can connect to a read replica just as they would to any DB instance. Amazon RDS replicates all databases in the source DB instance.

When you create a read replica for Amazon RDS for MySQL, MariaDB, PostgreSQL, and Oracle, Amazon RDS sets up a secure communications channel using public-key encryption between the source DB instance and the read replica, even when replicating across regions. Amazon RDS establishes any AWS security configurations such as adding security group entries needed to enable the secure channel.

You can also create read replicas within a Region or between Regions for your Amazon RDS for MySQL, MariaDB, PostgreSQL, and Oracle database instances encrypted at rest with AWS Key Management Service (KMS).

Hence, the correct answers are:

- It elastically scales out beyond the capacity constraints of a single DB instance for read-heavy database workloads.

- Provides asynchronous replication and improves the performance of the primary database by taking read-heavy database workloads from it.

The option that says: Allows both read and write operations on the read replica to complement the primary database is incorrect as Read Replicas are primarily used to offload read-only operations from the primary database instance. By default, you can't do a write operation to your Read Replica.

The option that says: Provides synchronous replication and automatic failover in the case of Availability Zone service failures is incorrect as this is a benefit of Multi-AZ and not of a Read Replica. Moreover, Read Replicas provide an asynchronous type of replication and not synchronous replication.

The option that says: It enhances the read performance of your primary database by increasing its IOPS and accelerates its query processing via AWS Global Accelerator is incorrect because Read Replicas do not do anything to upgrade or increase the read throughput on the primary DB instance per se, but it provides a way for your application to fetch data from replicas. In this way, it improves the overall performance of your entire database-tier (and not just the primary DB instance). It doesn't increase the IOPS nor use AWS Global Accelerator to accelerate the compute capacity of your primary database. AWS Global Accelerator is a networking service, not related to RDS, that direct user traffic to the nearest application endpoint to the client, thus reducing internet latency and jitter. It simply routes the traffic to the closest edge location via Anycast.

References:

https://aws.amazon.com/rds/details/read-replicas/

https://aws.amazon.com/rds/features/multi-az/

Additional tutorial - How do I make my RDS MySQL read replica writable?

https://youtu.be/j5da6d2TIPc

Question 62:

You are a Solutions Architect for a global news company. You are configuring a fleet of EC2 instances in a subnet which currently is in a VPC with an Internet gateway attached. All of these EC2 instances can be accessed from the Internet. You then launch another subnet and launch an EC2 instance in it, however you are not able to access the EC2 instance from the Internet.

What could be the possible reasons for this issue? (Select TWO.)

1. The Amazon EC2 instance does not have a public IP address associated with it.
2. The Amazon EC2 instance is not a member of the same Auto Scaling group.
3. The Amazon EC2 instance does not have an attached Elastic Fabric Adapter (EFA).
4. The route table is not configured properly to send traffic from the EC2 instance to the Internet through the customer gateway (CGW).
5. The route table is not configured properly to send traffic from the EC2 instance to the Internet through the Internet gateway.

Answer(s): 1, 5

Explanation

Your VPC has an implicit router, and you use route tables to control where network traffic is directed. Each subnet in your VPC must be associated with a route table, which controls the routing for the subnet (subnet route table). You can explicitly associate a subnet with a particular route table. Otherwise, the subnet is implicitly associated with the main route table.

A subnet can only be associated with one route table at a time, but you can associate multiple subnets with the same subnet route table. You can optionally associate a route table with an internet gateway or a virtual private gateway (gateway route table). This enables you to specify routing rules for inbound traffic that enters your VPC through the gateway

Be sure that the subnet route table also has a route entry to the internet gateway. If this entry doesn't exist, the instance is in a private subnet and is inaccessible from the internet.

In cases where your EC2 instance cannot be accessed from the Internet (or vice versa), you usually have to check two things:

- Does it have an EIP or public IP address?

- Is the route table properly configured?

 Below are the correct answers:

- Amazon EC2 instance does not have a public IP address associated with it.

- The route table is not configured properly to send traffic from the EC2 instance to the Internet through the Internet gateway.

The option that says: The Amazon EC2 instance is not a member of the same Auto Scaling group is incorrect since Auto Scaling Groups do not affect Internet connectivity of EC2 instances.

The option that says: The Amazon EC2 instance doesn't have an attached Elastic Fabric Adapter (EFA) is incorrect because the Elastic Fabric Adapter is just a network device that you can attach to your Amazon EC2 instance to accelerate High Performance Computing (HPC) and machine learning applications. EFA enables you to achieve the application performance of an on-premises HPC cluster, with the scalability, flexibility, and elasticity provided by AWS. However, this component is not required in order for your EC2 instance to access the public Internet.

The option that says: The route table is not configured properly to send traffic from the EC2 instance to the Internet through the customer gateway (CGW) is incorrect since CGW is used when you are setting up a VPN. The correct gateway should be an Internet gateway.

References:

http://docs.aws.amazon.com/AmazonVPC/latest/UserGuide/VPC_Scenario2.html

https://docs.aws.amazon.com/vpc/latest/userguide/VPC_Route_Tables.html

uestion 63:

An online job site is using NGINX for its application servers hosted in EC2 instances and MongoDB Atlas for its database-tier. MongoDB Atlas is a fully automated third-party cloud service which is not provided by AWS, but supports VPC peering to connect to your VPC.

Which of the following items are invalid VPC peering configurations? (Select TWO.)

1. Two VPCs peered to a specific CIDR block in one VPC
2. Transitive Peering
3. Edge to Edge routing via a gateway
4. One VPC Peered with two VPCs using longest prefix match
5. One to one relationship between two Virtual Private Cloud networks

Answer(s): 2, 3

Explanation

Transitive Peering and Edge to Edge routing via a gateway are invalid VPC Peering configurations, while the other options are valid ones.

The following VPC peering connection configurations are not supported.

Overlapping CIDR Blocks

Transitive Peering

Edge to Edge Routing Through a Gateway or Private Connection

Overlapping CIDR Blocks

You cannot create a VPC peering connection between VPCs with matching or overlapping IPv4 CIDR blocks.

If the VPCs have multiple IPv4 CIDR blocks, you cannot create a VPC peering connection if any of the CIDR blocks overlap (regardless of whether you intend to use the VPC peering connection for communication between the non-overlapping CIDR blocks only).

(xyx)c

This limitation also applies to VPCs that have non-overlapping IPv6 CIDR blocks. Even if you intend to use the VPC peering connection for IPv6 communication only, you cannot create a VPC peering connection if the VPCs have matching or overlapping IPv4 CIDR blocks. Communication over IPv6 is not supported for an inter-region VPC peering connection.

Transitive Peering

You have a VPC peering connection between VPC A and VPC B (pcx-aaaabbbb), and between VPC A and VPC C (pcx-aaaacccc). There is no VPC peering connection between VPC B and VPC C. You cannot route packets directly from VPC B to VPC C through VPC A.

Edge to Edge Routing Through a Gateway or Private Connection

If either VPC in a peering relationship has one of the following connections, you cannot extend the peering relationship to that connection:

A VPN connection or an AWS Direct Connect connection to a corporate network

An internet connection through an internet gateway

An internet connection in a private subnet through a NAT device

A gateway VPC endpoint to an AWS service; for example, an endpoint to Amazon S3.

(IPv6) A ClassicLink connection. You can enable IPv4 communication between a linked EC2-Classic instance and instances in a VPC on the other side of a VPC peering connection. However, IPv6 is not supported in EC2-Classic, so you cannot extend this connection for IPv6 communication.

For example, if VPC A and VPC B are peered, and VPC A has any of these connections, then instances in VPC B cannot use the connection to access resources on the other side of the connection. Similarly, resources on the other side of a connection cannot use the connection to access VPC B.

References:

http://docs.aws.amazon.com/AmazonVPC/latest/PeeringGuide/invalid-peering-configurations.html

https://docs.aws.amazon.com/vpc/latest/peering/peering-configurations-partial-access.html

Here is a quick introduction to VPC Peering:

https://youtu.be/i1A1eH8vLtk

Question 64:

You are working as a Solutions Architect for a multinational financial firm. They have a global online trading platform in which the users from all over the world regularly upload terabytes of transactional data to a centralized S3 bucket. What AWS feature should you use in your present system to improve throughput and ensure consistently fast data transfer to the Amazon S3 bucket, regardless of your user's location?

1. FTP
2. Amazon S3 Transfer Acceleration
3. AWS Direct Connect
4. Use CloudFront Origin Access Identity

Answer(s): 2

Explanation

Amazon S3 Transfer Acceleration enables fast, easy, and secure transfers of files over long distances between your client and your Amazon S3 bucket. Transfer Acceleration leverages Amazon CloudFront's globally distributed AWS Edge Locations. As data arrives at an AWS Edge Location, data is routed to your Amazon S3 bucket over an optimized network path.

FTP is incorrect because the File Transfer Protocol does not guarantee fast throughput and consistent, fast data transfer.

AWS Direct Connect is incorrect because you have users all around the world and not just on your on-premises data center. Direct Connect would be too costly and is definitely not suitable for this purpose.

Using CloudFront Origin Access Identity is incorrect because this is a feature which ensures that only CloudFront can serve S3 content. It does not increase throughput and ensure fast delivery of content to your customers.

Reference:

http://docs.aws.amazon.com/AmazonS3/latest/dev/transfer-acceleration.html

Question 65:

A tech company is currently using Auto Scaling for their web application. A new AMI now needs to be used for launching a fleet of EC2 instances.

Which of the following changes needs to be done?

1. Create a new target group and launch configuration.
2. Do nothing. You can start directly launching EC2 instances in the Auto Scaling group with the same launch configuration.
3. Create a new launch configuration.
4. Create a new target group.

Answer(s): 3

Explanation

A launch configuration is a template that an Auto Scaling group uses to launch EC2 instances. When you create a launch configuration, you specify information for the instances such as the ID of the Amazon Machine Image (AMI), the instance type, a key pair, one or more security groups, and a block device mapping. If you've launched an EC2 instance before, you specified the same information in order to launch the instance.

You can specify your launch configuration with multiple Auto Scaling groups. However, you can only specify one launch configuration for an Auto Scaling group at a time, and you can't modify a launch configuration after you've created it. Therefore, if you want to change the launch configuration for an Auto Scaling group, you must create a launch configuration and then update your Auto Scaling group with the new launch configuration.

For this scenario, you have to create a new launch configuration. Remember that you can't modify a launch configuration after you've created it.

Hence, the correct answer is: Create a new launch configuration.

The option that says: Do nothing. You can start directly launching EC2 instances in the Auto Scaling group with the same launch configuration is incorrect because what you are trying to achieve is change the AMI being used by your fleet of EC2 instances. Therefore, you need to change the launch configuration to update what your instances are using.

The option that says: create a new target group and create a new target group and launch configuration are both incorrect because you only want to change the AMI being used by your instances, and not the instances themselves. Target groups are primarily used in ELBs and not in Auto Scaling. The scenario didn't mention that the architecture has a load balancer. Therefore, you should be updating your launch configuration, not the target group.

References:

http://docs.aws.amazon.com/autoscaling/latest/userguide/LaunchConfiguration.html

https://docs.aws.amazon.com/autoscaling/ec2/userguide/AutoScalingGroup.html

PRACTICE TEST 4

AWS CERTIFIED SOLUTIONS ARCHITECT ASSOCIATE

AWS CERTIFIED SOLUTIONS ARCHITECT ASSOCIATE PRACTICE TEST 4

Question 1:

You are managing a global news website which is deployed to AWS and is using MySQL RDS. The website has millions of viewers from all over the world which means that the website has read-heavy database workloads. All database transactions must be ACID compliant to ensure data integrity.

In this scenario, which of the following is the best option to use to increase the read throughput on the MySQL database?

1. Enable Amazon RDS Read Replicas
2. Use SQS to queue up the requests
3. Enable Multi-AZ deployments
4. Enable Amazon RDS Standby Replicas

Correct Answer(s): 1

Answer(s):

Explanation

Amazon RDS Read Replicas provide enhanced performance and durability for database (DB) instances. This feature makes it easy to elastically scale out beyond the capacity constraints of a single DB instance for read-heavy database workloads. You can create one or more replicas of a given source DB Instance and serve high-volume application read traffic from multiple copies of your data, thereby increasing aggregate read throughput. Read replicas can also be promoted when needed to become standalone DB instances. Read replicas are available in Amazon RDS for MySQL, MariaDB, Oracle and PostgreSQL as well as Amazon Aurora.

Enabling Multi-AZ deployments is incorrect because the Multi-AZ deployments feature is mainly used to achieve high availability and failover support for your database.

Enabling Amazon RDS Standby Replicas is incorrect because a Standby replica is used in Multi-AZ deployments and hence, it is not a solution to reduce read-heavy database workloads.

Using SQS to queue up the requests is incorrect because although an SQS queue can effectively manage the requests, it won't be able to entirely improve the read-throughput of the database by itself.

References:

https://aws.amazon.com/rds/details/read-replicas/

https://docs.aws.amazon.com/AmazonRDS/latest/UserGuide/USER_ReadRepl.ht
ml

Here is a quick introduction to Amazon RDS:

https://youtu.be/eMzCI7S1P9M

Question 2:

You launched an EC2 instance in your newly created VPC. You have noticed that the generated instance does not have an associated DNS hostname.

Which of the following options could be a valid reason for this issue?

1. The newly created VPC has an invalid CIDR block.
2. Amazon Route53 is not enabled.
3. The DNS resolution and DNS hostname of the VPC configuration should be enabled.
4. The security group of the EC2 instance needs to be modified.

Correct Answer(s): 3

Explanation

When you launch an EC2 instance into a default VPC, AWS provides it with public and private DNS hostnames that correspond to the public IPv4 and private IPv4 addresses for the instance.

However, when you launch an instance into a non-default VPC, AWS provides the instance with a private DNS hostname only. New instances will only be provided with public DNS hostname depending on these two DNS attributes: the DNS resolution and DNS hostnames, that you have specified for your VPC, and if your instance has a public IPv4 address.

In this case, the new EC2 instance does not automatically get a DNS hostname because the DNS resolution and DNS hostnames attributes are disabled in the newly created VPC.

The option that says: The newly created VPC has an invalid CIDR block is incorrect since it's very unlikely that a VPC has an invalid CIDR block because of AWS validation schemes.

The option that says: Amazon Route 53 is not enabled is incorrect since Route 53 does not need to be enabled. Route 53 is the DNS service of AWS, but the VPC is the one that enables assigning of instance hostnames.

255

The option that says: The security group of the EC2 instance needs to be modified is incorrect since security groups are just firewalls for your instances. They filter traffic based on a set of security group rules.

References:

https://docs.aws.amazon.com/AmazonVPC/latest/UserGuide/vpc-dns.html

https://aws.amazon.com/vpc/

Question 3:

A financial company instructed you to automate the recurring tasks in your department such as patch management, infrastructure selection, and data synchronization to improve their current processes. You need to have a service which can coordinate multiple AWS services into serverless workflows.

Which of the following is the most cost-effective service to use in this scenario?

1. AWS Step Functions
2. AWS Lambda
3. SWF
4. AWS Batch

Correct Answer(s): 1

Explanation

AWS Step Functions provides serverless orchestration for modern applications. Orchestration centrally manages a workflow by breaking it into multiple steps, adding flow logic, and tracking the inputs and outputs between the steps. As your applications execute, Step Functions maintains application state, tracking exactly which workflow step your application is in, and stores an event log of data that is passed between application components. That means that if networks fail or components hang, your application can pick up right where it left off.

Application development is faster and more intuitive with Step Functions, because you can define and manage the workflow of your application independently from its business logic. Making changes to one does not affect the other. You can easily update and modify workflows in one place, without having to struggle with managing, monitoring and maintaining multiple point-to-point integrations. Step Functions frees your functions and containers from excess code, so your applications are faster to write, more resilient, and easier to maintain.

SWF is incorrect because this is a fully-managed state tracker and task coordinator service. It does not provide serverless orchestration to multiple AWS resources.

AWS Lambda is incorrect because although Lambda is used for serverless computing, it does not provide a direct way to coordinate multiple AWS services into serverless workflows.

AWS Batch is incorrect because this is primarily used to efficiently run hundreds of thousands of batch computing jobs in AWS.

Reference:

https://aws.amazon.com/step-functions/features/

Question 4:

A technology company is building a new cryptocurrency trading platform that allows buying and selling of Bitcoin, Ethereum, XRP, Ripple and many others. You were hired as a Cloud Engineer to build the required infrastructure needed for this new trading platform. On your first week at work, you started to create CloudFormation YAML scripts that defines all of the needed AWS resources for the application. Your manager was shocked that you haven't created the EC2 instances, S3 buckets and other AWS resources straight away. He does not understand the text-based scripts that you have done and was disappointed that you are just slacking off at your job.

In this scenario, what are the benefits of using the Amazon CloudFormation service that you should tell your manager to clarify his concerns? (Select TWO.)

1. Enables modeling, provisioning, and version-controlling of your entire AWS infrastructure
2. Using CloudFormation itself is free, including the AWS resources that have been created.
3. A storage location for the code of your application
4. Allows you to model your entire infrastructure in a text file
5. Provides highly durable and scalable data storage

Correct Answer(s): 1, 4

Explanation

AWS CloudFormation provides a common language for you to describe and provision all the infrastructure resources in your cloud environment. CloudFormation allows you to use a simple text file to model and provision, in an automated and secure manner, all the resources needed for your applications across all regions and accounts. This file serves as the single source of truth for your cloud environment. AWS CloudFormation is available at no additional charge, and you pay only for the AWS resources needed to run your applications.

Hence, the correct answers are:

Enables modeling, provisioning, and version-controlling of your entire AWS infrastructure

Allows you to model your entire infrastructure in a text file

The option that says: Provides highly durable and scalable data storage is incorrect because CloudFormation is not a data storage service.

The option that says: A storage location for the code of your application is incorrect because CloudFormation is not used to store your application code. You have to use CodeCommit as a code repository and not CloudFormation.

The option that says: Using CloudFormation itself is free, including the AWS resources that have been created is incorrect because although the use of CloudFormation service is free, you have to pay the AWS resources that you created.

References:

https://aws.amazon.com/cloudformation/

https://aws.amazon.com/cloudformation/faqs/

Question 5:

A real-time data analytics application is using AWS Lambda to process data and store results in JSON format to an S3 bucket. To speed up the existing workflow, you have to use a service where you can run sophisticated Big Data analytics on your data without moving them into a separate analytics system.

Which of the following group of services can you use to meet this requirement?

1. S3 Select, Amazon Athena, Amazon Redshift Spectrum
2. S3 Select, Amazon Neptune, DynamoDB DAX
3. Amazon Glue, Glacier Select, Amazon Redshift
4. Amazon X-Ray, Amazon Neptune, DynamoDB

Correct Answer(s): 1

Explanation

Amazon S3 allows you to run sophisticated Big Data analytics on your data without moving the data into a separate analytics system. In AWS, there is a suite of tools that make analyzing and processing large amounts of data in the cloud faster, including ways to optimize and integrate existing workflows with Amazon S3:

1. S3 Select

Amazon S3 Select is designed to help analyze and process data within an object in Amazon S3 buckets, faster and cheaper. It works by providing the ability to retrieve a subset of data from an object in Amazon S3 using simple SQL expressions. Your applications no longer have to use compute resources to scan and filter the data from an object, potentially increasing query performance by up to 400%, and reducing query costs as much as 80%. You simply change your application to use SELECT instead of GET to take advantage of S3 Select.

2. Amazon Athena

Amazon Athena is an interactive query service that makes it easy to analyze data in Amazon S3 using standard SQL expressions. Athena is serverless, so there is no infrastructure to manage, and you pay only for the queries you run. Athena is easy to use. Simply point to your data in Amazon S3, define the schema, and start querying using standard SQL expressions. Most results are delivered within seconds. With Athena, there's no need for complex ETL jobs to prepare your data for analysis. This makes it easy for anyone with SQL skills to quickly analyze large-scale datasets.

3. Amazon Redshift Spectrum

Amazon Redshift also includes Redshift Spectrum, allowing you to directly run SQL queries against exabytes of unstructured data in Amazon S3. No loading or transformation is required, and you can use open data formats, including Avro, CSV, Grok, ORC, Parquet, RCFile, RegexSerDe, SequenceFile, TextFile, and TSV. Redshift Spectrum automatically scales query compute capacity based on the data being retrieved, so queries against Amazon S3 run fast, regardless of data set size.

Reference:

https://aws.amazon.com/s3/features/#Query_in_Place

Question 6:

An online trading platform with thousands of clients across the globe is hosted in AWS. To reduce latency, you have to direct user traffic to the nearest application endpoint to the client. The traffic should be routed to the closest edge location via an Anycast static IP address. AWS Shield should also be integrated into the solution for DDoS protection.

Which of the following is the MOST suitable service that the Solutions Architect should use to satisfy the above requirements?

1. AWS WAF
2. Amazon CloudFront
3. AWS PrivateLink
4. AWS Global Accelerator

Correct Answer(s): 4

Explanation

AWS Global Accelerator is a service that improves the availability and performance of your applications with local or global users. It provides static IP addresses that act as a fixed entry point to your application endpoints in a single or multiple AWS Regions, such as your Application Load Balancers, Network Load Balancers or Amazon EC2 instances.

AWS Global Accelerator uses the AWS global network to optimize the path from your users to your applications, improving the performance of your TCP and UDP traffic. AWS Global Accelerator continually monitors the health of your application endpoints and will detect an unhealthy endpoint and redirect traffic to healthy endpoints in less than 1 minute.

Many applications, such as gaming, media, mobile applications, and financial applications, need very low latency for a great user experience. To improve the user experience, AWS Global Accelerator directs user traffic to the nearest application endpoint to the client, thus reducing internet latency and jitter. It routes the traffic to the closest edge location via Anycast, then by routing it to the closest regional endpoint over the AWS global network. AWS Global Accelerator quickly reacts to changes in network performance to improve your users' application performance.

AWS Global Accelerator and Amazon CloudFront are separate services that use the AWS global network and its edge locations around the world. CloudFront improves performance for both cacheable content (such as images and videos) and dynamic content (such as API acceleration and dynamic site delivery). Global Accelerator improves performance for a wide range of applications over TCP or UDP by proxying packets at the edge to applications running in one or more AWS Regions. Global Accelerator is a good fit for non-HTTP use cases, such as gaming (UDP), IoT (MQTT), or Voice over IP, as well as for HTTP use cases that specifically require static IP addresses or deterministic, fast regional failover. Both services integrate with AWS Shield for DDoS protection.

Hence, the correct answer is AWS Global Accelerator.

Amazon CloudFront is incorrect because although this service uses edge locations, it doesn't have the capability to route the traffic to the closest edge location via an Anycast static IP address.

AWS WAF is incorrect because the this service is just a web application firewall that helps protect your web applications or APIs against common web exploits that may affect availability, compromise security, or consume excessive resources

AWS PrivateLink is incorrect because this service simply provides private connectivity between VPCs, AWS services, and on-premises applications, securely on the Amazon network. It doesn't route traffic to the closest edge location via an Anycast static IP address.

References:

https://aws.amazon.com/global-accelerator/

https://aws.amazon.com/global-accelerator/faqs/

Question 7:

A web application is hosted in an Auto Scaling group of EC2 instances deployed across multiple Availability Zones in front of an Application Load Balancer. You need to implement an SSL solution for your system to improve its security which is why you requested an SSL/TLS certificate from a third-party certificate authority (CA).

Where can you safely import the SSL/TLS certificate of your application? (Select TWO.)

1. AWS Certificate Manager
2. An S3 bucket configured with server-side encryption with customer-provided encryption keys (SSE-C)
3. CloudFront
4. A private S3 bucket with versioning enabled
5. IAM certificate store

Answer(s): 1, 5

Explanation

If you got your certificate from a third-party CA, import the certificate into ACM or upload it to the IAM certificate store. Hence, AWS Certificate Manager and IAM certificate store are the correct answers.

ACM lets you import third-party certificates from the ACM console, as well as programmatically. If ACM is not available in your region, use AWS CLI to upload your third-party certificate to the IAM certificate store.

A private S3 bucket with versioning enabled and an S3 bucket configured with server-side encryption with customer-provided encryption keys (SSE-C) are both incorrect as S3 is not a suitable service to store the SSL certificate.

CloudFront is incorrect because although you can upload certificates to CloudFront, it doesn't mean that you can import SSL certificates on it. You would not be able to export the certificate that you have loaded in CloudFront nor assign them to your EC2 or ELB instances as it would be tied to a single CloudFront distribution.

Reference:

https://docs.aws.amazon.com/AmazonCloudFront/latest/DeveloperGuide/cnames
-and-https-procedures.html#cnames-and-https-uploading-certificates

Question 8:

The company you are working for has a set of AWS resources hosted in ap-northeast-1 region. You have been asked by your IT Manager to create an AWS CLI shell script that will call an AWS service which could create duplicate resources in another region in the event that ap-northeast-1 region fails. The duplicated resources should also contain the VPC Peering configuration and other networking components from the primary stack.

Which of the following AWS services could help fulfill this task?

1. Amazon SQS
2. Amazon SNS
3. AWS CloudFormation
4. Amazon LightSail

Answer(s): 3

Explanation

AWS CloudFormation is a service that helps you model and set up your Amazon Web Services resources so that you can spend less time managing those resources and more time focusing on your applications that run in AWS.

You can create a template that describes all the AWS resources that you want (like Amazon EC2 instances or Amazon RDS DB instances), and AWS CloudFormation takes care of provisioning and configuring those resources for you. With this, you can deploy an exact copy of your AWS architecture, along with all of the AWS resources which are hosted in one region to another.

Hence, the correct answer is AWS CloudFormation.

Amazon LightSail is incorrect because you can't use this to duplicate your resources in your VPC. You have to use CloudFormation instead.

Amazon SQS and Amazon SNS are both incorrect because SNS and SQS are just messaging services.

References:

https://docs.aws.amazon.com/AWSCloudFormation/latest/UserGuide/Welcome.h
tml

Question 9:

You are a Solutions Architect working for a large multinational investment bank. They have a web application that requires a minimum of 4 EC2 instances to run to ensure that it can cater to its users across the globe. You are instructed to ensure fault tolerance of this system.

Which of the following is the best option?

1. Deploy an Auto Scaling group with 2 instances in each of 3 Availability Zones behind an Application Load Balancer.
2. Deploy an Auto Scaling group with 2 instances in each of 2 Availability Zones behind an Application Load Balancer.
3. Deploy an Auto Scaling group with 4 instances in one Availability Zone behind an Application Load Balancer.
4. Deploy an Auto Scaling group with 1 instance in each of 4 Availability Zones behind an Application Load Balancer.

Answer(s): 1

Explanation

Fault Tolerance is the ability of a system to remain in operation even if some of the components used to build the system fail. In AWS, this means that in the event of server fault or system failures, the number of running EC2 instances should not fall below the minimum number of instances required by the system for it to work properly. So if the application requires a minimum of 4 instances, there should be at least 4 instances running in case there is an outage in one of the Availability Zones or if there are server issues.

One of the differences between Fault Tolerance and High Availability is that, the former refers to the minimum number of running instances. For example, you have a system that requires a minimum of 4 running instances and currently has 6 running instances deployed in two Availability Zones. There was a component failure in one of the Availability Zones which knocks out 3 instances. In this case, the system can still be regarded as Highly Available since there are still instances running that can accomodate the requests. However, it is not Fault Tolerant since the required minimum of four instances have not been met.

As such, deploying an Auto Scaling group with 2 instances in each of 3 Availability Zones behind an Application Load Balancer is the correct answer because even if there was an outage in one of the Availability Zones, the system still satisfies the requirement of a minimum of 4 running instances.

Deploying an Auto Scaling group with 2 instances in each of 2 Availability Zones behind an Application Load Balancer is incorrect because if one Availability Zone went out, there will only be 2 running instances available out of the required 4 minimum instances. Although the Auto Scaling group can spin up another 2 instances, the fault tolerance of the web application has already been compromised.

Deploying an Auto Scaling group with 4 instances in one Availability Zone behind an Application Load Balancer is incorrect because if the Availability Zone went out, there will be no running instance available to accommodate the request.

Deploying an Auto Scaling group with 1 instance in each of 4 Availability Zones behind an Application Load Balancer is incorrect because if one Availability Zone went out, there will only be 3 instances available to accommodate the request.

References:

https://media.amazonwebservices.com/AWS_Building_Fault_Tolerant_Application s.pdf

https://d1.awsstatic.com/whitepapers/aws-building-fault-tolerant-applications.pdf

Question 10:

A financial firm is designing an application architecture for its online trading platform that must have high availability and fault tolerance. Their Solutions Architect configured the application to use an Amazon S3 bucket located in the us-east-1 region to store large amounts of intraday financial data. The stored financial data in the bucket must not be affected even if there is an outage in one of the Availability Zones or if there's a regional service failure.

What should the Architect do to avoid any costly service disruptions and ensure data durability?

1. Create a new S3 bucket in another region and configure Cross-Account Access to the bucket located in us-east-1.
2. Create a Lifecycle Policy to regularly backup the S3 bucket to Amazon Glacier.
3. Enable Cross-Region Replication.
4. Copy the S3 bucket to an EBS-backed EC2 instance.

Answer(s): 3

Explanation

In this scenario, you need to enable Cross-Region Replication to ensure that your S3 bucket would not be affected even if there is an outage in one of the Availability Zones or a regional service failure in us-east-1. When you upload your data in S3, your objects are redundantly stored on multiple devices across multiple facilities within the region only, where you created the bucket. Thus, if there is an outage on the entire region, your S3 bucket will be unavailable if you do not enable Cross-Region Replication, which should make your data available to another region.

Note that an Availability Zone (AZ) is more related with Amazon EC2 instances rather than Amazon S3 so if there is any outage in the AZ, the S3 bucket is usually not affected but only the EC2 instances deployed on that zone.

Hence, the correct answer is: Enable Cross-Region Replication.

The option that says: Copy the S3 bucket to an EBS-backed EC2 instance is incorrect because EBS is not as durable as Amazon S3. Moreover, if the Availability Zone where the volume is hosted goes down then the data will also be inaccessible.

The option that says: Create a Lifecycle Policy to regularly backup the S3 bucket to Amazon Glacier is incorrect because Glacier is primarily used for data archival. You also need to replicate your data to another region for better durability.

The option that says: Create a new S3 bucket in another region and configure Cross-Account Access to the bucket located in us-east-1 is incorrect because Cross-Account Access in Amazon S3 is primarily used if you want to grant access to your objects to another AWS account, and not just to another AWS Region. For example, Account MANILA can grant another AWS account (Account CEBU) permission to access its resources such as buckets and objects. S3 Cross-Account Access does not replicate data from one region to another. A better solution is to enable Cross-Region Replication (CRR) instead.

References:

https://aws.amazon.com/s3/faqs/

https://aws.amazon.com/s3/features/replication/

Question 11:

You are working as a Solutions Architect for a major supermarket store chain. They have an e-commerce application which is running in eu-east-2 region that strictly requires six EC2 instances running at all times. In that region, there are 3 Availability Zones (AZ) - eu-east-2a, eu-east-2b, and eu-east-2c that you can use.

Which of the following deployments provide 100% fault tolerance if any single AZ in the region becomes unavailable? (Select TWO.)

1. eu-east-2a with two EC2 instances, eu-east-2b with four EC2 instances, and eu-east-2c with two EC2 instances
2. eu-east-2a with six EC2 instances, eu-east-2b with six EC2 instances, and eu-east-2c with no EC2 instances

3. eu-east-2a with two EC2 instances, eu-east-2b with two EC2 instances, and eu-east-2c with two EC2 instances
4. eu-east-2a with four EC2 instances, eu-east-2b with two EC2 instances, and eu-east-2c with two EC2 instances
5. eu-east-2a with three EC2 instances, eu-east-2b with three EC2 instances, and eu-east-2c with three EC2 instances

Answer(s): 2, 5

Explanation

Fault Tolerance is the ability of a system to remain in operation even if some of the components used to build the system fail. In AWS, this means that in the event of server fault or system failures, the number of running EC2 instance should not fall below the minimum number of instances required by the system for it to work properly. So if the application requires a minimum of 6 instances, there should be at least 6 instances running in case there is an outage in one of the Availability Zones or if there are server issues.

In this scenario, you have to simulate a situation where one Availability Zone became unavailable for each option and check whether it still has 6 running instances.

Hence, the correct answers are: eu-east-2a with six EC2 instances, eu-east-2b with six EC2 instances, and eu-east-2c with no EC2 instances and eu-east-2a with three EC2 instances, eu-east-2b with three EC2 instances, and eu-east-2c with three EC2 instances because even if there is an outage in one of the Availability Zones, there are still 6 running instances:

Reference:

https://media.amazonwebservices.com/AWS_Building_Fault_Tolerant_Applications.pdf

Question 12:

A Solutions Architect is designing the cloud architecture for the enterprise application suite of the company. Both the web and application tiers need to access the Internet to fetch data from public APIs. However, these servers should be inaccessible from the Internet.

Which of the following steps should the Architect implement to meet the above requirements?

1. Deploy a NAT gateway in the private subnet and add a route to it from the public subnet where the web and application tiers are hosted.

2. Deploy the web and application tier instances to a private subnet and then allocate an Elastic IP address to each EC2 instance.
3. Deploy a NAT gateway in the public subnet and add a route to it from the private subnet where the web and application tiers are hosted.
4. Deploy the web and application tier instances to a public subnet and then allocate an Elastic IP address to each EC2 instance.

Answer(s): 3

Explanation

You can use a network address translation (NAT) gateway to enable instances in a private subnet to connect to the internet or other AWS services, but prevent the internet from initiating a connection with those instances. You are charged for creating and using a NAT gateway in your account.

NAT gateway hourly usage and data processing rates apply. Amazon EC2 charges for data transfer also apply. NAT gateways are not supported for IPv6 traffic—use an egress-only internet gateway instead.

To create a NAT gateway, you must specify the public subnet in which the NAT gateway should reside. You must also specify an Elastic IP address to associate with the NAT gateway when you create it. The Elastic IP address cannot be changed once you associate it with the NAT Gateway.

After you've created a NAT gateway, you must update the route table associated with one or more of your private subnets to point Internet-bound traffic to the NAT gateway. This enables instances in your private subnets to communicate with the internet. Each NAT gateway is created in a specific Availability Zone and implemented with redundancy in that zone. You have a limit on the number of NAT gateways you can create in an Availability Zone.

Hence, the correct answer is to deploy a NAT gateway in the public subnet and add a route to it from the private subnet where the web and application tiers are hosted.

Deploying the web and application tier instances to a private subnet and then allocating an Elastic IP address to each EC2 instance is incorrect because an Elastic IP address is just a static, public IPv4 address. In this scenario, you have to use a NAT Gateway instead.

Deploying a NAT gateway in the private subnet and adding a route to it from the public subnet where the web and application tiers are hosted is incorrect because you have to deploy a NAT gateway in the public subnet instead and not on a private one.

Deploying the web and application tier instances to a public subnet and then allocating an Elastic IP address to each EC2 instance is incorrect because having an EIP address is irrelevant as it is only a static, public IPv4 address. Moreover, you should deploy the web and application tier in the private subnet instead of a public subnet to make it inaccessible from the Internet and then just add a NAT Gateway to allow outbound Internet connection.

Reference:

https://docs.aws.amazon.com/vpc/latest/userguide/vpc-nat-gateway.html

Question 13:

A web application requires a minimum of six Amazon Elastic Compute Cloud (EC2) instances running at all times. You are tasked to deploy the application to three availability zones in the EU Ireland region (eu-west-1a, eu-west-1b, and eu-west-1c). It is required that the system is fault-tolerant up to the loss of one Availability Zone.

Which of the following setup is the most cost-effective solution which also maintains the fault-tolerance of your system?

1. 2 instances in eu-west-1a, 2 instances in eu-west-1b, and 2 instances in eu-west-1c
2. 6 instances in eu-west-1a, 6 instances in eu-west-1b, and no instances in eu-west-1c
3. 6 instances in eu-west-1a, 6 instances in eu-west-1b, and 6 instances in eu-west-1c
4. 3 instances in eu-west-1a, 3 instances in eu-west-1b, and 3 instances in eu-west-1c

Answer(s): 4

Explanation

Basically, fault-tolerance is the ability of a system to remain in operation even in the event that some of its components fail, without any service degradation. In AWS, it can also refer to the minimum number of running EC2 instances or resources which should be running at all times in order for the system to properly operate and serve its consumers. Take note that this is quite different from the concept of High Availability, which is just concerned with having at least one running instance or resource in case of failure.

In this scenario, 3 instances in eu-west-1a, 3 instances in eu-west-1b, and 3 instances in eu-west-1c is the correct answer because even if there was an outage in one of the Availability Zones, the system still satisfies the requirement of having a minimum of 6 running instances. It is also the most cost-effective solution among other options.

The option that says: 6 instances in eu-west-1a, 6 instances in eu-west-1b, and 6 instances in eu-west-1c is incorrect because although this solution provides the maximum fault-tolerance for the system, it entails a significant cost to maintain a total of 18 instances across 3 AZs.

The option that says: 2 instances in eu-west-1a, 2 instances in eu-west-1b, and 2 instances in eu-west-1c is incorrect because if one Availability Zone goes down, there will only be 4 running instances available. Although this is the most cost-effective solution, it does not provide fault-tolerance.

The option that says: 6 instances in eu-west-1a, 6 instances in eu-west-1b, and no instances in eu-west-1c is incorrect because although it provides fault-tolerance, it is not the most cost-effective solution as compared with the options above. This solution has 12 running instances, unlike the correct answer which only has 9 instances.

References:

https://docs.aws.amazon.com/AWSEC2/latest/UserGuide/ec2-increase-availability.html

https://media.amazonwebservices.com/AWS_Building_Fault_Tolerant_Applications.pdf

Question 14:

To save cost, a company decided to change their third-party data analytics tool to a cheaper solution. They sent a full data export on a CSV file which contains all of their analytics information. You then save the CSV file to an S3 bucket for storage. Your manager asked you to do some validation on the provided data export.

In this scenario, what is the most cost-effective and easiest way to analyze export data using a standard SQL?

1. Use mysqldump client utility to load the CSV export file from S3 to a MySQL RDS instance. Run some SQL queries once the data has been loaded to complete your validation.
2. Create a migration tool to load the CSV export file from S3 to a DynamoDB instance. Once the data has been loaded, run queries using DynamoDB.
3. Use a migration tool to load the CSV export file from S3 to a database which is designed for online analytic processing (OLAP) such as AWS RedShift. Run some queries once the data has been loaded to complete your validation.
4. To be able to run SQL queries, use AWS Athena to analyze the export data file in S3.

Answer(s): 4

Explanation

Amazon Athena is an interactive query service that makes it easy to analyze data directly in Amazon Simple Storage Service (Amazon S3) using standard SQL. With a few actions in the AWS Management Console, you can point Athena at your data stored in Amazon S3 and begin using standard SQL to run ad-hoc queries and get results in seconds.

Athena is serverless, so there is no infrastructure to set up or manage, and you pay only for the queries you run. Athena scales automatically—executing queries in parallel—so results are fast, even with large datasets and complex queries.

Athena helps you analyze unstructured, semi-structured, and structured data stored in Amazon S3. Examples include CSV, JSON, or columnar data formats such as Apache Parquet and Apache ORC. You can use Athena to run ad-hoc queries using ANSI SQL, without the need to aggregate or load the data into Athena.

Hence, the most cost-effective and appropriate answer in this scenario is the option that says: To be able to run SQL queries, use Amazon Athena to analyze the export data file in S3.

The rest of the options are all incorrect because it is not necessary to set up a database to be able to analyze the CSV export file. You can use a cost-effective option (AWS Athena), which is a serverless service that enables you to pay only for the queries you run.

Reference:

https://docs.aws.amazon.com/athena/latest/ug/what-is.html

Question 15:

You are working for a large bank that is developing a web application that receives large amounts of object data. They are using the data to generate a report for their stockbrokers to use on a daily basis. Unfortunately, a recent financial crisis has left the bank short on cash and cannot afford to purchase expensive storage hardware. They had resorted to use AWS instead.

Which is the best service to use in order to store a virtually unlimited amount of object data without any effort to scale when demand unexpectedly increases?

1. Amazon S3
2. DynamoDB
3. Amazon EC2
4. Amazon Import/Export
5. Amazon S3 Glacier

Answer(s): 1

Explanation

In this scenario, you can use Amazon S3 and Amazon S3 Glacier as a storage service. And since we are looking for the best option, we have to consider that the object data being stored by the bank is used on a daily basis as well. Hence, Amazon S3 is the better choice as it provides frequent access to your object data.

Amazon S3 is a durable, secure, simple, and fast storage service designed to make web-scale computing easier for developers. Use Amazon S3 if you need low latency or frequent access to your data. Use Amazon S3 Glacier if low storage cost is paramount, and you do not require millisecond access to your data.

Reference:

http://docs.aws.amazon.com/AmazonS3/latest/dev/Welcome.html

Question 16:

You are managing an online platform which allows people to easily buy, sell, spend, and manage their cryptocurrency. To meet the strict IT audit requirements, each of the API calls on all of your AWS resources should be properly captured and recorded. You used CloudTrail in your VPC to help you in the compliance, operational auditing, and risk auditing of your AWS account.

In this scenario, where does CloudTrail store all of the logs that it creates?

1. Amazon Redshift
2. A RDS instance
3. DynamoDB
4. Amazon S3

Answer(s): 4

Explanation

CloudTrail is enabled on your AWS account when you create it. When activity occurs in your AWS account, that activity is recorded in a CloudTrail event. You can easily view events in the CloudTrail console by going to Event history.

Event history allows you to view, search, and download the past 90 days of supported activity in your AWS account. In addition, you can create a CloudTrail trail to further archive, analyze, and respond to changes in your AWS resources. A trail is a configuration that enables delivery of events to an Amazon S3 bucket that you specify. You can also deliver and analyze events in a trail with Amazon CloudWatch

Logs and Amazon CloudWatch Events. You can create a trail with the CloudTrail console, the AWS CLI, or the CloudTrail API.

The rest of the answers are incorrect. DynamoDB and an RDS instance are for database; Amazon Redshift is used for data warehouse that scales horizontally and allows you to store terabytes and petabytes of data.

References:

https://docs.aws.amazon.com/awscloudtrail/latest/userguide/how-cloudtrail-works.html

https://aws.amazon.com/cloudtrail/

uestion 17:

Your company has a two-tier environment in its on-premises data center which is composed of an application tier and database tier. You are instructed to migrate their environment to the AWS cloud, and to design the subnets in their VPC with the following requirements:

a) There is an application load balancer that would distribute the incoming traffic among the servers in the application tier.

b) The application tier and the database tier must not be accessible from the public Internet. The application tier should only accept traffic coming from the load balancer.

c) The database tier contains very sensitive data. It must not share the same subnet with other AWS resources and its custom route table with other instances in the environment.

d) The environment must be highly available and scalable to handle a surge of incoming traffic over the Internet.

How many subnets should you create to meet the above requirements?

1. 6
2. 4
3. 2
4. 3

Answer(s): 1

Explanation

The given scenario indicated 4 requirements that should be met in order to successfully migrate their two-tier environment from their on-premises data center to

AWS Cloud. The first requirement means that you have to use an application load balancer (ALB) to distribute the incoming traffic to your application servers.

The second requirement specifies that both your application and database tier should not be accessible from the public Internet. This means that you could create a single private subnet for both of your application and database tier. However, the third requirement mentioned that the database tier should not share the same subnet with other AWS resources to protect its sensitive data. This means that you should provision one private subnet for your application tier and another private subnet for your database tier.

The last requirement alludes to the need for using at least two Availability Zones to achieve high availability. This means that you have to distribute your application servers to two AZs as well as your database which can be set up with a master-slave configuration to properly replicate the data between two zones.

If you have more than one private subnet in the same Availability Zone that contains instances that need to be registered with the load balancer, you only need to create one public subnet. You need only one public subnet per Availability Zone; you can add the private instances in all the private subnets that reside in that particular Availability Zone.

Since you have a public internet-facing load balancer that has a group of backend Amazon EC2 instances that are deployed in a private subnet, you must create the corresponding public subnets in the same Availability Zones. This new public subnet is on top of the private subnet that is used by your private EC2 instances. Lastly, you should associate these public subnets to the internet-facing load balancer to complete the setup.

To summarize, we need to have one private subnet for the application tier and another one for the database tier. We then need to create another public subnet in the same Availability Zone where the private EC2 instances are hosted, in order to properly connect the public Internet-facing load balancer to your instances. This means that we have to use a total of 3 subnets consisting of 2 private subnets and 1 public subnet.

To meet the requirement of high availability, we have to deploy the stack to two Availability Zones. This means that you have to double the number of subnets you are using. Take note as well that you must create the corresponding public subnet in the same Availability Zone of your private EC2 servers in order for it to properly communicate with the load balancer.

Hence, the correct answer is 6 subnets.

References:

https://docs.aws.amazon.com/vpc/latest/userguide/VPC_Scenario2.html

https://aws.amazon.com/premiumsupport/knowledge-center/public-load-balancer-private-ec2/

uestion 18:

A Solutions Architect is designing a monitoring application which generates audit logs of all operational activities of the company's cloud infrastructure. Their IT Security and Compliance team mandates that the application retain the logs for 5 years before the data can be deleted.

How can the Architect meet the above requirement?

1. Store the audit logs in an EFS volume and use Network File System version 4 (NFSv4) file-locking mechanism.
2. Store the audit logs in an Amazon S3 bucket and enable Multi-Factor Authentication Delete (MFA Delete) on the S3 bucket.
3. Store the audit logs in an EBS volume and then take EBS snapshots every month.
4. Store the audit logs in a Glacier vault and use the Vault Lock feature.

Answer(s): 4

Explanation

An Amazon S3 Glacier (Glacier) vault can have one resource-based vault access policy and one Vault Lock policy attached to it. A Vault Lock policy is a vault access policy that you can lock. Using a Vault Lock policy can help you enforce regulatory and compliance requirements. Amazon S3 Glacier provides a set of API operations for you to manage the Vault Lock policies.

As an example of a Vault Lock policy, suppose that you are required to retain archives for one year before you can delete them. To implement this requirement, you can create a Vault Lock policy that denies users permissions to delete an archive until the archive has existed for one year. You can test this policy before locking it down. After you lock the policy, the policy becomes immutable. For more information about the locking process, see Amazon S3 Glacier Vault Lock. If you want to manage other user permissions that can be changed, you can use the vault access policy

Amazon S3 Glacier supports the following archive operations: Upload, Download, and Delete. Archives are immutable and cannot be modified. Hence, the correct answer is to store the audit logs in a Glacier vault and use the Vault Lock feature.

Storing the audit logs in an EBS volume and then taking EBS snapshots every month is incorrect because this is not a suitable and secure solution. Anyone who has access to the EBS Volume can simply delete and modify the audit logs. Snapshots can be deleted too.

Storing the audit logs in an Amazon S3 bucket and enabling Multi-Factor Authentication Delete (MFA Delete) on the S3 bucket is incorrect because this would still not meet the requirement. If someone has access to the S3 bucket and also has the proper MFA privileges then the audit logs can be edited.

Storing the audit logs in an EFS volume and using Network File System version 4 (NFSv4) file-locking mechanism is incorrect because the data integrity of the audit logs can still be compromised if it is stored in an EFS volume with Network File System version 4 (NFSv4) file-locking mechanism and hence, not suitable as storage for the files. Although it will provide some sort of security, the file lock can still be overridden and the audit logs might be edited by someone else.

References:

https://docs.aws.amazon.com/amazonglacier/latest/dev/vault-lock.html

https://docs.aws.amazon.com/amazonglacier/latest/dev/vault-lock-policy.html

https://aws.amazon.com/blogs/aws/glacier-vault-lock/

Question 19:

A company is looking to store their confidential financial files in AWS which are accessed every week. The Architect was instructed to set up the storage system which uses envelope encryption and automates key rotation. It should also provide an audit trail which shows who used the encryption key and by whom for security purposes.

Which of the following should the Architect implement to satisfy the requirement in the most cost-effective way? (Select TWO.)

1. Use Amazon S3 Glacier Deep Archive to store the data.
2. Amazon Certificate Manager
3. Configure Server-Side Encryption with AWS KMS-Managed Keys (SSE-KMS).
4. Configure Server-Side Encryption with Customer-Provided Keys (SSE-C).
5. Configure Server-Side Encryption with Amazon S3-Managed Keys (SSE-S3).
6. Use Amazon S3 to store the data.

Answer(s): 3, 5

Explanation

Server-side encryption is the encryption of data at its destination by the application or service that receives it. AWS Key Management Service (AWS KMS) is a service that combines secure, highly available hardware and software to provide a key management system scaled for the cloud. Amazon S3 uses AWS KMS customer master keys (CMKs) to encrypt your Amazon S3 objects. SSE-KMS encrypts only the object data. Any object metadata is not encrypted. If you use customer-managed CMKs, you use AWS KMS via the AWS Management Console or AWS KMS APIs to centrally create encryption keys, define the policies that control how keys can be used, and audit key usage to prove that they are being used correctly. You can use these keys to protect your data in Amazon S3 buckets.

A customer master key (CMK) is a logical representation of a master key. The CMK includes metadata, such as the key ID, creation date, description, and key state. The CMK also contains the key material used to encrypt and decrypt data. You can use a CMK to encrypt and decrypt up to 4 KB (4096 bytes) of data. Typically, you use CMKs to generate, encrypt, and decrypt the data keys that you use outside of AWS KMS to encrypt your data. This strategy is known as envelope encryption.

You have three mutually exclusive options depending on how you choose to manage the encryption keys:

Use Server-Side Encryption with Amazon S3-Managed Keys (SSE-S3) – Each object is encrypted with a unique key. As an additional safeguard, it encrypts the key itself with a master key that it regularly rotates. Amazon S3 server-side encryption uses one of the strongest block ciphers available, 256-bit Advanced Encryption Standard (AES-256), to encrypt your data.

Use Server-Side Encryption with Customer Master Keys (CMKs) Stored in AWS Key Management Service (SSE-KMS) – Similar to SSE-S3, but with some additional benefits and charges for using this service. There are separate permissions for the use of a CMK that provides added protection against unauthorized access of your objects in Amazon S3. SSE-KMS also provides you with an audit trail that shows when your CMK was used and by whom. Additionally, you can create and manage customer-managed CMKs or use AWS managed CMKs that are unique to you, your service, and your Region.

Use Server-Side Encryption with Customer-Provided Keys (SSE-C) – You manage the encryption keys and Amazon S3 manages the encryption, as it writes to disks, and decryption when you access your objects.

In the scenario, the company needs to store financial files in AWS which are accessed every week and the solution should use envelope encryption. This requirement can be fulfilled by using an Amazon S3 configured with Server-Side Encryption with AWS KMS-Managed Keys (SSE-KMS). Hence, using Amazon S3 to store the data and configuring Server-Side Encryption with AWS KMS-Managed Keys (SSE-KMS) are the correct answers.

Using Amazon S3 Glacier Deep Archive to store the data is incorrect because although this provides the most cost-effective storage solution, it is not the appropriate service to use if the files being stored are frequently accessed every week.

Configuring Server-Side Encryption with Customer-Provided Keys (SSE-C) and configuring Server-Side Encryption with Amazon S3-Managed Keys (SSE-S3) are incorrect because although you can configure automatic key rotation, these two do not provide you with an audit trail that shows when your CMK was used and by whom, unlike Server-Side Encryption with AWS KMS-Managed Keys (SSE-KMS).

References:

https://docs.aws.amazon.com/AmazonS3/latest/dev/serv-side-encryption.html

https://docs.aws.amazon.com/AmazonS3/latest/dev/UsingKMSEncryption.html

https://docs.aws.amazon.com/kms/latest/developerguide/services-s3.html

Question 20:

An application is using a RESTful API hosted in AWS which uses Amazon API Gateway and AWS Lambda. There is a requirement to trace and analyze user requests as they travel through your Amazon API Gateway APIs to the underlying services.

Which of the following is the most suitable service to use to meet this requirement?

1. CloudWatch
2. CloudTrail
3. VPC Flow Logs
4. AWS X-Ray

Answer(s): 4

Explanation

You can use AWS X-Ray to trace and analyze user requests as they travel through your Amazon API Gateway APIs to the underlying services. API Gateway supports AWS X-Ray tracing for all API Gateway endpoint types: regional, edge-optimized, and private. You can use AWS X-Ray with Amazon API Gateway in all regions where X-Ray is available.

X-Ray gives you an end-to-end view of an entire request, so you can analyze latencies in your APIs and their backend services. You can use an X-Ray service map to view the latency of an entire request and that of the downstream services that are integrated with X-Ray. And you can configure sampling rules to tell X-Ray which requests to record, at what sampling rates, according to criteria that you specify. If you call an API Gateway API from a service that's already being traced, API Gateway passes the trace through, even if X-Ray tracing is not enabled on the API.

You can enable X-Ray for an API stage by using the API Gateway management console, or by using the API Gateway API or CLI.

VPC Flow Logs is incorrect because this is a feature that enables you to capture information about the IP traffic going to and from network interfaces in your entire VPC. Although it can capture some details about the incoming user requests, it is still better to use AWS X-Ray as it provides a better way to debug and analyze your microservices applications with request tracing so you can find the root cause of your issues and performance.

CloudWatch is incorrect because this is a monitoring and management service. It does not have the capability to trace and analyze user requests as they travel through your Amazon API Gateway APIs.

CloudTrail is incorrect because this is primarily used for IT audits and API logging of all of your AWS resources. It does not have the capability to trace and analyze user requests as they travel through your Amazon API Gateway APIs, unlike AWS X-Ray.

Reference:

https://docs.aws.amazon.com/apigateway/latest/developerguide/apigateway-xray.html

Question 21:

You recently launched a new FTP server using an On-Demand EC2 instance in a newly created VPC with default settings. The server should not be accessible publicly but only through your IP address 175.45.116.100 and nowhere else.

Which of the following is the most suitable way to implement this requirement?

1. Create a new inbound rule in the security group of the EC2 instance with the following details:

    Protocol: UDP

    Port Range: 20 - 21

    Source: 175.45.116.100/32

2. Create a new Network ACL inbound rule in the subnet of the EC2 instance with the following details:

    Protocol: TCP

    Port Range: 20 - 21

    Source: 175.45.116.100/0

    Allow/Deny: ALLOW

3. Create a new Network ACL inbound rule in the subnet of the EC2 instance with the following details:

    Protocol: UDP

    Port Range: 20 - 21

    Source: 175.45.116.100/0

    Allow/Deny: ALLOW

4. Create a new inbound rule in the security group of the EC2 instance with the following details:

Protocol: TCP

Port Range: 20 - 21

Source: 175.45.116.100/32

Answer(s): 4

Explanation

The FTP protocol uses TCP via ports 20 and 21. This should be configured in your security groups or in your Network ACL inbound rules. As required by the scenario, you should only allow the individual IP of the client and not the entire network. Therefore, in the Source, the proper CIDR notation should be used. The /32 denotes one IP address and the /0 refers to the entire network.

Notice that the scenario says that you launched the EC2 instances in a newly created VPC with default settings. Your VPC automatically comes with a modifiable default network ACL. By default, it allows all inbound and outbound IPv4 traffic and, if applicable, IPv6 traffic. Hence, you actually don't need to explicitly add inbound rules to your Network ACL to allow inbound traffic, if your VPC has a default setting.

The below option is incorrect because although the configuration of the Security Group is valid, the provided Protocol is incorrect. Take note that FTP uses TCP and not UDP.

Create a new inbound rule in the security group of the EC2 instance with the following details:

Protocol: UDP

Port Range: 20 - 21

Source: 175.45.116.100/32

The below option is incorrect because although setting up an inbound Network ACL is valid, the source is invalid since it must be an IPv4 or IPv6 CIDR block. In the provided IP address, the /0 refers to the entire network and not a specific IP address. In addition, the scenario says that the newly created VPC has default settings and by default, the Network ACL allows all traffic. This means that there is actually no need to configure your Network ACL.

Create a new Network ACL inbound rule in the subnet of the EC2 instance with the following details:

Protocol: TCP

Port Range: 20 - 21

Source: 175.45.116.100/0

Allow/Deny: ALLOW

The below option is incorrect because, just like Option 3, the source is also invalid. Take note that FTP uses TCP and not UDP, which is one of the reasons why this option is wrong. In addition, the scenario says that the newly created VPC has default settings and by default, the Network ACL allows all traffic. This means that there is actually no need to configure your Network ACL.

Create a new Network ACL inbound rule in the subnet of the EC2 instance with the following details:

> Protocol: UDP
>
> Port Range: 20 - 21
>
> Source: 175.45.116.100/0
>
> Allow/Deny: ALLOW

References:

https://docs.aws.amazon.com/vpc/latest/userguide/VPC_SecurityGroups.html

https://docs.aws.amazon.com/vpc/latest/userguide/vpc-network-acls.html

Question 22:

A newly hired Solutions Architect is checking all of the security groups and network access control list rules of the company's AWS resources. For security purposes, the MS SQL connection via port 1433 of the database tier should be secured. Below is the security group configuration of their Microsoft SQL Server database:

Larger image

The application tier hosted in an Auto Scaling group of EC2 instances is the only identified resource that needs to connect to the database. The Architect should ensure that the architecture complies with the best practice of granting least privilege.

Which of the following changes should be made to the security group configuration?

1. For the MS SQL rule, change the Source to the static AnyCast IP address attached to the application tier.
2. For the MS SQL rule, change the Source to the EC2 instance IDs of the underlying instances of the Auto Scaling group.
3. For the MS SQL rule, change the Source to the Network ACL ID attached to the application tier.
4. For the MS SQL rule, change the Source to the security group ID attached to the application tier.

Answer(s): 4

Explanation

A security group acts as a virtual firewall for your instance to control inbound and outbound traffic. When you launch an instance in a VPC, you can assign up to five security groups to the instance. Security groups act at the instance level, not the subnet level. Therefore, each instance in a subnet in your VPC can be assigned to a different set of security groups.

If you launch an instance using the Amazon EC2 API or a command line tool and you don't specify a security group, the instance is automatically assigned to the default security group for the VPC. If you launch an instance using the Amazon EC2 console, you have an option to create a new security group for the instance.

For each security group, you add rules that control the inbound traffic to instances, and a separate set of rules that control the outbound traffic. This section describes the basic things that you need to know about security groups for your VPC and their rules.

Amazon security groups and network ACLs don't filter traffic to or from link-local addresses (169.254.0.0/16) or AWS reserved IPv4 addresses (these are the first four IPv4 addresses of the subnet, including the Amazon DNS server address for the VPC). Similarly, flow logs do not capture IP traffic to or from these addresses.

In the scenario, the security group configuration allows any server (0.0.0.0/0) from anywhere to establish an MS SQL connection to the database via the 1433 port. The most suitable solution here is to change the Source field to the security group ID attached to the application tier.

Hence, the correct answer is the option that says: For the MS SQL rule, change the Source to the security group ID attached to the application tier.

The option that says: For the MS SQL rule, change the Source to the EC2 instance IDs of the underlying instances of the Auto Scaling group is incorrect because using the EC2 instance IDs of the underlying instances of the Auto Scaling group as the source can cause intermittent issues. New instances will be added and old instances will be removed from the Auto Scaling group over time, which means that you have to manually update the security group setting once again. A better solution is to use the security group ID of the Auto Scaling group of EC2 instances.

The option that says: For the MS SQL rule, change the Source to the static AnyCast IP address attached to the application tier is incorrect because a static AnyCast IP address is primarily used for AWS Global Accelerator and not for security group configurations.

The option that says: For the MS SQL rule, change the Source to the Network ACL ID attached to the application tier is incorrect because you have to use the security group ID instead of the Network ACL ID of the application tier. Take note that the

Network ACL covers the entire subnet which means that other applications that use the same subnet will also be affected.

References:

https://docs.aws.amazon.com/vpc/latest/userguide/VPC_SecurityGroups.html

https://docs.aws.amazon.com/vpc/latest/userguide/VPC_Security.html

Question 23:

A multinational company with multiple on-premises data centers around the globe is heavily using AWS to serve its clients worldwide. The company already has hundreds of VPCs with multiple VPN connections to their data centers that span to multiple AWS Regions. As the number of its workloads running on AWS grows, the company must be able to scale its networks across multiple accounts and Amazon VPCs to keep up. A Solutions Architect is tasked to interconnect all of the company's on-premises networks, VPNs, and VPCs into a single gateway, that includes support for inter-region peering across multiple AWS regions.

Which of the following is the BEST solution that the Architect should set up to support the required interconnectivity?

1. Enable inter-region VPC peering that allows peering relationships to be established between multiple VPCs across different AWS regions. Set up a networking configuration that ensures that the traffic will always stay on the global AWS backbone and never traverse the public Internet.
2. Set up an AWS Transit Gateway to implement a hub-and-spoke network topology in each region that routes all traffic through a network transit center. Route traffic between VPCs and the on-premises data centers over AWS Site-to-Site VPNs.
3. Set up an AWS VPN CloudHub for inter-region VPC access and a Direct Connect gateway for the VPN connections to the on-premises data centers. Create a virtual private gateway in each VPC, then create a private virtual interface for each AWS Direct Connect connection to the Direct Connect gateway.
4. Set up an AWS Direct Connect Gateway to achieve inter-region VPC access to all of the AWS resources and on-premises data centers. Set up a link aggregation group (LAG) to aggregate multiple connections at a single AWS Direct Connect endpoint in order to treat them as a single, managed connection. Launch a virtual private gateway in each VPC and then create a public virtual interface for each AWS Direct Connect connection to the Direct Connect Gateway.

Answer(s): 2

Explanation

AWS Transit Gateway is a service that enables customers to connect their Amazon Virtual Private Clouds (VPCs) and their on-premises networks to a single gateway. As you grow the number of workloads running on AWS, you need to be able to scale your networks across multiple accounts and Amazon VPCs to keep up with the growth. Today, you can connect pairs of Amazon VPCs using peering. However, managing point-to-point connectivity across many Amazon VPCs, without the ability to centrally manage the connectivity policies, can be operationally costly and cumbersome. For on-premises connectivity, you need to attach your AWS VPN to each individual Amazon VPC. This solution can be time consuming to build and hard to manage when the number of VPCs grows into the hundreds.

With AWS Transit Gateway, you only have to create and manage a single connection from the central gateway in to each Amazon VPC, on-premises data center, or remote office across your network. Transit Gateway acts as a hub that controls how traffic is routed among all the connected networks which act like spokes. This hub and spoke model significantly simplifies management and reduces operational costs because each network only has to connect to the Transit Gateway and not to every other network. Any new VPC is simply connected to the Transit Gateway and is then automatically available to every other network that is connected to the Transit Gateway. This ease of connectivity makes it easy to scale your network as you grow.

It acts as a Regional virtual router for traffic flowing between your virtual private clouds (VPC) and VPN connections. A transit gateway scales elastically based on the volume of network traffic. Routing through a transit gateway operates at layer 3, where the packets are sent to a specific next-hop attachment, based on their destination IP addresses.

A transit gateway attachment is both a source and a destination of packets. You can attach the following resources to your transit gateway:

- One or more VPCs

- One or more VPN connections

- One or more AWS Direct Connect gateways

- One or more transit gateway peering connections

If you attach a transit gateway peering connection, the transit gateway must be in a different Region.

Hence, the correct answer is: Set up an AWS Transit Gateway to implement a hub-and-spoke network topology in each region that routes all traffic through a network transit center. Route traffic between VPCs and the on-premises data centers over AWS Site-to-Site VPNs.

The option that says: Set up an AWS Direct Connect Gateway to achieve inter-region VPC access to all of the AWS resources and on-premises data centers. Set up a link aggregation group (LAG) to aggregate multiple connections at a single AWS Direct Connect endpoint in order to treat them as a single, managed connection. Launch a virtual private gateway in each VPC and then create a public virtual interface for each AWS Direct Connect connection to the Direct Connect Gateway is incorrect because you can only create a private virtual interface to a Direct Connect gateway and not a public virtual interface. Using a link aggregation group (LAG) is also irrelevant in this scenario because it is just a logical interface that uses the Link Aggregation Control Protocol (LACP) to aggregate multiple connections at a single AWS Direct Connect endpoint, allowing you to treat them as a single, managed connection. Ultimately, an AWS Direct Connect Gateway is quite limited as opposed to a Transit Gateway as it can only manage a single connection for multiple VPCs or VPNs that are in the same Region. Remember that the multinational company has several VPCs and VPN connections in multiple AWS Regions.

The option that says: Enable inter-region VPC peering which allows peering relationships to be established between VPCs across different AWS regions. This will ensure that the traffic will always stay on the global AWS backbone and will never traverse the public Internet is incorrect because this solution would require a lot of manual setup and management overhead to successfully build a functional, error-free inter-region VPC network compared with just using a Transit Gateway. Although the Inter-Region VPC Peering provides a cost-effective way to share resources between regions or replicate data for geographic redundancy, its connections are not dedicated and highly available. Moreover, it doesn't support the company's on-premises data centers in multiple AWS Regions.

The option that says: Set up an AWS VPN CloudHub for inter-region VPC access and a Direct Connect gateway for the VPN connections to the on-premises data centers. Create a virtual private gateway in each VPC, then create a private virtual interface for each AWS Direct Connect connection to the Direct Connect gateway is incorrect because this solution doesn't meet the requirement of interconnecting all of the company's on-premises networks, VPNs, and VPCs into a single gateway, that includes support for inter-region peering across multiple AWS regions. As its name implies, the AWS VPN CloudHub is only for VPNs and not for VPCs. It is also not capable of managing hundreds of VPCs with multiple VPN connections to their data centers that span to multiple AWS Regions.

References:

https://aws.amazon.com/transit-gateway/

https://docs.aws.amazon.com/vpc/latest/tgw/how-transit-gateways-work.html

Question 24:

You have a prototype web application that uses one Spot EC2 instance. What will happen to the instance by default if it gets interrupted by Amazon EC2 for capacity requirements?

1. The instance will be terminated
2. The instance will be stopped
3. The instance will be restarted
4. This is not possible as only On-Demand instances can be interrupted by Amazon EC2

Answer(s): 1

Explanation

The main differences are that:

- Spot instances typically offer a significant discount off the On-Demand prices.

- Your instances can be interrupted by Amazon EC2 for capacity requirements with a 2-minute notification.

- Spot prices adjust gradually based on long term supply and demand for spare EC2 capacity.

You can choose to have your Spot instances terminated, stopped, or hibernated upon interruption. Stop and hibernate options are available for persistent Spot requests and Spot Fleets with the maintain option enabled. By default, your instances are terminated hence, the correct answer is the option that says: The instance will be terminated.

Reference:

https://aws.amazon.com/ec2/faqs/

Here is an in-depth look at Spot Instances:

https://youtu.be/PKvss-RgSjI

Question 25:

You are working as a Solutions Architect for a financial firm which is building an internal application that processes loans, accruals, and interest rates for their clients. They require a storage service that is able to handle future increases in storage capacity of up to 16 TB and can provide the lowest-latency access to their data. Their web application will be hosted in a single m5ad.24xlarge Reserved EC2 instance which will process and store data to the storage service.

Which of the following would be the most suitable storage service that you should use to meet this requirement?

1. EFS
2. S3
3. Storage Gateway
4. EBS

Answer(s): 4

Explanation

Amazon Web Services (AWS) offers cloud storage services to support a wide range of storage workloads such as Amazon S3, EFS and EBS. Amazon EFS is a file storage service for use with Amazon EC2. Amazon EFS provides a file system interface, file system access semantics (such as strong consistency and file locking), and concurrently-accessible storage for up to thousands of Amazon EC2 instances. Amazon S3 is an object storage service. Amazon S3 makes data available through an Internet API that can be accessed anywhere. Amazon EBS is a block-level storage service for use with Amazon EC2. Amazon EBS can deliver performance for workloads that require the lowest-latency access to data from a single EC2 instance. You can also increase EBS storage for up to 16TB or add new volumes for additional storage.

In this scenario, the company is looking for a storage service which can provide the lowest-latency access to their data which will be fetched by a single m5ad.24xlarge Reserved EC2 instance. This type of workloads can be supported better by using either EFS or EBS but in this case, the latter is the most suitable storage service. As mentioned above, EBS provides the lowest-latency access to the data for your EC2 instance since the volume is directly attached to the instance. In addition, the scenario does not require concurrently-accessible storage since they only have one instance.

Hence, the correct answer is EBS.

Storage Gateway is incorrect since this is primarily used to extend your on-premises storage to your AWS Cloud.

S3 is incorrect because although this is also highly available and highly scalable, it still does not provide the lowest-latency access to the data, unlike EBS. Remember that S3 does not reside within your VPC by default, which means the data will traverse the public Internet that may result to higher latency. You can set up a VPC Endpoint for S3 yet still, its latency is greater than that of EBS.

EFS is incorrect because the scenario does not require concurrently-accessible storage since the internal application is only hosted in one instance. Although EFS can provide low latency data access to the EC2 instance as compared with S3, the storage service that can provide the lowest latency access is still EBS.

References:

https://aws.amazon.com/ebs/

https://aws.amazon.com/efs/faq/

Question 26:

You are working as a Solutions Architect for a leading financial firm where you are responsible in ensuring that their applications are highly available and safe from common web security vulnerabilities. Which is the most suitable AWS service to use to mitigate Distributed Denial of Service (DDoS) attacks from hitting your back-end EC2 instances?

1. AWS Firewall Manager
2. Amazon GuardDuty
3. AWS Shield
4. AWS WAF

Answer(s): 3

Explanation

AWS Shield is a managed Distributed Denial of Service (DDoS) protection service that safeguards applications running on AWS. AWS Shield provides always-on detection and automatic inline mitigations that minimize application downtime and latency, so there is no need to engage AWS Support to benefit from DDoS protection. There are two tiers of AWS Shield - Standard and Advanced.

All AWS customers benefit from the automatic protections of AWS Shield Standard, at no additional charge. AWS Shield Standard defends against most common, frequently occurring network and transport layer DDoS attacks that target your web site or applications. When you use AWS Shield Standard with Amazon CloudFront and Amazon Route 53, you receive comprehensive availability protection against all known infrastructure (Layer 3 and 4) attacks.

AWS WAF is incorrect because this is a web application firewall service that helps protect your web apps from common exploits that could affect app availability, compromise security, or consume excessive resources. Although this can help you against DDoS attacks, AWS WAF alone is not enough to fully protect your VPC. You still need to use AWS Shield in this scenario.

AWS Firewall Manager is incorrect because this just simplifies your AWS WAF administration and maintenance tasks across multiple accounts and resources.

Amazon GuardDuty is incorrect because this is just an intelligent threat detection service to protect your AWS accounts and workloads. Using this alone will not fully protect your AWS resources against DDoS attacks.

References:

https://docs.aws.amazon.com/waf/latest/developerguide/waf-which-to-choose.html

https://aws.amazon.com/answers/networking/aws-ddos-attack-mitigation/

Question 27:

A company is using the AWS Directory Service to integrate their on-premises Microsoft Active Directory (AD) domain with their Amazon EC2 instances via an AD connector. The below identity-based policy is attached to the IAM Identities that use the AWS Directory service:

```
{
"Version":"2012-10-17",
"Statement":[
{
 "Sid":"DirectoryTutorialsfree1234",
 "Effect":"Allow",
 "Action":[
  "ds:*"
],
 "Resource":"arn:aws:ds:us-east-1:987654321012:directory/d-1234567890"
},
{
 "Effect":"Allow",
 "Action":[
 "ec2:*"
],
 "Resource":"*"
}
]
}
```

Which of the following BEST describes what the above resource policy does?

1. Allows all AWS Directory Service (ds) calls as long as the resource contains the directory ID: DirectoryTutorialsfree1234
2. Allows all AWS Directory Service (ds) calls as long as the resource contains the directory name of: DirectoryTutorialsfree1234
3. Allows all AWS Directory Service (ds) calls as long as the resource contains the directory ID: d-1234567890
4. Allows all AWS Directory Service (ds) calls as long as the resource contains the directory ID: 987654321012

Answer(s): 3

Explanation

AWS Directory Service provides multiple ways to use Amazon Cloud Directory and Microsoft Active Directory (AD) with other AWS services. Directories store information about users, groups, and devices, and administrators use them to manage access to information and resources. AWS Directory Service provides multiple directory choices for customers who want to use existing Microsoft AD or Lightweight Directory Access Protocol (LDAP)–aware applications in the cloud. It also offers those same choices to developers who need a directory to manage users, groups, devices, and access.

Every AWS resource is owned by an AWS account, and permissions to create or access the resources are governed by permissions policies. An account administrator can attach permissions policies to IAM identities (that is, users, groups, and roles), and some services (such as AWS Lambda) also support attaching permissions policies to resources.

The following resource policy example allows all ds calls as long as the resource contains the directory ID "d-1234567890".

```
{
"Version":"2012-10-17",
"Statement":[
  {
    "Sid":"VisualEditor0",
    "Effect":"Allow",
    "Action":[
      "ds:*"
    ],
        "Resource":"arn:aws:ds:us-east-1:123456789012:directory/d-1234567890"
```

```
  },
  {
  "Effect":"Allow",
  "Action":[
     "ec2:*"
  ],
  "Resource":"*"
  }
 ]
}
```

Hence, the correct answer is the option that says: Allows all AWS Directory Service (ds) calls as long as the resource contains the directory ID: d-1234567890.

The option that says: Allows all AWS Directory Service (ds) calls as long as the resource contains the directory ID: DirectoryTutorialsfree1234 is incorrect because DirectoryTutorialsfree1234 is the Statement ID (SID) and not the Directory ID.

The option that says: Allows all AWS Directory Service (ds) calls as long as the resource contains the directory ID: 987654321012 is incorrect because the numbers: 987654321012 is the Account ID and not the Directory ID.

The option that says: Allows all AWS Directory Service (ds) calls as long as the resource contains the directory name of: DirectoryTutorialsfree1234 is incorrect because DirectoryTutorialsfree1234 is the Statement ID (SID) and not the Directory name.

References:

https://docs.aws.amazon.com/directoryservice/latest/admin-guide/IAM_Auth_Access_IdentityBased.html

https://docs.aws.amazon.com/directoryservice/latest/admin-guide/IAM_Auth_Access_Overview.html

Question 28:

You have a web application hosted in an On-Demand EC2 instance in your VPC. You are creating a shell script that needs the instance's public and private IP addresses.

What is the best way to get the instance's associated IP addresses which your shell script can use?

1. By using a Curl or Get Command to get the latest user data information from http://169.254.169.254/latest/user-data/
2. By using IAM.
3. By using a CloudWatch metric.
4. By using a Curl or Get Command to get the latest metadata information from http://169.254.169.254/latest/meta-data/

Answer(s): 4

Explanation

Instance metadata is data about your EC2 instance that you can use to configure or manage the running instance. Because your instance metadata is available from your running instance, you do not need to use the Amazon EC2 console or the AWS CLI. This can be helpful when you're writing scripts to run from your instance. For example, you can access the local IP address of your instance from instance metadata to manage a connection to an external application.

To view the private IPv4 address, public IPv4 address, and all other categories of instance metadata from within a running instance, use the following URL:

http://169.254.169.254/latest/meta-data/

Reference:

http://docs.aws.amazon.com/AWSEC2/latest/UserGuide/ec2-instance-metadata.html

Question 29:

You are working as a Solutions Architect for a leading data analytics company in which you are tasked to process real-time streaming data of your users across the globe. This will enable you to track and analyze globally-distributed user activity on your website and mobile applications, including click stream analysis. Your cloud architecture should process the data in close geographical proximity to your users and to respond to user requests at low latencies.

Which of the following options is the most ideal solution that you should implement?

1. Use a CloudFront web distribution and Route 53 with a latency-based routing policy, in order to process the data in close geographical proximity to users and respond to user requests at low latencies. Process real-time streaming data using Kinesis and durably store the results to an Amazon S3 bucket.
2. Integrate CloudFront with Lambda@Edge in order to process the data in close geographical proximity to users and respond to user requests at low

latencies. Process real-time streaming data using Kinesis and durably store the results to an Amazon S3 bucket.

3. Integrate CloudFront with Lambda@Edge in order to process the data in close geographical proximity to users and respond to user requests at low latencies. Process real-time streaming data using Amazon Athena and durably store the results to an Amazon S3 bucket.

4. Use a CloudFront web distribution and Route 53 with a Geoproximity routing policy in order to process the data in close geographical proximity to users and respond to user requests at low latencies. Process real-time streaming data using Kinesis and durably store the results to an Amazon S3 bucket.

Answer(s): 2

Explanation

Lambda@Edge is a feature of Amazon CloudFront that lets you run code closer to users of your application, which improves performance and reduces latency. With Lambda@Edge, you don't have to provision or manage infrastructure in multiple locations around the world. You pay only for the compute time you consume - there is no charge when your code is not running.

With Lambda@Edge, you can enrich your web applications by making them globally distributed and improving their performance — all with zero server administration. Lambda@Edge runs your code in response to events generated by the Amazon CloudFront content delivery network (CDN). Just upload your code to AWS Lambda, which takes care of everything required to run and scale your code with high availability at an AWS location closest to your end user.

By using Lambda@Edge and Kinesis together, you can process real-time streaming data so that you can track and analyze globally-distributed user activity on your website and mobile applications, including clickstream analysis. Hence, the correct answer in this scenario is the option that says: Integrate CloudFront with Lambda@Edge in order to process the data in close geographical proximity to users and respond to user requests at low latencies. Process real-time streaming data using Kinesis and durably store the results to an Amazon S3 bucket.

The options that say: Use a CloudFront web distribution and Route 53 with a latency-based routing policy, in order to process the data in close geographical proximity to users and respond to user requests at low latencies. Process real-time streaming data using Kinesis and durably store the results to an Amazon S3 bucket and Use a CloudFront web distribution and Route 53 with a Geoproximity routing policy in order to process the data in close geographical proximity to users and respond to user requests at low latencies. Process real-time streaming data using Kinesis and durably store the results to an Amazon S3 bucket are both incorrect because you can only route traffic using Route 53 since it does not have any computing capability. This solution would not be able to process and return the data in close geographical proximity to your users since it is not using Lambda@Edge.

The option that says: Integrate CloudFront with Lambda@Edge in order to process the data in close geographical proximity to users and respond to user requests at low latencies. Process real-time streaming data using Amazon Athena and durably store the results to an Amazon S3 bucket is incorrect because although using Lambda@Edge is correct, Amazon Athena is just an interactive query service that enables you to easily analyze data in Amazon S3 using standard SQL. Kinesis should be used to process the streaming data in real-time.

References:

https://aws.amazon.com/lambda/edge/

https://aws.amazon.com/blogs/networking-and-content-delivery/global-data-ingestion-with-amazon-cloudfront-and-lambdaedge/

Question 30:

A bank portal application is hosted in an Auto Scaling group of EC2 instances behind a Classic Load Balancer (CLB). You are required to set up the architecture so that any back-end EC2 instances that you de-register should complete the in-progress requests first before the de-registration process takes effect. Conversely, if a back-end instance fails health checks, the load balancer should not send any new requests to the unhealthy instance but should allow existing requests to complete.

How will you configure your load balancer to satisfy the above requirement?

1. Configure Sticky Sessions
2. Configure Proxy Protocol
3. Configure both Cross-Zone Load Balancing and Sticky Sessions
4. Configure Connection Draining

Answer(s): 4

Explanation

To ensure that a Classic Load Balancer stops sending requests to instances that are de-registering or unhealthy while keeping the existing connections open, use connection draining. This enables the load balancer to complete in-flight requests made to instances that are de-registering or unhealthy. Hence, configuring Connection Draining is the correct answer.

When you enable connection draining, you can specify a maximum time for the load balancer to keep connections alive before reporting the instance as de-registered. The maximum timeout value can be set between 1 and 3,600 seconds (the default is 300 seconds). When the maximum time limit is reached, the load balancer forcibly closes connections to the de-registering instance.

Configuring Sticky Sessions is incorrect because the sticky sessions feature is mainly used to ensure that all requests from the user during the session are sent to the same instance.

Configuring both Cross-Zone Load Balancing and Sticky Sessions is incorrect because this will still not satisfy the requirement. Cross-Zone load balancing is mainly used to distribute requests evenly across the registered instances in all enabled Availability Zones. You have to enable Connection Draining.

Configuring Proxy Protocol is incorrect because this is an Internet protocol used to carry connection information from the source requesting the connection to the destination for which the connection was requested.

Reference:

https://docs.aws.amazon.com/elasticloadbalancing/latest/classic/config-conn-drain.html

Question 31:

There are a few, easily reproducible but confidential files that your client wants to store in AWS without worrying about storage capacity. For the first month, all of these files will be accessed frequently but after that, they will rarely be accessed at all. The old files will only be accessed by developers so there is no set retrieval time requirement. However, the files under a specific tutorialsfree-finance prefix in the S3 bucket will be used for post-processing that requires millisecond retrieval time.

Given these conditions, which of the following options would be the most cost-effective solution for your client's storage needs?

1. Store the files in S3 then after a month, change the storage class of the bucket to S3-IA using lifecycle policy.
2. Store the files in S3 then after a month, change the storage class of the tutorialsfree-finance prefix to S3-IA while the remaining go to Glacier using lifecycle policy.
3. Store the files in S3 then after a month, change the storage class of the tutorialsfree-finance prefix to One Zone-IA while the remaining go to Glacier using lifecycle policy.
4. Store the files in S3 then after a month, change the storage class of the bucket to Intelligent-Tiering using lifecycle policy.

Answer(s): 3

Explanation

Initially, the files will be accessed frequently, and S3 is a durable and highly available storage solution for that. After a month has passed, the files won't be accessed

294

frequently anymore, so it is a good idea to use lifecycle policies to move them to a storage class that would have a lower cost for storing them.

Since the files are easily reproducible and some of them are needed to be retrieved quickly based on a specific prefix filter (tutorialsfree-finance), S3-One Zone IA would be a good choice for storing them. The other files that do not contain such prefix would then be moved to Glacier for low cost archival. This setup would also be the most cost-effective for the client.

Hence, the correct answer is to store the files in S3 then after a month, change the storage class of the tutorialsfree-finance prefix to One Zone-IA while the remaining go to Glacier using lifecycle policy.

Storing the files in S3 then after a month, changing the storage class of the bucket to S3-IA using lifecycle policy is incorrect because although it is valid to move the files to S3-IA, this solution still costs more compared with using a combination of S3-One Zone IA and Glacier.

Storing the files in S3 then after a month, changing the storage class of the bucket to Intelligent-Tiering using lifecycle policy is incorrect because while S3 Intelligent-Tiering can automatically move data between two access tiers (frequent access and infrequent access) when access patterns change, it is more suitable for scenarios where you don't know the access patterns of your data. It may take some time for S3 Intellgent-Tiering to analyze the access patterns before it moves the data to a cheaper storage class like S3-IA which means you may still end up paying more in the beginning. In addition, you already know the access patterns of the files which means you can directly change the storage class immediately and save cost right away.

Storing the files in S3 then after a month, changing the storage class of the tutorialsfree-finance prefix to S3-IA while the remaining go to Glacier using lifecycle policy is incorrect because although S3-IA costs less than S3 Standard storage class, it is still more expensive than S3-One Zone IA. Remember that the files are easily reproducible so you can safely move the data to S3-One Zone IA and in case there is an outage, you can simply generate the missing data again.

References:

https://aws.amazon.com/blogs/compute/amazon-s3-adds-prefix-and-suffix-filters-for-lambda-function-triggering

https://docs.aws.amazon.com/AmazonS3/latest/dev/object-lifecycle-mgmt.html

https://docs.aws.amazon.com/AmazonS3/latest/dev/lifecycle-configuration-examples.html

https://aws.amazon.com/s3/pricing

Question 32:

A data analytics company has been building its new generation big data and analytics platform on their AWS cloud infrastructure. They need a storage service that provides the scale and performance that their big data applications require such as high throughput to compute nodes coupled with read-after-write consistency and low-latency file operations. In addition, their data needs to be stored redundantly across multiple AZs and allows concurrent connections from multiple EC2 instances hosted on multiple AZs.

Which of the following AWS storage services will you use to meet this requirement?

1. Glacier
2. EBS
3. S3
4. EFS

Answer(s): 4

Explanation

In this question, you should take note of the two keywords/phrases: "file operation" and "allows concurrent connections from multiple EC2 instances". There are various AWS storage options that you can choose but whenever these criteria show up, always consider using EFS instead of using EBS Volumes which is mainly used as a "block" storage and can only have one connection to one EC2 instance at a time. Amazon EFS provides the scale and performance required for big data applications that require high throughput to compute nodes coupled with read-after-write consistency and low-latency file operations.

Amazon EFS is a fully-managed service that makes it easy to set up and scale file storage in the Amazon Cloud. With a few clicks in the AWS Management Console, you can create file systems that are accessible to Amazon EC2 instances via a file system interface (using standard operating system file I/O APIs) and supports full file system access semantics (such as strong consistency and file locking).

Amazon EFS file systems can automatically scale from gigabytes to petabytes of data without needing to provision storage. Tens, hundreds, or even thousands of Amazon EC2 instances can access an Amazon EFS file system at the same time, and Amazon EFS provides consistent performance to each Amazon EC2 instance. Amazon EFS is designed to be highly durable and highly available.

EBS is incorrect because it does not allow concurrent connections from multiple EC2 instances hosted on multiple AZs and it does not store data redundantly across multiple AZs by default, unlike EFS.

S3 is incorrect because although it can handle concurrent connections from multiple EC2 instances, it does not have the ability to provide low-latency file operations, which is required in this scenario.

Glacier is incorrect because this is an archiving storage solution and is not applicable in this scenario.

References:

https://docs.aws.amazon.com/efs/latest/ug/performance.html

https://aws.amazon.com/efs/faq/

Here's a short video tutorial on Amazon EFS:

https://youtu.be/AvgAozsfCrY

Question 33:

A company has a High Performance Computing (HPC) cluster that is composed of EC2 Instances with Provisioned IOPS volume to process transaction-intensive, low-latency workloads. The Solutions Architect must maintain high IOPS while keeping the latency down by setting the optimal queue length for the volume. The size of each volume is 10 GiB.

Which of the following is the MOST suitable configuration that the Architect should set up?

1. Set the IOPS to 500 then maintain a low queue length.
2. Set the IOPS to 800 then maintain a low queue length.
3. Set the IOPS to 600 then maintain a high queue length.
4. Set the IOPS to 400 then maintain a low queue length.

Answer(s): 1

Explanation

Provisioned IOPS SSD (io1) volumes are designed to meet the needs of I/O-intensive workloads, particularly database workloads, that are sensitive to storage performance and consistency. Unlike gp2, which uses a bucket and credit model to calculate performance, an io1 volume allows you to specify a consistent IOPS rate when you create the volume, and Amazon EBS delivers within 10 percent of the provisioned IOPS performance 99.9 percent of the time over a given year.

An io1 volume can range in size from 4 GiB to 16 TiB. You can provision from 100 IOPS up to 64,000 IOPS per volume on Nitro system instance families and up to 32,000 on other instance families. The maximum ratio of provisioned IOPS to requested volume size (in GiB) is 50:1.

For example, a 100 GiB volume can be provisioned with up to 5,000 IOPS. On a supported instance type, any volume 1,280 GiB in size or greater allows provisioning up to the 64,000 IOPS maximum (50 × 1,280 GiB = 64,000).

An io1 volume provisioned with up to 32,000 IOPS supports a maximum I/O size of 256 KiB and yields as much as 500 MiB/s of throughput. With the I/O size at the maximum, peak throughput is reached at 2,000 IOPS. A volume provisioned with more than 32,000 IOPS (up to the cap of 64,000 IOPS) supports a maximum I/O size of 16 KiB and yields as much as 1,000 MiB/s of throughput.

The volume queue length is the number of pending I/O requests for a device. Latency is the true end-to-end client time of an I/O operation, in other words, the time elapsed between sending an I/O to EBS and receiving an acknowledgement from EBS that the I/O read or write is complete. Queue length must be correctly calibrated with I/O size and latency to avoid creating bottlenecks either on the guest operating system or on the network link to EBS.

Optimal queue length varies for each workload, depending on your particular application's sensitivity to IOPS and latency. If your workload is not delivering enough I/O requests to fully use the performance available to your EBS volume then your volume might not deliver the IOPS or throughput that you have provisioned.

Transaction-intensive applications are sensitive to increased I/O latency and are well-suited for SSD-backed io1 and gp2 volumes. You can maintain high IOPS while keeping latency down by maintaining a low queue length and a high number of IOPS available to the volume. Consistently driving more IOPS to a volume than it has available can cause increased I/O latency.

Throughput-intensive applications are less sensitive to increased I/O latency, and are well-suited for HDD-backed st1 and sc1 volumes. You can maintain high throughput to HDD-backed volumes by maintaining a high queue length when performing large, sequential I/O.

Therefore, for instance, a 10 GiB volume can be provisioned with up to 500 IOPS. Any volume 640 GiB in size or greater allows provisioning up to a maximum of 32,000 IOPS (50×640 GiB $= 32,000$). Hence, the correct answer is to set the IOPS to 500 then maintain a low queue length.

Setting the IOPS to 400 then maintaining a low queue length is incorrect because although a value of 400 is an acceptable value, it is not the maximum value for the IOPS. You will not fully utilize the available IOPS that the volume can offer if you just set it to 400.

The options that say: Set the IOPS to 600 then maintain a high queue length and Set the IOPS to 800 then maintain a low queue length are both incorrect because the maximum IOPS for the 10 GiB volume is only 500. Therefore, any value greater than the maximum amount, such as 600 or 800, is wrong. Moreover, you should keep the latency down by maintaining a low queue length, and not higher.

References:

http://docs.aws.amazon.com/AWSEC2/latest/UserGuide/EBSVolumeTypes.html

https://docs.aws.amazon.com/AWSEC2/latest/UserGuide/ebs-io-characteristics.html

Question 34:

You had recently set up a CloudWatch Alarm that performs status checks on your EBS volume. However, you noticed that the volume check has a status of insufficient-data. What does this status mean?

1. The check on the EBS volume is still in progress.
2. The EBS Volume is severely degraded or the volume performance is well below expectations.
3. All EBS Volume checks have failed.
4. All EBS Volume checks have been completed.

Answer(s): 1

Explanation

Volume status checks are automated tests that run every 5 minutes and return a pass or fail status. You can view the results of volume status checks to identify any impaired volumes and take any necessary actions.

If all checks pass, the status of the volume is ok. The option that says: All EBS Volume checks have been completed is therefore incorrect.

If a check fails, the status of the volume is impaired. The option that says: All EBS Volume checks have failed is therefore incorrect.

If the volume is severely degraded or the volume performance is well below expectations, then the status is warning. The option that says: The EBS Volume is severely degraded or the volume performance is well below expectations is therefore incorrect.

If the status is insufficient-data, the checks may still be in progress on the volume. The option that says: The check on the EBS volume is still in progress is therefore correct.

Reference:

http://docs.aws.amazon.com/AWSEC2/latest/UserGuide/monitoring-volume-status.html

Question 35:

You are responsible for running a global news website hosted in a fleet of EC2 Instances. Lately, the load on the website has increased which resulted to slower response time for the site visitors. This issue impacts the revenue of the company as some readers tend to leave the site if it does not load after 10 seconds.

Which of the below services in AWS can be used to solve this problem? (Select TWO.)

1. Deploy the website to all regions in different VPCs for faster processing.
2. Use Amazon ElastiCache for the website's in-memory data store or cache.
3. Use Amazon CloudFront with website as the custom origin.
4. For better read throughput, use AWS Storage Gateway to distribute the content across multiple regions.

Answer(s): 2, 3

Explanation

The global news website has a problem with latency considering that there are a lot of readers of the site from all parts of the globe. In this scenario, you can use a content delivery network (CDN) which is a geographically distributed group of servers which work together to provide fast delivery of Internet content. And since this is a news website, most of its data are read-only, which can be cached to improve the read throughput and avoid the repetitive requests from the server.

In AWS, Amazon CloudFront is the global content delivery network (CDN) service that you can use and for web caching, Amazon ElastiCache is the suitable service. Hence, the correct answers here are using Amazon CloudFront with website as the custom origin and using Amazon ElastiCache for the website's in-memory data store or cache.

The option that says: For better read throughput, use AWS Storage Gateway to distribute the content across multiple regions is incorrect as AWS Storage Gateway is used for storage.

Deploying the website to all regions in different VPCs for faster processing is incorrect as this would be costly and totally unnecessary considering that you can use Amazon CloudFront and ElastiCache to improve the performance of the website.

References:

https://aws.amazon.com/elasticache/

http://docs.aws.amazon.com/AmazonCloudFront/latest/DeveloperGuide/Introduction.html

Question 36:

You are the technical lead of the Cloud Infrastructure team in your company and you were consulted by a software developer regarding the required AWS resources of the web application that he is building. He knows that an Instance Store only provides ephemeral storage where the data is automatically deleted when the instance is terminated. To ensure that the data of his web application persists, the app should be launched in an EC2 instance that has a durable, block-level storage volume attached. He knows that they need to use an EBS volume, but they are not sure what type they need to use.

In this scenario, which of the following is true about Amazon EBS volume types and their respective usage? (Select TWO.)

1. Spot volumes provide the lowest cost per gigabyte of all EBS volume types and are ideal for workloads where data is accessed infrequently, and applications where the lowest storage cost is important.
2. Provisioned IOPS volumes offer storage with consistent and low-latency performance, and are designed for I/O intensive applications such as large relational or NoSQL databases.
3. Single root I/O virtualization (SR-IOV) volumes are suitable for a broad range of workloads, including small to medium sized databases, development and test environments, and boot volumes.
4. Magnetic volumes provide the lowest cost per gigabyte of all EBS volume types and are ideal for workloads where data is accessed infrequently, and applications where the lowest storage cost is important.
5. Reduced Redundancy Storage volumes offer consistent and low-latency performance, and are designed for I/O intensive applications such as large relational or NoSQL databases.

Answer(s): 2, 4

Explanation

Amazon EBS provides three volume types to best meet the needs of your workloads: General Purpose (SSD), Provisioned IOPS (SSD), and Magnetic.

General Purpose (SSD) is the new, SSD-backed, general purpose EBS volume type that we recommend as the default choice for customers. General Purpose (SSD) volumes are suitable for a broad range of workloads, including small to medium sized databases, development, and test environments, and boot volumes.

Provisioned IOPS (SSD) volumes offer storage with consistent and low-latency performance and are designed for I/O intensive applications such as large relational or NoSQL databases. Magnetic volumes provide the lowest cost per gigabyte of all EBS volume types.

Magnetic volumes are ideal for workloads where data are accessed infrequently, and applications where the lowest storage cost is important. Take note that this is a Previous Generation Volume. The latest low-cost magnetic storage types are Cold HDD (sc1) and Throughput Optimized HDD (st1) volumes.

Hence, the correct answers are:

Provisioned IOPS volumes offer storage with consistent and low-latency performance, and are designed for I/O intensive applications such as large relational or NoSQL databases.

Magnetic volumes provide the lowest cost per gigabyte of all EBS volume types and are ideal for workloads where data is accessed infrequently, and applications where the lowest storage cost is important.

The option that says: Spot volumes provide the lowest cost per gigabyte of all EBS volume types and are ideal for workloads where data is accessed infrequently, and applications where the lowest storage cost is important is incorrect because there is no EBS type called a "Spot volume" however, there is an Instance purchasing option for Spot Instances.

The option that says: Reduced Redundancy Storage volumes offer consistent and low-latency performance, and are designed for I/O intensive applications such as large relational or NoSQL databases is incorrect because there is no such thing as Reduced Redundancy Storage volumes. In Amazon S3, there is an obsolete storage type named: Reduced Redundancy Storage (RRS), but not in EBS.

The option that says: Single root I/O virtualization (SR-IOV) volumes are suitable for a broad range of workloads, including small to medium sized databases, development and test environments, and boot volumes is incorrect because SR-IOV is related with Enhanced Networking on Linux and not in EBS.

References:

https://docs.aws.amazon.com/AWSEC2/latest/UserGuide/EBSVolumeTypes.html

https://docs.aws.amazon.com/AWSEC2/latest/UserGuide/AmazonEBS.html

Question 37:

You are working for a media company and you need to configure an Amazon S3 bucket to serve static assets for your public-facing web application. Which methods ensure that all of the objects uploaded to the S3 bucket can be read publicly all over the Internet? (Select TWO.)

1. Configure the S3 bucket policy to set all objects to public read.
2. Grant public read access to the object when uploading it using the S3 Console.
3. Create an IAM role to set the objects inside the S3 bucket to public read.
4. Configure the ACL of the S3 bucket to set all objects to be publicly readable and writeable.
5. Do nothing. Amazon S3 objects are already public by default.

Answer(s): 1, 2

Explanation

By default, all Amazon S3 resources such as buckets, objects, and related subresources are private which means that only the AWS account holder (resource owner) that created it has access to the resource. The resource owner can optionally grant access permissions to others by writing an access policy. In S3, you also set the permissions of the object during upload to make it public.

Amazon S3 offers access policy options broadly categorized as resource-based policies and user policies. Access policies you attach to your resources (buckets and objects) are referred to as resource-based policies.

For example, bucket policies and access control lists (ACLs) are resource-based policies. You can also attach access policies to users in your account. These are called user policies. You may choose to use resource-based policies, user policies, or some combination of these to manage permissions to your Amazon S3 resources.

You can also manage the public permissions of your objects during upload. Under Manage public permissions you can grant read access to your objects to the general public (everyone in the world), for all of the files that you're uploading. Granting public read access is applicable to a small subset of use cases such as when buckets are used for websites.

Hence, the correct answers are:

Grant public read access to the object when uploading it using the S3 Console.

Configure the S3 bucket policy to set all objects to public read.

Configuring the ACL of the S3 bucket to set all objects to be publicly readable and writeable is incorrect as ACLs are primarily used to grant basic read/write permissions to AWS accounts and are not suitable for providing public access over the Internet.

Creating an IAM role to set the objects inside the S3 bucket to public read is incorrect. You can create an IAM role and attach it to an EC2 instance in order to retrieve objects from the S3 bucket or add new ones. An IAM Role, in itself, cannot directly make the S3 objects public or change the permissions of each individual object.

The option that says: Do nothing. Amazon S3 objects are already public by default is incorrect because by default, all the S3 resources are private, so only the AWS account that created the resources can access them.

References:

http://docs.aws.amazon.com/AmazonS3/latest/dev/s3-access-control.html

https://docs.aws.amazon.com/AmazonS3/latest/dev/BucketRestrictions.html

Additional learning material: How do I configure an S3 bucket policy to Deny all actions unless they meet certain conditions?

https://youtu.be/8ew8MSXBiA4

Question 38:

You are working for a tech company which currently has an on-premises infrastructure. They are currently running low on storage and want to have the ability to extend their storage using AWS cloud.

Which AWS service can help you achieve this requirement?

1. Amazon Storage Gateway
2. Amazon SQS
3. Amazon EC2
4. Amazon Elastic Block Storage

Answer(s): 1

Explanation

AWS Storage Gateway connects an on-premises software appliance with cloud-based storage to provide seamless integration with data security features between your on-premises IT environment and the AWS storage infrastructure. You can use the service to store data in the AWS Cloud for scalable and cost-effective storage that helps maintain data security.

Amazon EC2 is incorrect since this is a compute service, not a storage service.

Amazon Elastic Block Storage is incorrect since EBS is primarily used as a storage of your EC2 instances.

Amazon SQS is incorrect since this is a message queuing service, and does not extend your on-premises storage capacity.

Reference:

http://docs.aws.amazon.com/storagegateway/latest/userguide/WhatIsStorageGateway.html

Question 39:

To save costs, your manager instructed you to analyze and review the setup of your AWS cloud infrastructure. You should also provide an estimate of how much your company will pay for all of the AWS resources that they are using. In this scenario, which of the following will incur costs? (Select TWO.)

1. A stopped On-Demand EC2 Instance
2. EBS Volumes attached to stopped EC2 Instances
3. Using an Amazon VPC
4. Public Data Set
5. A running EC2 Instance

Answer(s): 2, 5

Explanation

Billing commences when Amazon EC2 initiates the boot sequence of an AMI instance. Billing ends when the instance terminates, which could occur through a web services command, by running "shutdown -h", or through instance failure. When you stop an instance, AWS shuts it down but don't charge hourly usage for a stopped instance or data transfer fees, but AWS does charge for the storage of any Amazon EBS volumes.

Hence, a running EC2 Instance and EBS Volumes attached to stopped EC2 Instances are the right answers and conversely, a stopped On-Demand EC2 Instance is incorrect as there is no charge for a terminated EC2 instance that you have shut down.

Using Amazon VPC is incorrect because there are no additional charges for creating and using the VPC itself. Usage charges for other Amazon Web Services, including Amazon EC2, still apply at published rates for those resources, including data transfer charges.

Public Data Set is incorrect due to the fact that Amazon stores the data sets at no charge to the community and, as with all AWS services, you pay only for the compute and storage you use for your own applications.

References:

https://aws.amazon.com/cloudtrail/

https://aws.amazon.com/vpc/faqs

https://docs.aws.amazon.com/AWSEC2/latest/UserGuide/using-public-data-sets.html

Question 40:

An automotive company is working on an autonomous vehicle development and deployment project using AWS. The solution requires High Performance Computing (HPC) in order to collect, store and manage massive amounts of data as well as to support deep learning frameworks. The Linux EC2 instances that will be used should have a lower latency and higher throughput than the TCP transport traditionally used in cloud-based HPC systems. It should also enhance the performance of inter-instance communication and must include an OS-bypass functionality to allow the HPC to communicate directly with the network interface hardware to provide low-latency, reliable transport functionality.

Which of the following is the MOST suitable solution that you should implement to achieve the above requirements?

1. Attach an Elastic Network Adapter (ENA) on each Amazon EC2 instance to accelerate High Performance Computing (HPC).
2. Attach an Elastic Fabric Adapter (EFA) on each Amazon EC2 instance to accelerate High Performance Computing (HPC).
3. Attach a Private Virtual Interface (VIF) on each Amazon EC2 instance to accelerate High Performance Computing (HPC).
4. Attach an Elastic Network Interface (ENI) on each Amazon EC2 instance to accelerate High Performance Computing (HPC).

Answer(s): 2

Explanation

An Elastic Fabric Adapter (EFA) is a network device that you can attach to your Amazon EC2 instance to accelerate High Performance Computing (HPC) and machine learning applications. EFA enables you to achieve the application performance of an on-premises HPC cluster, with the scalability, flexibility, and elasticity provided by the AWS Cloud.

EFA provides lower and more consistent latency and higher throughput than the TCP transport traditionally used in cloud-based HPC systems. It enhances the performance of inter-instance communication that is critical for scaling HPC and machine learning applications. It is optimized to work on the existing AWS network infrastructure and it can scale depending on application requirements.

EFA integrates with Libfabric 1.9.0 and it supports Open MPI 4.0.2 and Intel MPI 2019 Update 6 for HPC applications, and Nvidia Collective Communications Library (NCCL) for machine learning applications.

The OS-bypass capabilities of EFAs are not supported on Windows instances. If you attach an EFA to a Windows instance, the instance functions as an Elastic Network Adapter, without the added EFA capabilities.

Elastic Network Adapters (ENAs) provide traditional IP networking features that are required to support VPC networking. EFAs provide all of the same traditional IP networking features as ENAs, and they also support OS-bypass capabilities. OS-bypass enables HPC and machine learning applications to bypass the operating system kernel and to communicate directly with the EFA device.

Hence, the correct answer is to attach an Elastic Fabric Adapter (EFA) on each Amazon EC2 instance to accelerate High Performance Computing (HPC).

Attaching an Elastic Network Adapter (ENA) on each Amazon EC2 instance to accelerate High Performance Computing (HPC) is incorrect because Elastic Network Adapter (ENA) doesn't have OS-bypass capabilities, unlike EFA.

Attaching an Elastic Network Interface (ENI) on each Amazon EC2 instance to accelerate High Performance Computing (HPC) is incorrect because an Elastic Network Interface (ENI) is simply a logical networking component in a VPC that represents a virtual network card. It doesn't have OS-bypass capabilities that allow the HPC to communicate directly with the network interface hardware to provide low-latency, reliable transport functionality.

Attaching a Private Virtual Interface (VIF) on each Amazon EC2 instance to accelerate High Performance Computing (HPC) is incorrect because Private Virtual Interface just allows you to connect to your VPC resources on your private IP address or endpoint.

References:

https://docs.aws.amazon.com/AWSEC2/latest/UserGuide/efa.html

https://docs.aws.amazon.com/AWSEC2/latest/UserGuide/enhanced-networking-ena

Question 41:

A data analytics company, which uses machine learning to collect and analyze consumer data, is using Redshift cluster as their data warehouse. You are instructed to implement a disaster recovery plan for their systems to ensure business continuity even in the event of an AWS region outage.

Which of the following is the best approach to meet this requirement?

1. Use Automated snapshots of your Redshift Cluster.
2. Do nothing because Amazon Redshift is a highly available, fully-managed data warehouse which can withstand an outage of an entire AWS region.
3. Enable Cross-Region Snapshots Copy in your Amazon Redshift Cluster.
4. Create a scheduled job that will automatically take the snapshot of your Redshift Cluster and store it to an S3 bucket. Restore the snapshot in case of an AWS region outage.

Answer(s): 3

Explanation

You can configure Amazon Redshift to copy snapshots for a cluster to another region. To configure cross-region snapshot copy, you need to enable this copy feature for each cluster and configure where to copy snapshots and how long to keep copied automated snapshots in the destination region. When cross-region copy is enabled for a cluster, all new manual and automatic snapshots are copied to the specified region.

The option that says: Create a scheduled job that will automatically take the snapshot of your Redshift Cluster and store it to an S3 bucket. Restore the snapshot in case of an AWS region outage is incorrect because although this option is possible, this entails a lot of manual work and hence, not the best option. You should configure cross-region snapshot copy instead.

The option that says: Do nothing because Amazon Redshift is a highly available, fully-managed data warehouse which can withstand an outage of an entire AWS region is incorrect because although Amazon Redshift is a fully-managed data warehouse, you will still need to configure cross-region snapshot copy to ensure that your data is properly replicated to another region.

Using Automated snapshots of your Redshift Cluster is incorrect because using automated snapshots is not enough and will not be available in case the entire AWS region is down.

Reference:

https://docs.aws.amazon.com/redshift/latest/mgmt/managing-snapshots-console.html

Question 42:

You are working for a large global media company with multiple office locations all around the world. You are instructed to build a system to distribute training videos to all employees. Using CloudFront, what method would be used to serve content that is stored in S3, but not publicly accessible from S3 directly?

1. Add the CloudFront account security group.
2. Create an S3 bucket policy that lists the CloudFront distribution ID as the principal and the target bucket as the Amazon Resource Name (ARN).
3. Create an Origin Access Identity (OAI) for CloudFront and grant access to the objects in your S3 bucket to that OAI.
4. Create an Identity and Access Management (IAM) user for CloudFront and grant access to the objects in your S3 bucket to that IAM user.

Answer(s): 3

Explanation

When you create or update a distribution in CloudFront, you can add an origin access identity (OAI) and automatically update the bucket policy to give the origin access identity permission to access your bucket. Alternatively, you can choose to manually change the bucket policy or change ACLs, which control permissions on individual objects in your bucket.

You can update the Amazon S3 bucket policy using either the AWS Management Console or the Amazon S3 API:

- Grant the CloudFront origin access identity the applicable permissions on the bucket.

- Deny access to anyone that you don't want to have access using Amazon S3 URLs.

Reference:

https://docs.aws.amazon.com/AmazonCloudFront/latest/DeveloperGuide/private-content-restricting-access-to-s3.html#private-content-granting-permissions-to-oai

Question 43:

You are working as a Solutions Architect for a startup in which you are tasked to develop a custom messaging service that will also be used to train their AI for an automatic response feature which they plan to implement in the future. Based on their research and tests, the service can receive up to thousands of messages a day, and all of these data are to be sent to Amazon EMR for further processing. It is crucial that none of the messages will be lost, no duplicates will be produced and that they are processed in EMR in the same order as their arrival.

Which of the following options should you implement to meet the startup's requirements?

1. Create a pipeline using AWS Data Pipeline to handle the messages.
2. Set up a default Amazon SQS queue to handle the messages.
3. Create an Amazon Kinesis Data Stream to collect the messages.
4. Set up an Amazon SNS Topic to handle the messages.

Answer(s): 3

Explanation

Two important requirements that the chosen AWS service should fulfill is that data should not go missing, is durable, and streams data in the sequence of arrival. Kinesis can do the job just fine because of its architecture. A Kinesis data stream is a set of shards that has a sequence of data records, and each data record has a sequence number that is assigned by Kinesis Data Streams. Kinesis can also easily handle the high volume of messages being sent to the service.

Amazon Kinesis Data Streams enables real-time processing of streaming big data. It provides ordering of records, as well as the ability to read and/or replay records in the same order to multiple Amazon Kinesis Applications. The Amazon Kinesis

Client Library (KCL) delivers all records for a given partition key to the same record processor, making it easier to build multiple applications reading from the same Amazon Kinesis data stream (for example, to perform counting, aggregation, and filtering).

Setting up a default Amazon SQS queue to handle the messages is incorrect because although SQS is a valid messaging service, it is not suitable for scenarios where you need to process the data based on the order they were received. Take note that a default queue in SQS is just a standard queue and not a FIFO (First-In-First-Out) queue. In addition, SQS does not guarantee that no duplicates will be sent.

Setting up an Amazon SNS Topic to handle the messages is incorrect because SNS is a pub-sub messaging service in AWS. SNS might not be capable of handling such a large volume of messages being received and sent at a time. It does not also guarantee that the data will be transmitted in the same order they were received.

Creating a pipeline using AWS Data Pipeline to handle the messages is incorrect because this is primarily used as a cloud-based data workflow service that helps you process and move data between different AWS services and on-premises data sources. It is not suitable for collecting data from distributed sources such as users, IoT devices, or clickstreams.

References:

https://docs.aws.amazon.com/streams/latest/dev/introduction.html

For additional information, read the When should I use Amazon Kinesis Data Streams, and when should I use Amazon SQS? section of the Kinesis Data Stream FAQ:

https://aws.amazon.com/kinesis/data-streams/faqs/

Question 44:

You have an Auto Scaling group which is configured to launch new t2.micro EC2 instances when there is a significant load increase in the application. To cope with the demand, you now need to replace those instances with a larger t2.2xlarge instance type. How would you implement this change?

1. Change the instance type of each EC2 instance manually.
2. Just change the instance type to t2.2xlarge in the current launch configuration
3. Create another Auto Scaling Group and attach the new instance type.
4. Create a new launch configuration with the new instance type and update the Auto Scaling Group.

Answer(s): 4

Explanation

You can only specify one launch configuration for an Auto Scaling group at a time, and you can't modify a launch configuration after you've created it. Therefore, if you want to change the launch configuration for an Auto Scaling group, you must create a launch configuration and then update your Auto Scaling group with the new launch configuration.

Hence, the correct answer is: Create a new launch configuration with the new instance type and update the Auto Scaling Group.

The option that says: Just change the instance type to t2.2xlarge in the current launch configuration is incorrect because you can't change your launch configuration once it is created. You have to create a new one instead.

The option that says: Create another Auto Scaling Group and attach the new instance type is incorrect because you can't directly attach or declare the new instance type to your Auto Scaling group. You have to create a new launch configuration first, with a new instance type, then attach it to your existing Auto Scaling group.

The option that says: Change the instance type of each EC2 instance manually is incorrect because you can't directly change the instance type of your EC2 instance. This should be done by creating a brand new launch configuration then attaching it to your existing Auto Scaling group.

References:

https://docs.aws.amazon.com/autoscaling/ec2/userguide/LaunchConfiguration.html

https://docs.aws.amazon.com/autoscaling/ec2/userguide/create-asg.html

Question 45:

A tech startup has recently received a Series A round of funding to continue building their mobile forex trading application. You are hired to set up their cloud architecture in AWS and to implement a highly available, fault tolerant system. For their database, they are using DynamoDB and for authentication, they have chosen to use Cognito. Since the mobile application contains confidential financial transactions, there is a requirement to add a second authentication method that doesn't rely solely on user name and password.

How can you implement this in AWS?

1. Add a new IAM policy to a user pool in Cognito.
2. Develop a custom application that integrates with Cognito that implements a second layer of authentication.

3. Add multi-factor authentication (MFA) to a user pool in Cognito to protect the identity of your users.
4. Integrate Cognito with Amazon SNS Mobile Push to allow additional authentication via SMS.

Answer(s): 3

Explanation

You can add multi-factor authentication (MFA) to a user pool to protect the identity of your users. MFA adds a second authentication method that doesn't rely solely on user name and password. You can choose to use SMS text messages, or time-based one-time (TOTP) passwords as second factors in signing in your users. You can also use adaptive authentication with its risk-based model to predict when you might need another authentication factor. It's part of the user pool advanced security features, which also include protections against compromised credentials.

Reference:

https://docs.aws.amazon.com/cognito/latest/developerguide/managing-security.html

Question 46:

An auto-scaling group of Linux EC2 instances is created with basic monitoring enabled in CloudWatch. You noticed that your application is slow so you asked one of your engineers to check all of your EC2 instances. After checking your instances, you noticed that the auto scaling group is not launching more instances as it should be, even though the servers already have high memory usage.

Which of the following are possible solutions that an Architect can implement to solve this issue? (Select TWO.)

1. Enable detailed monitoring on the instances.
2. Install CloudWatch monitoring scripts in the instances. Send custom metrics to CloudWatch which will trigger your Auto Scaling group to scale up.
3. Install the CloudWatch agent to the EC2 instances which will trigger your Auto Scaling group to scale up.
4. Install AWS SDK in the EC2 instances. Create a script that will trigger the Auto Scaling event if there is a high memory usage.
5. Modify the scaling policy to increase the threshold to scale up the number of instances.

Answer(s): 2, 3

Explanation

The Amazon CloudWatch Monitoring Scripts for Amazon Elastic Compute Cloud (Amazon EC2) Linux-based instances demonstrate how to produce and consume Amazon CloudWatch custom metrics. These sample Perl scripts comprise a fully functional example that reports memory, swap, and disk space utilization metrics for a Linux instance.

The premise of the scenario is that the EC2 servers have high memory usage, but since this specific metric is not tracked by the Auto Scaling group by default, the scaling up activity is not being triggered. Remember that by default, CloudWatch doesn't monitor memory usage but only the CPU utilization, Network utilization, Disk performance and Disk Reads/Writes.

This is the reason why you have to install CloudWatch Monitoring Scripts in your EC2 instances to collect and monitor the custom metric (memory usage), which will be used by your Auto Scaling Group as a trigger for scaling activities.

CloudWatch does not monitor EC2 memory usage as well as disk space utilization. You would have to collect the metrics using a script or by using a CloudWatch agent then send the data to CloudWatch. Hence, the correct answers are:

- Install CloudWatch monitoring scripts in the instances. Send custom metrics to CloudWatch which will trigger your Auto Scaling group to scale up.

- Install the CloudWatch agent to the EC2 instances which will trigger your Auto Scaling group to scale up.

The option that says: Install AWS SDK in the EC2 instances. Create a script that will trigger the Auto Scaling event if there is a high memory usage is incorrect because AWS SDK is a set of programming tools that allow you to create applications that run using Amazon cloud services. You would have to program the alert which is not the best strategy for this scenario.

The option that says: Enable detailed monitoring on the instances is incorrect because detailed monitoring does not provide metrics for memory usage. CloudWatch does not monitor memory usage in its default set of EC2 metrics and detailed monitoring just provides a higher frequency of metrics (1-minute frequency).

The option that says: Modify the scaling policy to increase the threshold to scale up the number of instances is incorrect because you are already maxing out your usage, which should in effect cause an auto-scaling event.

References:

https://docs.aws.amazon.com/AWSEC2/latest/UserGuide/mon-scripts.html

https://docs.aws.amazon.com/AWSEC2/latest/UserGuide/viewing_metrics_with_cloudwatch.html

https://docs.aws.amazon.com/AWSEC2/latest/UserGuide/monitoring_ec2.html

Question 47:

You are using an On-Demand EC2 instance to host a legacy web application that uses an Amazon Instance Store-Backed AMI. The web application should be decommissioned as soon as possible and hence, you need to terminate the EC2 instance.

When the instance is terminated, what happens to the data on the root volume?

1. Data is automatically saved as an EBS snapshot.
2. Data is automatically deleted.
3. Data is automatically saved as an EBS volume.
4. Data is unavailable until the instance is restarted.

Answer(s): 2

Explanation

AMIs are categorized as either backed by Amazon EBS or backed by instance store. The former means that the root device for an instance launched from the AMI is an Amazon EBS volume created from an Amazon EBS snapshot. The latter means that the root device for an instance launched from the AMI is an instance store volume created from a template stored in Amazon S3.

The option that says: Data is automatically deleted is the correct answer because the data on instance store volumes persist only during the life of the instance which means that if the instance is terminated, the data will be automatically deleted.

Reference:

https://docs.aws.amazon.com/AWSEC2/latest/UserGuide/ComponentsAMIs.html

Question 48:

A popular augmented reality (AR) mobile game is heavily using a RESTful API which is hosted in AWS. The API uses Amazon API Gateway and a DynamoDB table with a preconfigured read and write capacity. Based on your systems monitoring, the DynamoDB table begins to throttle requests during high peak loads which causes the slow performance of the game.

Which of the following can you do to improve the performance of your app?

1. Create an SQS queue in front of the DynamoDB table.
2. Integrate an Application Load Balancer with your DynamoDB table.
3. Add the DynamoDB table to an Auto Scaling Group.
4. Use DynamoDB Auto Scaling

Answer(s): 4

Explanation

DynamoDB auto scaling uses the AWS Application Auto Scaling service to dynamically adjust provisioned throughput capacity on your behalf, in response to actual traffic patterns. This enables a table or a global secondary index to increase its provisioned read and write capacity to handle sudden increases in traffic, without throttling. When the workload decreases, Application Auto Scaling decreases the throughput so that you don't pay for unused provisioned capacity.

Using DynamoDB Auto Scaling is the best answer. DynamoDB Auto Scaling uses the AWS Application Auto Scaling service to dynamically adjust provisioned throughput capacity on your behalf.

Integrating an Application Load Balancer with your DynamoDB table is incorrect because an Application Load Balancer is not suitable to be used with DynamoDB and in addition, this will not increase the throughput of your DynamoDB table.

Adding the DynamoDB table to an Auto Scaling Group is incorrect because you usually put EC2 instances on an Auto Scaling Group, and not a DynamoDB table.

Creating an SQS queue in front of the DynamoDB table is incorrect because this is not a design principle for high throughput DynamoDB table. Using SQS is for handling queuing and polling the request. This will not increase the throughput of DynamoDB which is required in this situation.

Reference:

https://docs.aws.amazon.com/amazondynamodb/latest/developerguide/AutoScalin g.html

Question 49:

There is a new compliance rule in your company that audits every Windows and Linux EC2 instances each month to view any performance issues. They have more than a hundred EC2 instances running in production, and each must have a logging function that collects various system details regarding that instance. The SysOps team will periodically review these logs and analyze their contents using AWS Analytics tools, and the result will need to be retained in an S3 bucket.

In this scenario, what is the most efficient way to collect and analyze logs from the instances with minimal effort?

1. Install the AWS Systems Manager Agent (SSM Agent) in each instance which will automatically collect and push data to CloudWatch Logs. Analyze the log data with CloudWatch Logs Insights.
2. Install AWS SDK in each instance and create a custom daemon script that would collect and push data to CloudWatch Logs periodically. Enable CloudWatch detailed monitoring and use CloudWatch Logs Insights to analyze the log data of all instances.
3. Install the unified CloudWatch Logs agent in each instance which will automatically collect and push data to CloudWatch Logs. Analyze the log data with CloudWatch Logs Insights.
4. Install AWS Inspector Agent in each instance which will collect and push data to CloudWatch Logs periodically. Set up a CloudWatch dashboard to properly analyze the log data of all instances.

Answer(s): 3

Explanation

To collect logs from your Amazon EC2 instances and on-premises servers into CloudWatch Logs, AWS offers both a new unified CloudWatch agent, and an older CloudWatch Logs agent. It is recommended to use the unified CloudWatch agent which has the following advantages:

- You can collect both logs and advanced metrics with the installation and configuration of just one agent.

- The unified agent enables the collection of logs from servers running Windows Server.

- If you are using the agent to collect CloudWatch metrics, the unified agent also enables the collection of additional system metrics, for in-guest visibility.

- The unified agent provides better performance.

CloudWatch Logs Insights enables you to interactively search and analyze your log data in Amazon CloudWatch Logs. You can perform queries to help you quickly and effectively respond to operational issues. If an issue occurs, you can use CloudWatch Logs Insights to identify potential causes and validate deployed fixes.

CloudWatch Logs Insights includes a purpose-built query language with a few simple but powerful commands. CloudWatch Logs Insights provides sample queries, command descriptions, query autocompletion, and log field discovery to help you get started quickly. Sample queries are included for several types of AWS service logs.

The option that says: Install AWS SDK in each instance and create a custom daemon script that would collect and push data to CloudWatch Logs periodically. Enable

CloudWatch detailed monitoring and use CloudWatch Logs Insights to analyze the log data of all instances is incorrect. Although this is a valid solution, this entails a lot of effort to implement as you have to allocate time to install the AWS SDK to each instance and develop a custom monitoring solution. Remember that the question is specifically looking for a solution that can be implemented with minimal effort. In addition, it is unnecessary and not cost-efficient to enable detailed monitoring in CloudWatch in order to meet the requirements of this scenario since this can be done using CloudWatch Logs.

The option that says: Install the AWS Systems Manager Agent (SSM Agent) in each instance which will automatically collect and push data to CloudWatch Logs. Analyze the log data with CloudWatch Logs Insights is incorrect as although this is also a valid solution, it is more efficient to use CloudWatch agent than an SSM agent. Manually connecting to an instance to view log files and troubleshoot an issue with SSM Agent is time-consuming hence, for more efficient instance monitoring, you can use the CloudWatch Agent instead to send the log data to Amazon CloudWatch Logs.

The option that says: Install AWS Inspector Agent in each instance which will collect and push data to CloudWatch Logs periodically. Set up a CloudWatch dashboard to properly analyze the log data of all instances is incorrect because AWS Inspector is simply a security assessments service which only helps you in checking for unintended network accessibility of your EC2 instances and for vulnerabilities on those EC2 instances. Furthermore, setting up an Amazon CloudWatch dashboard is not suitable since its primarily used for scenarios where you have to monitor your resources in a single view, even those resources that are spread across different AWS Regions. It is better to use CloudWatch Logs Insights instead since it enables you to interactively search and analyze your log data.

References:

https://docs.aws.amazon.com/AmazonCloudWatch/latest/logs/WhatIsCloudWatchLogs.html

https://docs.aws.amazon.com/systems-manager/latest/userguide/monitoring-ssm-agent.html

https://docs.aws.amazon.com/AmazonCloudWatch/latest/logs/AnalyzingLogData.html

Question 50:

You have a web application hosted in AWS cloud where the application logs are sent to Amazon CloudWatch. Lately, the web application has recently been encountering some errors which can be resolved simply by restarting the instance.

What will you do to automatically restart the EC2 instances whenever the same application error occurs?

1. First, look at the existing Flow logs for keywords related to the application error to create a custom metric. Then, create a CloudWatch alarm for that custom metric which calls a Lambda function that invokes an action to restart the EC2 instance.
2. First, look at the existing CloudWatch logs for keywords related to the application error to create a custom metric. Then, create an alarm in Amazon SNS for that custom metric which invokes an action to restart the EC2 instance.
3. First, look at the existing Flow logs for keywords related to the application error to create a custom metric. Then, create a CloudWatch alarm for that custom metric which invokes an action to restart the EC2 instance.
4. First, look at the existing CloudWatch logs for keywords related to the application error to create a custom metric. Then, create a CloudWatch alarm for that custom metric which invokes an action to restart the EC2 instance.

Answer(s): 4

Explanation

In this scenario, you can look at the existing CloudWatch logs for keywords related to the application error to create a custom metric. Then, create a CloudWatch alarm for that custom metric which invokes an action to restart the EC2 instance.

You can create alarms that automatically stop, terminate, reboot, or recover your EC2 instances using Amazon CloudWatch alarm actions. You can use the stop or terminate actions to help you save money when you no longer need an instance to be running. You can use the reboot and recover actions to automatically reboot those instances or recover them onto new hardware if a system impairment occurs.

The option that says: First, look at the existing CloudWatch logs for keywords related to the application error to create a custom metric. Then, create an alarm in Amazon SNS for that custom metric which invokes an action to restart the EC2 instance is incorrect because you can't create an alarm in Amazon SNS.

The options that say: First, look at the existing Flow logs for keywords related to the application error to create a custom metric. Then, create a CloudWatch alarm for that custom metric which invokes an action to restart the EC2 instance and First, look at the existing Flow logs for keywords related to the application error to create a custom metric. Then, create a CloudWatch alarm for that custom metric which calls a Lambda function that invokes an action to restart the EC2 instance are incorrect because Flow Logs are used in VPC and not on specific EC2 instance.

Reference:

https://docs.aws.amazon.com/AmazonCloudWatch/latest/monitoring/UsingAlarm Actions.html

Question 51:

You have a requirement to integrate the Lightweight Directory Access Protocol (LDAP) directory service of your on-premises data center to your AWS VPC using IAM. The identity store which is currently being used is not compatible with SAML.

Which of the following provides the most valid approach to implement the integration?

1. Use AWS Single Sign-On (SSO) service to enable single sign-on between AWS and your LDAP.
2. Use IAM roles to rotate the IAM credentials whenever LDAP credentials are updated.
3. Develop an on-premises custom identity broker application and use STS to issue short-lived AWS credentials.
4. Use an IAM policy that references the LDAP identifiers and AWS credentials.

Answer(s): 3

Explanation

If your identity store is not compatible with SAML 2.0, then you can build a custom identity broker application to perform a similar function. The broker application authenticates users, requests temporary credentials for users from AWS, and then provides them to the user to access AWS resources.

The application verifies that employees are signed into the existing corporate network's identity and authentication system, which might use LDAP, Active Directory, or another system. The identity broker application then obtains temporary security credentials for the employees.

To get temporary security credentials, the identity broker application calls either AssumeRole or GetFederationToken to obtain temporary security credentials, depending on how you want to manage the policies for users and when the temporary credentials should expire. The call returns temporary security credentials consisting of an AWS access key ID, a secret access key, and a session token. The identity broker application makes these temporary security credentials available to the internal company application. The app can then use the temporary credentials to make calls to AWS directly. The app caches the credentials until they expire, and then requests a new set of temporary credentials.

Using an IAM policy that references the LDAP identifiers and AWS credentials is incorrect because using an IAM policy is not enough to integrate your LDAP service to IAM. You need to use SAML, STS or a custom identity broker.

Using AWS Single Sign-On (SSO) service to enable single sign-on between AWS and your LDAP is incorrect because the scenario did not require SSO and in addition, the identity store that you are using is not SAML-compatible.

Using IAM roles to rotate the IAM credentials whenever LDAP credentials are updated is incorrect because manually rotating the IAM credentials is not an optimal solution to integrate your on-premises and VPC network. You need to use SAML, STS or a custom identity broker.

References:

https://docs.aws.amazon.com/IAM/latest/UserGuide/id_roles_common-scenarios_federated-users.html

https://aws.amazon.com/blogs/aws/aws-identity-and-access-management-now-with-identity-federation/

Question 52:

A data analytics application requires a service that can collect, process, and analyze clickstream data from various websites in real-time. Which of the following is the most suitable service to use for the application?

1. Kinesis
2. AWS Glue
3. Amazon EMR with Compute Optimized Instances
4. Redshift Spectrum

Answer(s): 1

Explanation

Amazon Kinesis makes it easy to collect, process, and analyze real-time, streaming data so you can get timely insights and react quickly to new information. Amazon Kinesis offers key capabilities to cost-effectively process streaming data at any scale, along with the flexibility to choose the tools that best suit the requirements of your application. With Amazon Kinesis, you can ingest real-time data such as video, audio, application logs, website clickstreams, and IoT telemetry data for machine learning, analytics, and other applications. Amazon Kinesis enables you to process and analyze data as it arrives and responds instantly instead of having to wait until all your data is collected before the processing can begin.

Redshift Spectrum is incorrect because this is primarily used to directly query open data formats stored in Amazon S3 without the need for unnecessary data movement, which enables you to analyze data across your data warehouse and data lake, together, with a single service. It does not provide the ability to process your data in real-time, unlike Kinesis.

AWS Glue is incorrect because this is a fully managed extract, transform, and load (ETL) service that makes it easy for customers to prepare and load their data for analytics. It does not provide the ability to process your data in real-time, unlike Kinesis.

Amazon EMR with Compute Optimized Instances is incorrect because this is a web service that uses an open-source Hadoop framework to quickly & cost-effectively process vast amounts of data. It does not provide the ability to process your data in real-time, unlike Kinesis. Compute-optimized instances are ideal for compute-bound applications that benefit from high-performance processors but not for analyzing clickstream data from various websites in real-time.

References:

https://aws.amazon.com/kinesis/

https://docs.aws.amazon.com/AWSEC2/latest/UserGuide/compute-optimized-instances.html

Question 53:

You have a set of Linux servers running on multiple On-Demand EC2 Instances. The Audit team wants to collect and process the application log files generated from these servers for their report.

Which of the following services is the best to use in this case?

1. Amazon S3 Glacier for storing the application log files and Spot EC2 Instances for processing them.
2. Amazon S3 for storing the application log files and Amazon Elastic MapReduce for processing the log files.
3. Amazon S3 Glacier Deep Archive for storing the application log files and AWS ParallelCluster for processing the log files.
4. A single On-Demand Amazon EC2 instance for both storing and processing the log files

Answer(s): 2

Explanation

Amazon EMR is a managed cluster platform that simplifies running big data frameworks, such as Apache Hadoop and Apache Spark, on AWS to process and analyze vast amounts of data. By using these frameworks and related open-source projects such as Apache Hive and Apache Pig, you can process data for analytics purposes and business intelligence workloads. Additionally, you can use Amazon EMR to transform and move large amounts of data into and out of other AWS data stores and databases such as Amazon Simple Storage Service (Amazon S3) and Amazon DynamoDB.

Hence, the correct answer is: Amazon S3 for storing the application log files and Amazon Elastic MapReduce for processing the log files.

The option that says: Amazon S3 Glacier for storing the application log files and Spot EC2 Instances for processing them is incorrect as Amazon S3 Glacier is used for data archive only.

The option that says: A single On-Demand Amazon EC2 instance for both storing and processing the log files is incorrect as an EC2 instance is not a recommended storage service. In addition, Amazon EC2 does not have a built-in data processing engine to process large amounts of data.

The option that says: Amazon S3 Glacier Deep Archive for storing the application log files and AWS ParallelCluster for processing the log files is incorrect because the long retrieval time of Amazon S3 Glacier Deep Archive makes this option unsuitable. Moreover, AWS ParallelCluster is just an AWS-supported open-source cluster management tool that makes it easy for you to deploy and manage High-Performance Computing (HPC) clusters on AWS. ParallelCluster uses a simple text file to model and provision all the resources needed for your HPC applications in an automated and secure manner.

References:

http://docs.aws.amazon.com/emr/latest/ManagementGuide/emr-what-is-emr.html

https://aws.amazon.com/hpc/parallelcluster/

Here is an in-depth tutorial on Amazon EMR:

https://youtu.be/jylp2atrZjc

Question 54:

You are a Big Data Engineer who is assigned to handle the online enrollment system database of a prestigious university, which is hosted in RDS. You are required to monitor the database metrics in Amazon CloudWatch to ensure the availability of the enrollment system.

What are the enhanced monitoring metrics that Amazon CloudWatch gathers from Amazon RDS DB instances which provide a more accurate information? (Select TWO.)

1. OS processes
2. RDS child processes.
3. Freeable Memory
4. Database Connections
5. CPU Utilization

Answer(s): 1, 2

Explanation

Amazon RDS provides metrics in real time for the operating system (OS) that your DB instance runs on. You can view the metrics for your DB instance using the console, or consume the Enhanced Monitoring JSON output from CloudWatch Logs in a monitoring system of your choice.

CloudWatch gathers metrics about CPU utilization from the hypervisor for a DB instance, and Enhanced Monitoring gathers its metrics from an agent on the instance. As a result, you might find differences between the measurements, because the hypervisor layer performs a small amount of work. The differences can be greater if your DB instances use smaller instance classes, because then there are likely more virtual machines (VMs) that are managed by the hypervisor layer on a single physical instance. Enhanced Monitoring metrics are useful when you want to see how different processes or threads on a DB instance use the CPU.

In RDS, the Enhanced Monitoring metrics shown in the Process List view are organized as follows:

RDS child processes – Shows a summary of the RDS processes that support the DB instance, for example aurora for Amazon Aurora DB clusters and mysqld for MySQL DB instances. Process threads appear nested beneath the parent process. Process threads show CPU utilization only as other metrics are the same for all threads for the process. The console displays a maximum of 100 processes and threads. The results are a combination of the top CPU consuming and memory consuming processes and threads. If there are more than 50 processes and more than 50 threads, the console displays the top 50 consumers in each category. This display helps you identify which processes are having the greatest impact on performance.

RDS processes – Shows a summary of the resources used by the RDS management agent, diagnostics monitoring processes, and other AWS processes that are required to support RDS DB instances.

OS processes – Shows a summary of the kernel and system processes, which generally have minimal impact on performance.

CPU Utilization, Database Connections, and Freeable Memory are incorrect because these are just the regular items provided by Amazon RDS Metrics in CloudWatch. Remember that the scenario is asking for the Enhanced Monitoring metrics.

References:

https://docs.aws.amazon.com/AmazonCloudWatch/latest/monitoring/rds-metricscollected.html

https://docs.aws.amazon.com/AmazonRDS/latest/UserGuide/USER_Monitoring.OS.html#USER_Monitoring.OS.CloudWatchLogs

Question 55:

You are employed by a large electronics company that uses Amazon Simple Storage Service. For reporting purposes, they want to track and log every request access to their S3 buckets including the requester, bucket name, request time, request action, referrer, turnaround time, and error code information. The solution should also provide more visibility into the object-level operations of the bucket.

Which is the best solution among the following options that can satisfy the requirement?

1. Enable the Requester Pays option to track access via AWS Billing.
2. Enable Amazon S3 Event Notifications for PUT and POST.
3. Enable server access logging for all required Amazon S3 buckets.
4. Enable AWS CloudTrail to audit all Amazon S3 bucket access.

Answer(s): 3

Explanation

You can use AWS CloudTrail logs together with server access logs for Amazon S3. CloudTrail logs provide you with detailed API tracking for Amazon S3 bucket-level and object-level operations, while server access logs for Amazon S3 provide you visibility into object-level operations on your data in Amazon S3.

You can also use CloudTrail logs together with CloudWatch for Amazon S3. CloudTrail integration with CloudWatch Logs delivers S3 bucket-level API activity captured by CloudTrail to a CloudWatch log stream in the CloudWatch log group you specify. You can create CloudWatch alarms for monitoring specific API activity and receive email notifications when the specific API activity occurs

For this scenario, you can use CloudTrail and the Server Access Logging feature of Amazon S3. However, the question mentioned that it needs detailed information about every access request sent to the S3 bucket including the referrer and turn-around time information. These two records are not available in CloudTrail which is why the correct answer is to enable server access logging for all required Amazon S3 buckets.

Enabling the Requester Pays option to track access via AWS Billing is incorrect because this action refers to AWS billing and not for logging.

Enabling Amazon S3 Event Notifications for PUT and POST is incorrect because we are looking for a logging solution and not an event notification.

References:

https://docs.aws.amazon.com/AmazonS3/latest/dev/cloudtrail-logging.html#cloudtrail-logging-vs-server-logs

https://docs.aws.amazon.com/AmazonS3/latest/dev/LogFormat.html

https://docs.aws.amazon.com/AmazonS3/latest/dev/ServerLogs.html

Question 56:

A tech company is currently using Amazon Simple Workflow (SWF) service with a default configuration for their order processing system. The system works fine but you noticed that some of the orders seem to be stuck for almost 4 weeks.

What could be the possible reason for this?

1. The workflow has exceeded SWF's 14-day maximum workflow execution time.
2. SWF should be restarted.
3. The workflow has exceeded SWF's 15-day maximum workflow execution time.
4. It is because SWF is waiting human input from an activity task.

Answer(s): 4

Explanation

By default, each workflow execution can run for a maximum of 1 year in Amazon SWF. This means that it is possible that in your workflow, there are some tasks which require manual action that renders it idle. As a result, some orders get stuck for almost 4 weeks.

Amazon SWF does not take any special action if a workflow execution is idle for an extended period of time. Idle executions are subject to the timeouts that you configure. For example, if you have set the maximum duration for an execution to be 1 day, then an idle execution will be timed out if it exceeds the 1 day limit. Idle executions are also subject to the Amazon SWF limit on how long an execution can run (1 year).

The options that say: The workflow has exceeded SWF's 15-day maximum workflow execution time and The workflow has exceeded SWF's 14-day maximum workflow execution time are incorrect as the maximum execution time is 1 year.

The option that says: SWF should be restarted is incorrect as there is no problem with SWF and you can't manually restart this service.

Reference:

https://aws.amazon.com/swf/

Question 57:

You have a distributed application in AWS that periodically processes large volumes of data across multiple instances. You designed the application to recover gracefully from any instance failures. You are required to launch the application in the most cost-effective way.

Which type of EC2 instance will meet your requirements?

1. Spot Instances
2. Reserved instances
3. Dedicated instances
4. On-Demand instances

Answer(s): 1

Explanation

You require an EC2 instance that is the most cost-effective among other types. In addition, the application it will host is designed to gracefully recover in case of instance failures.

In terms of cost-effectiveness, Spot and Reserved instances are the top options. And since the application can gracefully recover from instance failures, the Spot instance is the best option for this case as it is the cheapest type of EC2 instance. Remember that when you use Spot Instances, there will be interruptions. Amazon EC2 can interrupt your Spot Instance when the Spot price exceeds your maximum price, when the demand for Spot Instances rise, or when the supply of Spot Instances decreases. This makes Spot Instances the correct answer.

Reserved instances is incorrect because although you could also use reserved instances to save costs, it entails a commitment of 1-year or 3-year terms of usage. Since your processes only run periodically, you won't be able to maximize the discounted price of using reserved instances.

Dedicated instances and On-Demand instances are also incorrect because Dedicated and on-demand instances are not a cost-effective solution to use for your application.

Reference:

http://docs.aws.amazon.com/AWSEC2/latest/UserGuide/how-spot-instances-work.html

Here is an in-depth look at Spot Instances:

https://youtu.be/PKvss-RgSjI

Question 58:

A Fortune 500 company which has numerous offices and customers around the globe has hired you as their Principal Architect. You have staff and customers that upload gigabytes to terabytes of data to a centralized S3 bucket from the regional data centers, across continents, all over the world on a regular basis. At the end of the financial year, there are thousands of data being uploaded to the central S3 bucket which is in ap-southeast-2 (Sydney) region and a lot of employees are starting to complain about the slow upload times. You were instructed by the CTO to resolve this issue as soon as possible to avoid any delays in processing their global end of financial year (EOFY) reports.

Which feature in Amazon S3 enables fast, easy, and secure transfer of your files over long distances between your client and your Amazon S3 bucket?

1. Multipart Upload
2. AWS Global Accelerator
3. Cross-Region Replication
4. Transfer Acceleration

Answer(s): 4

Explanation

Amazon S3 Transfer Acceleration enables fast, easy, and secure transfer of files over long distances between your client and your Amazon S3 bucket. Transfer Acceleration leverages Amazon CloudFront's globally distributed AWS Edge Locations. As data arrives at an AWS Edge Location, data is routed to your Amazon S3 bucket over an optimized network path.

Amazon S3 Transfer Acceleration can speed up content transfers to and from Amazon S3 by as much as 50-500% for long-distance transfer of larger objects. Customers who have either web or mobile applications with widespread users or applications hosted far away from their S3 bucket can experience long and variable upload and download speeds over the Internet. S3 Transfer Acceleration (S3TA) reduces the variability in Internet routing, congestion and speeds that can affect transfers, and logically shortens the distance to S3 for remote applications. S3TA improves transfer performance by routing traffic through Amazon CloudFront's globally distributed Edge Locations and over AWS backbone networks, and by using network protocol optimizations.

Hence, Transfer Acceleration is the correct answer.

AWS Global Accelerator is incorrect because this service is primarily used to optimize the path from your users to your applications which improves the performance of your TCP and UDP traffic. Using Amazon S3 Transfer Acceleration is a more suitable service for this scenario.

Cross-Region Replication is incorrect because this simply enables you to automatically copy S3 objects from one bucket to another bucket that is placed in a different AWS Region or within the same Region.

Multipart Upload is incorrect because this feature simply allows you to upload a single object as a set of parts. You can upload these object parts independently and in any order. If transmission of any part fails, you can retransmit that part without affecting other parts. After all parts of your object are uploaded, Amazon S3 assembles these parts and creates the object. In general, when your object size reaches 100 MB, you should consider using multipart uploads instead of uploading the object in a single operation.

References:

https://aws.amazon.com/s3/faqs/

https://aws.amazon.com/s3/transfer-acceleration/

Question 59:

You are a Cloud Migration Engineer in a media company which uses EC2, ELB, and S3 for its video-sharing portal for filmmakers. They are using a standard S3 storage class to store all high-quality videos that are frequently accessed only during the first three months of posting. What should you do if the company needs to automatically transfer or archive media data from an S3 bucket to Glacier?

1. Use Amazon SWF
2. Use Lifecycle Policies
3. Use Amazon SQS
4. Use a custom shell script that transfers data from the S3 bucket to Glacier

Answer(s): 2

Explanation

You can create a lifecycle policy in S3 to automatically transfer your data to Glacier.

Lifecycle configuration enables you to specify the lifecycle management of objects in a bucket. The configuration is a set of one or more rules, where each rule defines an action for Amazon S3 to apply to a group of objects.

These actions can be classified as follows:

Transition actions – In which you define when objects transition to another storage class. For example, you may choose to transition objects to the STANDARD_IA (IA, for infrequent access) storage class 30 days after creation, or archive objects to the GLACIER storage class one year after creation.

Expiration actions – In which you specify when the objects expire. Then Amazon S3 deletes the expired objects on your behalf.

Reference:

https://docs.aws.amazon.com/AmazonS3/latest/dev/object-lifecycle-mgmt.html

Question 60:

A customer is transitioning their ActiveMQ messaging broker service onto the AWS cloud in which they require an alternative asynchronous service that supports NMS and MQTT messaging protocol. The customer does not have the time and resources needed to recreate their messaging service in the cloud. The service has to be highly available and should require almost no management overhead.

Which of the following is the most suitable service to use to meet the above requirement?

1. Amazon SNS
2. Amazon SWF
3. Amazon SQS
4. Amazon MQ

Answer(s): 4

Explanation

Amazon MQ is a managed message broker service for Apache ActiveMQ that makes it easy to set up and operate message brokers in the cloud. Connecting your current applications to Amazon MQ is easy because it uses industry-standard APIs and protocols for messaging, including JMS, NMS, AMQP, STOMP, MQTT, and WebSocket. Using standards means that in most cases, there's no need to rewrite any messaging code when you migrate to AWS.

Amazon MQ, Amazon SQS, and Amazon SNS are messaging services that are suitable for anyone from startups to enterprises. If you're using messaging with existing applications and want to move your messaging service to the cloud quickly and easily, it is recommended that you consider Amazon MQ. It supports industry-standard APIs and protocols so you can switch from any standards-based message broker to Amazon MQ without rewriting the messaging code in your applications.

If you are building brand new applications in the cloud, then it is highly recommended that you consider Amazon SQS and Amazon SNS. Amazon SQS and SNS are lightweight, fully managed message queue and topic services that scale almost infinitely and provide simple, easy-to-use APIs. You can use Amazon SQS and SNS to decouple and scale microservices, distributed systems, and serverless applications, and improve reliability.

Hence, Amazon MQ is the correct answer.

Amazon SNS is incorrect because this is more suitable as a pub/sub messaging service instead of a message broker service.

Amazon SQS is incorrect because although this is a fully managed message queuing service, it does not support an extensive list of industry-standard messaging APIs and protocol, unlike Amazon MQ. Moreover, using Amazon SQS requires you to do additional changes in the messaging code of applications to make it compatible.

Amazon SWF is incorrect because this is a fully-managed state tracker and task coordinator service and not a messaging service, unlike Amazon MQ, AmazonSQS, and Amazon SNS.

References:

https://aws.amazon.com/amazon-mq/

https://aws.amazon.com/messaging/

https://docs.aws.amazon.com/AWSSimpleQueueService/latest/SQSDeveloperGuide/welcome.html#sqs-difference-from-amazon-mq-sns

Question 61:

You are a Solutions Architect for a large London-based software company. You are assigned to improve the performance and current processes of supporting the AWS resources in your VPC. Upon checking, you noticed that the Operations team does not have an automated way to monitor and resolve issues with their on-demand EC2 instances.

What can be used to automatically monitor your EC2 instances and notify the Operations team for any incidents?

1. Amazon SWF
2. Amazon CloudWatch
3. AWS Cloudtrail
4. Amazon SQS

Answer(s): 2

Explanation

Amazon CloudWatch is a monitoring service for AWS cloud resources and the applications you run on AWS. You can use Amazon CloudWatch to collect and track metrics, collect and monitor log files, and set alarms.

Amazon CloudWatch can monitor AWS resources such as Amazon EC2 instances, Amazon DynamoDB tables, and Amazon RDS DB instances, as well as custom metrics generated by your applications and services, and any log files your applications generate. You can use Amazon CloudWatch to gain system-wide visibility into resource utilization, application performance, and operational health. You can use these insights to react and keep your application running smoothly.

AWS CloudTrail is incorrect as this is mainly used for logging and not for monitoring.

Amazon SWF and Amazon SQS are incorrect as both are used for creating distributed application with decoupled components and not for monitoring.

Reference:

https://aws.amazon.com/cloudwatch/faqs/

Question 62:

A leading IT consulting company has an application which processes a large stream of financial data by an Amazon ECS Cluster then stores the result to a DynamoDB table. You have to design a solution to detect new entries in the DynamoDB table then automatically trigger a Lambda function to run some tests to verify the processed data.

What solution can be easily implemented to alert the Lambda function of new entries while requiring minimal configuration change to your architecture?

1. Use Systems Manager Automation to detect new entries in the DynamoDB table then automatically invoke the Lambda function for processing.
2. Invoke the Lambda functions using SNS each time that the ECS Cluster successfully processed financial data.
3. Enable DynamoDB Streams to capture table activity and automatically trigger the Lambda function.
4. Use CloudWatch Alarms to trigger the Lambda function whenever a new entry is created in the DynamoDB table.

Answer(s): 3

Explanation

Amazon DynamoDB is integrated with AWS Lambda so that you can create triggers—pieces of code that automatically respond to events in DynamoDB Streams. With triggers, you can build applications that react to data modifications in DynamoDB tables.

If you enable DynamoDB Streams on a table, you can associate the stream ARN with a Lambda function that you write. Immediately after an item in the table is modified, a new record appears in the table's stream. AWS Lambda polls the stream and invokes your Lambda function synchronously when it detects new stream records.

You can create a Lambda function which can perform a specific action that you specify, such as sending a notification or initiating a workflow. For instance, you can set up a Lambda function to simply copy each stream record to persistent storage, such as EFS or S3, to create a permanent audit trail of write activity in your table.

Suppose you have a mobile gaming app that writes to a TutorialsfreeCourses table. Whenever the TopCourse attribute of the TutorialsfreeScores table is updated, a corresponding stream record is written to the table's stream. This event could then trigger a Lambda function that posts a congratulatory message on a social media network. (The function would simply ignore any stream records that are not updates to TutorialsfreeCourses or that do not modify the TopCourse attribute.)

Hence, enabling DynamoDB Streams to capture table activity and automatically trigger the Lambda function is the correct answer because the requirement can be met with minimal configuration change using DynamoDB streams which can automatically trigger Lambda functions whenever there is a new entry.

Using CloudWatch Alarms to trigger the Lambda function whenever a new entry is created in the DynamoDB table is incorrect because CloudWatch Alarms only monitor service metrics, not changes in DynamoDB table data.

Invoking the Lambda functions using SNS each time that the ECS Cluster successfully processed financial data is incorrect because you don't need to create an SNS topic just to invoke Lambda functions. You can enable DynamoDB streams instead to meet the requirement with less configuration.

Using Systems Manager Automation to detect new entries in the DynamoDB table then automatically invoking the Lambda function for processing is incorrect because the Systems Manager Automation service is primarily used to simplify common maintenance and deployment tasks of Amazon EC2 instances and other AWS resources. It does not have the capability to detect new entries in a DynamoDB table.

References:

https://docs.aws.amazon.com/amazondynamodb/latest/developerguide/Streams.Lambda.html

https://docs.aws.amazon.com/amazondynamodb/latest/developerguide/Streams.html

Question 63:

A company has an OLTP (Online Transactional Processing) application that is hosted in an Amazon ECS cluster using the Fargate launch type. It has an Amazon RDS database that stores data of its production website. The Data Analytics team needs to run queries against the database to track and audit all user transactions.

These query operations against the production database must not impact application performance in any way.

Which of the following is the MOST suitable and cost-effective solution that you should implement?

1. Set up a Multi-AZ deployments configuration of your production database in RDS. Direct the Data Analytics team to query the production data from the standby instance.
2. Set up a new Amazon RDS Read Replica of the production database. Direct the Data Analytics team to query the production data from the replica.
3. Set up a new Amazon Redshift database cluster. Migrate the product database into Redshift and allow the Data Analytics team to fetch data from it.
4. Upgrade the instance type of the RDS database to a large instance.

Answer(s): 2

Explanation

Amazon RDS Read Replicas provide enhanced performance and durability for database (DB) instances. This feature makes it easy to elastically scale out beyond the capacity constraints of a single DB instance for read-heavy database workloads.

You can create one or more replicas of a given source DB Instance and serve high-volume application read traffic from multiple copies of your data, thereby increasing aggregate read throughput. Read replicas can also be promoted when needed to become standalone DB instances. Read replicas are available in Amazon RDS for MySQL, MariaDB, Oracle and PostgreSQL, as well as Amazon Aurora.

You can reduce the load on your source DB instance by routing read queries from your applications to the read replica. These replicas allow you to elastically scale out beyond the capacity constraints of a single DB instance for read-heavy database workloads.

Because read replicas can be promoted to master status, they are useful as part of a sharding implementation. To shard your database, add a read replica and promote it to master status, then, from each of the resulting DB Instances, delete the data that belongs to the other shard.

Hence, the correct answer is: Set up a new Amazon RDS Read Replica of the production database. Direct the Data Analytics team to query the production data from the replica.

The option that says: Set up a new Amazon Redshift database cluster. Migrate the product database into Redshift and allow the Data Analytics team to fetch data from it is incorrect because Redshift is primarily used for OLAP (Online Analytical Processing) applications and not for OLTP.

The option that says: Set up a Multi-AZ deployments configuration of your production database in RDS. Direct the Data Analytics team to query the production data from the standby instance is incorrect because you can't directly connect to the standby instance. This is only used in the event of a database failover when your primary instance encountered an outage.

The option that says: Upgrade the instance type of the RDS database to a large instance is incorrect because this entails a significant amount of cost. Moreover, the production database could still be affected by the queries done by the Data Analytics team. A better solution for this scenario is to use a Read Replica instead.

References:

https://aws.amazon.com/caching/database-caching/

https://aws.amazon.com/rds/details/read-replicas/

https://aws.amazon.com/elasticache/

Question 64:

You have a web-based order processing system which is currently using a standard queue in Amazon SQS. The support team noticed that there are a lot of cases where an order was processed twice. This issue has caused a lot of trouble in your processing and made your customers very unhappy. Your IT Manager has asked you to ensure that this issue will not recur.

What can you do to prevent this from happening again in the future? (Select TWO.)

1. Replace Amazon SQS and instead, use Amazon Simple Workflow service.
2. Change the message size in SQS.
3. Alter the visibility timeout of SQS.
4. Alter the retention period in Amazon SQS.
5. Use an Amazon SQS FIFO Queue instead.

Answer(s): 1, 5

Explanation

Amazon SQS FIFO (First-In-First-Out) Queues have all the capabilities of the standard queue with additional capabilities designed to enhance messaging between applications when the order of operations and events is critical, or where duplicates can't be tolerated, for example:

- Ensure that user-entered commands are executed in the right order.

- Display the correct product price by sending price modifications in the right order.

- Prevent a student from enrolling in a course before registering for an account.

Amazon SWF provides useful guarantees around task assignments. It ensures that a task is never duplicated and is assigned only once. Thus, even though you may have multiple workers for a particular activity type (or a number of instances of a decider), Amazon SWF will give a specific task to only one worker (or one decider instance). Additionally, Amazon SWF keeps at most one decision task outstanding at a time for a workflow execution. Thus, you can run multiple decider instances without worrying about two instances operating on the same execution simultaneously. These facilities enable you to coordinate your workflow without worrying about duplicate, lost, or conflicting tasks.

The main issue in this scenario is that the order management system produces duplicate orders at times. Since the company is using SQS, there is a possibility that a message can have a duplicate in case an EC2 instance failed to delete the already processed message. To prevent this issue from happening, you have to use Amazon Simple Workflow service instead of SQS.

Therefore, the correct answers are:

- Replace Amazon SQS and instead, use Amazon Simple Workflow service.

- Use an Amazon SQS FIFO Queue instead.

Altering the retention period in Amazon SQS is incorrect because the retention period simply specifies if the Amazon SQS should delete the messages that have been in a queue for a certain period of time.

Altering the visibility timeout of SQS is incorrect because for standard queues, the visibility timeout isn't a guarantee against receiving a message twice. To avoid duplicate SQS messages, it is better to design your applications to be idempotent (they should not be affected adversely when processing the same message more than once).

Changing the message size in SQS is incorrect because this is not related at all in this scenario.

References:

https://aws.amazon.com/swf/faqs/

https://aws.amazon.com/swf/

https://docs.aws.amazon.com/AWSSimpleQueueService/latest/SQSDeveloperGuide/sqs-visibility-timeout.html

Question 65:

You are planning to reduce the amount of data that Amazon S3 transfers to your servers in order to lower your operating costs as well as to lower the latency of retrieving the data. To accomplish this, you need to use simple structured query language (SQL) statements to filter the contents of Amazon S3 objects and retrieve just the subset of data that you need.

Which of the following services will help you accomplish this requirement?

1. RDS
2. S3 Select
3. AWS Step Functions
4. Redshift Spectrum

Answer(s): 2

Explanation

With Amazon S3 Select, you can use simple structured query language (SQL) statements to filter the contents of Amazon S3 objects and retrieve just the subset of data that you need. By using Amazon S3 Select to filter this data, you can reduce the amount of data that Amazon S3 transfers, which reduces the cost and latency to retrieve this data.

Amazon S3 Select works on objects stored in CSV, JSON, or Apache Parquet format. It also works with objects that are compressed with GZIP or BZIP2 (for CSV and JSON objects only), and server-side encrypted objects. You can specify the format of the results as either CSV or JSON, and you can determine how the records in the result are delimited.

RDS is incorrect because although RDS is an SQL database where you can perform SQL operations, it is still not valid because you want to apply SQL transactions on S3 itself, and not on the database, which RDS cannot do.

Redshift Spectrum is incorrect because although Amazon Redshift Spectrum provides a similar in-query functionality like S3 Select, this service is more suitable for querying your data from the Redshift external tables hosted in S3. The Redshift queries are run on your cluster resources against local disk. Redshift Spectrum queries run using per-query scale-out resources against data in S3 which can entail additional costs compared with S3 Select.

AWS Step Functions is incorrect because this only lets you coordinate multiple AWS services into serverless workflows so you can build and update apps quickly.

References:

https://docs.aws.amazon.com/AmazonS3/latest/dev/selecting-content-from-objects.html

https://docs.aws.amazon.com/redshift/latest/dg/c-using-spectrum.html

PRACTICE
TEST
5

AWS CERTIFIED
SOLUTIONS
ARCHITECT
ASSOCIATE

AWS CERTIFIED SOLUTIONS ARCHITECT ASSOCIATE PRACTICE TEST 5

Question 1:

You are working for a startup that builds Internet of Things (IOT) devices and monitoring application. They are using IOT sensors to monitor all data by using Amazon Kinesis configured with default settings. You then send the data to an Amazon S3 bucket after 2 days. When you checked the data in S3, there are only data for the last day and nothing for the first day.

What is the root cause of this issue?

1. Amazon S3 bucket has encountered a data loss.
2. The access of the Kinesis stream to the S3 bucket is insufficient.
3. By default, data records in Kinesis are only accessible for 24 hours from the time they are added to a stream.
4. Someone has manually deleted the record in Amazon S3.

Answer(s): 3

Explanation

By default, records of a stream in Amazon Kinesis are accessible for up to 24 hours from the time they are added to the stream. You can raise this limit to up to 7 days by enabling extended data retention.

The option that says: Amazon S3 bucket has encountered a data loss is incorrect because Amazon S3 rarely experiences data loss. Amazon has an SLA for S3 that it commits to its customers. Amazon S3 Standard, S3 Standard–IA, S3 One Zone-IA, and S3 Glacier are all designed to provide 99.999999999% durability of objects over a given year. This durability level corresponds to an average annual expected loss of 0.000000001% of objects. Hence, Amazon S3 bucket data loss is highly unlikely.

The option that says: Someone has manually deleted the record in Amazon S3 is incorrect because if someone has deleted the data, this should have been visible in CloudTrail. Also, deleting that much data manually shouldn't have occurred in the first place if you have put in the appropriate security measures.

The option that says: The access of the Kinesis stream to the S3 bucket is insufficient is incorrect because having insufficient access is highly unlikely since you are able to access the bucket and view the contents of the previous day's data collected by Kinesis.

Reference:

https://aws.amazon.com/kinesis/data-streams/faqs/

https://docs.aws.amazon.com/AmazonS3/latest/dev/DataDurability.html

Question 2:

Your IT Manager asks you to create a decoupled application whose process includes dependencies on EC2 instances and servers located in your company's on-premises data center.

Which of these options are you least likely to recommend as part of that process?

1. SQS polling from an EC2 instance using IAM user credentials
2. SQS polling from an EC2 instance deployed with an IAM role
3. (Incorrect)
4. Establish a Direct Connect connection from your on-premises network and VPC
5. An SWF workflow

Answer(s): 1

Explanation

For decoupled applications, it is best to use SWF and SQS which are both available in all options. Note that this question asks you for the option that you would LEAST likely to recommend.

SQS polling from an EC2 instance using IAM user credentials is not the recommended way to do so. It should use an IAM role instead.

The rest of the options are the recommended steps to satisfy the given requirement. You have to establish first a Direct Connect connection from your data center to your VPC to allow the on-premises servers to connect to SQS. You can either use SWF or SQS to create a decoupled application and you have to use an IAM Role, not an IAM user credential, on the EC2 instance to allow polling to the SQS queue.

Reference:

http://docs.aws.amazon.com/IAM/latest/UserGuide/id_roles.html

Question 3:

You are working as the Solutions Architect for a global technology consultancy firm which has an application that uses multiple EC2 instances located in various AWS regions such as US East (Ohio), US West (N. California), and EU (Ireland). Your manager instructed you to set up a latency-based routing to route incoming traffic for www. sample.com to all the EC2 instances across all AWS regions.

Which of the following options can satisfy the given requirement?

1. Use Route 53 to distribute the load to the multiple EC2 instances across all AWS Regions.
2. Use a Network Load Balancer to distribute the load to the multiple EC2 instances across all AWS Regions.
3. Use AWS DataSync to distribute the load to the multiple EC2 instances across all AWS Regions.
4. Use an Application Load Balancer to distribute the load to the multiple EC2 instances across all AWS Regions.

Answer(s): 1

Explanation

If your application is hosted in multiple AWS Regions, you can improve performance for your users by serving their requests from the AWS Region that provides the lowest latency.

You can create latency records for your resources in multiple AWS Regions by using latency-based routing. In the event that Route 53 receives a DNS query for your domain or subdomain such as sample.com or portal.sample.com, it determines which AWS Regions you've created latency records for, determines which region gives the user the lowest latency and then selects a latency record for that region. Route 53 responds with the value from the selected record which can be the IP address for a web server or the CNAME of your elastic load balancer.

Hence, using Route 53 to distribute the load to the multiple EC2 instances across all AWS Regions is the correct answer.

Using a Network Load Balancer to distribute the load to the multiple EC2 instances across all AWS Regions and using an Application Load Balancer to distribute the load to the multiple EC2 instances across all AWS Regions are both incorrect because load balancers distribute traffic only within their respective regions and not to other AWS regions. It is best to use Route 53 instead to balance the incoming load to two or more AWS regions.

Using AWS DataSync to distribute the load to the multiple EC2 instances across all AWS Regions is incorrect because the AWS DataSync service simply provides a fast way to move large amounts of data online between on-premises storage and Amazon S3 or Amazon Elastic File System (Amazon EFS).

References:

https://docs.aws.amazon.com/Route53/latest/DeveloperGuide/routing-policy.html#routing-policy-latency

https://docs.aws.amazon.com/Route53/latest/DeveloperGuide/TutorialAddingLBRRegion.html

Question 4:

You are working as a Cloud Engineer in a leading technology consulting firm which is using a fleet of Windows-based EC2 instances with IPv4 addresses launched in a private subnet. Several software installed in the EC2 instances are required to be updated via the Internet.

Which of the following services can provide you with a highly available solution to safely allow the instances to fetch the software patches from the Internet but prevent outside network from initiating a connection?

1. NAT Instance
2. VPC Endpoint
3. NAT Gateway
4. Egress-Only Internet Gateway

Answer(s): 3

Explanation

AWS offers two kinds of NAT devices — a NAT gateway or a NAT instance. It is recommended to use NAT gateways, as they provide better availability and bandwidth over NAT instances. The NAT Gateway service is also a managed service that does not require your administration efforts. A NAT instance is launched from a NAT AMI.

Just like a NAT instance, you can use a network address translation (NAT) gateway to enable instances in a private subnet to connect to the internet or other AWS services, but prevent the internet from initiating a connection with those instances.

Egress-Only Internet Gateway is incorrect because this is primarily used for VPCs that use IPv6 to enable instances in a private subnet to connect to the Internet or other AWS services, but prevent the Internet from initiating a connection with those instances, just like what NAT Instance and NAT Gateway do. The scenario explicitly says that the EC2 instances are using IPv4 addresses which is why Egress-only Internet gateway is invalid, even though it can provide the required high availability.

VPC Endpoint is incorrect because this simply enables you to privately connect your VPC to supported AWS services and VPC endpoint services powered by PrivateLink without requiring an Internet gateway, NAT device, VPN connection, or AWS Direct Connect connection.

NAT Instance is incorrect because although this can also enable instances in a private subnet to connect to the Internet or other AWS services and prevent the Internet from initiating a connection with those instances, it is not as highly available compared to a NAT Gateway.

References:

https://docs.aws.amazon.com/AmazonVPC/latest/UserGuide/vpc-nat-gateway.html

https://docs.aws.amazon.com/vpc/latest/userguide/vpc-nat-comparison.html

https://docs.aws.amazon.com/vpc/latest/userguide/egress-only-internet-gateway.html

Question 5:

An online shopping platform has been deployed to AWS using Elastic Beanstalk. They simply uploaded their Node.js application, and Elastic Beanstalk automatically handles the details of capacity provisioning, load balancing, scaling, and application health monitoring. Since the entire deployment process is automated, the DevOps team is not sure where to get the application log files of their shopping platform.

In Elastic Beanstalk, where does it store the application files and server log files?

1. Application files are stored in S3. The server log files can be stored directly in Glacier or in CloudWatch Logs.
2. Application files are stored in S3. The server log files can be optionally stored in CloudTrail or in CloudWatch Logs.
3. Application files are stored in S3. The server log files can only be stored in the attached EBS volumes of the EC2 instances, which were launched by AWS Elastic Beanstalk.
4. Application files are stored in S3. The server log files can also optionally be stored in S3 or in CloudWatch Logs.

Answer(s): 4

Explanation

The correct answer is the option that says: Application files are stored in S3. The server log files can also optionally be stored in S3 or in CloudWatch Logs. AWS Elastic Beanstalk stores your application files and optionally, server log files in Amazon S3. If you are using the AWS Management Console, the AWS Toolkit for Visual Studio, or AWS Toolkit for Eclipse, an Amazon S3 bucket will be created in your account and the files you upload will be automatically copied from your local client to Amazon S3. Optionally, you may configure Elastic Beanstalk to copy your server log files every hour to Amazon S3. You do this by editing the environment configuration settings.

With CloudWatch Logs, you can monitor and archive your Elastic Beanstalk application, system, and custom log files from Amazon EC2 instances of your environments. You can also configure alarms that make it easier for you to react to specific log stream events that your metric filters extract. The CloudWatch Logs agent installed on each Amazon EC2 instance in your environment publishes metric data points to the CloudWatch service for each log group you configure. Each log group applies its own filter patterns to determine what log stream events to send to CloudWatch as data points. Log streams that belong to the same log group share the same retention, monitoring, and access control settings. You can configure Elastic Beanstalk to automatically stream logs to the CloudWatch service.

The option that says: Application files are stored in S3. The server log files can only be stored in the attached EBS volumes of the EC2 instances, which were launched by AWS Elastic Beanstalk is incorrect because the server log files can also be stored in either S3 or CloudWatch Logs, and not only on the EBS volumes of the EC2 instances which are launched by AWS Elastic Beanstalk.

The option that says: Application files are stored in S3. The server log files can be stored directly in Glacier or in CloudWatch Logs is incorrect because the server log files can optionally be stored in either S3 or CloudWatch Logs, but not directly to Glacier. You can create a lifecycle policy to the S3 bucket to store the server logs and archive it in Glacier, but there is no direct way of storing the server logs to Glacier using Elastic Beanstalk unless you do it programmatically.

The option that says: Application files are stored in S3. The server log files can be optionally stored in CloudTrail or in CloudWatch Logs is incorrect because the server log files can optionally be stored in either S3 or CloudWatch Logs, but not directly to CloudTrail as this service is primarily used for auditing API calls.

Reference:

https://aws.amazon.com/elasticbeanstalk/faqs/

Question 6:

A fast food company is using AWS to host their online ordering system which uses an Auto Scaling group of EC2 instances deployed across multiple Availability Zones with an Application Load Balancer in front. To better handle the incoming traffic from various digital devices, you are planning to implement a new routing system where requests which have a URL of <server>/api/android are forwarded to one specific target group named "Android-Target-Group". Conversely, requests which have a URL of <server>/api/ios are forwarded to another separate target group named "iOS-Target-Group".

How can you implement this change in AWS?

1. Replace your ALB with a Classic Load Balancer then use path conditions to define rules that forward requests to different target groups based on the URL in the request.
2. Use path conditions to define rules that forward requests to different target groups based on the URL in the request.
3. Use host conditions to define rules that forward requests to different target groups based on the host name in the host header. This enables you to support multiple domains using a single load balancer.
4. Replace your ALB with a Network Load Balancer then use host conditions to define rules that forward requests to different target groups based on the URL in the request.

Answer(s): 2

Explanation

You can use path conditions to define rules that forward requests to different target groups based on the URL in the request (also known as path-based routing). This type of routing is the most appropriate solution for this scenario hence, using path conditions to define rules that forward requests to different target groups based on the URL in the request is the correct answer.

Each path condition has one path pattern. If the URL in a request matches the path pattern in a listener rule exactly, the request is routed using that rule.

A path pattern is case-sensitive, can be up to 128 characters in length, and can contain any of the following characters. You can include up to three wildcard characters.

A–Z, a–z, 0–9

_ - . $ / ~ " ' @ : +

& (using &)

* (matches 0 or more characters)

? (matches exactly 1 character)

Example path patterns

/img/*

/js/*

The option that says: Use host conditions to define rules that forward requests to different target groups based on the host name in the host header. This enables you to support multiple domains using a single load balancer is incorrect because host-based routing defines rules that forward requests to different target groups based on the host name in the host header instead of the URL, which is what is needed in this scenario.

The option that says: Replace your ALB with a Classic Load Balancer then use path conditions to define rules that forward requests to different target groups based on the URL in the request is incorrect because a Classic Load Balancer does not support path-based routing. You must use an Application Load Balancer.

The option that says: Replace your ALB with a Network Load Balancer then use host conditions to define rules that forward requests to different target groups based on the URL in the request is incorrect because a Network Load Balancer is used for applications that need extreme network performance and static IP. It also does not support path-based routing which is what is needed in this scenario. Furthermore, the statement mentions host-based routing yet, the description is about path-based routing.

References:

https://docs.aws.amazon.com/elasticloadbalancing/latest/application/introduction.html#application-load-balancer-benefits

https://docs.aws.amazon.com/elasticloadbalancing/latest/application/load-balancer-listeners.html#path-conditions

Question 7:

You are a Solutions Architect working for a software development company. You are planning to launch a fleet of EBS-backed EC2 instances and want to automatically assign each instance with a static private IP address which does not change even if the instances are restarted.

What should you do to accomplish this?

1. Launch the instances in a Placement Group.
2. Launch the instances to a single Availability Zone.
3. Launch the instances in EC2-Classic.
4. Launch the instances to multiple Availability Zones.
5. Launch the instances in the Amazon Virtual Private Cloud (VPC).

Answer(s): 5

Explanation

In EC2-Classic, your EC2 instance receives a private IPv4 address from the EC2-Classic range each time it's started. In EC2-VPC on the other hand, your EC2 instance receives a static private IPv4 address from the address range of your default VPC. Hence, the correct answer is launching the instances in the Amazon Virtual Private Cloud (VPC) and not launching the instances in EC2-Classic.

Launching the instances to a single Availability Zone and launching the instances to multiple Availability Zones are incorrect due to the fact that Availability Zones do not provide static private IP addresses to EC2 instances.

Launching the instances in a Placement Group is incorrect as a Placement Group is just a grouping of instances.

References:

https://docs.aws.amazon.com/AWSEC2/latest/UserGuide/ec2-classic-platform.html#differences-ec2-classic-vpc

http://docs.aws.amazon.com/AWSEC2/latest/UserGuide/using-instance-addressing.html

Question 8:

You are working as an IT Consultant for a top investment firm. Your task is to ensure smooth upgrade of their accounting system in AWS to a new version without any system outages. The Technical Manager gave an advice to implement an in-place upgrade strategy while a DevOps Engineer suggested to use Blue/Green Deployment strategy instead.

Which of the following options are not the advantages of using Blue/Green Deployment over in-place upgrade strategy? (Select TWO.)

1. You can use Blue/Green Deployment with CodeCommit and CodeBuild to automatically deploy the new version of your application.
2. Blue/green deployments provide a level of isolation between your blue and green application environments, which reduce the deployment risk. The blue environment represents the current application version serving production traffic while the green one is staged running a different or upgrade version of your application.
3. It has the ability to simply roll the incoming traffic back to the currently working environment, in case of system failures, any time during the deployment process.
4. Blue/green deployment is more cost-effective than in-place upgrade. You don't need to launch a new environment with additional AWS resources.
5. Impaired operation or downtime is minimized because impact is limited to the window of time between green environment issue detection and shift of traffic back to the blue environment.

Answer(s): 1, 4

Explanation

All of the options are advantages of Blue/Green deployments, except for the following:

- You can use Blue/Green Deployment with CodeCommit and CodeBuild to automatically deploy the new version of your application.

Blue/green deployment is more cost-effective than in-place upgrade. You don't need to launch a new environment with additional AWS resources.

Take note that the Blue/Green deployment sets up a new green environment which uses entirely new AWS resources. In addition, CodeCommit and CodeBuild are not used for deployment and hence, it does not relate with Blue/Green deployments.

Traditionally, with in-place upgrades, it was difficult to validate your new application version in a production deployment while also continuing to run your old version of the application. Blue/green deployments provide a level of isolation between your blue and green application environments. It ensures that spinning up a parallel green environment does not affect resources underpinning your blue environment. This isolation reduces your deployment risk.

After you deploy the green environment, you have the opportunity to validate it. You might do that with test traffic before sending production traffic to the green environment, or by using a very small fraction of production traffic, to better reflect real user traffic. This is called canary analysis or canary testing. If you discover the green environment is not operating as expected, there is no impact on the blue environment. You can route traffic back to it, minimizing impaired operation or downtime, and limiting the blast radius of impact.

This ability to simply roll traffic back to the still-operating blue environment is a key benefit of blue/green deployments. You can roll back to the blue environment at any time during the deployment process. Blue/green deployments also fit well with continuous integration and continuous deployment (CI/CD) workflows, in many cases limiting their complexity. Your deployment automation would have to consider fewer dependencies on an existing environment, state, or configuration.

In AWS, blue/green deployments also provide cost optimization benefits. You're not tied to the same underlying resources. So if the performance envelope of the application changes from one version to another, you simply launch the new environment with optimized resources, whether that means fewer resources or just different compute resources. You also don't have to run an overprovisioned architecture for an extended period of time.

Reference:

https://d1.awsstatic.com/whitepapers/AWS_Blue_Green_Deployments.pdf#page=6

Question 9:

You were hired as an IT Consultant in a startup cryptocurrency company that wants to go global with their international money transfer app. Your project is to make sure that the database of the app is highly available on multiple regions.

What are the benefits of adding Multi-AZ deployments in Amazon RDS? (Select TWO.)

1. Creates a primary DB Instance and synchronously replicates the data to a standby instance in a different Availability Zone (AZ) in a different region.
2. Increased database availability in the case of system upgrades like OS patching or DB Instance scaling.
3. Significantly increases the database performance.
4. Provides SQL optimization.
5. Provides enhanced database durability in the event of a DB instance component failure or an Availability Zone outage.

Answer(s): 2, 5

Explanation

Amazon RDS Multi-AZ deployments provide enhanced availability and durability for Database (DB) Instances, making them a natural fit for production database workloads. When you provision a Multi-AZ DB Instance, Amazon RDS automatically creates a primary DB Instance and synchronously replicates the data to a standby instance in a different Availability Zone (AZ). Each AZ runs on its own physically distinct, independent infrastructure, and is engineered to be highly reliable.

In case of an infrastructure failure, Amazon RDS performs an automatic failover to the standby (or to a read replica in the case of Amazon Aurora), so that you can resume database operations as soon as the failover is complete. Since the endpoint for your DB Instance remains the same after a failover, your application can resume database operation without the need for manual administrative intervention.

The chief benefits of running your DB instance as a Multi-AZ deployment are enhanced database durability and availability. The increased availability and fault tolerance offered by Multi-AZ deployments make them a natural fit for production environments.

Hence, the correct answers are the following options:

- Increased database availability in the case of system upgrades like OS patching or DB Instance scaling.

- Provides enhanced database durability in the event of a DB instance component failure or an Availability Zone outage.

The option that says: Creates a primary DB Instance and synchronously replicates the data to a standby instance in a different Availability Zone (AZ) in a different region is almost correct. RDS synchronously replicates the data to a standby instance in a different Availability Zone (AZ) that is in the same region and not in a different one.

The options that say: Significantly increases the database performance and Provides SQL optimization are incorrect as it does not affect the performance nor provide SQL optimization.

References:

https://aws.amazon.com/rds/details/multi-az/

https://aws.amazon.com/rds/faqs/

Question 10:

There is a technical requirement by a financial firm that does online credit card processing to have a secure application environment on AWS. They are trying to decide on whether to use KMS or CloudHSM.

Which of the following statements is right when it comes to CloudHSM and KMS?

1. You should consider using AWS CloudHSM over AWS KMS if you require your keys stored in dedicated, third-party validated hardware security modules under your exclusive control.
2. If you want a managed service for creating and controlling your encryption keys but don't want or need to operate your own HSM, consider using AWS CloudHSM.
3. No major difference. They both do the same thing.
4. AWS CloudHSM should always be used for any payment transactions.

Answer(s): 1

Explanation

AWS Key Management Service (AWS KMS) is a managed service that makes it easy for you to create and control the encryption keys used to encrypt your data. The master keys that you create in AWS KMS are protected by FIPS 140-2 validated cryptographic modules. AWS KMS is integrated with most other AWS services that encrypt your data with encryption keys that you manage. AWS KMS is also integrated with AWS CloudTrail to provide encryption key usage logs to help meet your auditing, regulatory and compliance needs.

By using AWS KMS, you gain more control over access to data you encrypt. You can use the key management and cryptographic features directly in your applications or through AWS services that are integrated with AWS KMS. Whether you are writing applications for AWS or using AWS services, AWS KMS enables you to maintain control over who can use your customer master keys and gain access to your encrypted data. AWS KMS is integrated with AWS CloudTrail, a service that delivers log files to an Amazon S3 bucket that you designate. By using CloudTrail you can monitor and investigate how and when your master keys have been used and by whom.

If you want a managed service for creating and controlling your encryption keys, but you don't want or need to operate your own HSM, consider using AWS Key Management Service.

Hence, the correct answer is: You should consider using AWS CloudHSM over AWS KMS if you require your keys stored in dedicated, third-party validated hardware security modules under your exclusive control.

The option that says: No major difference. They both do the same thing is incorrect because KMS and CloudHSM are two different services. If you want a managed service for creating and controlling your encryption keys, without operating your own HSM, you have to consider using AWS Key Management Service.

The option that says: If you want a managed service for creating and controlling your encryption keys, but you don't want or need to operate your own HSM, consider using AWS CloudHSM is incorrect because you have to consider using AWS KMS if you want a managed service for creating and controlling your encryption keys, without operating your own HSM.

The option that says: AWS CloudHSM should always be used for any payment transactions is incorrect because this is not always the case. AWS CloudHSM is a cloud-based hardware security module (HSM) that enables you to easily generate and use your own encryption keys on the AWS Cloud.

References:

https://docs.aws.amazon.com/kms/latest/developerguide/overview.html

https://docs.aws.amazon.com/kms/latest/developerguide/concepts.html#data-keys

https://docs.aws.amazon.com/cloudhsm/latest/userguide/introduction.html

Question 11:

A Solutions Architect designed a real-time data analytics system based on Kinesis Data Stream and Lambda. A week after the system has been deployed, the users noticed that it performed slowly as the data rate increases. The Architect identified that the performance of the Kinesis Data Streams is causing this problem.

Which of the following should the Architect do to improve performance?

1. Replace the data stream with Amazon Kinesis Data Firehose instead.
2. Implement Step Scaling to the Kinesis Data Stream.

3. Increase the number of shards of the Kinesis stream by using the UpdateShardCount command.
4. Improve the performance of the stream by decreasing the number of its shards using the MergeShard command.

Answer(s): 3

Explanation

Amazon Kinesis Data Streams supports resharding, which lets you adjust the number of shards in your stream to adapt to changes in the rate of data flow through the stream. Resharding is considered an advanced operation.

There are two types of resharding operations: shard split and shard merge. In a shard split, you divide a single shard into two shards. In a shard merge, you combine two shards into a single shard. Resharding is always pairwise in the sense that you cannot split into more than two shards in a single operation, and you cannot merge more than two shards in a single operation. The shard or pair of shards that the resharding operation acts on are referred to as parent shards. The shard or pair of shards that result from the resharding operation are referred to as child shards.

Splitting increases the number of shards in your stream and therefore increases the data capacity of the stream. Because you are charged on a per-shard basis, splitting increases the cost of your stream. Similarly, merging reduces the number of shards in your stream and therefore decreases the data capacity—and cost—of the stream.

If your data rate increases, you can also increase the number of shards allocated to your stream to maintain the application performance. You can reshard your stream using the UpdateShardCount API. The throughput of an Amazon Kinesis data stream is designed to scale without limits via increasing the number of shards within a data stream. Hence, the correct answer is to increase the number of shards of the Kinesis stream by using the UpdateShardCount command.

Replacing the data stream with Amazon Kinesis Data Firehose instead is incorrect because the throughput of Kinesis Firehose is not exceptionally higher than Kinesis Data Streams. In fact, the throughput of an Amazon Kinesis data stream is designed to scale without limits via increasing the number of shards within a data stream.

Improving the performance of the stream by decreasing the number of its shards using the MergeShard command is incorrect because merging the shards will effectively decrease the performance of the stream rather than improve it.

Implementing Step Scaling to the Kinesis Data Stream is incorrect because there is no Step Scaling feature for Kinesis Data Streams. This is only applicable for EC2.

References:

https://aws.amazon.com/blogs/big-data/scale-your-amazon-kinesis-stream-capacity-with-updateshardcount/

https://aws.amazon.com/kinesis/data-streams/faqs/

https://docs.aws.amazon.com/streams/latest/dev/kinesis-using-sdk-java-resharding.html

Question 12:

A large Philippine-based Business Process Outsourcing company is building a two-tier web application in their VPC to serve dynamic transaction-based content. The data tier is leveraging an Online Transactional Processing (OLTP) database but for the web tier, they are still deciding what service they will use.

What AWS services should you leverage to build an elastic and scalable web tier?

1. Amazon RDS with Multi-AZ and Auto Scaling
2. Elastic Load Balancing, Amazon RDS with Multi-AZ, and Amazon S3
3. Amazon EC2, Amazon DynamoDB, and Amazon S3
4. Elastic Load Balancing, Amazon EC2, and Auto Scaling

Answer(s): 4

Explanation

Amazon RDS is a suitable database service for online transaction processing (OLTP) applications. However, the question asks for a list of AWS services for the web tier and not the database tier. Also, when it comes to services providing scalability and elasticity for your web tier, you should always consider using Auto Scaling and Elastic Load Balancer.

To build an elastic and a highly-available web tier, you can use Amazon EC2, Auto Scaling, and Elastic Load Balancing. You can deploy your web servers on a fleet of EC2 instances to an Auto Scaling group, which will automatically monitor your applications and automatically adjust capacity to maintain steady, predictable performance at the lowest possible cost. Load balancing is an effective way to increase the availability of a system. Instances that fail can be replaced seamlessly behind the load balancer while other instances continue to operate. Elastic Load Balancing can be used to balance across instances in multiple availability zones of a region.

The rest of the options are all incorrect since they don't mention all of the required services in building a highly available and scalable web tier, such as EC2, Auto Scaling, and Elastic Load Balancer. Although Amazon RDS with Multi-AZ and DynamoDB are highly scalable databases, the scenario is more focused on building its web tier and not the database tier.

Hence, the correct answer is Elastic Load Balancing, Amazon EC2, and Auto Scaling.

The option that says: Elastic Load Balancing, Amazon RDS with Multi-AZ, and Amazon S3 is incorrect because you can't host your web tier using Amazon S3 since the application is doing a dynamic transactions. Amazon S3 is only suitable if you plan to have a static website.

The option that says: Amazon RDS with Multi-AZ and Auto Scaling is incorrect because the focus of the question is building a scalable web tier. You need a service, like EC2, in which you can run your web tier.

The option that says: Amazon EC2, Amazon DynamoDB, and Amazon S3 is incorrect because you need Auto Scaling and ELB in order to scale the web tier.

References:

https://media.amazonwebservices.com/AWS_Building_Fault_Tolerant_Applications.pdf

https://d1.awsstatic.com/whitepapers/aws-building-fault-tolerant-applications.pdf

https://docs.aws.amazon.com/AWSEC2/latest/UserGuide/ec2-increase-availability.html

Question 13:

You are working as an AWS Engineer in a major telecommunications company in which you are tasked to make a network monitoring system. You launched an EC2 instance to host the monitoring system and used CloudWatch to monitor, store, and access the log files of your instance.

Which of the following provides an automated way to send log data to CloudWatch Logs from your Amazon EC2 instance?

1. CloudTrail
2. VPC Flow Logs
3. CloudTrail Logs agent
4. CloudWatch Logs agent

Answer(s): 4

Explanation

CloudWatch Logs agent provides an automated way to send log data to CloudWatch Logs from Amazon EC2 instances hence, CloudWatch Logs agent is the correct answer.

The CloudWatch Logs agent is comprised of the following components:

- A plug-in to the AWS CLI that pushes log data to CloudWatch Logs.

- A script (daemon) that initiates the process to push data to CloudWatch Logs.

- A cron job that ensures that the daemon is always running.

CloudTrail is incorrect as this is mainly used for tracking the API calls of your AWS resources and not for sending EC2 logs to CloudWatch.

VPC Flow Logs is incorrect as this is mainly used for tracking the traffic coming into the VPC and not for EC2 instance monitoring.

CloudTrail Logs agent is incorrect because this does not exist.

Reference:

https://docs.aws.amazon.com/AmazonCloudWatch/latest/logs/AgentReference.ht
ml

Question 14:

You are a Solutions Architect of a tech company. You are having an issue whenever you try to connect to your newly created EC2 instance using a Remote Desktop connection from your computer. Upon checking, you have verified that the instance has a public IP and the Internet gateway and route tables are in place.

What else should you do for you to resolve this issue?

1. You should adjust the security group to allow traffic from port 22
2. You should restart the EC2 instance since there might be some issue with the instance
3. You should adjust the security group to allow traffic from port 3389
4. You should create a new instance since there might be some issue with the instance

Answer(s): 3

Explanation

Since you are using a Remote Desktop connection to access your EC2 instance, you have to ensure that the Remote Desktop Protocol is allowed in the security group. By default, the server listens on TCP port 3389 and UDP port 3389.

The option that says: You should adjust the security group to allow traffic from port 22 is incorrect as the port 22 is used for SSH connections and not for RDP.

The options that say: You should restart the EC2 instance since there might be some issue with the instance and You should create a new instance since there might be some issue with the instance are incorrect as the EC2 instance is newly created and hence, unlikely to cause the issue. You have to check the security group first if it allows the Remote Desktop Protocol (3389) before investigating if there is indeed an issue on the specific instance.

Reference:

https://docs.aws.amazon.com/AWSEC2/latest/WindowsGuide/troubleshooting-windows-instances.html#rdp-issues

Question 15:

As the Solutions Architect, you have built a photo-sharing site for an entertainment company. The site was hosted using 3 EC2 instances in a single availability zone with a Classic Load Balancer in front to evenly distribute the incoming load.

What should you do to enable your Classic Load Balancer to bind a user's session to a specific instance?

1. Security Group
2. Availability Zone
3. Sticky Sessions
4. Placement Group

Answer(s): 3

Explanation

By default, a Classic Load Balancer routes each request independently to the registered instance with the smallest load. However, you can use the sticky session feature (also known as session affinity), which enables the load balancer to bind a user's session to a specific instance. This ensures that all requests from the user during the session are sent to the same instance.

The key to managing sticky sessions is to determine how long your load balancer should consistently route the user's request to the same instance. If your application has its own session cookie, then you can configure Elastic Load Balancing so that the session cookie follows the duration specified. If your application does not have its own session cookie, then you can configure Elastic Load Balancing to create a session cookie by specifying your own stickiness duration.

Reference:

https://docs.aws.amazon.com/elasticloadbalancing/latest/classic/elb-sticky-sessions.html

Question 16:

You are planning to launch an application that tracks the GPS coordinates of delivery trucks in your country. The coordinates are transmitted from each delivery truck every five seconds. You need to design an architecture that will enable real-time processing of these coordinates from multiple consumers. The aggregated data will be analyzed in a separate reporting application.

Which AWS service should you use for this scenario?

1. Amazon Kinesis
2. AWS Data Pipeline
3. Amazon AppStream
4. Amazon Simple Queue Service

Answer(s): 1

Explanation

Amazon Kinesis makes it easy to collect, process, and analyze real-time, streaming data so you can get timely insights and react quickly to new information. It offers key capabilities to cost-effectively process streaming data at any scale, along with the flexibility to choose the tools that best suit the requirements of your application.

With Amazon Kinesis, you can ingest real-time data such as video, audio, application logs, website clickstreams, and IoT telemetry data for machine learning, analytics, and other applications. Amazon Kinesis enables you to process and analyze data as it arrives and responds instantly instead of having to wait until all your data are collected before the processing can begin.

Reference:

https://aws.amazon.com/kinesis/

Question 17:

A startup is building an AI-based face recognition application in AWS, where they store millions of images in an S3 bucket. As the Solutions Architect, you have to ensure that each and every image uploaded to their system is stored without any issues.

What is the correct indication that an object was successfully stored when you put objects in Amazon S3?

1. HTTP 200 result code and MD5 checksum.
2. You will receive an SMS from Amazon SNS informing you that the object is successfully stored.

3. Amazon S3 has 99.999999999% durability hence, there is no need to confirm that data was inserted.
4. You will receive an email from Amazon SNS informing you that the object is successfully stored.

Answer(s): 1

Explanation

If you triggered an S3 API call and got HTTP 200 result code and MD5 checksum, then it is considered as a successful upload. The S3 API will return an error code in case the upload is unsuccessful.

The option that says: Amazon S3 has 99.999999999% durability hence, there is no need to confirm that data was inserted is incorrect because although S3 is durable, it is not an assurance that all objects uploaded using S3 API calls will be successful.

The options that say: You will receive an SMS from Amazon SNS informing you that the object is successfully stored and You will receive an email from Amazon SNS informing you that the object is successfully stored are both incorrect because you don't receive an SMS nor an email notification by default, unless you added an event notification.

Reference:

https://docs.aws.amazon.com/AmazonS3/latest/API/RESTObjectPOST.html

Question 18:

You are working for a computer animation film studio that has a web application running on an Amazon EC2 instance. It uploads 5 GB video objects to an Amazon S3 bucket. Video uploads are taking longer than expected, which impacts the performance of your application.

Which method will help improve the performance of your application?

1. Use Amazon S3 Multipart Upload API.
2. Enable Enhanced Networking with the Elastic Network Adapter (ENA) on your EC2 Instances.
3. Use Amazon Elastic Block Store Provisioned IOPS and an Amazon EBS-optimized instance.
4. Leverage on Amazon CloudFront and use HTTP POST method to reduce latency.

Answer(s): 1

Explanation

The main issue is the slow upload time of the video objects to Amazon S3. To address this issue, you can use Multipart upload in S3 to improve the throughput. It allows you to upload parts of your object in parallel thus, decreasing the time it takes to upload big objects. Each part is a contiguous portion of the object's data.

You can upload these object parts independently and in any order. If transmission of any part fails, you can retransmit that part without affecting other parts. After all parts of your object are uploaded, Amazon S3 assembles these parts and creates the object. In general, when your object size reaches 100 MB, you should consider using multipart uploads instead of uploading the object in a single operation.

Using multipart upload provides the following advantages:

Improved throughput - You can upload parts in parallel to improve throughput.

Quick recovery from any network issues - Smaller part size minimizes the impact of restarting a failed upload due to a network error.

Pause and resume object uploads - You can upload object parts over time. Once you initiate a multipart upload, there is no expiry; you must explicitly complete or abort the multipart upload.

Begin an upload before you know the final object size - You can upload an object as you are creating it.

Enabling Enhanced Networking with the Elastic Network Adapter (ENA) on your EC2 Instances is incorrect because even though this will improve network performance, the issue will still persist since the problem lies in the upload time of the object to Amazon S3. You should use the Multipart upload feature instead.

Leveraging on Amazon CloudFront and using HTTP POST method to reduce latency is incorrect because CloudFront is a CDN service and is not used to expedite the upload process of objects to Amazon S3. Amazon CloudFront is a fast content delivery network (CDN) service that securely delivers data, videos, applications, and APIs to customers globally with low latency, high transfer speeds, all within a developer-friendly environment.

Using Amazon Elastic Block Store Provisioned IOPS and an Amazon EBS-optimized instance is incorrect because although the use of Amazon Elastic Block Store Provisioned IOPS will speed up the I/O performance of the EC2 instance, the root cause is still not resolved since the primary problem here is the slow video upload to Amazon S3. There is no network contention in the EC2 instance.

References:

https://docs.aws.amazon.com/AmazonS3/latest/dev/uploadobjusingmpu.html

http://docs.aws.amazon.com/AmazonS3/latest/dev/qfacts.html

Question 19:

A game development company operates several virtual reality (VR) and augmented reality (AR) games which use various RESTful web APIs hosted on their on-premises data center. Due to the unprecedented growth of their company, they decided to migrate their system to AWS Cloud to scale out their resources as well to minimize costs.

Which of the following should you recommend as the most cost-effective and scalable solution to meet the above requirement?

1. Use AWS Lambda and Amazon API Gateway.
2. Use a Spot Fleet of Amazon EC2 instances, each with an Elastic Fabric Adapter (EFA) for more consistent latency and higher network throughput. Set up an Application Load Balancer to distribute traffic to the instances.
3. Set up a micro-service architecture with ECS, ECR, and Fargate.
4. Host the APIs in a static S3 web hosting bucket behind a CloudFront web distribution.

Answer(s): 1

Explanation

With AWS Lambda, you pay only for what you use. You are charged based on the number of requests for your functions and the duration, the time it takes for your code to execute.

Lambda counts a request each time it starts executing in response to an event notification or invoke call, including test invokes from the console. You are charged for the total number of requests across all your functions. Duration is calculated from the time your code begins executing until it returns or otherwise terminates, rounded up to the nearest 100ms. The price depends on the amount of memory you allocate to your function. The Lambda free tier includes 1M free requests per month and over 400,000 GB-seconds of compute time per month.

The best possible answer here is to use Lambda and API Gateway because this solution is both scalable and cost-effective. You will only be charged when you use your Lambda function, unlike having an EC2 instance which always runs even though you don't use it.

Setting up a micro-service architecture with ECS, ECR, and Fargate is incorrect because ECS is mainly used to host Docker applications and in addition, using ECS, ECR, and Fargate alone is not scalable and not recommended for this type of scenarios.

Hosting the APIs in a static S3 web hosting bucket behind a CloudFront web distribution is not a suitable option as there is no compute capability for S3 and you can only use it as a static website. Although this solution is scalable since it is using CloudFront, the use of S3 to host the web APIs or the dynamic website is still incorrect.

The option that says: Use a Spot Fleet of Amazon EC2 instances, each with an Elastic Fabric Adapter (EFA) for more consistent latency and higher network throughput. Set up an Application Load Balancer to distribute traffic to the instances is incorrect because EC2 alone, without Auto Scaling, is not scalable. Even though you use Spot EC2 instance, it is still more expensive compared to Lambda because you will be charged only when your function is being used. An Elastic Fabric Adapter (EFA) is simply a network device that you can attach to your Amazon EC2 instance that enables you to achieve the application performance of an on-premises HPC cluster, with the scalability, flexibility, and elasticity provided by the AWS Cloud. Although EFA is scalable, the Spot Fleet configuration of this option doesn't have Auto Scaling involved.

References:

https://docs.aws.amazon.com/apigateway/latest/developerguide/getting-started-with-lambda-integration.html

https://aws.amazon.com/lambda/pricing/

Question 20:

You are working as a Solutions Architect in a well-funded financial startup. The CTO instructed you to launch a cryptocurrency mining server on a Reserved EC2 instance in us-east-1 region's private subnet which is using IPv6. Due to the financial data that the server contains, the system should be secured to avoid any unauthorized access and to meet the regulatory compliance requirements.

In this scenario, which VPC feature allows the EC2 instance to communicate to the Internet but prevents inbound traffic?

1. Egress-only Internet gateway
2. Internet Gateway
3. NAT instances
4. NAT Gateway

Answer(s): 1

Explanation

An egress-only Internet gateway is a horizontally scaled, redundant, and highly available VPC component that allows outbound communication over IPv6 from instances in your VPC to the Internet, and prevents the Internet from initiating an IPv6 connection with your instances.

Take note that an egress-only Internet gateway is for use with IPv6 traffic only. To enable outbound-only Internet communication over IPv4, use a NAT gateway instead.

NAT Gateway and NAT instances are incorrect because these are only applicable for IPv4 and not IPv6. Even though these two components can enable the EC2 instance in a private subnet to communicate to the Internet and prevent inbound traffic, it is only limited with instances which are using IPv4 address and not IPv6. The most suitable VPC component to use is egress-only Internet gateway.

Internet Gateway is incorrect because this is primarily used to provide Internet access to your instances in the public subnet of your VPC, and not for private subnets. However, with an Internet gateway, traffic originating from the public Internet will also be able to reach your instances. The scenario is asking you to prevent inbound access, so this is not the correct answer.

Reference:

https://docs.aws.amazon.com/vpc/latest/userguide/egress-only-internet-gateway.html

Question 21:

A tech company is running two production web servers hosted on Reserved EC2 instances with EBS-backed root volumes. These instances have a consistent CPU load of 90%. Traffic is being distributed to these instances by an Elastic Load Balancer. In addition, they also have Multi-AZ RDS MySQL databases for their production, test, and development environments.

What recommendation would you make to reduce cost in this AWS environment without affecting availability and performance of mission-critical systems? Choose the best answer.

1. Consider removing the Elastic Load Balancer
2. Consider using On-demand instances instead of Reserved EC2 instances
3. Consider not using a Multi-AZ RDS deployment for the development and test database
4. Consider using Spot instances instead of reserved EC2 instances

Answer(s): 3

Explanation

One thing that you should notice here is that the company is using Multi-AZ databases in all of their environments, including their development and test environment. This is costly and unnecessary as these two environments are not critical. It is better to use Multi-AZ for production environments to reduce costs, which is why the option that says: Consider not using a Multi-AZ RDS deployment for the development and test database is the correct answer.

The option that says: Consider using On-demand instances instead of Reserved EC2 instances is incorrect because selecting Reserved instances is cheaper than On-demand instances for long term usage due to the discounts offered when purchasing reserved instances.

The option that says: Consider using Spot instances instead of reserved EC2 instances is incorrect because the web servers are running in a production environment. Never use Spot instances for production level web servers unless you are sure that they are not that critical in your system. This is because your spot instances can be terminated once the maximum price goes over the maximum amount that you specified.

The option that says: Consider removing the Elastic Load Balancer is incorrect because the Elastic Load Balancer is crucial in maintaining the elasticity and reliability of your system.

Reference:

https://aws.amazon.com/rds/details/multi-az/

https://aws.amazon.com/pricing/cost-optimization/

Question 22:

A web application, which is hosted in your on-premises data center and uses a MySQL database, must be migrated to AWS Cloud. You need to ensure that the network traffic to and from your RDS database instance is encrypted using SSL. For improved security, you have to use the profile credentials specific to your EC2 instance to access your database, instead of a password.

Which of the following should you do to meet the above requirement?

1. Configure your RDS database to enable encryption.
2. Launch a new RDS database instance with the Backtrack feature enabled.
3. Launch the mysql client using the --ssl-ca parameter when connecting to the database.
4. Set up an RDS database and enable the IAM DB Authentication.

Answer(s): 4

Explanation

You can authenticate to your DB instance using AWS Identity and Access Management (IAM) database authentication. IAM database authentication works with MySQL and PostgreSQL. With this authentication method, you don't need to use a password when you connect to a DB instance. Instead, you use an authentication token.

An authentication token is a unique string of characters that Amazon RDS generates on request. Authentication tokens are generated using AWS Signature Version 4. Each token has a lifetime of 15 minutes. You don't need to store user credentials in the database, because authentication is managed externally using IAM. You can also still use standard database authentication.

IAM database authentication provides the following benefits:

- Network traffic to and from the database is encrypted using Secure Sockets Layer (SSL).

- You can use IAM to centrally manage access to your database resources, instead of managing access individually on each DB instance.

- For applications running on Amazon EC2, you can use profile credentials specific to your EC2 instance to access your database instead of a password, for greater security

Hence, setting up an RDS database and enable the IAM DB Authentication is the correct answer based on the above reference.

Launching a new RDS database instance with the Backtrack feature enabled is incorrect because the Backtrack feature simply "rewinds" the DB cluster to the time you specify. Backtracking is not a replacement for backing up your DB cluster so that you can restore it to a point in time. However, you can easily undo mistakes using the backtrack feature if you mistakenly perform a destructive action, such as a DELETE without a WHERE clause.

Configuring your RDS database to enable encryption is incorrect because this encryption feature in RDS is mainly for securing your Amazon RDS DB instances and snapshots at rest. The data that is encrypted at rest includes the underlying storage for DB instances, its automated backups, Read Replicas, and snapshots.

Launching the mysql client using the --ssl-ca parameter when connecting to the database is incorrect because even though using the --ssl-ca parameter can provide SSL connection to your database, you still need to use IAM database connection to use the profile credentials specific to your EC2 instance to access your database instead of a password.

Reference:

https://docs.aws.amazon.com/AmazonRDS/latest/UserGuide/UsingWithRDS.IA MDBAuth.html

Question 23:

An application is using a Lambda function to process complex financial data that run for 15 minutes on average. Most invocations were successfully processed. However, you noticed that there are a few terminated invocations throughout the day, which caused data discrepancy in the application.

Which of the following is the most likely cause of this issue?

1. The Lambda function contains a recursive code and has been running for over 15 minutes.
2. The concurrent execution limit has been reached.
3. The failed Lambda Invocations contain a ServiceException error which means that the AWS Lambda service encountered an internal error.
4. The failed Lambda functions have been running for over 15 minutes and reached the maximum execution time.

Answer(s): 4

Explanation

A Lambda function consists of code and any associated dependencies. In addition, a Lambda function also has configuration information associated with it. Initially, you specify the configuration information when you create a Lambda function. Lambda provides an API for you to update some of the configuration data.

You pay for the AWS resources that are used to run your Lambda function. To prevent your Lambda function from running indefinitely, you specify a timeout. When the specified timeout is reached, AWS Lambda terminates execution of your Lambda function. It is recommended that you set this value based on your expected execution time. The default timeout is 3 seconds and the maximum execution duration per request in AWS Lambda is 900 seconds, which is equivalent to 15 minutes.

Hence, the correct answer is the option that says: The failed Lambda functions have been running for over 15 minutes and reached the maximum execution time.

Take note that you can invoke a Lambda function synchronously either by calling the Invoke operation or by using an AWS SDK in your preferred runtime. If you anticipate a long-running Lambda function, your client may time out before function execution completes. To avoid this, update the client timeout or your SDK configuration.

The option that says: The concurrent execution limit has been reached is incorrect because, by default, the AWS Lambda limits the total concurrent executions across all functions within a given region to 1000. By setting a concurrency limit on a function, Lambda guarantees that allocation will be applied specifically to that function, regardless of the amount of traffic processing the remaining functions. If that limit is exceeded, the function will be throttled but not terminated, which is in contrast with what is happening in the scenario.

The option that says: The Lambda function contains a recursive code and has been running for over 15 minutes is incorrect because having a recursive code in your Lambda function does not directly result to an abrupt termination of the function execution. This is a scenario wherein the function automatically calls itself until some arbitrary criteria is met. This could lead to an unintended volume of function invocations and escalated costs, but not an abrupt termination because Lambda will throttle all invocations to the function.

The option that says: The failed Lambda Invocations contain a ServiceException error which means that the AWS Lambda service encountered an internal error is incorrect because although this is a valid root cause, it is unlikely to have several ServiceException errors throughout the day unless there is an outage or disruption in AWS. Since the scenario says that the Lambda function runs for about 10 to 15 minutes, the maximum execution duration is the most likely cause of the issue and not the AWS Lambda service encountering an internal error.

Reference:

https://docs.aws.amazon.com/lambda/latest/dg/limits.html

https://docs.aws.amazon.com/lambda/latest/dg/resource-model.html

Question 24:

You have designed and built a new AWS architecture. After deploying your application to an On-demand EC2 instance, you found that there is an issue in your application when connecting to port 443. After troubleshooting the issue, you added port 443 to the security group of the instance.

How long will it take before the changes are applied to all of the resources in your VPC?

1. Immediately.
2. It takes exactly one minute for the rules to apply to all availability zones within the AWS region.
3. Roughly around 5-8 minutes in order for the security rules to propagate.
4. Immediately after a reboot of the EC2 instances which belong to that security group.

Answer(s): 1

Explanation

A security group acts as a virtual firewall for your instance to control inbound and outbound traffic. When you launch an instance in a VPC, you can assign up to five security groups to the instance. Security groups act at the instance level, not the subnet level. Therefore, each instance in a subnet in your VPC could be assigned to a different set of security groups. If you don't specify a particular group at launch time, the instance is automatically assigned to the default security group for the VPC.

The correct answer is Immediately. Changes made in a security group are immediately implemented. There is no need to wait for some amount of time for propagation nor reboot any instances for your changes to take effect.

The options that say: Roughly around 5-8 minutes in order for the security rules to propagate and It takes exactly one minute for the rules to apply to all availability zones within the AWS region are incorrect because the changes in your security group are implemented immediately and not after a minute or after a few minutes.

The option that says: Immediately after a reboot of the EC2 instances which belong to that security group is incorrect because there is no need to reboot your EC2 instance before the security group changes are fully applied. The change takes effect immediately.

Reference:

http://docs.aws.amazon.com/AmazonVPC/latest/UserGuide/VPC_SecurityGroups.html

Question 25:

You have a fleet of running Spot EC2 instances behind an Application Load Balancer. The incoming traffic comes from various users across multiple AWS regions and you would like to have the user's session shared among your fleet of instances. You are required to set up a distributed session management layer that will provide a scalable and shared data storage for the user sessions.

Which of the following would be the best choice to meet the requirement while still providing sub-millisecond latency for your users?

1. ELB sticky sessions
2. Multi-AZ RDS
3. Multi-master DynamoDB
4. ElastiCache in-memory caching

Answer(s): 4

Explanation

For sub-millisecond latency caching, ElastiCache is the best choice. In order to address scalability and to provide a shared data storage for sessions that can be accessed from any individual web server, you can abstract the HTTP sessions from the web servers themselves. A common solution to for this is to leverage an In-Memory Key/Value store such as Redis and Memcached.

ELB sticky sessions is incorrect because the scenario does not require you to route a user to the particular web server that is managing that individual user's session. Since the session state is shared among the instances, the use of the ELB sticky sessions feature is not recommended in this scenario.

Multi-master DynamoDB and Multi-AZ RDS are incorrect because although you can use DynamoDB and RDS for storing session state, these two are not the best choices in terms of cost-effectiveness and performance when compared to ElastiCache. There is a significant difference in terms of latency if you used DynamoDB and RDS when you store the session data.

References:

https://aws.amazon.com/caching/session-management/

https://d0.awsstatic.com/whitepapers/performance-at-scale-with-amazon-elasticache.pdf

Question 26:

An application is hosted in an Auto Scaling group of EC2 instances and a Microsoft SQL Server on Amazon RDS. There is a requirement that all in-flight data between your web servers and RDS should be secured.

Which of the following options is the MOST suitable solution that you should implement? (Select TWO.)

1. Force all connections to your DB instance to use SSL by setting the rds.force_ssl parameter to true. Once done, reboot your DB instance. Configure the security group of your RDS to only allow traffic from port 443.
2. Specify the TDE option in an RDS option group that is associated with that DB instance to enable transparent data encryption (TDE).
3. Download the Amazon RDS Root CA certificate. Import the certificate to your servers and configure your application to use SSL to encrypt the connection to RDS.
4. Configure the security groups of your EC2 instances and RDS to only allow traffic to and from port 443.

5.   Enable the IAM DB authentication in RDS using the AWS Management Console.

Answer(s): 1, 3

Explanation

You can use Secure Sockets Layer (SSL) to encrypt connections between your client applications and your Amazon RDS DB instances running Microsoft SQL Server. SSL support is available in all AWS regions for all supported SQL Server editions.

When you create a SQL Server DB instance, Amazon RDS creates an SSL certificate for it. The SSL certificate includes the DB instance endpoint as the Common Name (CN) for the SSL certificate to guard against spoofing attacks.

There are 2 ways to use SSL to connect to your SQL Server DB instance:

- Force SSL for all connections — this happens transparently to the client, and the client doesn't have to do any work to use SSL.

- Encrypt specific connections — this sets up an SSL connection from a specific client computer, and you must do work on the client to encrypt connections.

You can force all connections to your DB instance to use SSL, or you can encrypt connections from specific client computers only. To use SSL from a specific client, you must obtain certificates for the client computer, import certificates on the client computer, and then encrypt the connections from the client computer.

If you want to force SSL, use the rds.force_ssl parameter. By default, the rds.force_ssl parameter is set to false. Set the rds.force_ssl parameter to true to force connections to use SSL. The rds.force_ssl parameter is static, so after you change the value, you must reboot your DB instance for the change to take effect.

Hence, the correct answers for this scenario are the options that say:

- Force all connections to your DB instance to use SSL by setting the rds.force_ssl parameter to true. Once done, reboot your DB instance. Configure the security group of your RDS to only allow traffic from port 443.

- Download the Amazon RDS Root CA certificate. Import the certificate to your servers and configure your application to use SSL to encrypt the connection to RDS.

Specifying the TDE option in an RDS option group that is associated with that DB instance to enable transparent data encryption (TDE) is incorrect because transparent data encryption (TDE) is primarily used to encrypt stored data on your DB instances running Microsoft SQL Server, and not the data that are in-transit.

Enabling the IAM DB authentication in RDS using the AWS Management Console is incorrect because IAM database authentication is only supported in MySQL and PostgreSQL database engines. With IAM database authentication, you don't need to use a password when you connect to a DB instance but instead, you use an authentication token.

Configuring the security groups of your EC2 instances and RDS to only allow traffic to and from port 443 is incorrect because it is not enough to do this. You need to either force all connections to your DB instance to use SSL, or you can encrypt connections from specific client computers, just as mentioned above.

References:

https://docs.aws.amazon.com/AmazonRDS/latest/UserGuide/SQLServer.Concept s.General.SSL.Using.html

https://docs.aws.amazon.com/AmazonRDS/latest/UserGuide/Appendix.SQLServ er.Options.TDE.html

https://docs.aws.amazon.com/AmazonRDS/latest/UserGuide/UsingWithRDS.IA MDBAuth.html

Question 27:

Your boss has asked you to launch a new MySQL RDS which ensures that you are available to recover from a database crash.

Which of the below is not a recommended practice for RDS?

1. Use MyISAM as the storage engine for MySQL.
2. Ensure that automated backups are enabled for the RDS
3. Use InnoDB as the storage engine for MySQL.
4. Partition your large tables so that file sizes does not exceed the 16 TB limit.

Answer(s): 1

Explanation

Using MyISAM as the storage engine for MySQL is not recommended. The recommended storage engine for MySQL is InnoDB and not MyISAM.

The rest of the options are best practices in the AWS MySQL RDS documentation. Again, InnoDB is the recommended storage engine for MySQL. However, in case you require intense, full-text search capability, use MyISAM storage engine instead.

Reference:

https://docs.aws.amazon.com/AmazonRDS/latest/UserGuide/CHAP_BestPractice s.html#CHAP_BestPractices.MySQLStorage

Question 28:

You recently created a brand new IAM User with a default setting using AWS CLI. This is intended to be used to send API requests to your S3, DynamoDB, Lambda, and other AWS resources of your cloud infrastructure.

Which of the following must be done to allow the user to make API calls to your AWS resources?

1. Do nothing as the IAM User is already capable of sending API calls to your AWS resources.
2. Enable Multi-Factor Authentication for the user.
3. Create a set of Access Keys for the user and attach the necessary permissions.
4. Assign an IAM Policy to the user to allow it to send API calls.

Answer(s): 3

Explanation

You can choose the credentials that are right for your IAM user. When you use the AWS Management Console to create a user, you must choose to at least include a console password or access keys. By default, a brand new IAM user created using the AWS CLI or AWS API has no credentials of any kind. You must create the type of credentials for an IAM user based on the needs of your user.

Access keys are long-term credentials for an IAM user or the AWS account root user. You can use access keys to sign programmatic requests to the AWS CLI or AWS API (directly or using the AWS SDK). Users need their own access keys to make programmatic calls to AWS from the AWS Command Line Interface (AWS CLI), Tools for Windows PowerShell, the AWS SDKs, or direct HTTP calls using the APIs for individual AWS services.

To fill this need, you can create, modify, view, or rotate access keys (access key IDs and secret access keys) for IAM users. When you create an access key, IAM returns the access key ID and secret access key. You should save these in a secure location and give them to the user.

The option that says: Do nothing as the IAM User is already capable of sending API calls to your AWS resources is incorrect because by default, a brand new IAM user created using the AWS CLI or AWS API has no credentials of any kind. Take note that in the scenario, you created the new IAM user using the AWS CLI and not via the AWS Management Console, where you must choose to at least include a console password or access keys when creating a new IAM user.

Enabling Multi-Factor Authentication for the user is incorrect because this will still not provide the required Access Keys needed to send API calls to your AWS resources. You have to grant the IAM user with Access Keys to meet the requirement.

Assigning an IAM Policy to the user to allow it to send API calls is incorrect because adding a new IAM policy to the new user will not grant the needed Access Keys needed to make API calls to the AWS resources.

References:

https://docs.aws.amazon.com/IAM/latest/UserGuide/id_credentials_access-keys.html

https://docs.aws.amazon.com/IAM/latest/UserGuide/id_users.html#id_users_creds

Question 29:

You are the Solutions Architect of a software development company where you are required to connect the on-premises infrastructure to their AWS cloud. Which of the following AWS services can you use to accomplish this? (Select TWO.)

1. AWS Direct Connect
2. VPC Peering
3. NAT Gateway
4. Amazon Connect
5. IPsec VPN connection

Answer(s): 1, 5

Explanation

You can connect your VPC to remote networks by using a VPN connection which can be Direct Connect, IPsec VPN connection, AWS VPN CloudHub, or a third party software VPN appliance. Hence, IPsec VPN connection and AWS Direct Connect are the correct answers.

Amazon Connect is incorrect because this is not a VPN connectivity option. It is actually a self-service, cloud-based contact center service in AWS that makes it easy for any business to deliver better customer service at a lower cost. Amazon Connect is based on the same contact center technology used by Amazon customer service associates around the world to power millions of customer conversations.

VPC Peering is incorrect because this is a networking connection between two VPCs only, which enables you to route traffic between them privately. This can't be used to connect your on-premises network to your VPC.

NAT Gateway is incorrect because you only use a network address translation (NAT) gateway to enable instances in a private subnet to connect to the Internet or other AWS services, but prevent the Internet from initiating a connection with those instances. This is not used to connect to your on-premises network.

References:

https://docs.aws.amazon.com/AmazonVPC/latest/UserGuide/vpn-connections.html

https://aws.amazon.com/connect/

Question 30:

A global medical research company has a molecular imaging system which provides each client with frequently updated images of what is happening inside the human body at the molecular and cellular level. The system is hosted in AWS and the images are hosted in an S3 bucket behind a CloudFront web distribution. There was a new batch of updated images that were uploaded in S3, however, the users were reporting that they were still seeing the old content. You need to control which image will be returned by the system even when the user has another version cached either locally or behind a corporate caching proxy.

Which of the following is the most suitable solution to solve this issue?

1. Invalidate the files in your CloudFront web distribution
2. Use versioned objects
3. Add Cache-Control no-cache, no-store, or private directives in the S3 bucket
4. Add a separate cache behavior path for the content and configure a custom object caching with a Minimum TTL of 0

Answer(s): 2

Explanation

To control the versions of files that are served from your distribution, you can either invalidate files or give them versioned file names. If you want to update your files frequently, AWS recommends that you primarily use file versioning for the following reasons:

- Versioning enables you to control which file a request returns even when the user has a version cached either locally or behind a corporate caching proxy. If you invalidate the file, the user might continue to see the old version until it expires from those caches.

- CloudFront access logs include the names of your files, so versioning makes it easier to analyze the results of file changes.

- Versioning provides a way to serve different versions of files to different users.

- Versioning simplifies rolling forward and back between file revisions.

- Versioning is less expensive. You still have to pay for CloudFront to transfer new versions of your files to edge locations, but you don't have to pay for invalidating files.

Invalidating the files in your CloudFront web distribution is incorrect because even though using invalidation will solve this issue, this solution is more expensive as compared to using versioned objects.

Adding a separate cache behavior path for the content and configuring a custom object caching with a Minimum TTL of 0 is incorrect because this alone is not enough to solve the problem. A cache behavior is primarily used to configure a variety of CloudFront functionality for a given URL path pattern for files on your website. Although this solution may work, it is still better to use versioned objects where you can control which image will be returned by the system even when the user has another version cached either locally or behind a corporate caching proxy.

Adding Cache-Control no-cache, no-store, or private directives in the S3 bucket is incorrect because although it is right to configure your origin to add the Cache-Control or Expires header field, you should do this to your objects and not on the entire S3 bucket.

References:

https://docs.aws.amazon.com/AmazonCloudFront/latest/DeveloperGuide/UpdatingExistingObjects.html

https://aws.amazon.com/premiumsupport/knowledge-center/prevent-cloudfront-from-caching-files/

https://docs.aws.amazon.com/AmazonCloudFront/latest/DeveloperGuide/Invalidation.html#PayingForInvalidation

Question 31:

In a tech company that you are working for, there is a requirement to allow one IAM user to modify the configuration of one of your Elastic Load Balancers (ELB) which is used in a specific project. Each developer in your company has an individual IAM user and they usually move from one project to another.

Which of the following would be the best way to allow this access?

1. Provide the user temporary access to the root account for 8 hours only. Afterwards, change the password once the activity is completed.
2. Open up the port that ELB uses in a security group and then give the user access to that security group via a policy.
3. Create a new IAM user that has access to modify the ELB. Delete that user when the work is completed.

4. Create a new IAM Role which will be assumed by the IAM user. Attach a policy allowing access to modify the ELB and once it is done, remove the IAM role from the user.

Answer(s): 4

Explanation

In this scenario, the best option is to use IAM Role to provide access. You can create a new IAM Role then associate it to the IAM user. Attach a policy allowing access to modify the ELB and once it is done, remove the IAM role to the user.

An IAM role is similar to a user in that it is an AWS identity with permission policies that determine what the identity can and cannot do in AWS. However, instead of being uniquely associated with one person, a role is intended to be assumable by anyone who needs it. Also, a role does not have standard long-term credentials (password or access keys) associated with it. Instead, if a user assumes a role, temporary security credentials are created dynamically and provided to the user.

You can use roles to delegate access to users, applications, or services that don't normally have access to your AWS resources. For example, you might want to grant users in your AWS account access to resources they don't usually have, or grant users in one AWS account access to resources in another account. Or you might want to allow a mobile app to use AWS resources, but not want to embed AWS keys within the app (where they can be difficult to rotate and where users can potentially extract them). Sometimes you want to give AWS access to users who already have identities defined outside of AWS, such as in your corporate directory. Or, you might want to grant access to your account to third parties so that they can perform an audit on your resources.

Reference:

https://docs.aws.amazon.com/IAM/latest/UserGuide/id_roles_create_for-user.html

Question 32:

You have several EC2 Reserved Instances in your account that needs to be decommissioned and shut down since they are no longer required. The data is still required by the Audit team.

Which of the following steps can be taken for this scenario? (Select TWO.)

1. Take snapshots of the EBS volumes and terminate the EC2 instances.
2. Convert the EC2 instance to On-Demand instances
3. You can opt to sell these EC2 instances on the AWS Reserved Instance Marketplace

4. Convert the EC2 instances to Spot instances with a persistent Spot request type.

Answer(s): 1, 3

Explanation

You can create a snapshot of the instance to save its data and then sell the instance to the Reserved Instance Marketplace.

The Reserved Instance Marketplace is a platform that supports the sale of third-party and AWS customers' unused Standard Reserved Instances, which vary in terms of length and pricing options. For example, you may want to sell Reserved Instances after moving instances to a new AWS region, changing to a new instance type, ending projects before the term expiration, when your business needs change, or if you have unneeded capacity.

Reference:

http://docs.aws.amazon.com/AWSEC2/latest/UserGuide/ri-market-general.html

Question 33:

You are working for a global news network where you have set up a CloudFront distribution for your web application. However, you noticed that your application's origin server is being hit for each request instead of the AWS Edge locations, which serve the cached objects. The issue occurs even for the commonly requested objects.

What could be a possible cause of this issue?

1. The Cache-Control max-age directive is set to zero.
2. The file sizes of the cached objects are too large for CloudFront to handle.
3. You did not add an SSL certificate.
4. An object is only cached by Cloudfront once a successful request has been made hence, the objects were not requested before, which is why the request is still directed to the origin server.

Answer(s): 1

Explanation

In this scenario, the main culprit is that the Cache-Control max-age directive is set to a low value, which is why the request is always directed to your origin server. Hence the correct answer is the option that says: The Cache-Control max-age directive is set to zero.

The option that says: An object is only cached by CloudFront once a successful request has been made hence, the objects were not requested before, which is why the request is still directed to the origin server is incorrect because the issue also occurs even for the commonly requested objects. This means that these objects were successfully requested before but due to a zero Cache-Control max-age directive value, it causes this issue in CloudFront.

The options that say: The file sizes of the cached objects are too large for CloudFront to handle and You did not add an SSL certificate are incorrect because they are not related to the issue in caching.

You can control how long your objects stay in a CloudFront cache before CloudFront forwards another request to your origin. Reducing the duration allows you to serve dynamic content. Increasing the duration means your users get better performance because your objects are more likely to be served directly from the edge cache. A longer duration also reduces the load on your origin.

Typically, CloudFront serves an object from an edge location until the cache duration that you specified passes — that is, until the object expires. After it expires, the next time the edge location gets a user request for the object, CloudFront forwards the request to the origin server to verify that the cache contains the latest version of the object.

The Cache-Control and Expires headers control how long objects stay in the cache. The Cache-Control max-age directive lets you specify how long (in seconds) you want an object to remain in the cache before CloudFront gets the object again from the origin server. The minimum expiration time CloudFront supports is 0 seconds for web distributions and 3600 seconds for RTMP distributions.

Reference:

http://docs.aws.amazon.com/AmazonCloudFront/latest/DeveloperGuide/Expiration.html

Question 34:

You are instructed by your manager to create a publicly accessible EC2 instance by using an Elastic IP (EIP) address and also to give him a report on how much it will cost to use that EIP.

Which of the following statements is correct regarding the pricing of EIP?

1. There is no cost if the instance is running and it has only one associated EIP.
2. There is no cost if the instance is running and it has at least two associated EIP.
3. There is no cost if the instance is terminated and it has only one associated EIP.

4. There is no cost if the instance is stopped and it has only one associated EIP.

Answer(s): 1

Explanation

An Elastic IP address doesn't incur charges as long as the following conditions are true:

-The Elastic IP address is associated with an Amazon EC2 instance.

-The instance associated with the Elastic IP address is running.

-The instance has only one Elastic IP address attached to it.

If you've stopped or terminated an EC2 instance with an associated Elastic IP address and you don't need that Elastic IP address anymore, consider disassociating or releasing the Elastic IP address .

References:

https://aws.amazon.com/premiumsupport/knowledge-center/elastic-ip-charges/

Question 35:

AWS hosts a variety of public datasets such as satellite imagery, geospatial, or genomic data that you want to use for your web application hosted in Amazon EC2.

If you use these datasets, how much will it cost you?

1. $10 per month for all datasets.
2. No charge.
3. A one-time charge of $10.
4. $10 per month for each dataset.

Answer(s): 2

Explanation

AWS hosts a variety of public datasets that anyone can access for free.

Previously, large datasets such as satellite imagery or genomic data have required hours or days to locate, download, customize, and analyze. When data is made publicly available on AWS, anyone can analyze any volume of data without needing to download or store it themselves.

Reference:

https://aws.amazon.com/public-datasets/

Question 36:

You are building a microservices architecture in which a software is composed of small independent services that communicate over well-defined APIs. In building large-scale systems, fine-grained decoupling of microservices is a recommended practice to implement. The decoupled services should scale horizontally from each other to improve scalability.

What is the difference between Horizontal scaling and Vertical scaling?

1. Horizontal scaling means running the same software on smaller containers such as Docker and Kubernetes using ECS or EKS. Vertical scaling is adding more servers to the existing pool and doesn't run into limitations of individual servers.
2. Vertical scaling means running the same software on a fully serverless architecture using Lambda. Horizontal scaling means adding more servers to the existing pool and it doesn't run into limitations of individual servers.
3. Vertical scaling means running the same software on bigger machines which is limited by the capacity of the individual server. Horizontal scaling is adding more servers to the existing pool and doesn't run into limitations of individual servers.
4. Horizontal scaling means running the same software on bigger machines which is limited by the capacity of individual servers. Vertical scaling is adding more servers to the existing pool and doesn't run into limitations of individual servers.

Answer(s): 3

Explanation

Vertical scaling means running the same software on bigger machines which is limited by the capacity of the individual server. Horizontal scaling is adding more servers to the existing pool and doesn't run into limitations of individual servers.

Fine-grained decoupling of microservices is a best practice for building large-scale systems. It's a prerequisite for performance optimization since it allows choosing the appropriate and optimal technologies for a specific service. Each service can be implemented with the appropriate programming languages and frameworks, leverage the optimal data persistence solution, and be fine-tuned with the best performing service configurations.

Properly decoupled services can be scaled horizontally and independently from each other. Vertical scaling, which is running the same software on bigger machines, is limited by the capacity of individual servers and can incur downtime during the scaling process. Horizontal scaling, which is adding more servers to the existing pool, is highly dynamic and doesn't run into limitations of individual servers. The scaling process can be completely automated.

Furthermore, the resiliency of the application can be improved because failing components can be easily and automatically replaced. Hence, the correct answer is the option that says: Vertical scaling means running the same software on bigger machines which is limited by the capacity of the individual server. Horizontal scaling is adding more servers to the existing pool and doesn't run into limitations of individual servers.

The option that says: Vertical scaling means running the same software on a fully serverless architecture using Lambda. Horizontal scaling means adding more servers to the existing pool and it doesn't run into limitations of individual servers is incorrect because Vertical scaling is not about running the same software on a fully serverless architecture. AWS Lambda is not required for scaling.

The option that says: Horizontal scaling means running the same software on bigger machines which is limited by the capacity of individual servers. Vertical scaling is adding more servers to the existing pool and doesn't run into limitations of individual servers is incorrect because the definitions for the two concepts were switched. Vertical scaling means running the same software on bigger machines which is limited by the capacity of the individual server. Horizontal scaling is adding more servers to the existing pool and doesn't run into limitations of individual servers.

The option that says: Horizontal scaling means running the same software on smaller containers such as Docker and Kubernetes using ECS or EKS. Vertical scaling is adding more servers to the existing pool and doesn't run into limitations of individual servers is incorrect because Horizontal scaling is not related to using ECS or EKS containers on a smaller instance.

Reference:

https://docs.aws.amazon.com/aws-technical-content/latest/microservices-on-aws/microservices-on-aws.pdf#page=8

Question 37:

A new DevOps engineer has created a CloudFormation template for a web application and she raised a pull-request in GIT for you to check and review. After checking the template, you immediately told her that the template will not work.

Which of the following is the reason why this CloudFormation template will fail to deploy the stack?

{ "AWSTemplateFormatVersion":"2010-09-09",

```
"Parameters":{
 "VPCId":{
  "Type":"String",
  "Description":"tutorialsfree"
 },
 "SubnetId":{
  "Type":"String",
  "Description":"subnet-b46032ec"
 }
},
"Outputs":{
 "InstanceId":{
  "Value":{
   "Ref":"TutorialsfreeInstance"
  }, "Description":"Instance Id"
 }
}
}
```

1. An invalid section named Parameters is present. This will cause the CloudFormation stack to fail.
2. The Conditions section is missing.
3. The Resources section is missing.
4. The value of the AWSTemplateFormatVersion is incorrect. It should be 2017-06-06.

Answer(s): 3

Explanation

In CloudFormation, a template is a JSON or a YAML-formatted text file that describes your AWS infrastructure. Templates include several major sections. The Resources section is the only required section. Some sections in a template can be in any order. However, as you build your template, it might be helpful to use the logical ordering of the following list, as values in one section might refer to values from a previous section. Take note that all of the sections here are optional, except for Resources, which is the only one required.

-Format Version

-Description

-Metadata

-Parameters

-Mappings

-Conditions

-Transform

-Resources (required)

-Outputs

Reference:

http://docs.aws.amazon.com/AWSCloudFormation/latest/UserGuide/template-anatomy.html

Question 38:

You are setting up the required compute resources in your VPC for your application which have workloads that require high, sequential read and write access to very large data sets on local storage. Which of the following instance type is the most suitable one to use in this scenario?

1. Compute Optimized Instances
2. Memory Optimized Instances
3. Storage Optimized Instances
4. General Purpose Instances

Answer(s): 3

Explanation

Storage Optimized Instances is the correct answer. Storage optimized instances are designed for workloads that require high, sequential read and write access to very large data sets on local storage. They are optimized to deliver tens of thousands of low-latency, random I/O operations per second (IOPS) to applications.

Memory Optimized Instances is incorrect because these are designed to deliver fast performance for workloads that process large data sets in memory, which is quite different from handling high read and write capacity on local storage.

Compute Optimized Instances is incorrect because these are ideal for compute-bound applications that benefit from high-performance processors, such as batch processing workloads and media transcoding.

General Purpose Instances is incorrect because these are the most basic type of instances. They provide a balance of compute, memory, and networking resources, and can be used for a variety of workloads. Since you are requiring higher read and write capacity, storage optimized instances should be selected instead.

Reference:

https://docs.aws.amazon.com/AWSEC2/latest/UserGuide/storage-optimized-instances.html

Question 39:

You are working as a Senior Solutions Architect in a digital media services startup. Your current project is about a movie streaming app where you are required to launch several EC2 instances on multiple availability zones. Which of the following will configure your load balancer to distribute incoming requests evenly to all EC2 instances across multiple Availability Zones?

1. Cross-zone load balancing
2. Elastic Load Balancing request routing
3. An Amazon Route 53 latency routing policy
4. An Amazon Route 53 weighted routing policy

Answer(s): 1

Explanation

The right answer is to enable cross-zone load balancing.

If the load balancer nodes for your Classic Load Balancer can distribute requests regardless of Availability Zone, this is known as cross-zone load balancing. With cross-zone load balancing enabled, your load balancer nodes distribute incoming requests evenly across the Availability Zones enabled for your load balancer. Otherwise, each load balancer node distributes requests only to instances in its Availability Zone.

For example, if you have 10 instances in Availability Zone us-west-2a and 2 instances in us-west-2b, the requests are distributed evenly across all 12 instances if cross-zone load balancing is enabled. Otherwise, the 2 instances in us-west-2b serve the same number of requests as the 10 instances in us-west-2a.

Cross-zone load balancing reduces the need to maintain equivalent numbers of instances in each enabled Availability Zone, and improves your application's ability to handle the loss of one or more instances. However, we still recommend that you maintain approximately equivalent numbers of instances in each enabled Availability Zone for higher fault tolerance.

Reference:

http://docs.aws.amazon.com/elasticloadbalancing/latest/classic/enable-disable-crosszone-lb.html

Question 40:

A WordPress website hosted in an EC2 instance, which has an additional EBS volume attached, was mistakenly deployed in the us-east-1a Availability Zone due to a misconfiguration in your CloudFormation template. There is a requirement to quickly rectify the issue by moving and attaching the EBS volume to a new EC2 instance in the us-east-1b Availability Zone.

As the Solutions Architect of the company, which of the following should you do to solve this issue?

1. Detach the EBS volume and attach it to an EC2 instance residing in another Availability Zone.
2. First, create a new volume in the other Availability Zone. Next, perform a disk copy of the contents from the source volume to the new volume that you have created.
3. First, create a snapshot of the EBS volume. Afterwards, create a volume using the snapshot in the other Availability Zone.
4. Create a new EBS volume in another Availability Zone and then specify the current EBS volume as the source.

Answer(s): 3

Explanation

The first step is to create a snapshot of the EBS volume. Create a volume using this snapshot and then specify the new Availability Zone accordingly.

A point-in-time snapshot of an EBS volume, can be used as a baseline for new volumes or for data backup. If you make periodic snapshots of a volume, the snapshots are incremental—only the blocks on the device that have changed after your last snapshot are saved in the new snapshot. Even though snapshots are saved incrementally, the snapshot deletion process is designed so that you need to retain only the most recent snapshot in order to restore the entire volume.

Snapshots occur asynchronously; the point-in-time snapshot is created immediately, but the status of the snapshot is pending until the snapshot is complete (when all of the modified blocks have been transferred to Amazon S3), which can take several hours for large initial snapshots or subsequent snapshots where many blocks have changed. While it is completing, an in-progress snapshot is not affected by ongoing reads and writes to the volume.

Creating a new EBS volume in another Availability Zone and then specifying the current EBS volume as the source is incorrect. There is no such action like this in AWS since EBS volumes do not require a source from other EBS volumes.

Detaching the EBS volume and attaching it to an EC2 instance residing in another Availability Zone is incorrect because an EBS volume is only available in the Availability Zone it was created in and cannot be attached directly to other Availability Zones.

The option that says: First, create a new volume in the other Availability Zone. Next, perform a disk copy of the contents from the source volume to the new volume that you have created is incorrect because doing that is not the safest way to copy EBS contents. Create a snapshot instead for better reliability of the process.

References:

http://docs.aws.amazon.com/AWSEC2/latest/UserGuide/EBSSnapshots.html

https://docs.aws.amazon.com/AWSEC2/latest/UserGuide/ebs-restoring-volume.html

Question 41:

You are trying to enable Cross-Region Replication to your S3 bucket but this option is disabled.

Which of the following options is a valid reason for this?

1. The Cross-Region Replication feature is only available for Amazon S3 - Infrequent Access.
2. The Cross-Region Replication feature is only available for Amazon S3 - RRS.
3. In order to use the Cross-Region Replication feature in S3, you need to first enable versioning on the bucket.
4. This is a premium feature which is only for AWS Enterprise accounts.

Answer(s): 3

Explanation

To enable the cross-region replication feature in S3, the following items should be met:

The source and destination buckets must have versioning enabled.

The source and destination buckets must be in different AWS Regions.

Amazon S3 must have permissions to replicate objects from that source bucket to the destination bucket on your behalf.

The options that say: The Cross-Region Replication feature is only available for Amazon S3 - RRS and The Cross-Region Replication feature is only available for Amazon S3 - Infrequent Access are incorrect as this feature is available to all types of S3 classes.

The option that says: This is a premium feature which is only for AWS Enterprise accounts is incorrect as this CRR feature is available to all Support Plans.

Reference:

https://docs.aws.amazon.com/AmazonS3/latest/dev/crr.html

Question 42:

A mobile application stores pictures in Amazon Simple Storage Service (S3) and allows application sign-in using an OpenID Connect-compatible identity provider.

Which AWS Security Token Service approach to temporary access should you use for this scenario?

1. SAML-based Identity Federation
2. AWS Identity and Access Management roles
3. Cross-Account Access
4. Web Identity Federation

Answer(s): 4

Explanation

With web identity federation, you don't need to create custom sign-in code or manage your own user identities. Instead, users of your app can sign in using a well-known identity provider (IdP) —such as Login with Amazon, Facebook, Google, or any other OpenID Connect (OIDC)-compatible IdP, receive an authentication token, and then exchange that token for temporary security credentials in AWS that map to an IAM role with permissions to use the resources in your AWS account. Using an IdP helps you keep your AWS account secure because you don't have to embed and distribute long-term security credentials with your application.

Reference:

http://docs.aws.amazon.com/IAM/latest/UserGuide/id_roles_providers_oidc.html

Question 43:

Your company has developed a financial analytics web application hosted in a Docker container using MEAN (MongoDB, Express.js, AngularJS, and Node.js) stack. You want to easily port that web application to AWS Cloud which can automatically handle all the tasks such as balancing load, auto-scaling, monitoring, and placing your containers across your cluster.

Which of the following services can be used to fulfill this requirement?

1. ECS
2. AWS CodeDeploy
3. OpsWorks
4. AWS Elastic Beanstalk

Answer(s): 4

Explanation

Elastic Beanstalk supports the deployment of web applications from Docker containers. With Docker containers, you can define your own runtime environment. You can choose your own platform, programming language, and any application dependencies (such as package managers or tools), that aren't supported by other platforms. Docker containers are self-contained and include all the configuration information and software your web application requires to run.

By using Docker with Elastic Beanstalk, you have an infrastructure that automatically handles the details of capacity provisioning, load balancing, scaling, and application health monitoring. You can manage your web application in an environment that supports the range of services that are integrated with Elastic Beanstalk, including but not limited to VPC, RDS, and IAM. Hence, AWS Elastic Beanstalk is the correct answer.

ECS is incorrect because although it also provides Service Auto Scaling, Service Load Balancing and Monitoring with CloudWatch, these features are not automatically enabled by default unlike with Elastic Beanstalk. Take note that the scenario requires a service that will automatically handle all the tasks such as balancing load, auto-scaling, monitoring, and placing your containers across your cluster. You will have to manually configure these things if you wish to use ECS. With Elastic Beanstalk, you can manage your web application in an environment that supports the range of services easier.

OpsWorks and AWS CodeDeploy are incorrect because these are primarily used for application deployment and configuration only, without providing load balancing, auto-scaling, monitoring or ECS cluster management.

Reference:

https://docs.aws.amazon.com/elasticbeanstalk/latest/dg/create_deploy_docker.html

Question 44:

A web application is hosted on a fleet of EC2 instances inside an Auto Scaling Group with a couple of Lambda functions for ad hoc processing. Whenever you release updates to your application every week, there are inconsistencies where some resources are not updated properly. You need a way to group the resources together and deploy the new version of your code consistently among the groups with minimal downtime.

Which among these options should you do to satisfy the given requirement with the least effort?

1. Use deployment groups in CodeDeploy to automate code deployments in a consistent manner.
2. Create CloudFormation templates that have the latest configurations and code in them.
3. Use CodeCommit to publish your code quickly in a private repository and push them to your resources for fast updates.
4. Create OpsWorks recipes that will automatically launch resources containing the latest version of the code.

Answer(s): 1

Explanation

CodeDeploy is a deployment service that automates application deployments to Amazon EC2 instances, on-premises instances, or serverless Lambda functions. It allows you to rapidly release new features, update Lambda function versions, avoid downtime during application deployment, and handle the complexity of updating your applications, without many of the risks associated with error-prone manual deployments.

Creating CloudFormation templates that have the latest configurations and code in them is incorrect since it is used for provisioning and managing stacks of AWS resources based on templates you create to model your infrastructure architecture. CloudFormation is recommended if you want a tool for granular control over the provisioning and management of your own infrastructure.

Using CodeCommit to publish your code quickly in a private repository and pushing them to your resources for fast updates is incorrect as you mainly use CodeCommit for managing a source-control service that hosts private Git repositories. You can store anything from code to binaries and work seamlessly with your existing Git-based tools. CodeCommit integrates with CodePipeline and CodeDeploy to streamline your development and release process.

You could also use OpsWorks to deploy your code, however, creating OpsWorks recipes that will automatically launch resources containing the latest version of the code is still incorrect because you don't need to launch new resources containing your new code when you can just update the ones that are already running.

References:

https://docs.aws.amazon.com/codedeploy/latest/userguide/deployment-groups.html

https://docs.aws.amazon.com/codedeploy/latest/userguide/welcome.html

Overview of Deployment Options on AWS whitepaper

https://d0.awsstatic.com/whitepapers/overview-of-deployment-options-on-aws.pdf

Question 45:

You are working as a Solutions Architect for a major accounting firm, and they have a legacy general ledger accounting application that needs to be moved to AWS. However, the legacy application has a dependency on multicast networking. On this scenario, which of the following options should you consider to ensure the legacy application works in AWS?

1. All of the above.
2. Provision Elastic Network Interfaces between the subnets.
3. Create a virtual overlay network running on the OS level of the instance.
4. Create all the subnets on another VPC and enable VPC peering.

Answer(s): 3

Explanation

Multicast is a network capability that allows one-to-many distribution of data. With multicasting, one or more sources can transmit network packets to subscribers that typically reside within a multicast group. However, take note that Amazon VPC does not support multicast or broadcast networking.

You can use an overlay multicast in order to migrate the legacy application. An overlay multicast is a method of building IP level multicast across a network fabric supporting unicast IP routing, such as Amazon Virtual Private Cloud (Amazon VPC).

Creating a virtual overlay network running on the OS level of the instance is correct because overlay multicast is a method of building IP level multicast across a network fabric supporting unicast IP routing, such as Amazon Virtual Private Cloud (Amazon VPC).

Provisioning Elastic Network Interfaces between the subnets is incorrect because just providing ENIs between the subnets would not resolve the dependency on multicast.

Creating all the subnets on another VPC and enabling VPC peering is incorrect because VPC peering and multicast are not the same.

The option that says: All of the options are correct is incorrect because the only option that will work in this scenario is creating a virtual overlay network.

Reference:

https://aws.amazon.com/articles/overlay-multicast-in-amazon-virtual-private-cloud

Question 46:

A startup company wants to launch a fleet of EC2 instances on AWS. Your manager wants to ensure that the Java programming language is installed automatically when the instance is launched. In which of the below configurations can you achieve this requirement?

1. User data
2. EC2Config service
3. AWS Config
4. IAM roles

Answer(s): 1

Explanation

When you launch an instance in Amazon EC2, you have the option of passing user data to the instance that can be used to perform common automated configuration tasks and even run scripts after the instance starts. You can write and run scripts that install new packages, software, or tools in your instance when it is launched.

You can pass two types of user data to Amazon EC2: shell scripts and cloud-init directives. You can also pass this data into the launch wizard as plain text, as a file (this is useful for launching instances using the command line tools), or as base64-encoded text (for API calls).

Reference:

https://docs.aws.amazon.com/AWSEC2/latest/UserGuide/user-data.html

Question 47:

You are working for a weather station in Asia with a weather monitoring system that needs to be migrated to AWS. Since the monitoring system requires a low network latency and high network throughput, you decided to launch your EC2 instances to a new cluster placement group. The system was working fine for a couple of weeks, however, when you try to add new instances to the placement group that already has running EC2 instances, you receive an 'insufficient capacity error'.

How will you fix this issue?

1. Submit a capacity increase request to AWS as you are initially limited to only 12 instances per Placement Group.
2. Stop and restart the instances in the Placement Group and then try the launch again.
3. Create another Placement Group and launch the new instances in the new group.
4. Verify all running instances are of the same size and type and then try the launch again.

Answer(s): 2

Explanation

It is recommended that you launch the number of instances that you need in the placement group in a single launch request and that you use the same instance type for all instances in the placement group. If you try to add more instances to the placement group later, or if you try to launch more than one instance type in the placement group, you increase your chances of getting an insufficient capacity error.

If you stop an instance in a placement group and then start it again, it still runs in the placement group. However, the start fails if there isn't enough capacity for the instance.

If you receive a capacity error when launching an instance in a placement group that already has running instances, stop and start all of the instances in the placement group, and try the launch again. Restarting the instances may migrate them to hardware that has capacity for all the requested instances.

The option that says: Stop and restart the instances in the Placement Group and then try the launch again is correct because you can resolve this issue just by launching again. If the instances are stopped and restarted, AWS may move the instances to a hardware that has capacity for all the requested instances.

The option that says: Create another Placement Group and launch the new instances in the new group is incorrect because to benefit from the enhanced networking, all the instances should be in the same Placement Group. Launching the new ones in a new Placement Group will not work in this case.

The option that says: Verify all running instances are of the same size and type and then try the launch again is incorrect because the capacity error is not related to the instance size.

The option that says: Submit a capacity increase request to AWS as you are initially limited to only 12 instances per Placement Group is incorrect because there is no such limit on the number of instances in a Placement Group.

References:

https://docs.aws.amazon.com/AWSEC2/latest/UserGuide/placement-groups.html#placement-groups-cluster

http://docs.amazonaws.cn/en_us/AWSEC2/latest/UserGuide/troubleshooting-launch.html#troubleshooting-launch-capacity

Question 48:

A construction company has an online system that tracks all of the status and progress of their projects. The system is hosted in AWS and there is a requirement to monitor the read and write IOPs metrics for their MySQL RDS instance and send real-time alerts to their DevOps team.

Which of the following services in AWS can you use to meet the requirements? (Select TWO.)

1. Route 53
2. CloudWatch
3. Amazon Simple Queue Service
4. SWF
5. Amazon Simple Notification Service

Answer(s): 2, 5

Explanation

In this scenario, you can use CloudWatch to monitor your AWS resources and SNS to provide notification. Hence, the correct answers are CloudWatch and Amazon Simple Notification Service.

Amazon Simple Notification Service (SNS) is a flexible, fully managed pub/sub messaging and mobile notifications service for coordinating the delivery of messages to subscribing endpoints and clients.

Amazon CloudWatch is a monitoring service for AWS cloud resources and the applications you run on AWS. You can use Amazon CloudWatch to collect and track metrics, collect and monitor log files, set alarms, and automatically react to changes in your AWS resources.

SWF is incorrect because this is mainly used for managing workflows and not for monitoring and notifications.

Amazon Simple Queue Service is incorrect because this is a messaging queue service and not suitable for this kind of scenario.

Route 53 is incorrect because this is primarily used for routing and domain name registration and management.

References:

http://docs.aws.amazon.com/AmazonCloudWatch/latest/monitoring/CW_Support_For_AWS.html

https://aws.amazon.com/sns/

Question 49:

You are working as a Solution Architect for a startup in Silicon Valley. Their application architecture is currently set up to store both the access key ID and the secret access key in a plain text file on a custom Amazon Machine Image (AMI). The EC2 instances, which are created by using this AMI, are using the stored access keys to connect to a DynamoDB table.   What should you do to make the current architecture more secure?

1. Put the access keys in an Amazon S3 bucket instead.
2. Remove the stored access keys in the AMI. Create a new IAM role with permissions to access the DynamoDB table and assign it to the EC2 instances.
3. Put the access keys in Amazon Glacier instead.
4. Do nothing. The architecture is already secure because the access keys are already in the Amazon Machine Image.

Answer(s): 2

Explanation

You should use an IAM role to manage temporary credentials for applications that run on an EC2 instance. When you use an IAM role, you don't have to distribute long-term credentials (such as a user name and password or access keys) to an EC2 instance.

Instead, the role supplies temporary permissions that applications can use when they make calls to other AWS resources. When you launch an EC2 instance, you specify an IAM role to associate with the instance. Applications that run on the instance can then use the role-supplied temporary credentials to sign API requests.

Hence, the best option here is to remove the stored access keys first in the AMI. Then, create a new IAM role with permissions to access the DynamoDB table and assign it to the EC2 instances.

Putting the access keys in Amazon Glacier or in an Amazon S3 bucket are incorrect because S3 and Glacier are mainly used as a storage option. It is better to use an IAM role instead of storing access keys in these storage services.

The option that says: Do nothing. The architecture is already secure because the access keys are already in the Amazon Machine Image is incorrect because you can make the architecture more secure by using IAM.

Reference:

https://docs.aws.amazon.com/IAM/latest/UserGuide/id_roles_use_switch-role-ec2.html

Question 50:

A multinational company has been building its new data analytics platform with high-performance computing workloads (HPC) which requires a scalable, POSIX-compliant storage service. The data need to be stored redundantly across multiple AZs and allows concurrent connections from thousands of EC2 instances hosted on multiple Availability Zones.

Which of the following AWS storage service is the most suitable one to use in this scenario?

1. Amazon S3
2. EBS Volumes
3. Elastic File System
4. ElastiCache

Answer(s): 3

Explanation

In this question, you should take note of this phrase: "allows concurrent connections from multiple EC2 instances". There are various AWS storage options that you can choose but whenever these criteria show up, always consider using EFS instead of using EBS Volumes which is mainly used as a "block" storage and can only have one connection to one EC2 instance at a time.

Amazon EFS is a fully-managed service that makes it easy to set up and scale file storage in the Amazon Cloud. With a few clicks in the AWS Management Console, you can create file systems that are accessible to Amazon EC2 instances via a file system interface (using standard operating system file I/O APIs) and supports full file system access semantics (such as strong consistency and file locking).

Amazon EFS file systems can automatically scale from gigabytes to petabytes of data without needing to provision storage. Tens, hundreds, or even thousands of Amazon EC2 instances can access an Amazon EFS file system at the same time, and Amazon EFS provides consistent performance to each Amazon EC2 instance. Amazon EFS is designed to be highly durable and highly available.

References:

https://docs.aws.amazon.com/efs/latest/ug/performance.html

https://aws.amazon.com/efs/faq/

Here's a short video tutorial on Amazon EFS:

https://www.youtube.com/embed/AvgAozsfCrY

Question 51:

A multinational manufacturing company has multiple accounts in AWS to separate their various departments such as finance, human resources, engineering and many others. There is a requirement to ensure that certain access to services and actions are properly controlled to comply with the security policy of the company.

As the Solutions Architect, which is the most suitable way to set up the multi-account AWS environment of the company?

1. Set up a common IAM policy that can be applied across all AWS accounts.
2. Use AWS Organizations and Service Control Policies to control services on each account.
3. Provide access to externally authenticated users via Identity Federation. Set up an IAM role to specify permissions for users from each department whose identity is federated from your organization or a third-party identity provider.
4. Connect all departments by setting up a cross-account access to each of the AWS accounts of the company. Create and attach IAM policies to your resources based on their respective departments to control access.

Answer(s): 2

Explanation

Using AWS Organizations and Service Control Policies to control services on each account is the correct answer. Refer to the diagram below:

AWS Organizations offers policy-based management for multiple AWS accounts. With Organizations, you can create groups of accounts, automate account creation, apply and manage policies for those groups. Organizations enables you to centrally manage policies across multiple accounts, without requiring custom scripts and manual processes. It allows you to create Service Control Policies (SCPs) that centrally control AWS service use across multiple AWS accounts.

Setting up a common IAM policy that can be applied across all AWS accounts is incorrect because it is not possible to create a common IAM policy for multiple AWS accounts.

The option that says: Connect all departments by setting up a cross-account access to each of the AWS accounts of the company. Create and attach IAM policies to your resources based on their respective departments to control access is incorrect because although you can set up cross-account access to each department, this entails a lot of configuration compared with using AWS Organizations and Service Control Policies (SCPs). Cross-account access would be a more suitable choice if you only have two accounts to manage, but not for multiple accounts.

The option that says: Provide access to externally authenticated users via Identity Federation. Set up an IAM role to specify permissions for users from each department whose identity is federated from your organization or a third-party identity provider is incorrect as this option is focused on the Identity Federation authentication set up for your AWS accounts but not the IAM policy management for multiple AWS accounts. A combination of AWS Organizations and Service Control Policies (SCPs) is a better choice compared to this option.

Reference:

https://aws.amazon.com/organizations/

Question 52:

A company is planning to deploy a High Performance Computing (HPC) cluster in its VPC that requires a scalable, high-performance file system. The storage service must be optimized for efficient workload processing, and the data must be accessible via a fast and scalable file system interface. It should also work natively with Amazon S3 that enables you to easily process your S3 data with a high-performance POSIX interface.

Which of the following is the MOST suitable service that you should use for this scenario?

1. Amazon Elastic File System (EFS)
2. Amazon FSx for Windows File Server
3. Amazon Elastic Block Storage (EBS)
4. Amazon FSx for Lustre

Answer(s): 4

Explanation

Amazon FSx for Lustre provides a high-performance file system optimized for fast processing of workloads such as machine learning, high performance computing (HPC), video processing, financial modeling, and electronic design automation (EDA). These workloads commonly require data to be presented via a fast and scalable file system interface, and typically have data sets stored on long-term data stores like Amazon S3.

Operating high-performance file systems typically require specialized expertise and administrative overhead, requiring you to provision storage servers and tune complex performance parameters. With Amazon FSx, you can launch and run a file system that provides sub-millisecond access to your data and allows you to read and write data at speeds of up to hundreds of gigabytes per second of throughput and millions of IOPS.

Amazon FSx for Lustre works natively with Amazon S3, making it easy for you to process cloud data sets with high-performance file systems. When linked to an S3 bucket, an FSx for Lustre file system transparently presents S3 objects as files and allows you to write results back to S3. You can also use FSx for Lustre as a standalone high-performance file system to burst your workloads from on-premises to the cloud. By copying on-premises data to an FSx for Lustre file system, you can make that data available for fast processing by compute instances running on AWS. With Amazon FSx, you pay for only the resources you use. There are no minimum commitments, upfront hardware or software costs, or additional fees.

For Windows-based applications, Amazon FSx provides fully managed Windows file servers with features and performance optimized for "lift-and-shift" business-critical application workloads including home directories (user shares), media workflows, and ERP applications. It is accessible from Windows and Linux instances via the SMB protocol. If you have Linux-based applications, Amazon EFS is a cloud-native fully managed file system that provides simple, scalable, elastic file storage accessible from Linux instances via the NFS protocol.

For compute-intensive and fast processing workloads, like high-performance computing (HPC), machine learning, EDA, and media processing, Amazon FSx for Lustre, provides a file system that's optimized for performance, with input and output stored on Amazon S3.

Hence, the correct answer is: Amazon FSx for Lustre.

Amazon Elastic File System (EFS) is incorrect because although the EFS service can be used for HPC applications, it doesn't natively work with Amazon S3. It doesn't have the capability to easily process your S3 data with a high-performance POSIX interface, unlike Amazon FSx for Lustre.

Amazon FSx for Windows File Server is incorrect because although this service is a type of Amazon FSx, it does not work natively with Amazon S3. This service is a fully managed native Microsoft Windows file system that is primarily used for your Windows-based applications that require shared file storage to AWS.

Amazon Elastic Block Storage (EBS) is incorrect because this service is not a scalable, high-performance file system.

References:

https://aws.amazon.com/fsx/lustre/

https://aws.amazon.com/getting-started/use-cases/hpc/3/

Question 53:

A Solutions Architect is developing a three-tier cryptocurrency web application for a FinTech startup. The Architect has been instructed to restrict access to the database tier to only accept traffic from the application-tier and deny traffic from other sources. The application-tier is composed of application servers hosted in an Auto Scaling group of EC2 instances.

Which of the following options is the MOST suitable solution to implement in this scenario?

1. Set up the security group of the database tier to allow database traffic from a specified list of application server IP addresses.
2. Set up the Network ACL of the database subnet to deny all inbound non-database traffic from the subnet of the application-tier.
3. Set up the security group of the database tier to allow database traffic from the security group of the application servers.
4. Set up the Network ACL of the database subnet to allow inbound database traffic from the subnet of the application-tier.

Answer(s): 3

Explanation

A security group acts as a virtual firewall for your instance to control inbound and outbound traffic. When you launch an instance in a VPC, you can assign up to five security groups to the instance. Security groups act at the instance level, not the subnet level. Therefore, each instance in a subnet in your VPC could be assigned to a different set of security groups. If you don't specify a particular group at launch time, the instance is automatically assigned to the default security group for the VPC.

For each security group, you add rules that control the inbound traffic to instances, and a separate set of rules that control the outbound traffic. This section describes the basic things you need to know about security groups for your VPC and their rules.

You can add or remove rules for a security group which is also referred to as authorizing or revoking inbound or outbound access. A rule applies either to inbound traffic (ingress) or outbound traffic (egress). You can grant access to a specific CIDR range, or to another security group in your VPC or in a peer VPC (requires a VPC peering connection).

In the scenario, the servers of the application-tier are in an Auto Scaling group which means that the number of EC2 instances could grow or shrink over time. An Auto Scaling group could also cover one or more Availability Zones (AZ) which have their own subnets. Hence, the most suitable solution would be to set up the security group of the database tier to allow database traffic from the security group of the application servers since you can utilize the security group of the application-tier Auto Scaling group as the source for the security group rule in your database tier.

Setting up the security group of the database tier to allow database traffic from a specified list of application server IP addresses is incorrect because the list of application server IP addresses will change over time since an Auto Scaling group can add or remove EC2 instances based on the configured scaling policy. This will create inconsistencies in your application because the newly launched instances, which are not included in the initial list of IP addresses, will not be able to access the database.

Setting up the Network ACL of the database subnet to deny all inbound non-database traffic from the subnet of the application-tier is incorrect because doing this could affect the other EC2 instances of other applications, which are also hosted in the same subnet of the application-tier. For example, a large subnet with a CIDR block of /16 could be shared by several applications. Denying all inbound non-database traffic from the entire subnet will impact other applications which use this subnet.

Setting up the Network ACL of the database subnet to allow inbound database traffic from the subnet of the application-tier is incorrect because although this solution can work, the subnet of the application-tier could be shared by another tier or another set of EC2 instances other than the application-tier. This means that you would inadvertently be granting database access to unauthorized servers hosted in the same subnet other than the application-tier.

References:

https://docs.aws.amazon.com/vpc/latest/userguide/VPC_Security.html#VPC_Security_Comparison

http://docs.aws.amazon.com/AmazonVPC/latest/UserGuide/VPC_SecurityGroups.html

Question 54:

You are working as a Solutions Architect in a global investment bank which requires corporate IT governance and cost oversight of all of their AWS resources across their divisions around the world. Their corporate divisions want to maintain administrative control of the discrete AWS resources they consume and ensure that those resources are separate from other divisions.

Which of the following options will support the autonomy of each corporate division while enabling the corporate IT to maintain governance and cost oversight? (Select TWO.)

1. Use AWS Trusted Advisor
2. Enable IAM cross-account access for all corporate IT administrators in each child account.
3. Use AWS Consolidated Billing by creating AWS Organizations to link the divisions' accounts to a parent corporate account.
4. Create separate VPCs for each division within the corporate IT AWS account.
5. Create separate Availability Zones for each division within the corporate IT AWS account.

Answer(s): 2, 3

Explanation

In this scenario, enabling IAM cross-account access for all corporate IT administrators in each child account and using AWS Consolidated Billing by creating AWS Organizations to link the divisions' accounts to a parent corporate account are the correct choices. The combined use of IAM and Consolidated Billing will support the autonomy of each corporate division while enabling corporate IT to maintain governance and cost oversight.

You can use an IAM role to delegate access to resources that are in different AWS accounts that you own. You share resources in one account with users in a different account. By setting up cross-account access in this way, you don't need to create individual IAM users in each account. In addition, users don't have to sign out of one account and sign into another in order to access resources that are in different AWS accounts.

You can use the consolidated billing feature in AWS Organizations to consolidate payment for multiple AWS accounts or multiple AISPL accounts. With consolidated billing, you can see a combined view of AWS charges incurred by all of your accounts. You can also get a cost report for each member account that is associated with your master account. Consolidated billing is offered at no additional charge. AWS and AISPL accounts can't be consolidated together.

Using AWS Trusted Advisor is incorrect. Trusted Advisor is an online tool that provides you real-time guidance to help you provision your resources following AWS best practices. It only provides you alerts on areas where you do not adhere to best practices and tells you how to improve them. It does not assist in maintaining governance over your AWS accounts.

Creating separate VPCs for each division within the corporate IT AWS account is incorrect because creating separate VPCs would not separate the divisions from each other since they will still be operating under the same account and therefore contribute to the same billing each month.

Creating separate Availability Zones for each division within the corporate IT AWS account is incorrect because you do not need to create Availability Zones. They are already provided for you by AWS right from the start, and not all services support multiple AZ deployments. In addition, having separate Availability Zones in your VPC does not meet the requirement of supporting the autonomy of each corporate division.

References:

http://docs.aws.amazon.com/awsaccountbilling/latest/aboutv2/consolidated-billing.html

https://docs.aws.amazon.com/IAM/latest/UserGuide/tutorial_cross-account-with-roles.html

Question 55:

You have created a VPC with a single subnet then you launched an On-Demand EC2 instance in that subnet. You have attached Internet gateway (IGW) to the VPC and verified that the EC2 instance has a public IP. The main route table of the VPC is as shown below:

Larger image

However, the instance still cannot be reached from the Internet when you tried to connect to it from your computer. Which of the following should be made to the route table to fix this issue?

1. Modify the above route table: 10.0.0.0/27 -> Your Internet Gateway
2. Add this new entry to the route table: 0.0.0.0/27 -> Your Internet Gateway
3. Add this new entry to the route table: 0.0.0.0/0 -> Your Internet Gateway
4. Add the following entry to the route table: 10.0.0.0/27 -> Your Internet Gateway

Answer(s): 3

Explanation

Apparently, the route table does not have an entry for the Internet Gateway. This is why you cannot connect to the EC2 instance. To fix this, you have to add a route with a destination of 0.0.0.0/0 for IPv4 traffic or ::/0 for IPv6 traffic, and then a target of the Internet gateway ID (igw-xxxxxxxx).

This should be the correct route table configuration after adding the new entry.

Reference:

http://docs.aws.amazon.com/AmazonVPC/latest/UserGuide/VPC_Route_Tables. html

Question 56:

A multinational corporate and investment bank is regularly processing steady workloads of accruals, loan interests, and other critical financial calculations every night at 10 PM to 3 AM on their on-premises data center for their corporate clients. Once the process is done, the results are then uploaded to the Oracle General Ledger which means that the processing should not be delayed nor interrupted. The CTO has decided to move their IT infrastructure to AWS to save cost and to improve the scalability of their digital financial services.

As the Senior Solutions Architect, how can you implement a cost-effective architecture in AWS for their financial system?

1. Use Dedicated Hosts which provide a physical host that is fully dedicated to running your instances, and bring your existing per-socket, per-core, or per-VM software licenses to reduce costs.
2. Use On-Demand EC2 instances which allows you to pay for the instances that you launch and use by the second.
3. Use Spot EC2 Instances launched by a persistent Spot request, which can significantly lower your Amazon EC2 costs.
4. Use Scheduled Reserved Instances, which provide compute capacity that is always available on the specified recurring schedule.

Answer(s): 4

Explanation

Scheduled Reserved Instances (Scheduled Instances) enable you to purchase capacity reservations that recur on a daily, weekly, or monthly basis, with a specified start time and duration, for a one-year term. You reserve the capacity in advance, so that you know it is available when you need it. You pay for the time that the instances are scheduled, even if you do not use them.

Scheduled Instances are a good choice for workloads that do not run continuously, but do run on a regular schedule. For example, you can use Scheduled Instances for an application that runs during business hours or for batch processing that runs at the end of the week.

Hence, the correct answer is to use Scheduled Reserved Instances, which provide compute capacity that is always available on the specified recurring schedule.

Using On-Demand EC2 instances which allows you to pay for the instances that you launch and use by the second is incorrect because although an On-Demand instance is stable and suitable for processing critical data, it costs more than any other option. Moreover, the critical financial calculations are only done every night from 10 PM to 3 AM only and not 24/7. This means that your compute capacity will not be utilized for a total of 19 hours every single day.

Using Spot EC2 Instances launched by a persistent Spot request, which can significantly lower your Amazon EC2 costs is incorrect because although this is the most cost-effective solution, this type is not suitable for processing critical financial data since a Spot Instance has a risk of being interrupted.

Using Dedicated Hosts which provide a physical host that is fully dedicated to running your instances, and bringing your existing per-socket, per-core, or per-VM software licenses to reduce costs is incorrect because the use of a fully dedicated physical host is not warranted in this scenario. Moreover, this will be underutilized since you only run the process for 5 hours (from 10 PM to 3 AM only), wasting 19 hours of compute capacity every single day.

References:

https://aws.amazon.com/blogs/aws/new-scheduled-reserved-instances/

https://docs.aws.amazon.com/AWSEC2/latest/UserGuide/ec2-scheduled-instances.html

Question 57:

A game company has a requirement of load balancing the incoming TCP traffic at the transport level (Layer 4) to their containerized gaming servers hosted in AWS Fargate. To maintain performance, it should handle millions of requests per second sent by gamers around the globe while maintaining ultra-low latencies.

Which of the following must be implemented in the current architecture to satisfy the new requirement?

1. Launch a new Application Load Balancer.
2. Create a new record in Amazon Route 53 with Weighted Routing policy to load balance the incoming traffic.
3. Launch a new microservice in AWS Fargate that acts as a load balancer since using an ALB or NLB with Fargate is not possible.
4. Launch a new Network Load Balancer.

Answer(s): 4

Explanation

Elastic Load Balancing automatically distributes incoming application traffic across multiple targets, such as Amazon EC2 instances, containers, IP addresses, and Lambda functions. It can handle the varying load of your application traffic in a single Availability Zone or across multiple Availability Zones. Elastic Load Balancing offers three types of load balancers that all feature the high availability, automatic scaling, and robust security necessary to make your applications fault-tolerant. They are: Application Load Balancer, Network Load Balancer, and Classic Load Balancer

Network Load Balancer is best suited for load balancing of TCP traffic where extreme performance is required. Operating at the connection level (Layer 4), Network Load Balancer routes traffic to targets within Amazon Virtual Private Cloud (Amazon VPC) and is capable of handling millions of requests per second while maintaining ultra-low latencies. Network Load Balancer is also optimized to handle sudden and volatile traffic patterns.

Hence, the correct answer is to launch a new Network Load Balancer.

The option that says: Launch a new Application Load Balancer is incorrect because it cannot handle TCP or Layer 4 connections, only Layer 7 (HTTP and HTTPS).

The option that says: Create a new record in Amazon Route 53 with Weighted Routing policy to load balance the incoming traffic is incorrect because although Route 53 can act as a load balancer by assigning each record a relative weight that corresponds to how much traffic you want to send to each resource, it is still not capable of handling millions of requests per second while maintaining ultra-low latencies. You have to use a Network Load Balancer instead.

The option that says: Launch a new microservice in AWS Fargate that acts as a load balancer since using an ALB or NLB with Fargate is not possible is incorrect because you can place an ALB and NLB in front of your AWS Fargate cluster.

References:

https://aws.amazon.com/elasticloadbalancing/features/#compare

https://docs.aws.amazon.com/AmazonECS/latest/developerguide/load-balancer-types.html

https://aws.amazon.com/getting-started/projects/build-modern-app-fargate-lambda-dynamodb-python/module-two/

Question 58:

You are working for a startup which develops an AI-based traffic monitoring service. You need to register a new domain called www.tutorialsfree-ai.com and set up other

DNS entries for the other components of your system in AWS. Which of the following is not supported by Amazon Route 53?

1. SPF (sender policy framework)
2. PTR (pointer record)
3. DNSSEC (Domain Name System Security Extensions)
4. SRV (service locator)

Answer(s): 3

Explanation

Amazon Route 53's DNS services does not support DNSSEC at this time. However, their domain name registration service supports configuration of signed DNSSEC keys for domains when DNS service is configured at another provider. More information on configuring DNSSEC for your domain name registration can be found here.

Amazon Route 53 currently supports the following DNS record types:

-A (address record)

-AAAA (IPv6 address record)

-CNAME (canonical name record)

-CAA (certification authority authorization)

-MX (mail exchange record)

-NAPTR (name authority pointer record)

-NS (name server record)

-PTR (pointer record)

-SOA (start of authority record)

-SPF (sender policy framework)

-SRV (service locator)

-TXT (text record)

Reference:

https://aws.amazon.com/route53/faqs/

http://docs.aws.amazon.com/Route53/latest/DeveloperGuide/domain-configure-dnssec.html

Question 59:

A commercial bank has designed their next generation online banking platform to use a distributed system architecture. As their Software Architect, you have to ensure that their architecture is highly scalable, yet still cost-effective. Which of the following will provide the most suitable solution for this scenario?

1. Launch multiple On-Demand EC2 instances to host your application services and an SQS queue which will act as a highly-scalable buffer that stores messages as they travel between distributed applications.
2. Launch an Auto-Scaling group of EC2 instances to host your application services and an SQS queue. Include an Auto Scaling trigger to watch the SQS queue size which will either scale in or scale out the number of EC2 instances based on the queue.
3. Launch multiple EC2 instances behind an Application Load Balancer to host your application services, and SWF which will act as a highly-scalable buffer that stores messages as they travel between distributed applications.
4. Launch multiple EC2 instances behind an Application Load Balancer to host your application services and SNS which will act as a highly-scalable buffer that stores messages as they travel between distributed applications.

Answer(s): 2

Explanation

There are three main parts in a distributed messaging system: the components of your distributed system which can be hosted on EC2 instance; your queue (distributed on Amazon SQS servers); and the messages in the queue.

To improve the scalability of your distributed system, you can add Auto Scaling group to your EC2 instances.

References:

https://docs.aws.amazon.com/autoscaling/ec2/userguide/as-using-sqs-queue.html

https://docs.aws.amazon.com/AWSSimpleQueueService/latest/SQSDeveloperGuid e/sqs-basic-architecture.html

Question 60:

A top university has recently launched its online learning portal where the students can take e-learning courses from the comforts of their homes. The portal is on a large On-Demand EC2 instance with a single Amazon Aurora database.

How can you improve the availability of your Aurora database to prevent any unnecessary downtime of the online portal?

1. Deploy Aurora to two Auto-Scaling groups of EC2 instances across two Availability Zones with an elastic load balancer which handles load balancing.
2. Use an Asynchronous Key Prefetch in Amazon Aurora to improve the performance of queries that join tables across indexes.
3. Enable Hash Joins to improve the database query performance.
4. Create Amazon Aurora Replicas.

Answer(s): 4

Explanation

Amazon Aurora MySQL and Amazon Aurora PostgreSQL support Amazon Aurora Replicas, which share the same underlying volume as the primary instance. Updates made by the primary are visible to all Amazon Aurora Replicas. With Amazon Aurora MySQL, you can also create MySQL Read Replicas based on MySQL's binlog-based replication engine. In MySQL Read Replicas, data from your primary instance is replayed on your replica as transactions. For most use cases, including read scaling and high availability, it is recommended using Amazon Aurora Replicas.

Read Replicas are primarily used for improving the read performance of the application. The most suitable solution in this scenario is to use Multi-AZ deployments instead but since this option is not available, you can still set up Read Replicas which you can promote as your primary stand-alone DB cluster in the event of an outage.

Hence, the correct answer here is to create Amazon Aurora Replicas.

Deploying Aurora to two Auto-Scaling groups of EC2 instances across two Availability Zones with an elastic load balancer which handles load balancing is incorrect because Aurora is a database engine for RDS and not deployed on a typical EC2 instance.

Enabling Hash Joins to improve the database query performance is incorrect because Hash Joins are mainly used if you need to join a large amount of data by using an equijoin and not for improving availability.

Using an Asynchronous Key Prefetch in Amazon Aurora to improve the performance of queries that join tables across indexes is incorrect because the Asynchronous Key Prefetch is mainly used to improve the performance of queries that join tables across indexes.

References:

https://docs.aws.amazon.com/AmazonRDS/latest/UserGuide/AuroraMySQL.Best Practices.html

https://aws.amazon.com/rds/aurora/faqs/

Question 61:

You are a Solutions Architect in an intelligence agency that is currently hosting a learning and training portal in AWS. Your manager instructed you to launch a large EC2 instance with an attached EBS Volume and enable Enhanced Networking. What are the valid case scenarios in using Enhanced Networking? (Select TWO.)

1. When you need a higher packet per second (PPS) performance
2. When you need a low packet-per-second performance
3. When you need a consistently lower inter-instance latencies
4. When you need high latency networking
5. When you need a dedicated connection to your on-premises data center

Answer(s): 1, 3

Explanation

Enhanced networking uses single root I/O virtualization (SR-IOV) to provide high-performance networking capabilities on supported instance types. SR-IOV is a method of device virtualization that provides higher I/O performance and lower CPU utilization when compared to traditional virtualized network interfaces. Enhanced networking provides higher bandwidth, higher packet per second (PPS) performance, and consistently lower inter-instance latencies. There is no additional charge for using enhanced networking.

The option that says: When you need a low packet-per-second performance is incorrect because you want to increase packet-per-second performance, and not lower it, when you enable enhanced networking.

The option that says: When you need high latency networking is incorrect because higher latencies means slower network, which is the opposite of what you want to happen when you enable enhanced networking.

The option that says: When you need a dedicated connection to your on-premises data center is incorrect because enabling enhanced networking does not provide a dedicated connection to your on-premises data center. Use AWS Direct Connect or enable VPN tunneling instead for this purpose.

Reference:

Question 62:

An online stock trading system is hosted in AWS and uses an Auto Scaling group of EC2 instances, an RDS database, and an Amazon ElastiCache for Redis. You need to improve the data security of your in-memory data store by requiring the user to enter a password before they are granted permission to execute Redis commands.

Which of the following should you do to meet the above requirement?

1. Authenticate the users using Redis AUTH by creating a new Redis Cluster with both the --transit-encryption-enabled and --auth-token parameters enabled.
2. Do nothing. This feature is already enabled by default.
3. Enable the in-transit encryption for Redis replication groups.
4. None of the above.
5. Create a new Redis replication group and set the AtRestEncryptionEnabled parameter to true.

Answer(s): 1

Explanation

Using Redis AUTH command can improve data security by requiring the user to enter a password before they are granted permission to execute Redis commands on a password-protected Redis server.

Hence, the correct answer is to authenticate the users using Redis AUTH by creating a new Redis Cluster with both the --transit-encryption-enabled and --auth-token parameters enabled.

To require that users enter a password on a password-protected Redis server, include the parameter --auth-token with the correct password when you create your replication group or cluster and on all subsequent commands to the replication group or cluster.

Enabling the in-transit encryption for Redis replication groups is incorrect because although in-transit encryption is part of the solution, it is missing the most important thing which is the Redis AUTH option.

Creating a new Redis replication group and setting the AtRestEncryptionEnabled parameter to true is incorrect because the Redis At-Rest Encryption feature only secures the data inside the in-memory data store. You have to use Redis AUTH option instead.

The option that says: Do nothing. This feature is already enabled by default is incorrect because the Redis AUTH option is disabled by default.

References:

https://docs.aws.amazon.com/AmazonElastiCache/latest/red-ug/auth.html

https://docs.aws.amazon.com/AmazonElastiCache/latest/red-ug/encryption.html

Question 63:

You are working as a Senior Solutions Architect for a data analytics company which has a VPC for their human resource department, and another VPC located on a different region for their finance department. You need to configure your architecture to allow the finance department to access all resources that are in the human resource department and vice versa.

Which type of networking connection in AWS should you set up to satisfy the above requirement?

1. VPC Endpoint
2. VPN Connection
3. Inter-Region VPC Peering
4. AWS Cloud Map

Answer(s): 3

Explanation

Amazon Virtual Private Cloud (Amazon VPC) offers a comprehensive set of virtual networking capabilities that provide AWS customers with many options for designing and implementing networks on the AWS cloud. With Amazon VPC, you can provision logically isolated virtual networks to host your AWS resources. You can create multiple VPCs within the same region or in different regions, in the same account or in different accounts. This is useful for customers who require multiple VPCs for security, billing, regulatory, or other purposes, and want to integrate AWS resources between their VPCs more easily. More often than not, these different VPCs need to communicate privately and securely with one another for sharing data or applications.

A VPC peering connection is a networking connection between two VPCs that enables you to route traffic between them privately. Instances in either VPC can communicate with each other as if they are within the same network. You can create a VPC peering connection between your own VPCs, with a VPC in another AWS account, or with a VPC in a different AWS Region.

AWS uses the existing infrastructure of a VPC to create a VPC peering connection; it is neither a gateway nor a VPN connection and does not rely on a separate piece of physical hardware. There is no single point of failure for communication or a bandwidth bottleneck.

Hence, the correct answer is: Inter-Region VPC Peering.

AWS Cloud Map is incorrect because this is simply a cloud resource discovery service. With Cloud Map, you can define custom names for your application resources, and it maintains the updated location of these dynamically changing resources. This increases your application availability because your web service always discovers the most up-to-date locations of its resources.

VPN Connection is incorrect because this does not let you share the resources of each VPC with each other. It only creates a network connection between the two VPCs.

VPC Endpoint is incorrect because this is primarily used to allow you to privately connect your VPC to supported AWS services and VPC endpoint services powered by PrivateLink, but not to the other VPC itself.

References:

https://docs.aws.amazon.com/AmazonVPC/latest/UserGuide/vpc-peering.html

https://aws.amazon.com/answers/networking/aws-multiple-region-multi-vpc-connectivity/

Here is a quick introduction to VPC Peering:

https://youtu.be/i1A1eH8vLtk

Question 64:

You deployed a web application to an EC2 instance that adds a variety of photo effects to a picture uploaded by the users. The application will put the generated photos to an S3 bucket by sending PUT requests to the S3 API.

What is the best option for this scenario considering that you need to have API credentials to be able to send a request to the S3 API?

1. Store the API credentials in the root web application directory of the EC2 instance.
2. Create a role in IAM. Afterwards, assign this role to a new EC2 instance.
3. Store your API credentials in Amazon Glacier.
4. Encrypt the API credentials and store in any directory of the EC2 instance.

Answer(s): 2

Explanation

The best option is to create a role in IAM. Afterwards, assign this role to a new EC2 instance. Applications must sign their API requests with AWS credentials. Therefore, if you are an application developer, you need a strategy for managing credentials for your applications that run on EC2 instances.

You can securely distribute your AWS credentials to the instances, enabling the applications on those instances to use your credentials to sign requests while protecting your credentials from other users. However, it's challenging to securely distribute credentials to each instance, especially those that AWS creates on your behalf such as Spot Instances or instances in Auto Scaling groups. You must also be able to update the credentials on each instance when you rotate your AWS credentials.

In this scenario, you have to use IAM roles so that your applications can securely make API requests from your instances without requiring you to manage the security credentials that the applications use. Instead of creating and distributing your AWS credentials, you can delegate permission to make API requests using IAM roles.

Encrypting the API credentials and storing in any directory of the EC2 instance and storing the API credentials in the root web application directory of the EC2 instance are incorrect. Though you can store and use the API credentials in the EC2 instance, it will be difficult to manage just as mentioned above. You have to use IAM Roles.

Storing your API credentials in Amazon S3 Glacier is incorrect as Amazon S3 Glacier is used for data archives and not for managing API credentials.

Reference:

http://docs.aws.amazon.com/AWSEC2/latest/UserGuide/iam-roles-for-amazon-ec2.html

Question 65:

A company would like to store their old yet confidential corporate files that are infrequently accessed. Which is the MOST cost-efficient solution in AWS that should you recommend?

1. Amazon S3
2. Amazon EBS
3. Amazon Storage Gateway
4. Amazon Glacier

Answer(s): 4

Explanation

Amazon Glacier is a secure, durable, and extremely low-cost cloud storage service for data archiving and long-term backup. It is designed to deliver 99.999999999% durability, and provides comprehensive security and compliance capabilities that can help meet even the most stringent regulatory requirements. Amazon Glacier provides query-in-place functionality, allowing you to run powerful analytics directly on your archive data at rest.

Reference:

https://aws.amazon.com/glacier/faqs/

PRACTICE TEST 6

AWS CERTIFIED SOLUTIONS ARCHITECT ASSOCIATE

AWS CERTIFIED SOLUTIONS ARCHITECT ASSOCIATE PRACTICE TEST 6

Question 1:

You are working for a large financial company. In their enterprise application, they want to apply a group of database-specific settings to their Relational Database Instances.

Which of the following options can be used to easily apply the settings in one go for all of the Relational database instances?

1. IAM Roles
2. Parameter Groups
3. Security Groups
4. NACL Groups

Answer(s): 2

Explanation

You manage your DB engine configuration through the use of parameters in a DB parameter group. DB parameter groups act as a container for engine configuration values that are applied to one or more DB instances.

Reference:

https://docs.aws.amazon.com/AmazonRDS/latest/UserGuide/USER_WorkingWit hParamGroups.html

Question 2:

A web application is hosted on an EC2 instance that processes sensitive financial information which is launched in a private subnet. All of the data are stored in an Amazon S3 bucket. The financial information is accessed by users over the Internet. The security team of the company is concerned that the Internet connectivity to Amazon S3 is a security risk.

In this scenario, what will you do to resolve this security vulnerability?

1. Change the web architecture to access the financial data hosted in your S3 bucket by creating a custom VPC endpoint service.
2. Change the web architecture to access the financial data through a Gateway VPC Endpoint.

3. Change the web architecture to access the financial data in S3 through an interface VPC endpoint, which is powered by AWS PrivateLink.
4. Change the web architecture to access the financial data in your S3 bucket through a VPN connection.

Answer(s): 2

Explanation

Take note that your VPC lives within a larger AWS network and the services, such as S3, DynamoDB, RDS and many others, are located outside of your VPC, but still within the AWS network. By default, the connection that your VPC uses to connect to your S3 bucket or any other service traverses the public Internet via your Internet Gateway.

A VPC endpoint enables you to privately connect your VPC to supported AWS services and VPC endpoint services powered by PrivateLink without requiring an internet gateway, NAT device, VPN connection, or AWS Direct Connect connection. Instances in your VPC do not require public IP addresses to communicate with resources in the service. Traffic between your VPC and the other service does not leave the Amazon network.

There are two types of VPC endpoints: interface endpoints and gateway endpoints. You have to create the type of VPC endpoint required by the supported service.

An interface endpoint is an elastic network interface with a private IP address that serves as an entry point for traffic destined to a supported service. A gateway endpoint is a gateway that is a target for a specified route in your route table, used for traffic destined to a supported AWS service. It is important to note that for Amazon S3 and DynamoDB service, you have to create a gateway endpoint and then use an interface endpoint for other services.

Changing the web architecture to access the financial data in your S3 bucket through a VPN connection is incorrect because a VPN connection still goes through the public Internet. You have to use a VPC Endpoint in this scenario and not VPN, to privately connect your VPC to supported AWS services such as S3.

Changing the web architecture to access the financial data hosted in your S3 bucket by creating a custom VPC endpoint service is incorrect because a "VPC endpoint service" is quite different from a "VPC endpoint". With VPC endpoint service, you are the service provider where you can create your own application in your VPC and configure it as an AWS PrivateLink-powered service (referred to as an endpoint service). Other AWS principals can create a connection from their VPC to your endpoint service using an interface VPC endpoint.

Changing the web architecture to access the financial data in S3 through an interface VPC endpoint, which is powered by AWS PrivateLink is incorrect because although you are correctly using a VPC Endpoint to satisfy the requirement, you chose a wrong type of VPC Endpoint. Remember that for S3 and DynamoDB service, you have to use a Gateway VPC Endpoint and not an Interface VPC Endpoint.

References:

https://docs.aws.amazon.com/AmazonVPC/latest/UserGuide/vpc-endpoints.html

https://docs.aws.amazon.com/vpc/latest/userguide/vpce-gateway.html

Question 3:

A company has an application hosted in an Amazon ECS Cluster behind an Application Load Balancer. The Solutions Architect is building a sophisticated web filtering solution that allows or blocks web requests based on the country that the requests originate from. However, the solution should still allow specific IP addresses from that country.

Which combination of steps should the Architect implement to satisfy this requirement? (Select TWO.)

1. Using AWS WAF, create a web ACL with a rule that explicitly allows requests from approved IP addresses declared in an IP Set.
2. Add another rule in the AWS WAF web ACL with a geo match condition that blocks requests that originate from a specific country.
3. Place a Transit Gateway in front of the VPC where the application is hosted and set up Network ACLs that block requests that originate from a specific country.
4. In the Application Load Balancer, create a listener rule that explicitly allows requests from approved IP addresses.
5. Set up a geo match condition in the Application Load Balancer that blocks requests from a specific country.

Answer(s): 1, 2

Explanation

If you want to allow or block web requests based on the country that the requests originate from, create one or more geo match conditions. A geo match condition lists countries that your requests originate from. Later in the process, when you create a web ACL, you specify whether to allow or block requests from those countries.

You can use geo match conditions with other AWS WAF Classic conditions or rules to build sophisticated filtering. For example, if you want to block certain countries but still allow specific IP addresses from that country, you could create a rule containing a geo match condition and an IP match condition. Configure the rule to block requests that originate from that country and do not match the approved IP addresses. As another example, if you want to prioritize resources for users in a particular country, you could include a geo match condition in two different rate-based rules. Set a higher rate limit for users in the preferred country and set a lower rate limit for all other users.

If you are using the CloudFront geo restriction feature to block a country from accessing your content, any request from that country is blocked and is not forwarded to AWS WAF Classic. So if you want to allow or block requests based on geography plus other AWS WAF Classic conditions, you should not use the CloudFront geo restriction feature. Instead, you should use an AWS WAF Classic geo match condition.

Hence, the correct answers are:

Using AWS WAF, create a web ACL with a rule that explicitly allows requests from approved IP addresses declared in an IP Set.

Add another rule in the AWS WAF web ACL with a geo match condition that blocks requests that originate from a specific country.

The option that says: In the Application Load Balancer, create a listener rule that explicitly allows requests from approved IP addresses is incorrect because a listener rule just checks for connection requests using the protocol and port that you configure. It only determines how the load balancer routes the requests to its registered targets.

The option that says: Set up a geo match condition in the Application Load Balancer that block requests that originate from a specific country is incorrect because you can't configure a geo match condition in an Application Load Balancer. You have to use AWS WAF instead.

The option that says: Place a Transit Gateway in front of the VPC where the application is hosted and set up Network ACLs that block requests that originate from a specific country is incorrect because AWS Transit Gateway is simply a service that enables customers to connect their Amazon Virtual Private Clouds (VPCs) and their on-premises networks to a single gateway. Using this type of gateway is not warranted in this scenario. Moreover, Network ACLs are not suitable for blocking requests from a specific country. You have to use AWS WAF instead.

References:

https://docs.aws.amazon.com/waf/latest/developerguide/classic-web-acl-geo-conditions.html

https://docs.aws.amazon.com/waf/latest/developerguide/how-aws-waf-works.html

Question 4:

A Solutions Architect is migrating several Windows-based applications to AWS that require a scalable file system storage for high-performance computing (HPC). The storage service must have full support for the SMB protocol and Windows NTFS, Active Directory (AD) integration, and Distributed File System (DFS).

Which of the following is the MOST suitable storage service that the Architect should use to fulfill this scenario?

1. Amazon FSx for Lustre
2. Amazon S3 Glacier Deep Archive
3. AWS DataSync
4. Amazon FSx for Windows File Server

Answer(s): 4

Explanation

Amazon FSx provides fully managed third-party file systems. Amazon FSx provides you with the native compatibility of third-party file systems with feature sets for workloads such as Windows-based storage, high-performance computing (HPC), machine learning, and electronic design automation (EDA). You don't have to worry about managing file servers and storage, as Amazon FSx automates the time-consuming administration tasks such as hardware provisioning, software configuration, patching, and backups. Amazon FSx integrates the file systems with cloud-native AWS services, making them even more useful for a broader set of workloads.

Amazon FSx provides you with two file systems to choose from: Amazon FSx for Windows File Server for Windows-based applications and Amazon FSx for Lustre for compute-intensive workloads.

For Windows-based applications, Amazon FSx provides fully managed Windows file servers with features and performance optimized for "lift-and-shift" business-critical application workloads including home directories (user shares), media workflows, and ERP applications. It is accessible from Windows and Linux instances via the SMB protocol. If you have Linux-based applications, Amazon EFS is a cloud-native fully managed file system that provides simple, scalable, elastic file storage accessible from Linux instances via the NFS protocol.

For compute-intensive and fast processing workloads, like high-performance computing (HPC), machine learning, EDA, and media processing, Amazon FSx for Lustre, provides a file system that's optimized for performance, with input and output stored on Amazon S3.

Hence, the correct answer is: Amazon FSx for Windows File Server.

Amazon S3 Glacier Deep Archive is incorrect because this service is primarily used as a secure, durable, and extremely low-cost cloud storage for data archiving and long-term backup.

AWS DataSync is incorrect because this service simply provides a fast way to move large amounts of data online between on-premises storage and Amazon S3 or Amazon Elastic File System (Amazon EFS).

Amazon FSx for Lustre is incorrect because this service doesn't support the Windows-based applications as well as Windows servers.

References:

https://aws.amazon.com/fsx/

https://aws.amazon.com/getting-started/use-cases/hpc/3/

Question 5:

You are working as an IT Consultant for a large media company where you are tasked to design a web application that stores static assets in an Amazon Simple Storage Service (S3) bucket. You expect this S3 bucket to immediately receive over 2000 PUT requests and 3500 GET requests per second at peak hour.

What should you do to ensure optimal performance?

1. Use a predictable naming scheme in the key names such as sequential numbers or date time sequences.
2. Use Byte-Range Fetches to retrieve multiple ranges of an object data per GET request.
3. Do nothing. Amazon S3 will automatically manage performance at this scale.
4. Add a random prefix to the key names.

Answer(s): 3

Explanation

Amazon S3 now provides increased performance to support at least 3,500 requests per second to add data and 5,500 requests per second to retrieve data, which can save significant processing time for no additional charge. Each S3 prefix can support these request rates, making it simple to increase performance significantly.

Applications running on Amazon S3 today will enjoy this performance improvement with no changes, and customers building new applications on S3 do not have to make any application customizations to achieve this performance. Amazon S3's support for parallel requests means you can scale your S3 performance by the factor of your compute cluster, without making any customizations to your application. Performance scales per prefix, so you can use as many prefixes as you need in parallel to achieve the required throughput. There are no limits to the number of prefixes.

This S3 request rate performance increase removes any previous guidance to randomize object prefixes to achieve faster performance. That means you can now use logical or sequential naming patterns in S3 object naming without any performance implications. This improvement is now available in all AWS Regions.

Using Byte-Range Fetches to retrieve multiple ranges of an object data per GET request is incorrect because although a Byte-Range Fetch helps you achieve higher aggregate throughput, Amazon S3 does not support retrieving multiple ranges of data per GET request. Using the Range HTTP header in a GET Object request, you can fetch a byte-range from an object, transferring only the specified portion. You can use concurrent connections to Amazon S3 to fetch different byte ranges from within the same object. Fetching smaller ranges of a large object also allows your application to improve retry times when requests are interrupted.

Adding a random prefix to the key names is incorrect. Adding a random prefix is not required in this scenario because S3 can now scale automatically to adjust perfomance. You do not need to add a random prefix anymore for this purpose since S3 has increased performance to support at least 3,500 requests per second to add data and 5,500 requests per second to retrieve data, which covers the workload in the scenario.

Using a predictable naming scheme in the key names such as sequential numbers or date time sequences is incorrect because Amazon S3 already maintains an index of object key names in each AWS region. S3 stores key names in alphabetical order. The key name dictates which partition the key is stored in. Using a sequential prefix increases the likelihood that Amazon S3 will target a specific partition for a large number of your keys, overwhelming the I/O capacity of the partition.

References:

https://docs.aws.amazon.com/AmazonS3/latest/dev/request-rate-perf-considerations.html

https://d1.awsstatic.com/whitepapers/AmazonS3BestPractices.pdf

https://docs.aws.amazon.com/AmazonS3/latest/dev/GettingObjectsUsingAPIs.html

Question 6:

You just joined a large tech company with an existing Amazon VPC. When reviewing the Auto Scaling events, you noticed that their web application is scaling up and down multiple times within the hour.

What design change could you make to optimize cost while preserving elasticity?

1. Increase the base number of Auto Scaling instances for the Auto Scaling group
2. Increase the instance type in the launch configuration

3. Change the cooldown period of the Auto Scaling group and set the CloudWatch metric to a higher threshold
4. Add provisioned IOPS to the instances

Answer(s): 3

Explanation

Since the application is scaling up and down multiple times within the hour, the issue lies on the cooldown period of the Auto Scaling group.

The cooldown period is a configurable setting for your Auto Scaling group that helps to ensure that it doesn't launch or terminate additional instances before the previous scaling activity takes effect. After the Auto Scaling group dynamically scales using a simple scaling policy, it waits for the cooldown period to complete before resuming scaling activities.

When you manually scale your Auto Scaling group, the default is not to wait for the cooldown period, but you can override the default and honor the cooldown period. If an instance becomes unhealthy, the Auto Scaling group does not wait for the cooldown period to complete before replacing the unhealthy instance.

Reference:

http://docs.aws.amazon.com/autoscaling/latest/userguide/as-scale-based-on-demand.html

Question 7:

You are assigned to design a highly available architecture in AWS. You have two target groups with three EC2 instances each, which are added to an Application Load Balancer. In the security group of the EC2 instance, you have verified that the port 80 for HTTP is allowed. However, the instances are still showing out of service from the load balancer.

What could be the root cause of this issue?

1. The wrong subnet was used in your VPC
2. The instances are using the wrong AMI.
3. The wrong instance type was used for the EC2 instance.
4. The health check configuration is not properly defined.

Answer(s): 4

Explanation

Since the security group is properly configured, the issue may be caused by a wrong health check configuration in the Target Group.

Your Application Load Balancer periodically sends requests to its registered targets to test their status. These tests are called health checks. Each load balancer node routes requests only to the healthy targets in the enabled Availability Zones for the load balancer. Each load balancer node checks the health of each target, using the health check settings for the target group with which the target is registered. After your target is registered, it must pass one health check to be considered healthy. After each health check is completed, the load balancer node closes the connection that was established for the health check.

Reference:

http://docs.aws.amazon.com/elasticloadbalancing/latest/classic/elb-healthchecks.html

Question 8:

You are consulted by a multimedia company that needs to deploy web services to an AWS region which they have never used before. The company currently has an IAM role for their Amazon EC2 instance which permits the instance to access Amazon DynamoDB. They want their EC2 instances in the new region to have the exact same privileges.

What should you do to accomplish this?

1. Assign the existing IAM role to instances in the new region.
2. In the new Region, create a new IAM role and associated policies then assign it to the new instance.
3. Duplicate the IAM role and associated policies to the new region and attach it to the instances.
4. Create an Amazon Machine Image (AMI) of the instance and copy it to the new region.

Answer(s): 1

Explanation

In this scenario, the company has an existing IAM role hence you don't need to create a new one. IAM roles are global service that are available to all regions hence, all you have to do is assign the existing IAM role to the instance in the new region.

The option that says: In the new Region, create a new IAM role and associated policies then assign it to the new instance is incorrect because you don't need to create another IAM role - there is already an existing one.

Duplicating the IAM role and associated policies to the new region and attaching it to the instances is incorrect as you don't need duplicate IAM roles for each region. One IAM role suffices for the instances on two regions.

Creating an Amazon Machine Image (AMI) of the instance and copying it to the new region is incorrect because creating an AMI image does not affect the IAM role of the instance.

Reference:

https://docs.aws.amazon.com/AmazonS3/latest/dev/NotificationHowTo.html

Question 9:

A Junior DevOps Engineer deployed a large EBS-backed EC2 instance to host a NodeJS web app in AWS which was developed by an IT contractor. He properly configured the security group and used a key pair named "tutorialsfreekey" which has a tutorialsfreekey.pem private key file. The EC2 instance works as expected and the junior DevOps engineer can connect to it using an SSH connection. The IT contractor was also given the key pair and he has made various changes in the instance as well to the files located in .ssh folder to make the NodeJS app work. After a few weeks, the IT contractor and the junior DevOps engineer cannot connect the EC2 instance anymore, even with a valid private key file. They are constantly getting a "Server refused our key" error even though their private key is valid.

In this scenario, which one of the following options is not a possible reason for this issue?

1. The SSH private key that you are using has a file permission of 0777.
2. You're using an SSH private key but the corresponding public key is not in the authorized_keys file.
3. You don't have permissions for the .ssh folder.
4. You don't have permissions for your authorized_keys file.

Answer(s): 1

Explanation

All of the options here are correct except for the option that says: The SSH private key that you are using has a file permission of 0777 because if the private key that you are using has a file permission of 0777, then it will throw an "Unprotected Private Key File" error and not a "Server refused our key" error.

You might be unable to log into an EC2 instance if:

- You're using an SSH private key but the corresponding public key is not in the authorized_keys file.

- You don't have permissions for your authorized_keys file.

- You don't have permissions for the .ssh folder.

- Your authorized_keys file or .ssh folder isn't named correctly.

- Your authorized_keys file or .ssh folder was deleted.

- Your instance was launched without a key, or it was launched with an incorrect key.

To connect to your EC2 instance after receiving the error "Server refused our key," you can update the instance's user data to append the specified SSH public key to the authorized_keys file, which sets the appropriate ownership and file permissions for the SSH directory and files contained in it.

Reference:

https://aws.amazon.com/premiumsupport/knowledge-center/ec2-server-refused-our-key/

Question 10:

A leading bank has an application that is hosted on an Auto Scaling group of EBS-backed EC2 instances. As the Solutions Architect, you need to provide the ability to fully restore the data stored in their EBS volumes by using EBS snapshots.

Which of the following approaches provide the lowest cost for Amazon Elastic Block Store snapshots?

1. Maintain two snapshots: the original snapshot and the latest incremental snapshot.
2. Maintain a volume snapshot; subsequent snapshots will overwrite one another.
3. Just maintain a single snapshot of the EBS volume since the latest snapshot is both incremental and complete.
4. Maintain the most current snapshot and then archive the original and incremental snapshots to Amazon Glacier.

Answer(s): 3

Explanation

To meet the requirement on this scenario, you can just maintain a single snapshot of the EBS volume since its latest snapshot is both incremental and complete.

You can back up the data on your Amazon EBS volumes to Amazon S3 by taking point-in-time snapshots. Snapshots are incremental backups, which means that only the blocks on the device that have changed after your most recent snapshot are saved. This minimizes the time required to create the snapshot and saves on storage costs by not duplicating data.

When you delete a snapshot, only the data unique to that snapshot is removed. Each snapshot contains all of the information needed to restore your data (from the moment the snapshot was taken) to a new EBS volume.

Reference:

http://docs.aws.amazon.com/AWSEC2/latest/UserGuide/EBSSnapshots.html

Question 11:

A financial company wants to store their data in Amazon S3 but at the same time, they want to store their frequently accessed data locally on their on-premises server. This is due to the fact that they do not have the option to extend their on-premises storage, which is why they are looking for a durable and scalable storage service to use in AWS.

What is the best solution for this scenario?

1. Use the Amazon Storage Gateway - Cached Volumes.
2. Use a fleet of EC2 instance with EBS volumes to store the commonly used data.
3. Use Amazon Glacier.
4. Use both Elasticache and S3 for frequently accessed data.

Answer(s): 1

Explanation

By using Cached volumes, you store your data in Amazon Simple Storage Service (Amazon S3) and retain a copy of frequently accessed data subsets locally in your on-premises network. Cached volumes offer substantial cost savings on primary storage and minimize the need to scale your storage on-premises. You also retain low-latency access to your frequently accessed data. This is the best solution for this scenario.

Using a fleet of EC2 instance with EBS volumes to store the commonly used data is incorrect because an EC2 instance is not a storage service and it does not provide the required durability and scalability.

Using both Elasticache and S3 for frequently accessed data is incorrect as this is not efficient. Moreover, the question explicitly said that the frequently accessed data should be stored locally on their on-premises server and not on AWS.

Using Amazon Glacier is incorrect as this is mainly used for data archiving.

Reference:

https://aws.amazon.com/storagegateway/faqs/

Question 12:

You are setting up a configuration management in your existing cloud architecture where you have to deploy and manage your EC2 instances including the other AWS resources using Chef and Puppet. Which of the following is the most suitable service to use in this scenario?

1. AWS OpsWorks
2. AWS CodeDeploy
3. AWS CloudFormation
4. AWS Elastic Beanstalk

Answer(s): 1

Explanation

AWS OpsWorks is a configuration management service that provides managed instances of Chef and Puppet. Chef and Puppet are automation platforms that allow you to use code to automate the configurations of your servers. OpsWorks lets you use Chef and Puppet to automate how servers are configured, deployed, and managed across your Amazon EC2 instances or on-premises compute environments.

Reference:

https://aws.amazon.com/opsworks/

Question 13:

An application is hosted in an On-Demand EC2 instance and is using Amazon SDK to communicate to other AWS services such as S3, DynamoDB, and many others. As part of the upcoming IT audit, you need to ensure that all API calls to your AWS resources are logged and durably stored.

Which is the most suitable service that you should use to meet this requirement?

1. AWS CloudTrail
2. Amazon API Gateway
3. AWS X-Ray
4. Amazon CloudWatch

Answer(s): 1

Explanation

AWS CloudTrail increases visibility into your user and resource activity by recording AWS Management Console actions and API calls. You can identify which users and accounts called AWS, the source IP address from which the calls were made, and when the calls occurred.

Amazon CloudWatch is incorrect because this is primarily used for systems monitoring based on the server metrics. It does not have the capability to track API calls to your AWS resources.

AWS X-Ray is incorrect because this is usually used to debug and analyze your microservices applications with request tracing so you can find the root cause of issues and performance. Unlike CloudTrail, it does not record the API calls that were made to your AWS resources.

Amazon API Gateway is incorrect because this is not used for logging each and every API call to your AWS resources. It is a fully managed service that makes it easy for developers to create, publish, maintain, monitor, and secure APIs at any scale.

Reference:

https://aws.amazon.com/cloudtrail/

Question 14:

You are working for a top IT Consultancy that has a VPC with two On-Demand EC2 instances with Elastic IP addresses. You were notified that your EC2 instances are currently under SSH brute force attacks over the Internet. Their IT Security team has identified the IP addresses where these attacks originated. You have to immediately implement a temporary fix to stop these attacks while the team is setting up AWS WAF, GuardDuty, and AWS Shield Advanced to permanently fix the security vulnerability.

Which of the following provides the quickest way to stop the attacks to your instances?

1. Assign a static Anycast IP address to each EC2 instance
2. Place the EC2 instances into private subnets
3. Remove the Internet Gateway from the VPC
4. Block the IP addresses in the Network Access Control List

Answer(s): 4

Explanation

A network access control list (ACL) is an optional layer of security for your VPC that acts as a firewall for controlling traffic in and out of one or more subnets. You might set up network ACLs with rules similar to your security groups in order to add an additional layer of security to your VPC.

The following are the basic things that you need to know about network ACLs:

- Your VPC automatically comes with a modifiable default network ACL. By default, it allows all inbound and outbound IPv4 traffic and, if applicable, IPv6 traffic.

- You can create a custom network ACL and associate it with a subnet. By default, each custom network ACL denies all inbound and outbound traffic until you add rules.

- Each subnet in your VPC must be associated with a network ACL. If you don't explicitly associate a subnet with a network ACL, the subnet is automatically associated with the default network ACL.

- You can associate a network ACL with multiple subnets; however, a subnet can be associated with only one network ACL at a time. When you associate a network ACL with a subnet, the previous association is removed.

- A network ACL contains a numbered list of rules that we evaluate in order, starting with the lowest numbered rule, to determine whether traffic is allowed in or out of any subnet associated with the network ACL. The highest number that you can use for a rule is 32766. We recommend that you start by creating rules in increments (for example, increments of 10 or 100) so that you can insert new rules where you need to later on.

- A network ACL has separate inbound and outbound rules, and each rule can either allow or deny traffic.

- Network ACLs are stateless; responses to allowed inbound traffic are subject to the rules for outbound traffic (and vice versa).

The scenario clearly states that it requires the quickest way to fix the security vulnerability. In this situation, you can manually block the offending IP addresses using Network ACLs since the IT Security team already identified the list of offending IP addresses. Alternatively, you can set up a bastion host however, this option entails additional time to properly set up as you have to configure the security configurations of your bastion host.

Hence, blocking the IP addresses in the Network Access Control List is the best answer since it can quickly resolve the issue by blocking the IP addresses using Network ACL.

Placing the EC2 instances into private subnets is incorrect because if you deploy the EC2 instance in the private subnet without public or EIP address, it would not be accessible over the Internet, even to you.

Removing the Internet Gateway from the VPC is incorrect because doing this will also make your EC2 instance inaccessible to you as it will cut down the connection to the Internet.

Assigning a static Anycast IP address to each EC2 instance is incorrect because a static Anycast IP address is primarily used by AWS Global Accelerator to enable organizations to seamlessly route traffic to multiple regions and improve availability and performance for their end-users.

References:

https://docs.aws.amazon.com/AmazonVPC/latest/UserGuide/VPC_ACLs.html

https://docs.aws.amazon.com/vpc/latest/userguide/VPC_Security.html

Question 15:

A news company is planning to use a Hardware Security Module (CloudHSM) in AWS for secure key storage of their web applications. You have launched the CloudHSM cluster but after just a few hours, a support staff mistakenly attempted to log in as the administrator three times using an invalid password in the Hardware Security Module. This has caused the HSM to be zeroized, which means that the encryption keys on it have been wiped. Unfortunately, you did not have a copy of the keys stored anywhere else.

How can you obtain a new copy of the keys that you have stored on Hardware Security Module?

1. Contact AWS Support and they will provide you a copy of the keys.
2. Use the Amazon CLI to get a copy of the keys.
3. Restore a snapshot of the Hardware Security Module.
4. The keys are lost permanently if you did not have a copy.

Answer(s): 4

Explanation

Attempting to log in as the administrator more than twice with the wrong password zeroizes your HSM appliance. When an HSM is zeroized, all keys, certificates, and other data on the HSM is destroyed. You can use your cluster's security group to prevent an unauthenticated user from zeroizing your HSM.

Amazon does not have access to your keys nor to the credentials of your Hardware Security Module (HSM) and therefore has no way to recover your keys if you lose your credentials. Amazon strongly recommends that you use two or more HSMs in separate Availability Zones in any production CloudHSM Cluster to avoid loss of cryptographic keys.

Refer to the CloudHSM FAQs for Reference:

Q: Could I lose my keys if a single HSM instance fails?

Yes. It is possible to lose keys that were created since the most recent daily backup if the CloudHSM cluster that you are using fails and you are not using two or more HSMs. Amazon strongly recommends that you use two or more HSMs, in separate Availability Zones, in any production CloudHSM Cluster to avoid loss of cryptographic keys.

Q: Can Amazon recover my keys if I lose my credentials to my HSM?

No. Amazon does not have access to your keys or credentials and therefore has no way to recover your keys if you lose your credentials.

References:

https://aws.amazon.com/premiumsupport/knowledge-center/stop-cloudhsm/

https://aws.amazon.com/cloudhsm/faqs/

https://d1.awsstatic.com/whitepapers/Security/security-of-aws-cloudhsm-backups.pdf

Question 16:

A company has recently adopted a hybrid cloud architecture and is planning to migrate a database hosted on-premises to AWS. The database currently has over 12 TB of consumer data, handles highly transactional (OLTP) workloads, and is expected to grow exponentially. The Solutions Architect should ensure that the database is ACID-compliant and can handle complex queries of the application.

Which type of database service should the Architect use?

1. Amazon RDS
2. Amazon DynamoDB
3. Amazon Aurora
4. Amazon Redshift

Answer(s): 3

Explanation

Amazon Aurora (Aurora) is a fully managed relational database engine that's compatible with MySQL and PostgreSQL. You already know how MySQL and

PostgreSQL combine the speed and reliability of high-end commercial databases with the simplicity and cost-effectiveness of open-source databases. The code, tools, and applications you use today with your existing MySQL and PostgreSQL databases can be used with Aurora. With some workloads, Aurora can deliver up to five times the throughput of MySQL and up to three times the throughput of PostgreSQL without requiring changes to most of your existing applications.

Aurora includes a high-performance storage subsystem. Its MySQL- and PostgreSQL-compatible database engines are customized to take advantage of that fast distributed storage. The underlying storage grows automatically as needed, up to 64 tebibytes (TiB). Aurora also automates and standardizes database clustering and replication, which are typically among the most challenging aspects of database configuration and administration.

For Amazon RDS MariaDB DB instances, the maximum provisioned storage limit constrains the size of a table to a maximum size of 16 TB when using InnoDB file-per-table tablespaces. This limit also constrains the system tablespace to a maximum size of 16 TB. InnoDB file-per-table tablespaces (with tables each in their own tablespace) is set by default for Amazon RDS MariaDB DB instances.

Hence, the correct answer is Amazon Aurora.

Amazon Redshift is incorrect because this is primarily used for OLAP applications and not for OLTP. Moreover, it doesn't scale automatically to handle the exponential growth of the database.

Amazon DynamoDB is incorrect because although you can use this to have an ACID-compliant database, it is not capable of handling complex queries and highly transactional (OLTP) workloads.

Amazon RDS is incorrect because although this service can host an ACID-compliant relational database that can handle complex queries and transactional (OLTP) workloads, it is still not scalable to handle the growth of the database. Amazon Aurora is the better choice as its underlying storage can grow automatically as needed.

References:

https://aws.amazon.com/rds/aurora/

https://docs.aws.amazon.com/amazondynamodb/latest/developerguide/SQLtoNoSQL.html

https://aws.amazon.com/nosql/

Question 17:

Your manager instructed you to use Route 53 instead of an ELB to load balance the incoming request to your web application. The system is deployed to two EC2 instances to which the traffic needs to be distributed to. You want to set a specific percentage of traffic to go to each instance.

Which routing policy would you use?

1. Geolocation
2. Weighted
3. Failover
4. Latency

Answer(s): 2

Explanation

Weighted routing lets you associate multiple resources with a single domain name (example.com) or subdomain name (acme.example.com) and choose how much traffic is routed to each resource. This can be useful for a variety of purposes including load balancing and testing new versions of software. You can set a specific percentage of how much traffic will be allocated to the resource by specifying the weights.

For example, if you want to send a tiny portion of your traffic to one resource and the rest to another resource, you might specify weights of 1 and 255. The resource with a weight of 1 gets 1/256th of the traffic (1/1+255), and the other resource gets 255/256ths (255/1+255).

You can gradually change the balance by changing the weights. If you want to stop sending traffic to a resource, you can change the weight for that record to 0.

Reference:

http://docs.aws.amazon.com/Route53/latest/DeveloperGuide/routing-policy.html

Question 18:

You are running an EC2 instance store-based instance. You shut it down and then start the instance. You noticed that the data which you have saved earlier is no longer available.

What might be the cause of this?

1. The volume of the instance was not big enough to handle all of the processing data.
2. The instance was hit by a virus that wipes out all data.
3. The EC2 instance was using EBS backed root volumes, which are ephemeral and only live for the life of the instance.

4. The EC2 instance was using instance store volumes, which are ephemeral and only live for the life of the instance.

Answer(s): 4

Explanation

An instance store provides temporary block-level storage for your instance. This storage is located on disks that are physically attached to the host computer. Instance store is ideal for temporary storage of information that changes frequently, such as buffers, caches, scratch data, and other temporary content, or for data that is replicated across a fleet of instances, such as a load-balanced pool of web servers.

An instance store consists of one or more instance store volumes exposed as block devices. The size of an instance store as well as the number of devices available varies by instance type. While an instance store is dedicated to a particular instance, the disk subsystem is shared among instances on a host computer.

The data in an instance store persists only during the lifetime of its associated instance. If an instance reboots (intentionally or unintentionally), data in the instance store persists. However, data in the instance store is lost under the following circumstances:

- The underlying disk drive fails

- The instance stops

- The instance terminates

Reference:

http://docs.aws.amazon.com/AWSEC2/latest/UserGuide/InstanceStorage.html

Question 19:

You are setting up a cost-effective architecture for a log processing application which has frequently accessed, throughput-intensive workloads with large, sequential I/O operations. The application should be hosted in an already existing On-Demand EC2 instance in your VPC. You have to attach a new EBS volume that will be used by the application.

Which of the following is the most suitable EBS volume type that you should use in this scenario?

1. EBS Throughput Optimized HDD (st1)
2. EBS Cold HDD (sc1)
3. EBS General Purpose SSD (gp2)
4. EBS Provisioned IOPS SSD (io1)

Answer(s): 1

Explanation

In the exam, always consider the difference between SSD and HDD as shown on the table below. This will allow you to easily eliminate specific EBS-types in the options which are not SSD or not HDD, depending on whether the question asks for a storage type which has small, random I/O operations or large, sequential I/O operations.

Since the scenario has workloads with large, sequential I/O operations, we can narrow down our options by selecting HDD volumes, instead of SDD volumes which are more suitable for small, random I/O operations.

Throughput Optimized HDD (st1) volumes provide low-cost magnetic storage that defines performance in terms of throughput rather than IOPS. This volume type is a good fit for large, sequential workloads such as Amazon EMR, ETL, data warehouses, and log processing. Bootable st1 volumes are not supported.

Throughput Optimized HDD (st1) volumes, though similar to Cold HDD (sc1) volumes, are designed to support frequently accessed data.

EBS Provisioned IOPS SSD (io1) is incorrect because Amazon EBS Provisioned IOPS SSD is not the most cost-effective EBS type and is primarily used for critical business applications that require sustained IOPS performance.

EBS General Purpose SSD (gp2) is incorrect because although an Amazon EBS General Purpose SSD volume balances price and performance for a wide variety of workloads, it is not suitable for frequently accessed, throughput-intensive workloads. Throughput Optimized HDD is a more suitable option to use than General Purpose SSD.

EBS Cold HDD (sc1) is incorrect because although this provides lower cost HDD volume compared to General Purpose SSD, it is much suitable for less frequently accessed workloads.

Reference:

https://docs.aws.amazon.com/AWSEC2/latest/UserGuide/EBSVolumeTypes.html #EBSVolumeTypes_st1

Question 20:

A company is planning to launch a High Performance Computing (HPC) cluster in AWS that does Computational Fluid Dynamics (CFD) simulations. The solution should scale-out their simulation jobs to experiment with more tunable parameters for faster and more accurate results. The cluster is composed of Windows servers hosted on t3a.medium EC2 instances. As the Solutions Architect, you should ensure that the architecture provides higher bandwidth, higher packet per second (PPS) performance, and consistently lower inter-instance latencies.

Which is the MOST suitable and cost-effective solution that the Architect should implement to achieve the above requirements?

Enable Enhanced Networking with Elastic Fabric Adapter (EFA) on the Windows EC2 Instances.

1. Enable Enhanced Networking with Intel 82599 Virtual Function (VF) interface on the Windows EC2 Instances.
2. Use AWS ParallelCluster to deploy and manage the HPC cluster to provide higher bandwidth, higher packet per second (PPS) performance, and lower inter-instance latencies.
3. Enable Enhanced Networking with Elastic Network Adapter (ENA) on the Windows EC2 Instances.

Answer(s): 3

Explanation

Enhanced networking uses single root I/O virtualization (SR-IOV) to provide high-performance networking capabilities on supported instance types. SR-IOV is a method of device virtualization that provides higher I/O performance and lower CPU utilization when compared to traditional virtualized network interfaces. Enhanced networking provides higher bandwidth, higher packet per second (PPS) performance, and consistently lower inter-instance latencies. There is no additional charge for using enhanced networking.

Amazon EC2 provides enhanced networking capabilities through the Elastic Network Adapter (ENA). It supports network speeds of up to 100 Gbps for supported instance types. Elastic Network Adapters (ENAs) provide traditional IP networking features that are required to support VPC networking.

An Elastic Fabric Adapter (EFA) is simply an Elastic Network Adapter (ENA) with added capabilities. It provides all of the functionality of an ENA, with additional OS-bypass functionality. OS-bypass is an access model that allows HPC and machine learning applications to communicate directly with the network interface hardware to provide low-latency, reliable transport functionality.

The OS-bypass capabilities of EFAs are not supported on Windows instances. If you attach an EFA to a Windows instance, the instance functions as an Elastic Network Adapter, without the added EFA capabilities.

Hence, the correct answer is to enable Enhanced Networking with Elastic Network Adapter (ENA) on the Windows EC2 Instances.

Enabling Enhanced Networking with Elastic Fabric Adapter (EFA) on the Windows EC2 Instances is incorrect because the OS-bypass capabilities of the Elastic Fabric

Adapter (EFA) are not supported on Windows instances. Although you can attach EFA to your Windows instances, this will just act as a regular Elastic Network Adapter, without the added EFA capabilities. Moreover, it doesn't support the t3a.medium instance type that is being used in the HPC cluster.

Enabling Enhanced Networking with Intel 82599 Virtual Function (VF) interface on the Windows EC2 Instances is incorrect because although you can attach an Intel 82599 Virtual Function (VF) interface on your Windows EC2 Instances to improve its networking capabilities, it doesn't support the t3a.medium instance type that is being used in the HPC cluster.

Using AWS ParallelCluster to deploy and manage the HPC cluster to provide higher bandwidth, higher packet per second (PPS) performance, and lower inter-instance latencies is incorrect because an AWS ParallelCluster is just an AWS-supported open-source cluster management tool that makes it easy for you to deploy and manage High Performance Computing (HPC) clusters on AWS. It does not provide higher bandwidth, higher packet per second (PPS) performance, and lower inter-instance latencies, unlike ENA or EFA.

References:

https://docs.aws.amazon.com/AWSEC2/latest/UserGuide/enhanced-networking.html

https://docs.aws.amazon.com/AWSEC2/latest/UserGuide/efa.html

Question 21:

The start-up company that you are working for has a batch job application that is currently hosted on an EC2 instance. It is set to process messages from a queue created in SQS with default settings. You configured the application to process the messages once a week. After 2 weeks, you noticed that not all messages are being processed by the application.

What is the root cause of this issue?

1. Amazon SQS has automatically deleted the messages that have been in a queue for more than the maximum message retention period.
2. Missing permissions in SQS.
3. The SQS queue is set to short-polling.
4. The batch job application is configured to long polling.

Answer(s): 1

Explanation

Amazon SQS automatically deletes messages that have been in a queue for more than the maximum message retention period. The default message retention period is 4 days. Since the queue is configured to the default settings and the batch job application only processes the messages once a week, the messages that are in the queue for more than 4 days are deleted. This is the root cause of the issue.

To fix this, you can increase the message retention period to a maximum of 14 days using the SetQueueAttributes action.

References:

https://aws.amazon.com/sqs/faqs/

https://docs.aws.amazon.com/AWSSimpleQueueService/latest/SQSDeveloperGuid e/sqs-message-lifecycle.html

Question 22:

Your IT Director instructed you to ensure that all of the AWS resources in your VPC don't go beyond their respective service limits. You should prepare a system that provides you real-time guidance in provisioning your resources that adheres to the AWS best practices.

Which of the following is the MOST appropriate service to use to satisfy this task?

1. AWS Budgets
2. Amazon Inspector
3. AWS Cost Explorer
4. AWS Trusted Advisor

Answer(s): 4

Explanation

AWS Trusted Advisor is an online tool that provides you real-time guidance to help you provision your resources following AWS best practices. It inspects your AWS environment and makes recommendations for saving money, improving system performance and reliability, or closing security gaps.

Whether establishing new workflows, developing applications, or as part of ongoing improvement, take advantage of the recommendations provided by Trusted Advisor on a regular basis to help keep your solutions provisioned optimally.

Trusted Advisor includes an ever-expanding list of checks in the following five categories:

Cost Optimization – recommendations that can potentially save you money by highlighting unused resources and opportunities to reduce your bill.

Security – identification of security settings that could make your AWS solution less secure.

Fault Tolerance – recommendations that help increase the resiliency of your AWS solution by highlighting redundancy shortfalls, current service limits, and over-utilized resources.

Performance – recommendations that can help to improve the speed and responsiveness of your applications.

Service Limits – recommendations that will tell you when service usage is more than 80% of the service limit.

Hence, the correct answer in this scenario is AWS Trusted Advisor.

AWS Cost Explorer is incorrect because this is just a tool that enables you to view and analyze your costs and usage. You can explore your usage and costs using the main graph, the Cost Explorer cost and usage reports, or the Cost Explorer RI reports. It has an easy-to-use interface that lets you visualize, understand, and manage your AWS costs and usage over time.

AWS Budgets is incorrect because it simply gives you the ability to set custom budgets that alert you when your costs or usage exceed (or are forecasted to exceed) your budgeted amount. You can also use AWS Budgets to set reservation utilization or coverage targets and receive alerts when your utilization drops below the threshold you define.

Amazon Inspector is incorrect because it is just an automated security assessment service that helps improve the security and compliance of applications deployed on AWS. Amazon Inspector automatically assesses applications for exposure, vulnerabilities, and deviations from best practices.

References:

https://aws.amazon.com/premiumsupport/technology/trusted-advisor/

https://aws.amazon.com/premiumsupport/technology/trusted-advisor/faqs/

Question 23:

You are working as a Principal Solutions Architect for a leading digital news company which has both an on-premises data center as well as an AWS cloud infrastructure. They store their graphics, audios, videos, and other multimedia assets primarily in their on-premises storage server and use an S3 Standard storage class bucket as a backup. Their data are heavily used for only a week (7 days) but after that period, it will only be infrequently used by their customers. You are instructed to save storage costs in AWS yet maintain the ability to fetch a subset of their media assets in a matter of minutes for a surprise annual data audit, which will be conducted on their cloud storage.

Which of the following are valid options that you can implement to meet the above requirement? (Select TWO.)

1. Set a lifecycle policy in the bucket to transition the data to Glacier after one week (7 days).
2. Set a lifecycle policy in the bucket to transition the data to S3 Glacier Deep Archive storage class after one week (7 days).
3. Set a lifecycle policy in the bucket to transition the data to S3 - One Zone-Infrequent Access storage class after one week (7 days).
4. Set a lifecycle policy in the bucket to transition the data to S3 - Standard IA storage class after one week (7 days).
5. Set a lifecycle policy in the bucket to transition to S3 - Standard IA after 30 days

Answer(s): 1, 5

Explanation

You can add rules in a lifecycle configuration to tell Amazon S3 to transition objects to another Amazon S3 storage class. For example: When you know that objects are infrequently accessed, you might transition them to the STANDARD_IA storage class. Or transition your data to the GLACIER storage class in case you want to archive objects that you don't need to access in real time.

In a lifecycle configuration, you can define rules to transition objects from one storage class to another to save on storage costs. When you don't know the access patterns of your objects or your access patterns are changing over time, you can transition the objects to the INTELLIGENT_TIERING storage class for automatic cost savings.

The lifecycle storage class transitions have a constraint when you want to transition from the STANDARD storage classes to either STANDARD_IA or ONEZONE_IA. The following constraints apply:

- For larger objects, there is a cost benefit for transitioning to STANDARD_IA or ONEZONE_IA. Amazon S3 does not transition objects that are smaller than 128 KB to the STANDARD_IA or ONEZONE_IA storage classes because it's not cost effective.

- Objects must be stored at least 30 days in the current storage class before you can transition them to STANDARD_IA or ONEZONE_IA. For example, you cannot create a lifecycle rule to transition objects to the STANDARD_IA storage class one day after you create them. Amazon S3 doesn't transition objects within the first 30 days because newer objects are often accessed more frequently or deleted sooner than is suitable for STANDARD_IA or ONEZONE_IA storage.

- If you are transitioning noncurrent objects (in versioned buckets), you can transition only objects that are at least 30 days noncurrent to STANDARD_IA or ONEZONE_IA storage.

Since there is a time constraint in transitioning objects in S3, you can only change the storage class of your objects from S3 Standard storage class to STANDARD_IA or ONEZONE_IA storage after 30 days. This limitation does not apply on INTELLIGENT_TIERING, GLACIER, and DEEP_ARCHIVE storage class.

In addition, the requirement says that the media assets should be fetched in a matter of minutes for a surprise annual data audit. This means that the retrieval will only happen once a year. You can use expedited retrievals in Glacier which will allow you to quickly access your data (within 1–5 minutes) when occasional urgent requests for a subset of archives are required.

In this scenario, you can set a lifecycle policy in the bucket to transition to S3 - Standard IA after 30 days or alternatively, you can directly transition your data to Glacier after one week (7 days).

Hence, the following are the correct answers:

- Set a lifecycle policy in the bucket to transition the data from Standard storage class to Glacier after one week (7 days).

- Set a lifecycle policy in the bucket to transition to S3 - Standard IA after 30 days.

Setting a lifecycle policy in the bucket to transition the data to S3 - Standard IA storage class after one week (7 days) and setting a lifecycle policy in the bucket to transition the data to S3 - One Zone-Infrequent Access storage class after one week (7 days) are both incorrect because there is a constraint in S3 that objects must be stored at least 30 days in the current storage class before you can transition them to STANDARD_IA or ONEZONE_IA. You cannot create a lifecycle rule to transition objects to either STANDARD_IA or ONEZONE_IA storage class 7 days after you create them because you can only do this after the 30-day period has elapsed. Hence, these options are incorrect.

Setting a lifecycle policy in the bucket to transition the data to S3 Glacier Deep Archive storage class after one week (7 days) is incorrect because although DEEP_ARCHIVE storage class provides the most cost-effective storage option, it does not have the ability to do expedited retrievals, unlike Glacier. In the event that the surprise annual data audit happens, it may take several hours before you can retrieve your data.

References:

https://docs.aws.amazon.com/AmazonS3/latest/dev/lifecycle-transition-general-considerations.html

https://docs.aws.amazon.com/AmazonS3/latest/dev/restoring-objects.html

https://aws.amazon.com/s3/storage-classes/

Question 24:

You have EC2 instances running on your VPC. You have both UAT and production EC2 instances running. You want to ensure that employees who are responsible for the UAT instances don't have the access to work on the production instances to minimize security risks.

Which of the following would be the best way to achieve this?

1. Provide permissions to the users via the AWS Resource Access Manager (RAM) service to only access EC2 instances that are used for production or development.
2. Define the tags on the UAT and production servers and add a condition to the IAM policy which allows access to specific tags.
3. Launch the UAT and production instances in different Availability Zones and use Multi Factor Authentication.
4. Launch the UAT and production EC2 instances in separate VPC's connected by VPC peering.

Answer(s): 2

Explanation

For this scenario, the best way to achieve the required solution is to use a combination of Tags and IAM policies. You can define the tags on the UAT and production EC2 instances and add a condition to the IAM policy which allows access to specific tags.

Tags enable you to categorize your AWS resources in different ways, for example, by purpose, owner, or environment. This is useful when you have many resources of the same type — you can quickly identify a specific resource based on the tags you've assigned to it.

By default, IAM users don't have permission to create or modify Amazon EC2 resources, or perform tasks using the Amazon EC2 API. (This means that they also can't do so using the Amazon EC2 console or CLI.) To allow IAM users to create or modify resources and perform tasks, you must create IAM policies that grant IAM users permission to use the specific resources and API actions they'll need, and then attach those policies to the IAM users or groups that require those permissions.

Hence, the correct answer is: Define the tags on the UAT and production servers and add a condition to the IAM policy which allows access to specific tags.

The option that says: Launch the UAT and production EC2 instances in separate VPC's connected by VPC peering is incorrect because these are just network changes to your cloud architecture and doesn't have any effect on the security permissions of your users to access your EC2 instances.

The option that says: Provide permissions to the users via the AWS Resource Access Manager (RAM) service to only access EC2 instances that are used for production or development is incorrect because the AWS Resource Access Manager (RAM) is primarily used to securely share your resources across AWS accounts or within your Organization and not on a single AWS account. You also have to set up a custom IAM Policy in order for this to work.

The option that says: Launch the UAT and production instances in different Availability Zones and use Multi Factor Authentication is incorrect because placing the EC2 instances to different AZs will only improve the availability of the systems but won't have any significance in terms of security. You have to set up an IAM Policy that allows access to EC2 instances based on their tags. In addition, a Multi-Factor Authentication is not a suitable security feature to be implemented for this scenario.

References:

http://docs.aws.amazon.com/AWSEC2/latest/UserGuide/Using_Tags.html

https://docs.aws.amazon.com/AWSEC2/latest/UserGuide/iam-policies-for-amazon-ec2.html

Question 25:

An application is hosted on an EC2 instance with multiple EBS Volumes attached and uses Amazon Neptune as its database. To improve data security, you encrypted all of the EBS volumes attached to the instance to protect the confidential data stored in the volumes.

Which of the following statements are true about encrypted Amazon Elastic Block Store volumes? (Select TWO.)

1. Only the data in the volume is encrypted and not all the data moving between the volume and the instance.
2. All data moving between the volume and the instance are encrypted.
3. The volumes created from the encrypted snapshot are not encrypted.
4. Snapshots are automatically encrypted.
5. Snapshots are not automatically encrypted.

Answer(s): 2, 4

Explanation

Amazon Elastic Block Store (Amazon EBS) provides block level storage volumes for use with EC2 instances. EBS volumes are highly available and reliable storage volumes that can be attached to any running instance that is in the same Availability Zone. EBS volumes that are attached to an EC2 instance are exposed as storage volumes that persist independently from the life of the instance.

When you create an encrypted EBS volume and attach it to a supported instance type, the following types of data are encrypted:

- Data at rest inside the volume

- All data moving between the volume and the instance

- All snapshots created from the volume

- All volumes created from those snapshots

Encryption operations occur on the servers that host EC2 instances, ensuring the security of both data-at-rest and data-in-transit between an instance and its attached EBS storage. You can encrypt both the boot and data volumes of an EC2 instance.

References:

http://docs.aws.amazon.com/AWSEC2/latest/UserGuide/AmazonEBS.html

https://docs.aws.amazon.com/AWSEC2/latest/UserGuide/EBSEncryption.html

Question 26:

You have just launched a new API Gateway service which uses AWS Lambda as a serverless computing service. In what type of protocol will your API endpoint be exposed?

1. HTTP/2
2. HTTP
3. WebSocket
4. HTTPS

Answer(s): 4

Explanation

All of the APIs created with Amazon API Gateway expose HTTPS endpoints only. Amazon API Gateway does not support unencrypted (HTTP) endpoints. By default, Amazon API Gateway assigns an internal domain to the API that automatically uses the Amazon API Gateway certificate. When configuring your APIs to run under a custom domain name, you can provide your own certificate for the domain.

Reference:

https://aws.amazon.com/api-gateway/faqs/

Question 27:

You have a web application hosted on a fleet of EC2 instances located in two Availability Zones that are all placed behind an Application Load Balancer. As a Solutions Architect, you have to add a health check configuration to ensure your application is highly-available.

Which health checks will you implement?

1. FTP health check
2. HTTP or HTTPS health check
3. ICMP health check
4. TCP health check

Answer(s): 2

Explanation

A load balancer takes requests from clients and distributes them across the EC2 instances that are registered with the load balancer. You can create a load balancer that listens on both the HTTP (80) and HTTPS (443) ports. If you specify that the HTTPS listener sends requests to the instances on port 80, the load balancer terminates the requests and communication from the load balancer to the instances is not encrypted. If the HTTPS listener sends requests to the instances on port 443, communication from the load balancer to the instances is encrypted.

If your load balancer uses an encrypted connection to communicate with the instances, you can optionally enable authentication of the instances. This ensures that the load balancer communicates with an instance only if its public key matches the key that you specified to the load balancer for this purpose.

The type of ELB that is mentioned in this scenario is an Application Elastic Load Balancer. This is used if you want a flexible feature set for your web applications with HTTP and HTTPS traffic. Conversely, it only allows 2 types of health check: HTTP and HTTPS.

Hence, the correct answer is: HTTP or HTTPS health check.

ICMP health check and FTP health check are incorrect as these are not supported.

TCP health check is incorrect. A TCP health check is only offered in Network Load Balancers and Classic Load Balancers.

References:

http://docs.aws.amazon.com/elasticloadbalancing/latest/classic/elb-healthchecks.html

https://docs.aws.amazon.com/elasticloadbalancing/latest/application/introduction.html

Question 28:

You are an IT Consultant for a top investment bank which is in the process of building its new Forex trading platform. To ensure high availability and scalability, you designed the trading platform to use an Elastic Load Balancer in front of an Auto Scaling group of On-Demand EC2 instances across multiple Availability Zones. For its database tier, you chose to use a single Amazon Aurora instance to take advantage of its distributed, fault-tolerant and self-healing storage system.

In the event of system failure on the primary database instance, what happens to Amazon Aurora during the failover?

1. Aurora will first attempt to create a new DB Instance in the same Availability Zone as the original instance. If unable to do so, Aurora will attempt to create a new DB Instance in a different Availability Zone.
2. Aurora will first attempt to create a new DB Instance in a different Availability Zone of the original instance. If unable to do so, Aurora will attempt to create a new DB Instance in the original Availability Zone in which the instance was first launched.
3. Amazon Aurora flips the A record of your DB Instance to point at the healthy replica, which in turn is promoted to become the new primary.
4. Amazon Aurora flips the canonical name record (CNAME) for your DB Instance to point at the healthy replica, which in turn is promoted to become the new primary.

Answer(s): 1

Explanation

Failover is automatically handled by Amazon Aurora so that your applications can resume database operations as quickly as possible without manual administrative intervention.

If you have an Amazon Aurora Replica in the same or a different Availability Zone, when failing over, Amazon Aurora flips the canonical name record (CNAME) for your DB Instance to point at the healthy replica, which in turn is promoted to become the new primary. Start-to-finish, failover typically completes within 30 seconds.

If you are running Aurora Serverless and the DB instance or AZ become unavailable, Aurora will automatically recreate the DB instance in a different AZ.

If you do not have an Amazon Aurora Replica (i.e. single instance) and are not running Aurora Serverless, Aurora will attempt to create a new DB Instance in the same Availability Zone as the original instance. This replacement of the original instance is done on a best-effort basis and may not succeed, for example, if there is an issue that is broadly affecting the Availability Zone.

Hence, the correct answer is the option that says: Aurora will first attempt to create a new DB Instance in the same Availability Zone as the original instance. If unable to do so, Aurora will attempt to create a new DB Instance in a different Availability Zone.

The options that say: Amazon Aurora flips the canonical name record (CNAME) for your DB Instance to point at the healthy replica, which in turn is promoted to become the new primary and Amazon Aurora flips the A record of your DB Instance to point at the healthy replica, which in turn is promoted to become the new primary are incorrect because this will only happen if you are using an Amazon Aurora Replica. In addition, Amazon Aurora flips the canonical name record (CNAME) and not the A record (IP address) of the instance.

The option that says: Aurora will first attempt to create a new DB Instance in a different Availability Zone of the original instance. If unable to do so, Aurora will attempt to create a new DB Instance in the original Availability Zone in which the instance was first launched is incorrect because Aurora will first attempt to create a new DB Instance in the same Availability Zone as the original instance. If unable to do so, Aurora will attempt to create a new DB Instance in a different Availability Zone and not the other way around.

Reference:

https://aws.amazon.com/rds/aurora/faqs/

Question 29:

You are working for a data analytics startup that collects clickstream data and stores them in an S3 bucket. You need to launch an AWS Lambda function to trigger your ETL jobs to run as soon as new data becomes available in Amazon S3.

Which of the following services can you use as an extract, transform, and load (ETL) service in this scenario?

1. AWS Step Functions
2. S3 Select
3. AWS Glue

4. Redshift Spectrum

Answer(s): 3

Explanation

AWS Glue is a fully managed extract, transform, and load (ETL) service that makes it easy for customers to prepare and load their data for analytics. You can create and run an ETL job with a few clicks in the AWS Management Console. You simply point AWS Glue to your data stored on AWS, and AWS Glue discovers your data and stores the associated metadata (e.g. table definition and schema) in the AWS Glue Data Catalog. Once cataloged, your data is immediately searchable, queryable, and available for ETL. AWS Glue generates the code to execute your data transformations and data loading processes.

Reference:

https://aws.amazon.com/glue/

Introduction to AWS Glue:

https://youtu.be/qgWMfNSN9f4

Question 30:

The social media company that you are working for needs to capture the detailed information of all HTTP requests that went through their public-facing application load balancer every five minutes. They want to use this data for analyzing traffic patterns and for troubleshooting their web applications in AWS.

Which of the following options meet the customer requirements?

1. Enable Amazon CloudWatch metrics on the application load balancer.
2. Enable access logs on the application load balancer.
3. Add an Amazon CloudWatch Logs agent on the application load balancer.
4. Enable AWS CloudTrail for their application load balancer.

Answer(s): 2

Explanation

Elastic Load Balancing provides access logs that capture detailed information about requests sent to your load balancer. Each log contains information such as the time the request was received, the client's IP address, latencies, request paths, and server responses. You can use these access logs to analyze traffic patterns and troubleshoot issues.

Access logging is an optional feature of Elastic Load Balancing that is disabled by default. After you enable access logging for your load balancer, Elastic Load Balancing captures the logs and stores them in the Amazon S3 bucket that you specify as compressed files. You can disable access logging at any time.

Reference:

http://docs.aws.amazon.com/elasticloadbalancing/latest/application/load-balancer-access-logs.html

Question 31:

You are working as a Solutions Architect for a leading technology company where you are instructed to troubleshoot the operational issues of your cloud architecture by logging the AWS API call history of your AWS resources. You need to quickly identify the most recent changes made to resources in your environment, including creation, modification, and deletion of AWS resources. One of the requirements is that the generated log files should be encrypted to avoid any security issues.

Which of the following is the most suitable approach to implement the encryption?

1. Use CloudTrail and configure the destination S3 bucket to use Server-Side Encryption (SSE).
2. Use CloudTrail and configure the destination Amazon Glacier archive to use Server-Side Encryption (SSE).
3. Use CloudTrail with its default settings
4. Use CloudTrail and ensure that the Server-Side Encryption (SSE) option is enabled for the trail in the CloudTrail console.

Answer(s): 3

Explanation

By default, CloudTrail event log files are encrypted using Amazon S3 server-side encryption (SSE). You can also choose to encrypt your log files with an AWS Key Management Service (AWS KMS) key. You can store your log files in your bucket for as long as you want. You can also define Amazon S3 lifecycle rules to archive or delete log files automatically. If you want notifications about log file delivery and validation, you can set up Amazon SNS notifications.

Using CloudTrail and configuring the destination Amazon Glacier archive to use Server-Side Encryption (SSE) is incorrect because CloudTrail stores the log files to S3 and not in Glacier. Take note that by default, CloudTrail event log files are already encrypted using Amazon S3 server-side encryption (SSE).

Using CloudTrail and configuring the destination S3 bucket to use Server-Side Encryption (SSE) is incorrect because CloudTrail event log files are already encrypted using the Amazon S3 server-side encryption (SSE) which is why you do not have to do this anymore.

Using CloudTrail and ensuring that the Server-Side Encryption (SSE) option is enabled for the trail in the CloudTrail console is incorrect because there is no available Server-Side Encryption (SSE) option in the CloudTrail console.

References:

https://docs.aws.amazon.com/awscloudtrail/latest/userguide/how-cloudtrail-works.html

https://aws.amazon.com/blogs/aws/category/cloud-trail/

Question 32:

In a startup company you are working for, you are asked to design a web application that requires a NoSQL database that has no limit on the storage size for a given table. The startup is still new in the market and it has very limited human resources who can take care of the database infrastructure.

Which is the most suitable service that you can implement that provides a fully managed, scalable and highly available NoSQL service?

1. SimpleDB
2. Amazon Aurora
3. DynamoDB
4. Amazon Neptune

Answer(s): 3

Explanation

The term "fully managed" means that Amazon will manage the underlying infrastructure of the service hence, you don't need an additional human resource to support or maintain the service. Therefore, Amazon DynamoDB is the right answer. Remember that Amazon RDS is a managed service but not "fully managed" as you still have the option to maintain and configure the underlying server of the database.

Amazon DynamoDB is a fast and flexible NoSQL database service for all applications that need consistent, single-digit millisecond latency at any scale. It is a fully managed cloud database and supports both document and key-value store models. Its flexible data model, reliable performance, and automatic scaling of throughput capacity make it a great fit for mobile, web, gaming, ad tech, IoT, and many other applications.

Amazon Neptune is incorrect because this is primarily used as a graph database.

Amazon Aurora is incorrect because this is a relational database and not a NoSQL database.

SimpleDB is incorrect because although SimpleDB is also a highly available and scalable NoSQL database, it has a limit on the request capacity or storage size for a given table, unlike DynamoDB.

Reference:

https://aws.amazon.com/dynamodb/

Question 33:

You are working as an IT Consultant for a large financial firm. They have a requirement to store irreproducible financial documents using Amazon S3. For their quarterly reporting, the files are required to be retrieved after a period of 3 months. There will be some occasions when a surprise audit will be held, which requires access to the archived data that they need to present immediately.

What will you do to satisfy this requirement in a cost-effective way?

1. Use Amazon S3 -Intelligent Tiering
2. Use Amazon S3 Standard - Infrequent Access
3. Use Amazon S3 Standard
4. Use Amazon Glacier Deep Archive

Answer(s): 2

Explanation

In this scenario, the requirement is to have a storage option that is cost-effective and has the ability to access or retrieve the archived data immediately. The cost-effective options are Amazon Glacier Deep Archive and Amazon S3 Standard- Infrequent Access (Standard - IA). However, the former option is not designed for rapid retrieval of data which is required for the surprise audit. Hence, using Amazon Glacier Deep Archive is incorrect and the best answer is to use Amazon S3 Standard - Infrequent Access.

Using Amazon S3 Standard is incorrect because the standard storage class is not cost-efficient in this scenario. It costs more than Glacier Deep Archive and S3 Standard - Infrequent Access.

Using Amazon S3 -Intelligent Tiering is incorrect because the Intelligent Tiering storage class entails an additional fee for monitoring and automation of each object in your S3 bucket vs. the Standard storage class and S3 Standard - Infrequent Access.

Amazon S3 Standard - Infrequent Access is an Amazon S3 storage class for data that is accessed less frequently, but requires rapid access when needed. Standard - IA offers the high durability, throughput, and low latency of Amazon S3 Standard, with a low per GB storage price and per GB retrieval fee.

This combination of low cost and high performance makes Standard - IA ideal for long-term storage, backups, and as a data store for disaster recovery. The Standard - IA storage class is set at the object level and can exist in the same bucket as Standard, allowing you to use lifecycle policies to automatically transition objects between storage classes without any application changes.

References:

https://aws.amazon.com/s3/storage-classes/

https://aws.amazon.com/s3/faqs/

Question 34:

You are working as a solutions architect for a large financial company. They have a web application hosted in their on-premises infrastructure which they want to migrate to AWS cloud. Your manager has instructed you to ensure that there is no downtime while the migration process is on-going. In order to achieve this, your team decided to divert 50% of the traffic to the new application in AWS and the other 50% to the application hosted in their on-premises infrastructure. Once the migration is over and the application works with no issues, a full diversion to AWS will be implemented. The company's VPC is connected to its on-premises network via an AWS Direct Connect connection.

Which of the following are the possible solutions that you can implement to satisfy the above requirement? (Select TWO.)

1. Use Route 53 with Weighted routing policy to divert the traffic between the on-premises and AWS-hosted application. Divert 50% of the traffic to the new application in AWS and the other 50% to the application hosted in their on-premises infrastructure.
2. Use AWS Global Accelerator to divert and proportion the HTTP and HTTPS traffic between the on-premises and AWS-hosted application. Ensure that the on-premises network has an AnyCast static IP address and is connected to your VPC via a Direct Connect Gateway.
3. Use a Network Load balancer with Weighted Target Groups to divert the traffic between the on-premises and AWS-hosted application. Divert 50% of the traffic to the new application in AWS and the other 50% to the application hosted in their on-premises infrastructure.
4. Use Route 53 with Failover routing policy to divert and proportion the traffic between the on-premises and AWS-hosted application. Divert 50% of the traffic to the new application in AWS and the other 50% to the application hosted in their on-premises infrastructure.
5. Use an Application Elastic Load balancer with Weighted Target Groups to divert and proportion the traffic between the on-premises and AWS-hosted

application. Divert 50% of the traffic to the new application in AWS and the other 50% to the application hosted in their on-premises infrastructure.

Answer(s): 1, 5

Explanation

Application Load Balancers support Weighted Target Groups routing. With this feature, you will be able to do weighted routing of the traffic forwarded by a rule to multiple target groups. This enables various use cases like blue-green, canary and hybrid deployments without the need for multiple load balancers. It even enables zero-downtime migration between on-premises and cloud or between different compute types like EC2 and Lambda.

To divert 50% of the traffic to the new application in AWS and the other 50% to the application, you can also use Route 53 with Weighted routing policy. This will divert the traffic between the on-premises and AWS-hosted application accordingly.

Weighted routing lets you associate multiple resources with a single domain name (sample.com) or subdomain name (portal.sample.com) and choose how much traffic is routed to each resource. This can be useful for a variety of purposes, including load balancing and testing new versions of software. You can set a specific percentage of how much traffic will be allocated to the resource by specifying the weights.

For example, if you want to send a tiny portion of your traffic to one resource and the rest to another resource, you might specify weights of 1 and 255. The resource with a weight of 1 gets 1/256th of the traffic (1/1+255), and the other resource gets 255/256ths (255/1+255).

You can gradually change the balance by changing the weights. If you want to stop sending traffic to a resource, you can change the weight for that record to 0.

When you create a target group in your Application Load Balancer, you specify its target type. This determines the type of target you specify when registering with this target group. You can select the following target types:

1. instance - The targets are specified by instance ID.

2. ip - The targets are IP addresses.

3. Lambda - The target is a Lambda function.

When the target type is ip, you can specify IP addresses from one of the following CIDR blocks:

- 10.0.0.0/8 (RFC 1918)

- 100.64.0.0/10 (RFC 6598)

- 172.16.0.0/12 (RFC 1918)

- 192.168.0.0/16 (RFC 1918)

- The subnets of the VPC for the target group

These supported CIDR blocks enable you to register the following with a target group: ClassicLink instances, instances in a VPC that is peered to the load balancer VPC, AWS resources that are addressable by IP address and port (for example, databases), and on-premises resources linked to AWS through AWS Direct Connect or a VPN connection.

Take note that you can not specify publicly routable IP addresses. If you specify targets using an instance ID, traffic is routed to instances using the primary private IP address specified in the primary network interface for the instance. If you specify targets using IP addresses, you can route traffic to an instance using any private IP address from one or more network interfaces. This enables multiple applications on an instance to use the same port. Each network interface can have its own security group.

Hence, the correct answers are the following options:

- Use an Application Elastic Load balancer with Weighted Target Groups to divert and proportion the traffic between the on-premises and AWS-hosted application. Divert 50% of the traffic to the new application in AWS and the other 50% to the application hosted in their on-premises infrastructure.

- Use Route 53 with Weighted routing policy to divert the traffic between the on-premises and AWS-hosted application. Divert 50% of the traffic to the new application in AWS and the other 50% to the application hosted in their on-premises infrastructure.

The option that says: Use a Network Load balancer with Weighted Target Groups to divert the traffic between the on-premises and AWS-hosted application. Divert 50% of the traffic to the new application in AWS and the other 50% to the application hosted in their on-premises infrastructure is incorrect because a Network Load balancer doesn't have Weighted Target Groups to divert the traffic between the on-premises and AWS-hosted application.

The option that says: Use Route 53 with Failover routing policy to divert and proportion the traffic between the on-premises and AWS-hosted application. Divert 50% of the traffic to the new application in AWS and the other 50% to the application hosted in their on-premises infrastructure is incorrect because you cannot divert and proportion the traffic between the on-premises and AWS-hosted application using Route 53 with Failover routing policy. This is primarily used if you want to configure active-passive failover to your application architecture.

The option that says: Use AWS Global Accelerator to divert and proportion the HTTP and HTTPS traffic between the on-premises and AWS-hosted application. Ensure that the on-premises network has an AnyCast static IP address and is connected to your VPC via a Direct Connect Gateway is incorrect because although you can control the proportion of traffic directed to each endpoint using AWS Global Accelerator by assigning weights across the endpoints, it is still wrong to use a

Direct Connect Gateway and an AnyCast IP address since these are not required at all. You can only associate static IP addresses provided by AWS Global Accelerator to regional AWS resources or endpoints, such as Network Load Balancers, Application Load Balancers, EC2 Instances, and Elastic IP addresses. Take note that a Direct Connect Gateway, per se, doesn't establish a connection from your on-premises network to your Amazon VPCs. It simply enables you to use your AWS Direct Connect connection to connect to two or more VPCs that are located in different AWS Regions.

References:

http://docs.aws.amazon.com/Route53/latest/DeveloperGuide/routing-policy.html

https://aws.amazon.com/blogs/aws/new-application-load-balancer-simplifies-deployment-with-weighted-target-groups/

https://docs.aws.amazon.com/elasticloadbalancing/latest/application/load-balancer-target-groups.html

Question 35:

Your company has a web-based ticketing service that utilizes Amazon SQS and a fleet of EC2 instances. The EC2 instances that consume messages from the SQS queue are configured to poll the queue as often as possible to keep end-to-end throughput as high as possible. You noticed that polling the queue in tight loops is using unnecessary CPU cycles, resulting in increased operational costs due to empty responses.

In this scenario, what will you do to make the system more cost-effective?

1. Configure Amazon SQS to use long polling by setting the ReceiveMessageWaitTimeSeconds to a number greater than zero.
2. Configure Amazon SQS to use short polling by setting the ReceiveMessageWaitTimeSeconds to a number greater than zero.
3. Configure Amazon SQS to use long polling by setting the ReceiveMessageWaitTimeSeconds to zero.
4. Configure Amazon SQS to use short polling by setting the ReceiveMessageWaitTimeSeconds to zero.

Answer(s): 1

Explanation

In this scenario, the application is deployed in a fleet of EC2 instances that are polling messages from a single SQS queue. Amazon SQS uses short polling by default, querying only a subset of the servers (based on a weighted random distribution) to determine whether any messages are available for inclusion in the

454

response. Short polling works for scenarios that require higher throughput. However, you can also configure the queue to use Long polling instead, to reduce cost.

The ReceiveMessageWaitTimeSeconds is the queue attribute that determines whether you are using Short or Long polling. By default, its value is zero which means it is using Short polling. If it is set to a value greater than zero, then it is Long polling.

Hence, configuring Amazon SQS to use long polling by setting the ReceiveMessageWaitTimeSeconds to a number greater than zero is the correct answer.

Quick facts about SQS Long Polling:

- Long polling helps reduce your cost of using Amazon SQS by reducing the number of empty responses when there are no messages available to return in reply to a ReceiveMessage request sent to an Amazon SQS queue and eliminating false empty responses when messages are available in the queue but aren't included in the response.

- Long polling reduces the number of empty responses by allowing Amazon SQS to wait until a message is available in the queue before sending a response. Unless the connection times out, the response to the ReceiveMessage request contains at least one of the available messages, up to the maximum number of messages specified in the ReceiveMessage action.

- Long polling eliminates false empty responses by querying all (rather than a limited number) of the servers. Long polling returns messages as soon any message becomes available.

Reference:

https://docs.aws.amazon.com/AWSSimpleQueueService/latest/SQSDeveloperGuide/sqs-long-polling.html

Question 36:

You recently launched a fleet of on-demand EC2 instances to host a massively multiplayer online role-playing game (MMORPG) server in your VPC. The EC2 instances are configured with Auto Scaling and AWS Systems Manager. What can you use to configure your EC2 instances without having to establish a RDP or SSH connection to each instance?

1. EC2Config
2. Run Command
3. AWS CodePipeline
4. AWS Config

Answer(s): 2

Explanation

You can use Run Command from the console to configure instances without having to login to each instance.

AWS Systems Manager Run Command lets you remotely and securely manage the configuration of your managed instances. A managed instance is any Amazon EC2 instance or on-premises machine in your hybrid environment that has been configured for Systems Manager. Run Command enables you to automate common administrative tasks and perform ad hoc configuration changes at scale. You can use Run Command from the AWS console, the AWS Command Line Interface, AWS Tools for Windows PowerShell, or the AWS SDKs. Run Command is offered at no additional cost.

Reference:

https://docs.aws.amazon.com/systems-manager/latest/userguide/execute-remote-commands.html

Question 37:

You are a Solutions Architect working for a startup which is currently migrating their production environment to AWS. Your manager asked you to set up access to the AWS console using Identity Access Management (IAM). Using the AWS CLI, you have created 5 users for your systems administrators.

What further steps do you need to take for your systems administrators to get access to the AWS console?

1. Provide a password for each user created and give these passwords to your system administrators.
2. Enable multi-factor authentication on their accounts and define a password policy.
3. Provide the system administrators the secret access key and access key id.
4. Add the administrators to the Security Group.

Answer(s): 1

Explanation

The AWS Management Console is the web interface used to manage your AWS resources using your web browser. To access this, your users should have a password that they can use to login to the web console.

Providing the system administrators the secret access key and access key id is incorrect as these are used to trigger AWS API calls.

Enabling multi-factor authentication on their accounts and defining a password policy is incorrect because the multi-factor authentication and a password policy are just additional security measures for the IAM user but these won't enable them to access the AWS Management Console.

Adding the administrators to the Security Group is incorrect as you can't add an IAM user to a security group. Remember that a security group is primarily used for EC2 instances, and not for IAM.

Reference:

http://docs.aws.amazon.com/IAM/latest/UserGuide/getting-started_how-users-sign-in.html

Question 38:

A data analytics company keeps a massive volume of data which they store in their on-premises data center. To scale their storage systems, they are looking for cloud-backed storage volumes that they can mount using Internet Small Computer System Interface (iSCSI) devices from their on-premises application servers. They have an on-site data analytics application which frequently access the latest data subsets locally while the older data are rarely accessed. You are required to minimize the need to scale the on-premises storage infrastructure while still providing their web application with low-latency access to the data.

Which type of AWS Storage Gateway service will you use to meet the above requirements?

1. Cached Volume Gateway
2. Tape Gateway
3. File Gateway
4. Stored Volume Gateway

Answer(s): 1

Explanation

In this scenario, the technology company is looking for a storage service that will enable their analytics application to frequently access the latest data subsets and not the entire data set because it was mentioned that the old data are rarely being used. This requirement can be fulfilled by setting up a Cached Volume Gateway in AWS Storage Gateway.

By using cached volumes, you can use Amazon S3 as your primary data storage, while retaining frequently accessed data locally in your storage gateway. Cached volumes minimize the need to scale your on-premises storage infrastructure, while still providing your applications with low-latency access to frequently accessed data. You can create storage volumes up to 32 TiB in size and afterwards, attach these volumes as iSCSI devices to your on-premises application servers. When you write to these volumes, your gateway stores the data in Amazon S3. It retains the recently read data in your on-premises storage gateway's cache and uploads buffer storage.

Cached volumes can range from 1 GiB to 32 TiB in size and must be rounded to the nearest GiB. Each gateway configured for cached volumes can support up to 32 volumes for a total maximum storage volume of 1,024 TiB (1 PiB).

In the cached volumes solution, AWS Storage Gateway stores all your on-premises application data in a storage volume in Amazon S3. Hence, the correct answer is Cached Volume Gateway.

Stored Volume Gateway is incorrect because the requirement is to provide low latency access to the frequently accessed data subsets locally. Stored Volume Gateway is used if you need low-latency access to your entire dataset.

Tape Gateway is incorrect because a this is just a cost-effective, durable, long-term offsite alternative for data archiving, which is not needed in this scenario.

File Gateway is incorrect because a this does not provide you the required low-latency access to the frequently accessed data that the on-site analytics application needs.

References:

https://docs.aws.amazon.com/storagegateway/latest/userguide/StorageGatewayConcepts.html#volume-gateway-concepts

https://docs.aws.amazon.com/storagegateway/latest/userguide/WhatIsStorageGateway.html

Question 39:

A website is running on an Auto Scaling group of On-Demand EC2 instances which are abruptly getting terminated from time to time. To automate the monitoring process, you started to create a simple script which uses the AWS CLI to find the root cause of this issue.

Which of the following is the most suitable command to use?

1. aws ec2 describe-volume-status
2. aws ec2 describe-instances
3. aws ec2 describe-images
4. aws ec2 get-console-screenshot

Answer(s): 2

Explanation

The describe-instances command shows the status of the EC2 instances including the recently terminated instances. It also returns a StateReason of why the instance was terminated.

Reference:

http://docs.aws.amazon.com/cli/latest/reference/ec2/describe-instances.html

Question 40:

A leading e-commerce company is in need of a storage solution that can be simultaneously accessed by 1000 Linux servers in multiple availability zones. The servers are hosted in EC2 instances that use a hierarchical directory structure via the NFSv4 protocol. The service should be able to handle the rapidly changing data at scale while still maintaining high performance. It should also be highly durable and highly available whenever the servers will pull data from it, with little need for management.

As the Solutions Architect, which of the following services is the most cost-effective choice that you should use to meet the above requirement?

1. S3
2. EBS
3. EFS
4. Storage Gateway

Answer(s): 3

Explanation

Amazon Web Services (AWS) offers cloud storage services to support a wide range of storage workloads such as EFS, S3 and EBS. You have to understand when you should use Amazon EFS, Amazon S3 and Amazon Elastic Block Store (EBS) based on the specific workloads. In this scenario, the keywords are rapidly changing data and 1000 Linux servers.

Amazon EFS is a file storage service for use with Amazon EC2. Amazon EFS provides a file system interface, file system access semantics (such as strong consistency and file locking), and concurrently-accessible storage for up to thousands of Amazon EC2 instances. EFS provides the same level of high availability and high scalability like S3 however, this service is more suitable for scenarios where it is

459

required to have a POSIX-compatible file system or if you are storing rapidly changing data.

Data that must be updated very frequently might be better served by storage solutions that take into account read and write latencies, such as Amazon EBS volumes, Amazon RDS, Amazon DynamoDB, Amazon EFS, or relational databases running on Amazon EC2.

Amazon EBS is a block-level storage service for use with Amazon EC2. Amazon EBS can deliver performance for workloads that require the lowest-latency access to data from a single EC2 instance.

Amazon S3 is an object storage service. Amazon S3 makes data available through an Internet API that can be accessed anywhere.

In this scenario, EFS is the best answer. As stated above, Amazon EFS provides a file system interface, file system access semantics (such as strong consistency and file locking), and concurrently-accessible storage for up to thousands of Amazon EC2 instances. EFS provides the performance, durability, high availability, and storage capacity needed by the 1000 Linux servers in the scenario.

S3 is incorrect because although this provides the same level of high availability and high scalability like EFS, this service is not suitable for storing data which are rapidly changing, just as mentioned in the above. It is still more effective to use EFS as it offers strong consistency and file locking which the S3 service lacks.

EBS is incorrect because an EBS Volume cannot be shared by multiple instances.

Storage Gateway is incorrect because this is primarily used to extend the storage of your on-premises data center to your AWS Cloud.

References:

https://docs.aws.amazon.com/efs/latest/ug/how-it-works.html

https://aws.amazon.com/efs/features/

https://d1.awsstatic.com/whitepapers/AWS%20Storage%20Services%20Whitepaper-v9.pdf#page=9

Question 41:

You are designing an online banking application which needs to have a distributed session data management. Currently, the application is hosted on an Auto Scaling group of On-Demand EC2 instances across multiple Availability Zones with a Classic Load Balancer that distributes the load.

Which of the following options should you do to satisfy the given requirement?

1. Use the GetSessionToken action in AWS STS for session management
2. Set up an AWS Systems Manager Session Manager

3. Enable the sticky session feature in the Classic Load Balancer
4. Use Amazon ElastiCache

Answer(s): 4

Explanation

In this question, the keyword is distributed session data management.

Sticky session feature of the Classic Load Balancer can also provide session management, however, take note that this feature has its limitations such as, in the event of a failure, you are likely to lose the sessions that were resident on the failed node. In the event that the number of your web servers change when your Auto Scaling kicks in, it's possible that the traffic may be unequally spread across the web servers as active sessions may exist on particular servers. If not mitigated properly, this can hinder the scalability of your applications. Hence, sticky session is not scalable or "distributed" as compared with ElastiCache.

You can manage HTTP session data from the web servers using an In-Memory Key/Value store such as Redis and Memcached. Redis is an open source, in-memory data structure store used as a database, cache, and message broker. Memcached is an in-memory key-value store for small arbitrary data (strings, objects) from results of database calls, API calls, or page rendering.

In AWS, you can use Amazon ElastiCache which offers fully managed Redis and Memcached service to manage and store session data for your web applications.

Setting up an AWS Systems Manager Session Manager is incorrect because the Session Manager is simply a capability that lets you manage your Amazon EC2 instances through an interactive one-click browser-based shell or through the AWS CLI. This does not act as a distributed session data management.

Enabling the sticky session feature in the Classic Load Balancer is incorrect because although you can use this to manage your session data, it is not a "distributed" solution compared to ElastiCache.

Using the GetSessionToken action in AWS STS for session management is incorrect because GetSessionToken is just one of the available actions in STS which returns a set of temporary credentials for an AWS account or IAM user. This is not used for distributed session data management

References:

https://aws.amazon.com/caching/session-management/

https://aws.amazon.com/elasticache/

Question 42:

You are implementing a hybrid architecture for your company where you are connecting their Amazon Virtual Private Cloud (VPC) to their on-premises network. Which of the following can be used to create a private connection between the VPC and your company's on-premises network?

1. Route 53
2. ClassicLink
3. Direct Connect
4. AWS Direct Link

Answer(s): 3

Explanation

Direct Connect creates a direct, private connection from your on-premises data center to AWS, letting you establish a 1-gigabit or 10-gigabit dedicated network connection using Ethernet fiber-optic cable.

Reference:

https://aws.amazon.com/premiumsupport/knowledge-center/connect-vpc/

Additional tutorial - how to configure a VPN over AWS Direct Connect:

https://youtu.be/dhpTTT6V1So

S3 Transfer Acceleration vs Direct Connect vs VPN vs Snowball vs Snowmobile:

Question 43:

A financial analytics application that collects, processes and analyzes stock data in real-time is using Kinesis Data Streams. The producers continually push data to Kinesis Data Streams while the consumers process the data in real time. In Amazon Kinesis, where can the consumers store their results? (Select TWO.)

1. Glacier Select
2. Amazon S3
3. AWS Glue
4. Amazon Athena
5. Amazon Redshift

Answer(s): 2, 5

Explanation

In Amazon Kinesis, the producers continually push data to Kinesis Data Streams and the consumers process the data in real time. Consumers (such as a custom application running on Amazon EC2, or an Amazon Kinesis Data Firehose delivery stream) can store their results using an AWS service such as Amazon DynamoDB, Amazon Redshift, or Amazon S3.

Hence, Amazon S3 and Amazon Redshift are the correct answers. The following diagram illustrates the high-level architecture of Kinesis Data Streams:

Glacier Select is incorrect because this is not a storage service. It is primarily used to run queries directly on data stored in Amazon Glacier, retrieving only the data you need out of your archives to use for analytics.

AWS Glue is incorrect because this is not a storage service. It is a fully managed extract, transform, and load (ETL) service that makes it easy for customers to prepare and load their data for analytics.

Amazon Athena is incorrect because this is just an interactive query service that makes it easy to analyze data in Amazon S3 using standard SQL. It is not a storage service where you can store the results processed by the consumers.

Reference:

http://docs.aws.amazon.com/streams/latest/dev/key-concepts.html

Question 44:

An e-commerce application is using a fanout messaging pattern for its order management system. For every order, it sends an Amazon SNS message to an SNS topic, and the message is replicated and pushed to multiple Amazon SQS queues for parallel asynchronous processing. A Spot EC2 instance retrieves the message from each SQS queue and processes the message. There was an incident that while an EC2 instance is currently processing a message, the instance was abruptly terminated, and the processing was not completed in time.

In this scenario, what happens to the SQS message?

1. The message is deleted and becomes duplicated in the SQS when the EC2 instance comes online.
2. The message will be sent to a Dead Letter Queue in AWS DataSync.
3. When the message visibility timeout expires, the message becomes available for processing by other EC2 instances
4. The message will automatically be assigned to the same EC2 instance when it comes back online within or after the visibility timeout.

Answer(s): 3

Explanation

A "fanout" pattern is when an Amazon SNS message is sent to a topic and then replicated and pushed to multiple Amazon SQS queues, HTTP endpoints, or email addresses. This allows for parallel asynchronous processing. For example, you could develop an application that sends an Amazon SNS message to a topic whenever an order is placed for a product. Then, the Amazon SQS queues that are subscribed to that topic would receive identical notifications for the new order. The Amazon EC2 server instance attached to one of the queues could handle the processing or fulfillment of the order, while the other server instance could be attached to a data warehouse for analysis of all orders received.

When a consumer receives and processes a message from a queue, the message remains in the queue. Amazon SQS doesn't automatically delete the message. Because Amazon SQS is a distributed system, there's no guarantee that the consumer actually receives the message (for example, due to a connectivity issue, or due to an issue in the consumer application). Thus, the consumer must delete the message from the queue after receiving and processing it.

Immediately after the message is received, it remains in the queue. To prevent other consumers from processing the message again, Amazon SQS sets a visibility timeout, a period of time during which Amazon SQS prevents other consumers from receiving and processing the message. The default visibility timeout for a message is 30 seconds. The maximum is 12 hours.

The option that says: The message will automatically be assigned to the same EC2 instance when it comes back online within or after the visibility timeout is incorrect because the message will not be automatically assigned to the same EC2 instance once it is abruptly terminated. When the message visibility timeout expires, the message becomes available for processing by other EC2 instances.

The option that says: The message is deleted and becomes duplicated in the SQS when the EC2 instance comes online is incorrect because the message will not be deleted and won't be duplicated in the SQS queue when the EC2 instance comes online.

The option that says: The message will be sent to a Dead Letter Queue in AWS DataSync is incorrect because although the message could be programmatically sent to a Dead Letter Queue (DLQ), it won't be handled by AWS DataSync but by Amazon SQS instead. AWS DataSync is primarily used to simplify your migration with AWS. It makes it simple and fast to move large amounts of data online between on-premises storage and Amazon S3 or Amazon Elastic File System (Amazon EFS).

References:

http://docs.aws.amazon.com/AWSSimpleQueueService/latest/SQSDeveloperGuide/sqs-visibility-timeout.html https://docs.aws.amazon.com/sns/latest/dg/sns-common-scenarios.html

Question 45:

You have an On-Demand EC2 instance with an attached non-root EBS volume. There is a scheduled job that creates a snapshot of this EBS volume every midnight at 12 AM when the instance is not used. On one night, there's been a production incident where you need to perform a change on both the instance and on the EBS volume at the same time, when the snapshot is currently taking place.

Which of the following scenario is true when it comes to the usage of an EBS volume while the snapshot is in progress?

1. The EBS volume cannot be detached or attached to an EC2 instance until the snapshot completes
2. The EBS volume can be used in read-only mode while the snapshot is in progress.
3. The EBS volume can be used while the snapshot is in progress.
4. The EBS volume cannot be used until the snapshot completes.

Answer(s): 3

Explanation

Snapshots occur asynchronously; the point-in-time snapshot is created immediately, but the status of the snapshot is pending until the snapshot is complete (when all of the modified blocks have been transferred to Amazon S3), which can take several hours for large initial snapshots or subsequent snapshots where many blocks have changed.

While it is completing, an in-progress snapshot is not affected by ongoing reads and writes to the volume hence, you can still use the EBS volume normally.

When you create an EBS volume based on a snapshot, the new volume begins as an exact replica of the original volume that was used to create the snapshot. The replicated volume loads data lazily in the background so that you can begin using it immediately. If you access data that hasn't been loaded yet, the volume immediately downloads the requested data from Amazon S3, and then continues loading the rest of the volume's data in the background.

A non-root EBS volume can be detached or attached to a new EC2 instance while the snapshot is in progress. The only exception here is if you are taking a snapshot of your root volume.

Hence, the correct answer is: The EBS volume can be used while the snapshot is in progress.

The option that says: The EBS volume cannot be detached or attached to an EC2 instance until the snapshot completes is not entirely correct. A non-root EBS volume can be detached or attached to a new EC2 instance while the snapshot is in progress. However, you cannot do this for your root volume.

The option that says: The EBS volume can be used in read-only mode while the snapshot is in progress is incorrect because you can perform both read and write operations in the volume while the snapshot is in progress.

The option that says: The EBS volume cannot be used until the snapshot completes is incorrect because just as shown in the previous option, the volume can be used even if the snapshot process is in progress.

References:

https://docs.aws.amazon.com/AWSEC2/latest/UserGuide/ebs-creating-snapshot.html

https://docs.aws.amazon.com/AWSEC2/latest/UserGuide/EBSSnapshots.html

Question 46:

You are planning to migrate a MySQL database from your on-premises data center to your AWS Cloud. This database will be used by a legacy batch application which has steady-state workloads in the morning but has its peak load at night for the end-of-day processing. You need to choose an EBS volume which can handle a maximum of 450 GB of data and can also be used as the system boot volume for your EC2 instance.

Which of the following is the most cost-effective storage type to use in this scenario?

1. Amazon EBS Cold HDD (sc1)
2. Amazon EBS Provisioned IOPS SSD (io1)
3. Amazon EBS Throughput Optimized HDD (st1)
4. Amazon EBS General Purpose SSD (gp2)

Answer(s): 4

Explanation

In this scenario, a legacy batch application which has steady-state workloads requires a relational MySQL database. The EBS volume that you should use has to handle a maximum of 450 GB of data and can also be used as the system boot volume for your EC2 instance. Since HDD volumes cannot be used as a bootable volume, we can narrow down our options by selecting SSD volumes. In addition, SSD volumes are more suitable for transactional database workloads, as shown in the table below:

General Purpose SSD (gp2) volumes offer cost-effective storage that is ideal for a broad range of workloads. These volumes deliver single-digit millisecond latencies and the ability to burst to 3,000 IOPS for extended periods of time. Between a minimum of 100 IOPS (at 33.33 GiB and below) and a maximum of 10,000 IOPS (at 3,334 GiB and above), baseline performance scales linearly at 3 IOPS per GiB of volume size. AWS designs gp2 volumes to deliver the provisioned performance 99% of the time. A gp2 volume can range in size from 1 GiB to 16 TiB.

Amazon EBS Provisioned IOPS SSD (io1) is incorrect because this is not the most cost-effective EBS type and is primarily used for critical business applications that require sustained IOPS performance.

Amazon EBS Throughput Optimized HDD (st1) is incorrect because this is primarily used for frequently accessed, throughput-intensive workloads. Although it is a low-cost HDD volume, it cannot be used as a system boot volume.

Amazon EBS Cold HDD (sc1) is incorrect because although Amazon EBS Cold HDD provides lower cost HDD volume compared to General Purpose SSD, it cannot be used as a system boot volume.

Reference:

https://docs.aws.amazon.com/AWSEC2/latest/UserGuide/EBSVolumeTypes.html#EBSVolumeTypes_gp2

Question 47:

A leading media company has recently adopted a hybrid cloud architecture which requires them to migrate their application servers and databases in AWS. One of their applications requires a heterogeneous database migration in which you need to transform your on-premises Oracle database to PostgreSQL in AWS. This entails a schema and code transformation before the proper data migration starts.

Which of the following options is the most suitable approach to migrate the database in AWS?

1. Heterogeneous database migration is not supported in AWS. You have to transform your database first to PostgreSQL and then migrate it to RDS.
2. Use Amazon Neptune to convert the source schema and code to match that of the target database in RDS. Use the AWS Batch to effectively migrate the data from the source database to the target database in a batch process.
3. Configure a Launch Template that automatically converts the source schema and code to match that of the target database. Then, use the AWS Database Migration Service to migrate data from the source database to the target database.
4. First, use the AWS Schema Conversion Tool to convert the source schema and application code to match that of the target database, and then use the

AWS Database Migration Service to migrate data from the source database to the target database.

Answer(s): 4

Explanation

AWS Database Migration Service helps you migrate databases to AWS quickly and securely. The source database remains fully operational during the migration, minimizing downtime to applications that rely on the database. The AWS Database Migration Service can migrate your data to and from most widely used commercial and open-source databases.

AWS Database Migration Service can migrate your data to and from most of the widely used commercial and open source databases. It supports homogeneous migrations such as Oracle to Oracle, as well as heterogeneous migrations between different database platforms, such as Oracle to Amazon Aurora. Migrations can be from on-premises databases to Amazon RDS or Amazon EC2, databases running on EC2 to RDS, or vice versa, as well as from one RDS database to another RDS database. It can also move data between SQL, NoSQL, and text based targets.

In heterogeneous database migrations the source and target databases engines are different, like in the case of Oracle to Amazon Aurora, Oracle to PostgreSQL, or Microsoft SQL Server to MySQL migrations. In this case, the schema structure, data types, and database code of source and target databases can be quite different, requiring a schema and code transformation before the data migration starts. That makes heterogeneous migrations a two step process. First use the AWS Schema Conversion Tool to convert the source schema and code to match that of the target database, and then use the AWS Database Migration Service to migrate data from the source database to the target database. All the required data type conversions will automatically be done by the AWS Database Migration Service during the migration. The source database can be located in your own premises outside of AWS, running on an Amazon EC2 instance, or it can be an Amazon RDS database. The target can be a database in Amazon EC2 or Amazon RDS.

The option that says: Configure a Launch Template that automatically converts the source schema and code to match that of the target database. Then, use the AWS Database Migration Service to migrate data from the source database to the target database is incorrect because Launch templates are primarily used in EC2 to enable you to store launch parameters so that you do not have to specify them every time you launch an instance.

The option that says: Use Amazon Neptune to convert the source schema and code to match that of the target database in RDS. Use the AWS Batch to effectively migrate the data from the source database to the target database in a batch process is incorrect because Amazon Neptune is a fully-managed graph database service and not a suitable service to use to convert the source schema. AWS Batch is not a database migration service and hence, it is not suitable to be used in this scenario.

You should use the AWS Schema Conversion Tool and AWS Database Migration Service instead.

The option that says: Heterogeneous database migration is not supported in AWS. You have to transform your database first to PostgreSQL and then migrate it to RDS is incorrect because heterogeneous database migration is supported in AWS using the Database Migration Service.

References:

https://aws.amazon.com/dms/

https://docs.aws.amazon.com/AWSEC2/latest/UserGuide/ec2-launch-templates.html

https://aws.amazon.com/batch/

Here is a case study on AWS Database Migration Service:

https://youtu.be/11IHvxjy4hw

Question 48:

You are building a prototype for a cryptocurrency news website of a small startup. The website will be deployed to a Spot EC2 Linux instance and will use Amazon Aurora as its database. You requested a spot instance at a maximum price of $0.04/hr which has been fulfilled immediately and after 90 minutes, the spot price increases to $0.06/hr and then your instance was terminated by AWS.

In this scenario, what would be the total cost of running your spot instance?

1. $0.00
2. $0.06
3. $0.07
4. $0.08

Answer(s): 2

Explanation

Since the Spot instance has been running for more than an hour, which is past the first instance hour, this means that you will be charged from the time it was launched till the time it was terminated by AWS. The computation for your 90 minute usage would be $0.04 (60 minutes) + $0.02 (30 minutes) = $0.06 hence, the correct answer is $0.06.

Based on the official EC2 FAQ:

Q. How will I be charged if my Spot instance is interrupted?

If your Spot instance is terminated or stopped by Amazon EC2 in the first instance hour, you will not be charged for that usage. However, if you terminate the instance yourself, you will be charged to the nearest second. If the Spot instance is terminated or stopped by Amazon EC2 in any subsequent hour, you will be charged for your usage to the nearest second. If you are running on Windows and you terminate the instance yourself, you will be charged for an entire hour.

Take note that there is one ambiguous AWS document which says:

Spot Instances perform exactly like other EC2 instances while running and can be terminated when you no longer need them. If you terminate your instance, you pay for any partial hour used (as you do for On-Demand or Reserved Instances). However, you are not charged for any partial hour of usage if the Spot price goes above your maximum price and Amazon EC2 interrupts your Spot Instance.

The above paragraph may seem to contradict what the official EC2 FAQ said that you will be charged for your usage to the nearest second if the Spot instance is terminated or stopped by Amazon EC2 in any subsequent hour. Therefore, please be reminded that the above paragraph is only applicable if the Spot Instance is terminated by Amazon EC2 in the first instance hour only, and not during any subsequent hour (more than 60 minutes) which is what the scenario depicts.

I have personally contacted AWS about this issue in their documentation:

https://github.com/awsdocs/amazon-ec2-user-guide/pull/65

Reference:

https://aws.amazon.com/ec2/faqs/

https://docs.aws.amazon.com/whitepapers/latest/cost-optimization-leveraging-ec2-spot-instances/how-spot-instances-work.html

Question 49:

An investment bank has a distributed batch processing application which is hosted in an Auto Scaling group of Spot EC2 instances with an SQS queue. You configured your components to use client-side buffering so that the calls made from the client will be buffered first and then sent as a batch request to SQS. What is a period of time during which the SQS queue prevents other consuming components from receiving and processing a message?

1. Receiving Timeout
2. Component Timeout
3. Processing Timeout
4. Visibility Timeout

Answer(s): 4

Explanation

The visibility timeout is a period of time during which Amazon SQS prevents other consuming components from receiving and processing a message.

When a consumer receives and processes a message from a queue, the message remains in the queue. Amazon SQS doesn't automatically delete the message. Because Amazon SQS is a distributed system, there's no guarantee that the consumer actually receives the message (for example, due to a connectivity issue, or due to an issue in the consumer application). Thus, the consumer must delete the message from the queue after receiving and processing it.

Immediately after the message is received, it remains in the queue. To prevent other consumers from processing the message again, Amazon SQS sets a visibility timeout, a period of time during which Amazon SQS prevents other consumers from receiving and processing the message. The default visibility timeout for a message is 30 seconds. The maximum is 12 hours.

References:

https://aws.amazon.com/sqs/faqs/

https://docs.aws.amazon.com/AWSSimpleQueueService/latest/SQSDeveloperGuid e/sqs-visibility-timeout.html

Question 50:

You created a new CloudFormation template that creates 4 EC2 instances and are connected to one Elastic Load Balancer (ELB). Which section of the template should you configure to get the Domain Name Server hostname of the ELB upon the creation of the AWS stack?

1. Parameters
2. Resources
3. Mappings
4. Outputs

Answer(s): 4

Explanation

Outputs is an optional section of the CloudFormation template that describes the values that are returned whenever you view your stack's properties.

Reference:

https://docs.aws.amazon.com/AWSCloudFormation/latest/UserGuide/template-anatomy.html

https://aws.amazon.com/cloudformation/

Question 51:

A company has an application hosted in an Auto Scaling group of Amazon EC2 instances across multiple Availability Zones behind an Application Load Balancer. There are several occasions where some instances are automatically terminated after failing the HTTPS health checks in the ALB and then purges all the ephemeral logs stored in the instance. A Solutions Architect must implement a solution that collects all of the application and server logs effectively. She should be able to perform a root cause analysis based on the logs, even if the Auto Scaling group immediately terminated the instance.

What is the EASIEST way for the Architect to automate the log collection from the Amazon EC2 instances?

1. Add a lifecycle hook to your Auto Scaling group to move instances in the Terminating state to the Pending:Wait state to delay the termination of the unhealthy Amazon EC2 instances. Configure a CloudWatch Events rule for the EC2 Instance-terminate Lifecycle Action Auto Scaling Event with an associated Lambda function. Set up an AWS Systems Manager Automation script that collects and uploads the application logs from the instance to a CloudWatch Logs group. Configure the solution to only resume the instance termination once all the logs were successfully sent.

2. Add a lifecycle hook to your Auto Scaling group to move instances in the Terminating state to the Terminating:Wait state to delay the termination of the unhealthy Amazon EC2 instances. Set up AWS Step Functions to collect the application logs and send them to a CloudWatch Log group. Configure the solution to resume the instance termination as soon as all the logs were successfully sent to CloudWatch Logs.

3. Add a lifecycle hook to your Auto Scaling group to move instances in the Terminating state to the Terminating:Wait state to delay the termination of unhealthy Amazon EC2 instances. Configure a CloudWatch Events rule for the EC2 Instance-terminate Lifecycle Action Auto Scaling Event with an associated Lambda function. Trigger the CloudWatch agent to push the application logs and then resume the instance termination once all the logs are sent to CloudWatch Logs.

4. Add a lifecycle hook to your Auto Scaling group to move instances in the Terminating state to the Terminating:Wait state to delay the termination of the unhealthy Amazon EC2 instances. Configure a CloudWatch Events rule for the EC2 Instance Terminate Successful Auto Scaling Event with an associated Lambda function. Set up the AWS Systems Manager Run Command service to run a script that collects and uploads the application

logs from the instance to a CloudWatch Logs group. Resume the instance termination once all the logs are sent.

Answer(s): 3

Explanation

The EC2 instances in an Auto Scaling group have a path, or lifecycle, that differs from that of other EC2 instances. The lifecycle starts when the Auto Scaling group launches an instance and puts it into service. The lifecycle ends when you terminate the instance, or the Auto Scaling group takes the instance out of service and terminates it.

You can add a lifecycle hook to your Auto Scaling group so that you can perform custom actions when instances launch or terminate.

When Amazon EC2 Auto Scaling responds to a scale out event, it launches one or more instances. These instances start in the Pending state. If you added an autoscaling:EC2_INSTANCE_LAUNCHING lifecycle hook to your Auto Scaling group, the instances move from the Pending state to the Pending:Wait state. After you complete the lifecycle action, the instances enter the Pending:Proceed state. When the instances are fully configured, they are attached to the Auto Scaling group and they enter the InService state.

When Amazon EC2 Auto Scaling responds to a scale in event, it terminates one or more instances. These instances are detached from the Auto Scaling group and enter the Terminating state. If you added an autoscaling:EC2_INSTANCE_TERMINATING lifecycle hook to your Auto Scaling group, the instances move from the Terminating state to the Terminating:Wait state. After you complete the lifecycle action, the instances enter the Terminating:Proceed state. When the instances are fully terminated, they enter the Terminated state.

Using CloudWatch agent is the most suitable tool to use to collect the logs. The unified CloudWatch agent enables you to do the following:

- Collect more system-level metrics from Amazon EC2 instances across operating systems. The metrics can include in-guest metrics, in addition to the metrics for EC2 instances. The additional metrics that can be collected are listed in Metrics Collected by the CloudWatch Agent.

- Collect system-level metrics from on-premises servers. These can include servers in a hybrid environment as well as servers not managed by AWS.

- Retrieve custom metrics from your applications or services using the StatsD and collectd protocols. StatsD is supported on both Linux servers and servers running Windows Server. collectd is supported only on Linux servers.

- Collect logs from Amazon EC2 instances and on-premises servers, running either Linux or Windows Server.

You can store and view the metrics that you collect with the CloudWatch agent in CloudWatch just as you can with any other CloudWatch metrics. The default namespace for metrics collected by the CloudWatch agent is CWAgent, although you can specify a different namespace when you configure the agent.

Hence, the correct answer is: Add a lifecycle hook to your Auto Scaling group to move instances in the Terminating state to the Terminating:Wait state to delay the termination of unhealthy Amazon EC2 instances. Configure a CloudWatch Events rule for the EC2 Instance-terminate Lifecycle Action Auto Scaling Event with an associated Lambda function. Trigger the CloudWatch agent to push the application logs and then resume the instance termination once all the logs are sent to CloudWatch Logs.

The option that says: Add a lifecycle hook to your Auto Scaling group to move instances in the Terminating state to the Pending:Wait state to delay the termination of the unhealthy Amazon EC2 instances. Configure a CloudWatch Events rule for the EC2 Instance-terminate Lifecycle Action Auto Scaling Event with an associated Lambda function. Set up an AWS Systems Manager Automation script that collects and uploads the application logs from the instance to a CloudWatch Logs group. Configure the solution to only resume the instance termination once all the logs were successfully sent is incorrect because the Pending:Wait state refers to the scale-out action in Amazon EC2 Auto Scaling and not for scale-in or for terminating the instances.

The option that says: Add a lifecycle hook to your Auto Scaling group to move instances in the Terminating state to the Terminating:Wait state to delay the termination of the unhealthy Amazon EC2 instances. Set up AWS Step Functions to collect the application logs and send them to a CloudWatch Log group. Configure the solution to resume the instance termination as soon as all the logs were successfully sent to CloudWatch Logs is incorrect because using AWS Step Functions is inappropriate in collecting the logs from your EC2 instances. You should use a CloudWatch agent instead.

The option that says: Add a lifecycle hook to your Auto Scaling group to move instances in the Terminating state to the Terminating:Wait state to delay the termination of the unhealthy Amazon EC2 instances. Configure a CloudWatch Events rule for the EC2 Instance Terminate Successful Auto Scaling Event with an associated Lambda function. Set up the AWS Systems Manager Run Command service to run a script that collects and uploads the application logs from the instance to a CloudWatch Logs group. Resume the instance termination once all the logs are sent is incorrect because although this solution could work, it entails a lot of effort to write a custom script that the AWS Systems Manager Run Command will run. Remember that the scenario asks for a solution that you can implement with the least amount of effort. This solution can be simplified by automatically uploading the logs using a CloudWatch Agent. You have to use the EC2 Instance-terminate Lifecycle Action event instead.

References:

https://docs.aws.amazon.com/autoscaling/ec2/userguide/AutoScalingGroupLifecy cle.html

https://docs.aws.amazon.com/autoscaling/ec2/userguide/cloud-watch-events.html#terminate-successful

https://aws.amazon.com/premiumsupport/knowledge-center/auto-scaling-delay-termination/

Question 52:

An On-Demand EC2 instance is launched into a VPC subnet with the Network ACL configured to allow all inbound traffic and deny all outbound traffic. The instance's security group has an inbound rule to allow SSH from any IP address and does not have any outbound rules.

In this scenario, what are the changes needed to allow SSH connection to the instance?

1. The outbound security group needs to be modified to allow outbound traffic.
2. Both the outbound security group and outbound network ACL need to be modified to allow outbound traffic.
3. No action needed. It can already be accessed from any IP address using SSH.
4. The outbound network ACL needs to be modified to allow outbound traffic.

Answer(s): 4

Explanation

In order for you to establish an SSH connection from your home computer to your EC2 instance, you need to do the following:

- On the Security Group, add an Inbound Rule to allow SSH traffic to your EC2 instance.

- On the NACL, add both an Inbound and Outbound Rule to allow SSH traffic to your EC2 instance.

The reason why you have to add both Inbound and Outbound SSH rule is due to the fact that Network ACLs are stateless which means that responses to allow inbound traffic are subject to the rules for outbound traffic (and vice versa). In other words, if you only enabled an Inbound rule in NACL, the traffic can only go in but the SSH response will not go out since there is no Outbound rule.

Security groups are stateful which means that if an incoming request is granted, then the outgoing traffic will be automatically granted as well, regardless of the outbound rules.

References:

https://docs.aws.amazon.com/AmazonVPC/latest/UserGuide/VPC_ACLs.html

https://docs.aws.amazon.com/AWSEC2/latest/UserGuide/authorizing-access-to-an-instance.html

Question 53:

You are managing a global news website which has a very high traffic. To improve the performance, you redesigned the application architecture to use a Classic Load Balancer with an Auto Scaling Group in multiple Availability Zones. However, you noticed that one of the Availability Zones is not receiving any traffic. What is the root cause of this issue?

1. By default, you are not allowed to use a load balancer with multiple Availability Zones. You have to send a request form to AWS in order for this to work.
2. The Classic Load Balancer is down
3. Auto Scaling should be disabled for the load balancer to route the traffic to multiple Availability Zones.
4. The Availability Zone is not properly added to the load balancer which is why it is not receiving any traffic.

Answer(s): 4

Explanation

In this scenario, one of the Availability Zones is not properly added to the Elastic load balancer. Hence, that Availability Zone is not receiving any traffic.

You can set up your load balancer in EC2-Classic to distribute incoming requests across EC2 instances in a single Availability Zone or multiple Availability Zones. First, launch EC2 instances in all the Availability Zones that you plan to use. Next, register these instances with your load balancer. Finally, add the Availability Zones to your load balancer. After you add an Availability Zone, the load balancer starts routing requests to the registered instances in that Availability Zone. Note that you can modify the Availability Zones for your load balancer at any time.

By default, the load balancer routes requests evenly across its Availability Zones. To route requests evenly across the registered instances in the Availability Zones, enable cross-zone load balancing.

Reference:

https://docs.aws.amazon.com/elasticloadbalancing/latest/classic/enable-disable-az.html

Question 54:

A company has 10 TB of infrequently accessed financial data files that would need to be stored in AWS. These data would be accessed infrequently during specific weeks when they are retrieved for auditing purposes. The retrieval time is not strict as long as it does not exceed 24 hours.

Which of the following would be a secure, durable, and cost-effective solution for this scenario?

1. Upload the data to S3 and set a lifecycle policy to transition data to Glacier after 0 days.
2. Upload the data to S3 then use a lifecycle policy to transfer data to S3 One Zone-IA.
3. Upload the data directly to Amazon Glacier through the AWS Management Console.
4. Upload the data to S3 then use a lifecycle policy to transfer data to S3-IA.

Answer(s): 1

Explanation

Glacier is a cost-effective archival solution for large amounts of data. Bulk retrievals are S3 Glacier's lowest-cost retrieval option, enabling you to retrieve large amounts, even petabytes, of data inexpensively in a day. Bulk retrievals typically complete within 5 – 12 hours. You can specify an absolute or relative time period (including 0 days) after which the specified Amazon S3 objects should be transitioned to Amazon Glacier.

Hence, the correct answer is the option that says: Upload the data to S3 and set a lifecycle policy to transition data to Glacier after 0 days.

Glacier has a management console which you can use to create and delete vaults. However, you cannot directly upload archives to Glacier by using the management console. To upload data, such as photos, videos, and other documents, you must either use the AWS CLI or write code to make requests, by using either the REST API directly or by using the AWS SDKs.

Take note that uploading data to the S3 Console and setting its storage class of "Glacier" is a different story as the proper way to upload data to Glacier is still via its API or CLI. In this way, you can set up your vaults and configure your retrieval options. If you uploaded your data using the S3 console then it will be managed via S3 even though it is internally, using a Glacier storage class. Hence, you won't be able to use Vaults, set your Retrieval Options or purchase Provisioned Capacity for your archives.

Uploading the data to S3 then using a lifecycle policy to transfer data to S3-IA is incorrect because using Glacier would be a more cost-effective solution than using S3-IA. Since required retrieval periods should not exceed more than a day, Glacier would be the best choice.

Uploading the data directly to Glacier through the Amazon Glacier Console is incorrect because you cannot upload objects to Amazon Glacier directly through the Management Console. To upload data, such as photos, videos, and other documents, you must either use the AWS CLI or write code to make requests, by using either the REST API directly or by using the AWS SDKs.

Uploading the data to S3 then using a lifecycle policy to transfer data to S3 One Zone-IA is incorrect because with S3 One Zone-IA, the data will only be stored in a single availability zone and thus, this storage solution is not durable. It also costs more compared with Glacier, which is why this option is wrong.

References:

https://aws.amazon.com/glacier/faqs/

https://docs.aws.amazon.com/AmazonS3/latest/dev/object-lifecycle-mgmt.html

https://docs.aws.amazon.com/amazonglacier/latest/dev/uploading-an-archive.html

Here is a deep dive on Amazon S3 and Glacier Best Practices:

https://youtu.be/rHeTn9pHNKo

Question 55:

A local bank has an in-house application which handles sensitive financial data in a private subnet. After the data is processed by the EC2 worker instances, they will be delivered to S3 for ingestion by other services.

How should you design this solution so that the data does not pass through the public Internet?

1. Create an Internet gateway in the public subnet with a corresponding route entry that directs the data to S3.
2. Configure a VPC Interface Endpoint along with a corresponding route entry that directs the data to S3.
3. Configure a VPC Gateway Endpoint along with a corresponding route entry that directs the data to S3.
4. Provision a NAT gateway in the private subnet with a corresponding route entry that directs the data to S3.

Answer(s): 3

Explanation

The important concept that you have to understand in the scenario is that your VPC and your S3 bucket are located within the larger AWS network. However, the traffic coming from your VPC to your S3 bucket is traversing the public Internet by default. To better protect your data in transit, you can set up a VPC endpoint so the incoming traffic from your VPC will not pass through the public Internet, but instead through the private AWS network.

A VPC endpoint enables you to privately connect your VPC to supported AWS services and VPC endpoint services powered by PrivateLink without requiring an Internet gateway, NAT device, VPN connection, or AWS Direct Connect connection. Instances in your VPC do not require public IP addresses to communicate with resources in the service. Traffic between your VPC and the other services do not leave the Amazon network.

Endpoints are virtual devices. They are horizontally scaled, redundant, and highly available VPC components that allow communication between instances in your VPC and services without imposing availability risks or bandwidth constraints on your network traffic.

There are two types of VPC endpoints: interface endpoints and gateway endpoints. You should create the type of VPC endpoint required by the supported service. As a rule of thumb, most AWS services use VPC Interface Endpoint except for S3 and DynamoDB, which use VPC Gateway Endpoint.

Configuring a VPC Gateway Endpoint along with a corresponding route entry that directs the data to S3 is correct because VPC Gateway Endpoint supports private connection to S3.

Creating an Internet gateway in the public subnet with a corresponding route entry that directs the data to S3 is incorrect because Internet gateway is used for instances in the public subnet to have accessibility to the Internet.

Configuring a VPC Interface Endpoint along with a corresponding route entry that directs the data to S3 is incorrect because VPC Interface Endpoint does not support the S3 service. You should use a VPC Gateway Endpoint instead. As mentioned in the above Explanation, most AWS services use VPC Interface Endpoint except for S3 and DynamoDB, which use VPC Gateway Endpoint.

Provisioning a NAT gateway in the private subnet with a corresponding route entry that directs the data to S3 is incorrect because NAT Gateway allows instances in the private subnet to gain access to the Internet, but not vice versa.

References:

https://docs.aws.amazon.com/vpc/latest/userguide/vpc-endpoints.html

https://docs.aws.amazon.com/vpc/latest/userguide/vpce-gateway.html

Question 56:

An application is hosted in an Auto Scaling group of EC2 instances. To improve the monitoring process, you have to configure the current capacity to increase or decrease based on a set of scaling adjustments. This should be done by specifying the scaling metrics and threshold values for the CloudWatch alarms that trigger the scaling process.

Which of the following is the most suitable type of scaling policy that you should use?

1. Step scaling
2. Scheduled Scaling
3. Simple scaling
4. Target tracking scaling

Answer(s): 1

Explanation

With step scaling, you choose scaling metrics and threshold values for the CloudWatch alarms that trigger the scaling process as well as define how your scalable target should be scaled when a threshold is in breach for a specified number of evaluation periods. Step scaling policies increase or decrease the current capacity of a scalable target based on a set of scaling adjustments, known as step adjustments. The adjustments vary based on the size of the alarm breach. After a scaling activity is started, the policy continues to respond to additional alarms, even while a scaling activity is in progress. Therefore, all alarms that are breached are evaluated by Application Auto Scaling as it receives the alarm messages.

When you configure dynamic scaling, you must define how to scale in response to changing demand. For example, you have a web application that currently runs on two instances and you want the CPU utilization of the Auto Scaling group to stay at around 50 percent when the load on the application changes. This gives you extra capacity to handle traffic spikes without maintaining an excessive amount of idle resources. You can configure your Auto Scaling group to scale automatically to meet this need. The policy type determines how the scaling action is performed.

Amazon EC2 Auto Scaling supports the following types of scaling policies:

Target tracking scaling - Increase or decrease the current capacity of the group based on a target value for a specific metric. This is similar to the way that your thermostat maintains the temperature of your home – you select a temperature and the thermostat does the rest.

Step scaling - Increase or decrease the current capacity of the group based on a set of scaling adjustments, known as step adjustments, that vary based on the size of the alarm breach.

Simple scaling - Increase or decrease the current capacity of the group based on a single scaling adjustment.

If you are scaling based on a utilization metric that increases or decreases proportionally to the number of instances in an Auto Scaling group, then it is recommended that you use target tracking scaling policies. Otherwise, it is better to use step scaling policies instead.

Hence, the correct answer in this scenario is Step Scaling.

Target tracking scaling is incorrect because the target tracking scaling policy increases or decreases the current capacity of the group based on a target value for a specific metric, instead of a set of scaling adjustments.

Simple scaling is incorrect because the simple scaling policy increases or decreases the current capacity of the group based on a single scaling adjustment, instead of a set of scaling adjustments.

Scheduled Scaling is incorrect because the scheduled scaling policy is based on a schedule that allows you to set your own scaling schedule for predictable load changes. This is not considered as one of the types of dynamic scaling.

References:

https://docs.aws.amazon.com/autoscaling/ec2/userguide/as-scale-based-on-demand.html

https://docs.aws.amazon.com/autoscaling/application/userguide/application-auto-scaling-step-scaling-policies.html

Question 57:

You are working for a multinational telecommunications company. Your IT Manager is willing to consolidate their log streams including the access, application, and security logs in one single system. Once consolidated, the company wants to analyze these logs in real-time based on heuristics. There will be some time in the future where the company will need to validate heuristics, which requires going back to data samples extracted from the last 12 hours.

What is the best approach to meet this requirement?

1. First, configure Amazon Cloud Trail to receive custom logs and then use EMR to apply heuristics on the logs.
2. First, send all the log events to Amazon SQS then set up an Auto Scaling group of EC2 servers to consume the logs and finally, apply the heuristics.

3. First, send all of the log events to Amazon Kinesis then afterwards, develop a client process to apply heuristics on the logs.
4. First, set up an Auto Scaling group of EC2 servers then store the logs on Amazon S3 then finally, use EMR to apply heuristics on the logs.

Answer(s): 3

Explanation

In this scenario, you need a service that can collect, process, and analyze data in real-time hence, the right service to use here is Amazon Kinesis.

Amazon Kinesis makes it easy to collect, process, and analyze real-time, streaming data so you can get timely insights and react quickly to new information. Amazon Kinesis offers key capabilities to cost-effectively process streaming data at any scale, along with the flexibility to choose the tools that best suit the requirements of your application.

With Amazon Kinesis, you can ingest real-time data such as video, audio, application logs, website clickstreams, and IoT telemetry data for machine learning, analytics, and other applications. Amazon Kinesis enables you to process and analyze data as it arrives and respond instantly instead of having to wait until all your data is collected before the processing can begin.

All other options are incorrect since these services do not have real-time processing capability, unlike Amazon Kinesis.

Reference:

https://aws.amazon.com/kinesis/

Question 58:

A client is hosting their company website on a cluster of web servers that are behind a public-facing load balancer. The client also uses Amazon Route 53 to manage their public DNS.

How should the client configure the DNS zone apex record to point to the load balancer?

1. Create an A record aliased to the load balancer DNS name.
2. Create an A record pointing to the IP address of the load balancer.
3. Create an alias for CNAME record to the load balancer DNS name.
4. Create a CNAME record pointing to the load balancer DNS name.

Answer(s): 1

Explanation

Route 53's DNS implementation connects user requests to infrastructure running inside (and outside) of Amazon Web Services (AWS). For example, if you have multiple web servers running on EC2 instances behind an Elastic Load Balancing load balancer, Route 53 will route all traffic addressed to your website (e.g. www.sample.com) to the load balancer DNS name (e.g. elbtutorialsfree123.elb.amazonaws.com).

Additionally, Route 53 supports the alias resource record set, which lets you map your zone apex (e.g. sample.com) DNS name to your load balancer DNS name. IP addresses associated with Elastic Load Balancing can change at any time due to scaling or software updates. Route 53 responds to each request for an Alias resource record set with one IP address for the load balancer.

Creating an A record pointing to the IP address of the load balancer is incorrect. You should be using an Alias record pointing to the DNS name of the load balancer since the IP address of the load balancer can change at any time.

Creating a CNAME record pointing to the load balancer DNS name and creating an alias for CNAME record to the load balancer DNS name are incorrect because CNAME records cannot be created for your zone apex. You should create an alias record at the top node of a DNS namespace which is also known as the zone apex. For example, if you register the DNS name sample.com, the zone apex is sample.com. You can't create a CNAME record directly for sample.com, but you can create an alias record for sample.com that routes traffic to www. sample.com.

References:

http://docs.aws.amazon.com/govcloud-us/latest/UserGuide/setting-up-route53-zoneapex-elb.html

https://docs.aws.amazon.com/Route53/latest/DeveloperGuide/resource-record-sets-choosing-alias-non-alias.html

Question 59:

You are a working as a Solutions Architect for a fast-growing startup which just started operations during the past 3 months. They currently have an on-premises Active Directory and 10 computers. To save costs in procuring physical workstations, they decided to deploy virtual desktops for their new employees in a virtual private cloud in AWS. The new cloud infrastructure should leverage on the existing security controls in AWS but can still communicate with their on-premises network.

Which set of AWS services will you use to meet these requirements?

1. AWS Directory Services, VPN connection, and ClassicLink
2. AWS Directory Services, VPN connection, and Amazon S3
3. AWS Directory Services, VPN connection, and Amazon Workspaces
4. AWS Directory Services, VPN connection, and AWS Identity and Access Management

Answer(s): 3

Explanation

For this scenario, the best answer is: AWS Directory Services, VPN connection, and Amazon Workspaces.

First, you need a VPN connection to connect the VPC and your on-premises network. Second, you need AWS Directory Services to integrate with your on-premises Active Directory and lastly, you need to use Amazon Workspace to create the needed virtual desktops in your VPC.

References:

https://aws.amazon.com/directoryservice/

https://docs.aws.amazon.com/AmazonVPC/latest/UserGuide/vpn-connections.html

https://aws.amazon.com/workspaces/

Question 60:

An online shopping platform is hosted on an Auto Scaling group of On-Demand EC2 instances with a default Auto Scaling termination policy and no instance protection configured. The system is deployed across three Availability Zones in the US West region (us-west-1) with an Application Load Balancer in front to provide high availability and fault tolerance for the shopping platform. The us-west-1a, us-west-1b, and us-west-1c Availability Zones have 10, 8 and 7 running instances respectively. Due to the low number of incoming traffic, the scale-in operation has been triggered.

Which of the following will the Auto Scaling group do to determine which instance to terminate first in this scenario? (Select THREE.)

1. Select the instance that is farthest to the next billing hour.
2. Select the instance that is closest to the next billing hour.
3. Select the instances with the most recent launch configuration.
4. Select the instances with the oldest launch configuration.
5. Choose the Availability Zone with the most number of instances, which is the us-west-1a Availability Zone in this scenario.

6. Choose the Availability Zone with the least number of instances, which is the us-west-1c Availability Zone in this scenario.

Answer(s): 2, 4, 5

Explanation

The default termination policy is designed to help ensure that your network architecture spans Availability Zones evenly. With the default termination policy, the behavior of the Auto Scaling group is as follows:

1. If there are instances in multiple Availability Zones, choose the Availability Zone with the most instances and at least one instance that is not protected from scale in. If there is more than one Availability Zone with this number of instances, choose the Availability Zone with the instances that use the oldest launch configuration.

2. Determine which unprotected instances in the selected Availability Zone use the oldest launch configuration. If there is one such instance, terminate it.

3. If there are multiple instances to terminate based on the above criteria, determine which unprotected instances are closest to the next billing hour. (This helps you maximize the use of your EC2 instances and manage your Amazon EC2 usage costs.) If there is one such instance, terminate it.

4. If there is more than one unprotected instance closest to the next billing hour, choose one of these instances at random.

The following flow diagram illustrates how the default termination policy works:

Reference:

https://docs.aws.amazon.com/autoscaling/ec2/userguide/as-instance-termination.html#default-termination-policy

Question 61:

A health organization is using a large Dedicated EC2 instance with multiple EBS volumes to host its health records web application. The EBS volumes must be encrypted due to the confidentiality of the data that they are handling and also to comply with the HIPAA (Health Insurance Portability and Accountability Act) standard.

In EBS encryption, what service does AWS use to secure the volume's data at rest? (Select TWO.)

1. By using S3 Server-Side Encryption.
2. By using your own keys in AWS Key Management Service (KMS).
3. By using Amazon-managed keys in AWS Key Management Service (KMS).

4. By using the SSL certificates provided by the AWS Certificate Manager (ACM).
5. By using S3 Client-Side Encryption.
6. By using a password stored in CloudHSM.

Answer(s): 2, 3

Explanation

Amazon EBS encryption offers seamless encryption of EBS data volumes, boot volumes, and snapshots, eliminating the need to build and maintain a secure key management infrastructure. EBS encryption enables data at rest security by encrypting your data using Amazon-managed keys, or keys you create and manage using the AWS Key Management Service (KMS). The encryption occurs on the servers that host EC2 instances, providing encryption of data as it moves between EC2 instances and EBS storage.

Hence, the correct answers are: using your own keys in AWS Key Management Service (KMS) and using Amazon-managed keys in AWS Key Management Service (KMS).

Using S3 Server-Side Encryption and using S3 Client-Side Encryption are both incorrect as these relate only to S3.

Using a password stored in CloudHSM is incorrect as you only store keys in CloudHSM and not passwords.

Using the SSL certificates provided by the AWS Certificate Manager (ACM) is incorrect as ACM only provides SSL certificates and not data encryption of EBS Volumes.

Reference:

https://aws.amazon.com/ebs/faqs/

Question 62:

You are required to deploy a Docker-based batch application to your VPC in AWS. The application will be used to process both mission-critical data as well as non-essential batch jobs. Which of the following is the most cost-effective option to use in implementing this architecture?

1. Use ECS as the container management service then set up On-Demand EC2 Instances for processing both mission-critical and non-essential batch jobs.

2. Use ECS as the container management service then set up a combination of Reserved and Spot EC2 Instances for processing mission-critical and non-essential batch jobs respectively.
3. Use ECS as the container management service then set up Spot EC2 Instances for processing both mission-critical and non-essential batch jobs.
4. Use ECS as the container management service then set up Reserved EC2 Instances for processing both mission-critical and non-essential batch jobs.

Answer(s): 2

Explanation

Amazon ECS lets you run batch workloads with managed or custom schedulers on Amazon EC2 On-Demand Instances, Reserved Instances, or Spot Instances. You can launch a combination of EC2 instances to set up a cost-effective architecture depending on your workload. You can launch Reserved EC2 instances to process the mission-critical data and Spot EC2 instances for processing non-essential batch jobs.

There are two different charge models for Amazon Elastic Container Service (ECS): Fargate Launch Type Model and EC2 Launch Type Model. With Fargate, you pay for the amount of vCPU and memory resources that your containerized application requests while for EC2 launch type model, there is no additional charge. You pay for AWS resources (e.g. EC2 instances or EBS volumes) you create to store and run your application. You only pay for what you use, as you use it; there are no minimum fees and no upfront commitments.

In this scenario, the most cost-effective solution is to use ECS as the container management service then set up a combination of Reserved and Spot EC2 Instances for processing mission-critical and non-essential batch jobs respectively. You can use Scheduled Reserved Instances (Scheduled Instances) which enables you to purchase capacity reservations that recur on a daily, weekly, or monthly basis, with a specified start time and duration, for a one-year term. This will ensure that you have an uninterrupted compute capacity to process your mission-critical batch jobs.

Hence, the correct answer is the option that says: Use ECS as the container management service then set up a combination of Reserved and Spot EC2 Instances for processing mission-critical and non-essential batch jobs respectively.

Using ECS as the container management service then setting up Reserved EC2 Instances for processing both mission-critical and non-essential batch jobs is incorrect because processing the non-essential batch jobs can be handled much cheaper by using Spot EC2 instances instead of Reserved Instances.

Using ECS as the container management service then setting up On-Demand EC2 Instances for processing both mission-critical and non-essential batch jobs is incorrect because an On-Demand instance costs more compared to Reserved and Spot EC2 instances. Processing the non-essential batch jobs can be handled much cheaper by using Spot EC2 instances instead of On-Demand instances.

Using ECS as the container management service then setting up Spot EC2 Instances for processing both mission-critical and non-essential batch jobs is incorrect because although this set up provides the cheapest solution among other options, it will not be able to meet the required workload. Using Spot instances to process mission-critical workloads is not suitable since these types of instances can be terminated by AWS at any time, which can affect critical processing.

References:

https://docs.aws.amazon.com/AmazonECS/latest/developerguide/Welcome.html

https://aws.amazon.com/ec2/spot/containers-for-less/get-started/

Question 63:

A web application is deployed in an On-Demand EC2 instance in your VPC. There is an issue with the application which requires you to connect to it via an SSH connection. Which of the following is needed in order to access an EC2 instance from the Internet? (Select THREE.)

1. A route entry to the Internet gateway in the Route table of the VPC.
2. A Public IP address attached to the EC2 instance.
3. A VPN Peering connection.
4. A Private Elastic IP address attached to the EC2 instance.
5. An Internet Gateway (IGW) attached to the VPC.
6. A Private IP address attached to the EC2 instance.

Answer(s): 1, 2, 5

Explanation

In order for you to access your EC2 instance from the Internet, you need to have:

- An Internet Gateway (IGW) attached to the VPC.

- A route entry to the Internet gateway in the Route table of the VPC.

- A Public IP address attached to the EC2 instance.

A Private IP address attached to the EC2 instance is incorrect as you only use a Private IP inside your VPC.

A Private Elastic IP address attached to the EC2 instance is incorrect as an Elastic IP Address is a public IPv4 address, not private. It is reachable from the Internet and is designed for dynamic cloud computing.

A VPN Peering connection is incorrect as you only use VPC Peering to connect two VPCs.

Reference:

http://docs.aws.amazon.com/AmazonVPC/latest/UserGuide/VPC_Scenario1.html

Question 64:

You recently launched a news website which is expected to be visited by millions of people around the world. You chose to deploy the website in AWS to take advantage of its extensive range of cloud services and global infrastructure. Aside from AWS Region and Availability Zones, which of the following is part of the AWS Global Infrastructure that is used for content distribution?

1. Edge Location
2. VPC Endpoint
3. Bastion Hosts
4. Hypervisor

Answer(s): 1

Explanation

An edge location helps deliver high availability, scalability, and performance of your application for all of your customers from anywhere in the world. This is used by other services such as Lambda and Amazon CloudFront.

Amazon CloudFront is a web service that gives businesses and web application developers an easy and cost-effective way to distribute content with low latency and high data transfer speeds. CloudFront delivers your files to end-users using a global network of edge locations.

Bastion Hosts is incorrect because a bastion host is not part of the AWS Global Infrastructure. It is just a host computer or a "jump server" used to allow SSH access to your EC2 instances from an outside network.

Hypervisor is incorrect because this is just a computer software, firmware or hardware that creates and runs virtual machines. This technology relates to EC2 instances but it is not part of the AWS Global Infrastructure.

VPC Endpoint is incorrect because this is not part of the AWS Global Infrastructure and is just used to privately connect your VPC to other AWS services and endpoint services.

References:

https://aws.amazon.com/cloudfront/

https://aws.amazon.com/about-aws/global-infrastructure/

Question 65:

A loan processing application is hosted in a single On-Demand EC2 instance in your VPC. To improve the scalability of your application, you have to use Auto Scaling to automatically add new EC2 instances to handle a surge of incoming requests.

Which of the following items should be done in order to add an existing EC2 instance to an Auto Scaling group? (Select TWO.)

1. You must stop the instance first.
2. You have to ensure that the instance is launched in one of the Availability Zones defined in your Auto Scaling group.
3. You have to ensure that the AMI used to launch the instance no longer exists.
4. You have to ensure that the instance is in a different Availability Zone as the Auto Scaling group.
5. You have to ensure that the AMI used to launch the instance still exists.

Answer(s): 2, 5

Explanation

Amazon EC2 Auto Scaling provides you with an option to enable automatic scaling for one or more EC2 instances by attaching them to your existing Auto Scaling group. After the instances are attached, they become a part of the Auto Scaling group.

The instance that you want to attach must meet the following criteria:

- The instance is in the running state.

- The AMI used to launch the instance must still exist.

- The instance is not a member of another Auto Scaling group.

- The instance is launched into one of the Availability Zones defined in your Auto Scaling group.

- If the Auto Scaling group has an attached load balancer, the instance and the load balancer must both be in EC2-Classic or the same VPC. If the Auto Scaling group has an attached target group, the instance and the load balancer must both be in the same VPC.

Based on the above criteria, the following are the correct answers among the given options:

- You have to ensure that the AMI used to launch the instance still exists.

- You have to ensure that the instance is launched in one of the Availability Zones defined in your Auto Scaling group.

The option that says: You must stop the instance first is incorrect because you can directly add a running EC2 instance to an Auto Scaling group without stopping it.

The option that says: You have to ensure that the AMI used to launch the instance no longer exists is incorrect because it should be the other way around. The AMI used to launch the instance should still exist.

The option that says: You have to ensure that the instance is in a different Availability Zone as the Auto Scaling group is incorrect because the instance should be launched in one of the Availability Zones defined in your Auto Scaling group.

References:

http://docs.aws.amazon.com/autoscaling/latest/userguide/attach-instance-asg.html

https://docs.aws.amazon.com/autoscaling/ec2/userguide/scaling_plan.html

www.ingramcontent.com/pod-product-compliance
Lightning Source LLC
LaVergne TN
LVHW051219050326
832903LV00028B/2167